WOMEN PLAYWRIGHTS
The Best Plays of 2002

SMITH AND KRAUS PUBLISHERS
Contemporary Playwrights / Full-Length Play Anthologies

If you require prepublication information about forthcoming Smith and Kraus books, you may receive our semiannual catalogue, free of charge, by sending your name and address to *Smith and Kraus Catalogue, PO Box 127, Lyme, NH 03768*. Or call us at (800) 895-4331, fax (603) 643-1831. www.SmithKraus.com.

WOMEN PLAYWRIGHTS

The Best Plays of 2002

Edited by D. L. Lepidus

CONTEMPORARY PLAYWRIGHTS
SERIES

SK
A Smith and Kraus Book

A Smith and Kraus Book
Published by Smith and Kraus, Inc.
177 Lyme Road, Hanover, NH 03755
www.SmithKraus.com

First Edition: August 2003
10 9 8 7 6 5 4 3 2 1
Manufactured in the United States of America

Cover and text design by Julia Hill Gignoux, Freedom Hill Design
Carson Kreitzer photo by Ian Hansen, Cathy Caplan photo by Ronald G. Harris,
Gina Gionfriddo photo by Peter Hocking

The Library of Congress Cataloging-In-Publication Data
Women playwrights : the best plays of 2002 / edited by D. L. Lepidus
p. cm. — (Contemporary playwrights series)
ISBN 1-57525-365-8
1. American drama—women authors. 2. American drama—20th century.
3. Women—drama.
I. Smith, Marisa. II. Series: Contemporary playwrights series.
PS628.W6W668   1994
812'.540809287—dc20
94-10071
CIP

CONTENTS

FOREWORD

Out of the hundreds of plays I read or saw in the past year, the plays in this book are the best ones by women I found. In my view, they represent the vibrancy and scope of the sort of writing women playwrights are producing in this country. Here you will find plays whose styles vary wildly. Some are set in the present, illuminating our world in comic or tragic ways. Some are set in the past, asking us to journey to yesteryear, to compare our world with that of the Italian Renaissance or of a Shaker community pre–Civil War. If there is one thing that all these plays have in common, it is that all are very compelling stories. In some circles, plays that tell a story, in a more or less linear way, are considered hopelessly passé. If you are one of those readers whose main interest is style rather than substance, metaphor rather than simile, these plays might not be weird enough for you. If, however, you value a good story, dramatically well told, you'll find one after another in this volume.

Aren't you sick of stylistic "innovation" endlessly being praised to the skies, while plays, book,s and films that don't try to reinvent the form itself get dissed for their "conventionality"? I know I am.

As it happens, two plays in this book deal (albeit in different ways) with the vital yet often thorny issue of faith. Arlene Hutton's *As It Is in Heaven* is a fascinating story of women living in a community of Shakers, some of whom may (or may not) have had visions of angels; while Donna Spector's *Golden Ladder* focuses on faith as individual identity. Both plays dare to take the whole idea of faith seriously. Omigod, how outré!

Lauren Weedman's *Homecoming* also deals with personal identity. It's about a woman's search for her birth mother — many characters, all played by one actress and highly dramatic, rather than static, narrative.

Lapis Blue Blood Red and *Degas in New Orleans* are both about artists and the scandals surrounding them. In Cathy Caplan's gripping play, the central character is the Renaissance painter Artemisia Gentileschi; in Rosary O'Neill's, it is Edgar Degas.

Finally, we get to Carson Kreitzer's *Self Defense* and Gina Gionfriddo's *U.S. Drag*. Ms. Kreitzer's is a brilliant, surreal drama based on the true story of a serial killer in Florida — a prostitute found guilty of murdering her johns. It exposes the dark underbelly of American criminal justice and asks some very trenchant questions about this shocking case. Ms. Gionfriddo, on the other hand, isn't into shock. *U.S. Drag* (which might remind you a little of some of the comedies of Christopher Durang) is an amusing satire of two educated women determined to make as much money for as little work as possible. It was a co-winner of the prestigious Susan Smith Blackburn Prize, perhaps the most prestigious award for women playwrights.

I hope you enjoy these plays as much as I do.

D. L. Lepidus

INTRODUCTION

At the close of the 1980s, I studied acting in New York City. I dreaded scene study. You had to find a partner. The women would run for the guys; everyone knew you couldn't find a decent scene for two women. If you got a guy, chances are you'd have the smaller part, or you'd get to be a stripper, or a spinster, or the one who just got out of bed in her underwear. Perfectly valid, till you saw what the guys got to play.

Then you had to find a scene. I spent hours in the theater bookstores, looking. I guess I thought that if I really flipped through all those plays, somewhere, hidden, I'd find a gem. I rarely did, but it wouldn't have occurred to me to question the plays themselves — or the worlds of the plays — even as I found it difficult to give myself over to the characters in them, something I'd have to do if I was going to be an actor. These were plays. These were the plays there were.

After drama school, I figured if I wanted to work, I'd have to self-produce. And after searching for plays to produce with the same fruitless urgency I'd put into finding a scene, it occurred to me that if I found a play by a woman, maybe there'd be a better part in it for me, and I'd learn something that would make me a better actor.

So I went back to the bookstores. Spent many more hours there, staring down the shelves. Found a book of plays that had won the Susan Smith Blackburn Prize (for plays by women); the appendix listed winners and finalists, maybe a hundred plays. I thought, "Well, here we go, they must have these here." I stood in the bookstore with that book in my hands and went through the shelves alphabetically. Nothing. I wandered the store till my feet hurt, all the time hoping the bookstore guy wouldn't stop to ask me what I was looking for. 'Cause that was starting to feel like a pretty big question. Where were those plays? Was there somewhere else to look? On the West Coast where I grew up, the playwrights I'd heard of had always been either very dead or very far away. But now here I was in New York, closer to where the work was —

only to find that it was no closer to me. I couldn't find myself on the shelves of the drama bookstore, and man, I had *looked.*

Now, with my company, I've produced and developed new plays by women for ten years — happily one is published here. I've met playwrights, communed with playwrights, bucked 'em up . . . become one. Tried to find audiences for their plays. Wished I could wrap them up and send them as gifts to all the girls (and boys!) in all the scene classes in the country.

I don't know that plays by women are different, or more relatable-to, or have better women characters. I just know they have to get out there — into the literature, into the culture, into the hands of curious young drama students who may not yet have discovered what their contribution will be. Reading Claire Chafee's *Why We Have a Body* in the 1993 edition of this anthology was a wake-up call for my own muddled ambitions: I'd started thinking up my first play before I was halfway through it. These plays give license and opportunity to us all. And now — hooray! — they're available in a bookstore near you.

Susan Bernfield
Artistic Director, New Georges

As It Is in Heaven

By Arlene Hutton

In memory of Randy Folger

PLAYWRIGHT'S BIOGRAPHY

Arlene Hutton is a MacDowell Fellow and a member of New Dramatists, the Dramatists Guild and Circle East.

Her Appalachian romance *Last Train to Nibroc* received a 2000 Best Play nomination from the New York Drama League for its Off Broadway run. It has had more than fifty productions across the country, including the Barrow Group, Miniature Theatre of Chester, Florida Studio Theatre, ArtStation, Nebraska Rep, ManBites Dog, Riverside, Coyote and Actors, and Guild of Lexington. It was published by Smith and Kraus, Inc. in the anthology *Women Playwrights: Best Plays 1999*. A second full-length *As It Is in Heaven* premiered in Edinburgh, opened in New York City at the 78th Street Theatre Lab, and moved to the ArcLight Theatre. *Last Train to Nibroc* and *As It Is in Heaven* are published by Dramatists Play Service.

Three of Ms. Hutton's one-act plays, *Studio Portrait, A Closer Look,* and *The Price You Pay,* are winners of the Samuel French Short Play Festival and have been published by French. Other New York credits include Circle-in-the-Square Downtown, Alice's Fourth Floor, Ensemble Studio Theatre, and HERE Arts Center. Her one-acts *Pushing Buttons, Cafeteria,* and *Cubicles* were finalists for the 2001 and 2002 Heidemann Award at Actor's Theatre of Louisville. Ms. Hutton's one-acts, including *I Dream Before I Take the Stand,* have been presented at theaters across the country and abroad, and her plays have been translated into Dutch, Chinese, and Catalan.

Arlene Hutton was born and raised in the southern United States and lives in New York City, where she began writing plays in 1994 at Alice's Fourth Floor. A recipient of the John Lipman Award, an ART/NY Nancy Quinn Fund grant, and a Cameron Macintosh Foundation grant, Hutton recently received a commission from Clear Channel Theatrical Division and is writing a new full-length play about the Bronté family. She is an adjunct professor at Fordham University.

ORIGINAL PRODUCTION

As It Is in Heaven premiered at the Assembly Rooms for the 2001 Edinburgh Festival Fringe, as a coproduction of the Journey Company (Beth Lincks, producing artistic director) and the 78th Street Theatre Lab (Eric Nightengale, artistic director), directed by Beth Lincks. The associate director was Stephanie Sandberg; costume design was by Shelley Norton; lighting design was by Tyler Micoleau; and the stage manager was Annie Levy. This production then played at the 78th Street Theatre Lab, New York City, opening September 13, 2001. The cast was as follows:

HANNAH	Priscilla Shanks
PEGGY	Julie Alderfer
BETSY	Ruth Nightengale
PHEBE	Margot Avery
RACHEL	Lisa Hayes
JANE	Judith Hawking
POLLY	Carla Cantrelle
FANNY	Alexandra Geis
JANE	Soline McLain

The play was subsequently produced by the Journey Company and the 78th Street Theatre Lab in association with Laine Valentino and Evan Bergman at the ArcLight Theatre on January 11, 2002 with the following cast:

HANNAH	Priscilla Shanks
PEGGY	Julie Alderfer
BETSY	Ruth Nightengale
PHEBE	Margot Avery
RACHEL	Lisa Hayes
JANE	Alana West
POLLY	Carla Cantrelle
FANNY	Sarah Gifford
JANE	Soline McLain

PRODUCTION NOTES

STAGING   There should be no blackouts between scenes. The movement is fluid, with first line of a new scene following the line in the previous scene with no break in rhythm. If additional time is needed, it should be filled with song. The set and staging should exemplify the simplicity of the Shakers and their dedication to work. The play can be performed with six benches, a few baskets, and some laundry. Or the set can resemble a meetinghouse, with Shaker pegs. The women should be constantly at their tasks.

CASTING   It would be historically accurate to cast one or more of the roles using ethnic types. As to the ages, it is more important to determine the difference in the ages than the ages themselves. For instance, Peggy could be as old as eighty, but could also be played by a college student if it were made clear that she was older than Fanny, Polly, and Izzy. A director may choose to present the play with a larger cast for the meetinghouse and other scenes. But we should never see the men in the village.

MUSIC   The songs in the script are all Shaker hymns, meant to be sung a cappella. A director may want to put additional songs and dances into the play. A booklet with all the hymns in the play, plus some extra ones, has been compiled by the Shaker Village of Pleasant Hill. Information about this can be obtained from Shaker Village of Pleasant Hill, Kentucky; Attn: Music Programs Coordinator, 3501 Lexington Road, Harrodsburg, KY 40330-8846; phone: 1-800-734-5611, ext. 115; e-mail: donna@shakervillageky.org.

SOURCE MATERIAL   Helpful works include *The Shaker Spiritual* by Daniel Patterson, recently reprinted by Dover, and *The Gift to Be Simple* by Edward Andrews, also by Dover. Especially helpful are Sharon Koomler's The *Gift Drawing Collection of Hancock Shaker Village* and *Shaker Style,* as well as Deborah Burns's *Shaker Cities of Peace, Love and Union. The Shaker Experience in America* by Stephen Stein remains one of the definitive works on the Shakers. Roger Hall has a Web site on Shaker music. *The Shaker Heritage Guidebook,* published by Golden Hill Press, is an excellent source of information about Shaker sites, including the villages at Pleasant Hill, Hancock, South Union, Enfield, Canterbury, Sabbathday Lake, Mount Lebanon, and the Shaker Museum and Library at Old Chatham.

ACKNOWLEDGMENTS
Randy Folger, Stephanie Sandberg, Larrie Curry, Sharon Koomler, Jerry Grant, Rhoda Pollace, Judith Royer, Donald Maass, Vivian Sorenson, Emily Morse, Thomas Edward West, Cameron Macintosh Foundation, the John Lippman family, the Playwright's Project at Healing Springs, New Dramatists, The Barrow Group, The MacDowell Colony.

A NOTE ON THE SHAKERS

The United Society of Believers in the Second Coming of Christ, more commonly known as the Shakers, was originally founded in Manchester, England, during the 1770s. Enduring religious persecution from the British government, the first nine Shakers set out for America. Mother Ann Lee, the charismatic and visionary leader of the early Shakers, was among those first Believers who set foot on American soil in 1774. In a two-year preaching tour of New England, Ann Lee won many new converts to the faith and lay the foundations of the first Shaker communities. Mother Ann Lee died in 1783, by which time there were several established Shaker communities beginning to flourish.

The Shakers were an exemplary group of early Americans, struggling to make a new life for themselves in the rich wilderness. The new country became a vast testing ground for utopian communities such as the Shakers. Of all the hundreds of utopian societies founded in early America, the Shakers, who emphasized a strong integration of faith and daily life, are the most enduring. They established a cooperative life of piety, work, and clean living. Personal property and individual rights were unimportant; all of which were sacrificed for the common good of the community.

The Shakers believed that God was dual in nature, both mother and father to their children. They believed that Jesus Christ was the first manifestation of God's presence on earth, and Mother Ann Lee was the second. The Shakers believed that they were living in the millennium leading up the final judgment, and so they were not to be focused on earthly concerns. Because of this last belief, they lived a celibate life dedicated to building the kingdom of heaven on earth. They lived separate from the outside world, "the world's people," in complete devotion to Mother and Father God.

Throughout the nineteenth century, the Shakers continued to gain converts, building their numbers to over four thousand Believers. Since they regarded themselves as the children of their holy Mother and Father, they saw one another as sisters and brothers who were to live in devotion and union, practicing a virtuous life together. They divided each village into "families" of brothers and sisters who lived, worked, and worshipped in a confessional community. Males and females lived in equality and all races were welcome to join in Shaker life. The only element required to join was the signing of a covenant at the age of twenty.

As It Is in Heaven is set in the Shaker village of Pleasant Hill, Kentucky — one of the most prosperous of all the Shaker communities during its time. Formally established as a village in 1814, Pleasant Hill, like its sister communities, flourished in antebellum America. Their dedication to hard work, simplicity, and cleanliness became evident in the beauty of their architecture and designs. They lived a good life by selling their manufactured goods to the world's people — goods such as seeds, canned and dried foods, furniture, brooms, herbal medicines, and crafts. To many outsiders, especially the poor and disenfranchised, Shaker life was exceedingly attractive, even more so in times of hardship. There are many stories of "winter Shakers" — individuals who joined the Shaker communities for the bleak winter months, but come spring, left to return to the world's people.

By the 1820s the Shaker way of life was well established. Like most religious communities, internal disruptions arose, and many felt that the original vision of Mother Ann had been lost. All this changed due to an intense spiritual revival that began in 1837, a period of Shaker history known as "Mother Ann's Work." *As It Is in Heaven* is set during this period of revival when believers experienced visions, trances, and all the phenomena of religious fervor. Intense periods of shaking and dancing, visions, and the channeling of spirits disrupted the orderly flow of the Shaker service. Many received what they termed "gifts," which were divine inspirations, experiences, or abilities. For example, during this revival many received gifts that manifested themselves in colorful spirit drawings. Others received visions and messages from Mother Ann. These revivalist experiences swept through all the Shaker communities, causing many to return to their beliefs and others to doubt.

In the rush of American industrialism and modernization after the Civil War, many of the Shaker communities disbanded. Their simple way of life was no longer attractive in a world of emerging materialist consumerism. The Shaker's story and experience is embraced by many Americans today as a national treasure. At its heart, the Shaker experience is about religious freedom and the American puritan values of hard work and endurance, brotherhood and sisterhood, and equality. Their beautiful utopian experiment will be cherished for generations.

Stephanie Sandberg
Associate Director
As It Is in Heaven

CHARACTERS

PEGGY: The cook. Meek, quiet and trustful, easily hurt.

HANNAH: An eldress. Tries to be merciful and kind.

PHEBE: A deaconess. Seeks righteousness.

BETSY: A deaconess. The peacemaker, but also a gossip.

RACHEL: A longtime Shaker. Pure in heart.

IZZY: The youngest. Raised with Shakers. Persecuted for righteousness sake.

NEWCOMERS

FANNY: A newcomer. Independent. Accused falsely.

POLLY: A newcomer. Poor in spirit, needy, bitter.

JANE: Mournful, sad.

TIME

Around 1838.

PLACE

A Shaker village at Pleasant Hill, Kentucky. Benches on a bare stage become both indoor and outdoor locations in the village.

AS IT IS IN HEAVEN 7

As It Is in Heaven

Act I

Scene One

A Shaker village in Pleasant Hill, Kentucky, 1838. The stage may subtly re-semble a Shaker meetinghouse. There are six to eight wooden benches on stage, which move around for the various scenes. There are no entrances and exits from or to offstage; when the actresses are not in a scene, they sit on the side benches and sew or knit. Their hands are always busy, even when they are out of the light.

There are no blackouts or pauses between scenes. The movement from scene to scene is fluid throughout the play; we do not wait for the set to change before the next scene starts. The actors frequently begin speaking the lines for the new scene while they are still in the previous scene. The benches are moved, or they move them, and they walk into the new scene. Sometimes a scene or song is happening in the foreground while a new scene is setting up behind the action, in full view of the audience. The downstage actors finish their scene and exit to the side benches, revealing the new scene upstage. Each scene has a task; none of the work of the Sisters should be totally mimed — there must always be a prop to represent the task.

The women all wear simple white sheer caps. The dresses are more col-orful than we would expect, and each woman wears a shawl-like kerchief. Occasionally an apron is worn.

At the start of the play the benches are set in rows like pews. The Sisters enter, singing as they dance a structured march. By the end of it they have taken their places in the meetinghouse.

PEGGY: *(Singing.)* Welcome, welcome precious gospel kindred.
ALL: *(Singing.)* We are happy you to meet
And make you freely welcome.
By the cords of union pure
Our hearts are bound together.
And the love we bear to you
No friendship e'er can sever.
(The song repeats as long as needed for the Sisters to get to their places. They all sit, except for Hannah.)

HANNAH: Let all confess their sins.

> (*Hannah sits. There is silence, and then the confessions come quickly. Each woman stands to make her confession and then sits.*)

PEGGY: I slept late last Thursday.

BETSY: I was angry at the hens. They nipped Izzy when she was gathering eggs. I was angry at them.

RACHEL: I, I, I forgot to pray for some of the Sisters this week.

BETSY: Yesterday I heard two boys quarreling and I passed them by without reporting them.

JANE: I pray that I keep my mind on my tasks.

BETSY: I ate bread between meals.

> (*A beat.*)

PEGGY: I wished that Sister Jane would fall asleep and not cry in her bed. I was prideful of my new apron.

BETSY: I wrung that rooster's neck in anger. 'Cause he pecked Izzy.

RACHEL: I threw a stone at a stray dog.

> (*Betsy, Jane, and Izzy all stand up at the same time to confess. Betsy and Izzy sit down.*)

JANE: I confess that my mind wandered while I should have been working.

IZZY: I teased the chickens. They nipped me 'cause I was teasing them. I confess that I was teasing the hens. Tryin' to pet the chicks.

> (*Betsy stands up, as if to respond to Izzy, but sits back down without speaking. There is a pause, and Betsy stands up again.*)

BETSY: I gossiped.

> (*A beat.*)

PHEBE: I became impatient when the children ran through the garden. I scolded them too harshly for trampling the seedlings and ruining the tomato plants.

POLLY: I fed my dinner to the cats. I confess that I couldn't eat it and I fed it to the cats.

BETSY: I didn't thank Sister Peggy for making waffles on my birthday.

RACHEL: I cursed at some raccoons.

POLLY: I forgot to throw out the food that the cats didn't eat. I confess that I forgot about the raccoons.

BETSY: I don't thank Sister Peggy often enough for her hard work in the kitchen.

PHEBE: I ate extra helpings of mashed potatoes without asking.

IZZY: I put extra gravy on my mashed potatoes.

BETSY: I had three helpings of soup beans.

RACHEL: At grace I forgot to give thanks for Sister Peggy's cooking. (*A pause.*)

PEGGY: I daydreamed and burned the muffins.

FANNY: May I be given strength to do my kitchen chores even better.

PHEBE: I am frequently impatient with the newcomers. With Sister Fanny and Sister Polly and Sister Jane. May I realize that they have much to learn about our ways.

(Sister Jane stands, starts to say something, but doesn't. She sits.)

PEGGY: I neglected to comfort Sister Jane in her sorrow.

POLLY: I looked at Brother Abraham in the meeting. Caught his eye.

FANNY: I went past the . . . *(She stops. Polly stares at her.)* Past the meetinghouse without saying a prayer. Walked right on by. *(Silence.)*

PHEBE: May we be forgiven and deserving in your eyes. Hear our prayers.

RACHEL: May we pray for our leaders and give thanks for their guidance. We pray for our deaconesses, Sister Betsy and Sister Phebe. We give thanks for the wisdom and love of our eldress, Sister Hannah.

PHEBE: *(Interrupting.)* We pray — we pray for the continued health and well-being of all the Sisters and the Brethren.

BETSY: Let us give thanks and praise. Let us work as if we were to live forever. Let us live as if we were to die tomorrow. Grant us grace and peace.

FANNY: Amen. *(When no one else says amen, Fanny realizes she responded too quickly.)*

HANNAH: May we go forth in the strength and the power of the gospel and labor for the spirit of conviction.

ALL:. Amen.

(Peggy, who clearly likes to sing, begins a song.)

PEGGY: *(Singing.)* Come life, shaker life

ALL: *(Standing and singing.)* Come life, eternal
Shake, shake out of me,
All that is carnal.

(The Sisters move to their positions in the next scene, moving the benches when necessary, singing all the while.)

I'll take nimble steps
I'll be a David
I'll show Michael twice
How he behavéd.

(Lights change. By the end of the song the stage is set for the next scene and the actors are in place.)

Scene Two

In a special light we see Polly sitting on one end of a bench which is perpendicular to the stage. On either side are Betsy and Jane standing, who interrogate her. The pace is very quick.

BETSY: *(To Polly.)* What did you see?

POLLY: I don't know.

BETSY: Must have been something powerful.

POLLY: Weren't much o' nothin'. Nothin' at'll.

JANE: We sometimes don't know what we see.

POLLY: Didn't see much of anything, I reckon.

BETSY: Well, then.

POLLY: You believe me?

JANE: No.

BETSY: If you say you didn't see anything, then, yes, I believe you.

JANE: She didn't say that. Didn't say she didn't see anything.

BETSY: *(To Polly.)* Then what did you see?

POLLY: I don't know.

JANE: She don't know what she saw. *(To Polly.)* You don't know what you saw.

POLLY: I don't know. It couldn't be —

BETSY: What couldn't it be?

POLLY: Fanny said.

JANE: We want to know what you saw.

POLLY: Fanny said it were angels. *(Lights change. We hear singing from the women sitting on the benches. Peggy, Phebe, Betsy, and Rachel sit and spread out a large cloth over their laps.)*

ALL: *(Singing.)* I will bow and be simple
I will bow and be free
I will bow and be humble
Yea, bow like the willow tree.
(Lights change. Still singing, the women move the benches to set up for the next scene.)

Scene Three

Peggy, Phebe, Betsy, Rachel are quilting, miming needles and thread. They hum or sing softly, obviously enjoying their work and their time together.

PEGGY, BETSY, PHEBE, RACHEL: *(Singing.)* I will bow this is the token
    I will wear the easy yoke
    I will bow and be broken
    Yea, I'll fall upon the rock.

BETSY: Sister Peggy, you look a little peakéd.

PHEBE: Indeed you do.

RACHEL: Hmm.

PHEBE: Too much close work.

PEGGY: I like it.

PHEBE: Quilting. Making labels for the jelly jars. Too much close work.

RACHEL: Hmm.

PEGGY: I'm quite well.

PHEBE: Fresh air would put color in your face.

BETSY: *(To Peggy.)* Would you like a respite from your quilting?

RACHEL: 'Taint the quilting that makes her look tired.

BETSY: Are you not sleeping well, Sister Peggy?

PEGGY: I've missed some nights.

RACHEL: Hmm.

PHEBE: You need your sleep.

RACHEL: Hmm.

BETSY: Should Sister Phebe administer herbs to you?

RACHEL: It's Sister Jane. She's in the room with Sister Jane.

PHEBE: That'll keep anybody from a good night's sleep.

BETSY: Is there a difficulty? Is there a difficulty with Sister Jane?

PEGGY: She cries all night.

PHEBE: Sister Jane can leave the community if she is not happy here.

BETSY: She signed the covenant.

PEGGY: Yes, she did.

BETSY: By her own free will.

PHEBE: Could leave if she liked.

RACHEL: I don't think Sister Jane would be happy anywhere.

PHEBE: I don't think Sister Jane was ever happy.

RACHEL: She's been here nigh on a year now.

BETSY: Came with her husband.

RACHEL: That's right.

BETSY: Brother James.

RACHEL: No.

PEGGY: It was Brother William.

BETSY: No.

PEGGY: Yes. It was Brother William.

BETSY: Of course it was.

RACHEL: Brother William.

BETSY: Brother William is good with the carpentry. Liked to raise that barn by himself.

PEGGY: He'll make deacon some day.

RACHEL: He'll make a good deacon.

PHEBE: Yes, he will.

RACHEL: Maybe make elder.

PEGGY: He looks like an elder.

RACHEL: He does look like an elder.

PEGGY: With that fine beard.

RACHEL: That is a fine beard on him. Full. Not scraggly like Brother Timothy's. Brother William keeps his beard in good trim. It's a tidy beard. You're right. He'll make a fine-looking elder some day.

BETSY: Always has a cheerful countenance.

PHEBE: Because he doesn't live with Sister Jane anymore.

(They laugh. Hannah enters and takes her place. The women focus on their work. Rachel hands Hannah a threaded needle. All sew in silence.)

HANNAH: Several of the brothers took the wagon to Lexington this morning. Taking the seed packets to sell. Going to bring us a new pot. I requested a new soup pot and a kettle.

PEGGY: The kitchen could use some new pots.

(All sew in silence.)

BETSY: My needle's gone dull.

PHEBE: Here is one. *(She mimes a needle.)*

BETSY: Thank you, Sister Phebe.

(All sew in silence.)

HANNAH: They'll be slaughtering that hog next week.

PEGGY: Izzy will be sad.

RACHEL: Hmm.

BETSY: Izzy raised that hog from a piglet.

RACHEL: *(Agreeing.)* Little piglet.

(They quilt in silence.)

HANNAH: The elders have a concern. *(All stop sewing and look at her.)* The Brethren mentioned to me that they have noticed some of the sisters gossiping.

PHEBE: Surely not.

BETSY: Must be the North Family they're talking about.

RACHEL: Hmm.

HANNAH: Surely you are right. Must be the North Family.

(They begin to sew again. Jane enters and takes her place at the quilt. She just touches it.)

HANNAH: Welcome, Sister Jane. *(Jane sits at the quilt but does not sew.)*

JANE: Reminds me of a baby quilt I made once. Wonder what happened to that quilt.

BETSY: Baby quilts are nice to make. Make 'em up quick, they're so small.

PEGGY: *(Kindly.)* Sister Jane, your babies are in heaven. They don't need quilts.

JANE: Oh, I recollect now! We buried one of my little boys in that quilt. My little boy Benjamin.

HANNAH: Sister Peggy, perhaps it would be wise to prepare the kitchen for the new pots.

PEGGY: I'll tend to that right now, Sister Hannah. *(Peggy knots off her thread and stands to leave.)*

HANNAH: Sister Jane, perhaps you could assist Sister Peggy.

JANE: Yes, I will do that. *(Jane stands and turns to go.)*

HANNAH: And Sister Jane

JANE: Yes, Sister Hannah?

HANNAH: *(As she begins folding the quilt.)* It was mentioned by a cousin of yours that you make fine oatmeal sweet cakes. Perhaps you would make some for us today. The brothers will be hungry after their journey.

JANE: But Sister Peggy always does the baking. *(Hannah stands, preparing to leave. The women take the quilt from her.)*

HANNAH: I understand that you are a fine baker, as well. Sometimes we need to change the way we do things. We look forward to your sweet cakes. *(Lights change as Peggy begins the next song. Jane and Hannah move two of the benches to the side and sit.)*

Scene Four

Peggy sings, as Rachel, Phebe, and Betsy dance. Or all four could sing and dance.

PEGGY: *(Singing.)* Who will bow and bend like a willow,
  Who will turn and twist and reel
  In the gale of simple freedom,
  From the bower of union flowing.
  Who will drink the wine of power,
  Dropping down like a shower, pride
  And bondage all forgetting,
  Mother's wine is freely working.
PEGGY, RACHEL, PHEBE, BETSY: *(Singing.)* Oh, ho! I will have it,
  I will bow and bend to get it,
  I'll be reeling, turning, twisting,
  Shake out all the starch and stiff'ning!
  (By the end of the song Peggy and Izzy have taken their place on a bench, and the other women have returned to their places on the side benches.)

Scene Five

Hannah and Fanny downstage. Peggy and Izzy on an upstage bench, in shadow.

HANNAH: Sister Fanny —
FANNY: Yes, Sister Hannah?
HANNAH: Your cousin came to the trustee's office again. Looking for you.
FANNY: I don't want to be no bother to anyone.
HANNAH: No bother. We sent him away.
FANNY: Thank you, Sister Hannah.
  (Hannah starts to leave but turns.)
HANNAH: You are safe here, Sister Fanny. And kindly welcome.
  (Hannah and Fanny exit, revealing . . . Lights up on Peggy, Izzy breaking green beans into a pot, tossing the ends and strings into a basket.)
PEGGY: Snap 'em.
IZZY: Beggin' your pardon.

PEGGY: You snap 'em, Izzy. Snap the beans. Don't just break 'em. Give it a little snap.

IZZY: Don't make much difference. They're going to the same pot.

PEGGY:. If they don't snap, they go back to the garden.

IZZY: Why don't you cut the beans? Slice 'em with a knife. Faster.

PEGGY: Cain't tell if it's a good bean, then. If the bean don't give a nice little snap when you break it, if it's soft, the bean's not good enough. If it don't snap, ya throw it back into the compost and give it another chance to be a better bean next time 'round.

IZZY: It'll still taste the same. Tastes the same in the pot. No one'll know if you cut it or snap it.

PEGGY: You will know. *(Izzy snaps a bean.)* And God will know.

(Lights change as Polly and Fanny begin the next scene in a different part of the stage.)

Scene Six

POLLY: *(Handing a broom to Fanny and beginning to sweep.)* Where were you?

FANNY: You seen the baby lambs?

POLLY: You were gone an awful long time.

FANNY: They're precious.

POLLY: Sister Phebe asked about you.

FANNY: Sister Rachel was there. With the lambs.

POLLY: Long time to be looking at lambs. Went back the meadow, didn't you? Izzy saw you go. She was up the stairs. Saw you go. No lambs past the meadow. You meet'n a bigger beast maybe? Maybe there's a stallion past the meadow. Big ole stallion await'n for you.

FANNY: Weren't no stallion there.

POLLY: I know'd you went, so you best be telling me where.

FANNY: Past the meadow. Past the big willow tree. I seen things. I heerd . . .

POLLY: Who'd ya see? Were it Jane? Out there a cryin'? Were it Jane?

FANNY: You wouldn't believe it.

POLLY: Who'd ya see?

FANNY: I seen angels. There's angels out there — past the meadow.

Scene Seven

Lights have changed to the special interrogation lights. The set has changed during the previous scene. We find Izzy seated at one end of a bench set perpendicular to the edge of the stage, flanked by Phebe and Rachel.

PHEBE: What did you see?
IZZY: *(To Rachel.)* They were from heaven.
PHEBE: What were?
RACHEL: Everything comes from heaven.
IZZY: They were beautiful. They were the most beautiful —
PHEBE: *(Overlapping.)* Tell us everything you saw.
IZZY: Gold. Lots of gold. And I heard music.
PHEBE: Maybe you were dreaming.
IZZY: It seemed like a dream. So beautiful.
PHEBE: What did it look like?
IZZY: Light. Beautiful light. Heavenly light.
PHEBE: *(To Rachel.)* She was dreaming.
IZZY: Weren't no dream.
PHEBE: I wasn't talking to you.
IZZY: Weren't no dream. I thought it was. I thought it was at first. I heard sounds. Like music, but not like music. I looked up and seen a light so bright. Brighter than the sun even, but it didn't hurt my eyes to look at it. I thought I must be dreaming, so I slapped my arm. And pinched at my hand. I pinched it hard. So hard. Look. Look at the bruise. Weren't no dream.
RACHEL: Surely that must be heaven she seen.
PHEBE: Dreams show us heaven sometimes. You pinched yourself in your sleep.
IZZY: No! Fanny seen it, too.

(Fanny stands from her side bench position and moves onstage purposefully. Izzy walks into the next scene and begins it immediately following her last line. Lights change, as Phebe and Rachel move the benches.)

Scene Eight

Izzy walks up to Fanny, who keeps moving around the stage.

IZZY: Fanny! *(No answer. Izzy follows her.)* Fanny! *(Izzy catches up to her. Fanny walks a while, Izzy behind.)*

FANNY: Don't you have chores?

IZZY: Finished. Fed the chickens. I can come with you.

FANNY: I don't recollect inviting you.

IZZY: I want to see . . . see the . . .

(Fanny turns to face her.)

FANNY: See what? What is it you wanting to see?

IZZY: What you've been seeing.

FANNY: I've been seeing blueberries. And I aim to pick us some. Gonna spoil that nice white apron o' yours if you come pickin' blueberries with me.

(Izzy turns to go as Polly runs on.)

POLLY: *(To Fanny.)* Was looking for you.

FANNY: Getting to be a party now, Polly.

IZZY: *(To Polly.)* Fanny's going to pick blueberries.

POLLY: Too early for blueberries.

FANNY: Found some early ones.

IZZY: Early ones'll be sour.

POLLY: She's going out past the meadow.

IZZY: *(To Fanny.)* You said you were going berry-picking.

POLLY: Where's her pail, then?

IZZY: You don't have a pail! *(A beat.)*

FANNY: Just wanted to be alone. Not used to spending every waking minute someone by my side. just like to go sit and look at the trees sometimes.

IZZY: I won't bother you. I won't even talk to you.

POLLY: You're seeing something in the trees.

FANNY: *(Starting to leave.)* Sure, I am. Birds. I'm seeing birds in the trees. And squirrels.

(Polly is following her throughout the following. Izzy tags along.)

IZZY: Are there baby squirrels? Funny how you never see baby squirrels. Baby birds. You see them. Once I found a baby bird fallen out of its nest. I put it back.

POLLY: It died.

IZZY: How do you know? I put it back.

POLLY: Mama bird won't touch a young'un after a person's handled it.

IZZY: Maybe it didn't die.

POLLY: Won't touch it once it's tainted with a human smell. Momma bird won't have anything to do with it.

FANNY: You saved it, Izzy. You saved its life.

(They keep walking.)

IZZY: Once I found a hummingbird caught in a spider web. I pulled that spider web off it. Flew off, happy as could be. Aren't hummingbirds the most beautiful thing? Little spirits flying around. Little angels, almost.

POLLY: Fanny sees angels. You told me you did. Unless it was a false gift.

FANNY: Weren't false. Ain't no false gift.

POLLY: If you're seeing something, then show us. I think it's a lying gift. I don't believe in spirits and angels no how.

IZZY: Mother Ann saw spirits.

POLLY: She's making it up. She's lying.

(Fanny stops and stares westward.)

IZZY: *(To Fanny.)* Are you making it up?

POLLY: She's making it up. I'm going back. I'm hungry.

FANNY: There's berries over there.

POLLY: Too early for berries.

(Izzy sees the berries.)

IZZY: Those are the biggest blueberries I ever saw. Don't see any squirrels or birds. Sure is quiet here.

POLLY: There it is! *(Polly gooses Izzy, who squeals.)*

IZZY: Where?

POLLY: Sun's about to set. There's nothing here.

FANNY: Over there.

POLLY: Where?

FANNY: There. *(She points.)*

IZZY: Where?

POLLY: An angel?

FANNY: Don't know.

IZZY: I should be getting back.

POLLY: You scared?

FANNY: Thought you wanted to see.

IZZY: I do.

FANNY: *(Suddenly stops.)* Then look.

IZZY: Don't see anything. Where am I supposed to look?

POLLY: It's getting warmer. Should be getting cooler, but it's getting warmer.

FANNY: Hush.

POLLY: What do you see?

FANNY: Hush.

IZZY: I'm scared.

FANNY: *(Whispers.)* Don't be scared, Izzy. It's the most beautiful thing you ever did see.

IZZY: *(Whispering back.)* More beautiful than a hummingbird?

FANNY: Like a hundred hummingbirds all at once.
  (The lights shift. Fanny holds out her arms.)
IZZY: Ohhhh. *(Fanny closes her eyes. Izzy and Polly look skyward.)* Ohhh, I see light.
FANNY: Hush.
POLLY: Where?
  (Fanny stands and faces the light as if it were sunlight streaming on her face after a long dark winter.)
POLLY: What do you see?
IZZY: So beautiful!
POLLY: Don't see anything except the pink clouds!
IZZY: The light!
POLLY: It's the sunset, silly.
IZZY: I hear the wings! Like a hundred hummingbirds! Oh, oh, oh . . .
POLLY: Just the breeze, Izzy. Just a warm breeze rustling though the trees. *(Polly shakes Izzy, who continues to look all around.)*
IZZY: Gold. All gold.
POLLY: Where?
FANNY: What do you hear, Izzy?
IZZY: Music? Singing? Sounds like I never heard before.
POLLY: *(Shouting.)* You're making it up! It's just a sunset.
FANNY: Look at the clouds, Polly.
POLLY: You're making it up!
FANNY: Look at the clouds!
POLLY: *(Covering her face.)* No!
FANNY: Does that look like any sunset you've ever seen before?
POLLY: *(In denial.)* No!
IZZY: Like a thousand hummingbirds!
  (Izzy and Fanny run off. Polly turns to go and runs into Rachel carrying a basket of laundry. Lights change.)

Scene Nine

RACHEL: Sister Polly, where's the fire?
POLLY: *(Out of breath.)* No, I, I, I don't know.
RACHEL: Catch your breath.
  (Betsy enters with a laundry basket and sets the benches with Rachel, all the time continuing the scene. They begin folding laundry.)

RACHEL: Something startled Sister Polly.

BETSY: *(Laughing.)* Seeing spirits, are you?

POLLY: No!

RACHEL: Hmm.

BETSY: Best not be. 'Til you sign the covenant.

POLLY: Really?

RACHEL: She's just funnin' you.

POLLY: How did you know you were ready to sign the covenant?

RACHEL: Just seemed like the thing to do, one day.

POLLY: Did you see . . . ? You just suddenly became a believer?

BETSY: Don't have to be a believer to sign the covenant.

RACHEL: Hmm.

BETSY: Don't have to believe. Just have to try.

POLLY: Were you always a believer?

BETSY: Sister Rachel was a minister's wife. She had to believe.

RACHEL: Joined with my late husband. And the entire congregation. Every last one of us believed.

BETSY: *(Beat.)* I didn't believe. When I came here. No. Didn't believe at all. Didn't have any family much, bringing me up. It's nicer here. Never had so many clothes to wear. And shoes. Shoes year-round. And if they wear out they get fixed. And if they wear out again, I get a new pair. Always like having shoes. I thought I'd be here a year, two at the most . . . Some people here eighty year old. Where else do I see so many people eighty year old? Being taken care of. Who's going to take care of me? Longer I'm here the more I believe.

RACHEL: Hmm. Have to want to believe. It's the journey that matters.

POLLY: I don't have to always believe?

RACHEL: We'll help you.

BETSY: Have faith and belief will come. Work like you believe. Sing like you believe.

RACHEL: You ever go to a barn dance? You twirl round and round 'til you're feeling dizzy? Same thing at the meetinghouse. You march round and round, you're bound to feel dizzy. You stop for just a minute to catch your breath, and the singing sweeps you up again, dancing and twirling and freeing yourself from earthly concerns.

BETSY: Listen to you, you old Methodist!

RACHEL: Don't miss being a Methodist. I like to dance.

POLLY: I'm always out of step.

RACHEL: You'll catch on to it after a while. Started forming the marches about ten years ago. Some people dancing the same dances for years. Singing the same songs. For years. You'll catch on.

POLLY: I don't like singing together all the time. Want some harmony.

RACHEL: Plain and simple.

POLLY: *(Confessing.)* And I don't like the circles. Afraid I'll go off in the wrong direction and end up dancing with the men.

RACHEL: That would be a dancin' gift! You a-twirlin' on the men's side. Give the old'uns palpitations.

POLLY: End up in the lap of Brother Timothy!

RACHEL: He's so blind, wouldn't know what was happening. Be thinking he'd got a gift from heaven and not be able to see what it was!

BETSY: Or end up twirlin' yourself into the arms of Brother Abraham.

POLLY: Hush!

RACHEL: *(Pointing.)* Rosy cheeks. Thinkin' of Brother Abraham.

(They giggle, as Jane enters with a basket of clothes.)

JANE: What about Brother Abraham?

POLLY: He's a looker!

JANE: I'm not looking. *(To Polly, pointedly.)* You shouldn't be, neither. *(Looks offstage.)* That ole bull Comet will be the death of me. Snortin' and runnin' at the fence. Pastured too close to the wash house. *(To Polly.)* You shouldn't be lookin' at the men.

POLLY: Weren't. We were just funnin'.

JANE: Gave all that up. Don't need any men anymore.

POLLY: Don't you miss bein' married sometimes?

JANE: Not one bit of it. Don't miss havin' a baby every year and wonderin' if they're gonna live long enough to walk. All that pain for nothin'. And if they do grow enough to walk and talk, you start lovin' on them every day and gettin' used to havin' your own family and then they get sickly and leave you quick as anything. I don't miss nursin' sick children who're gonna die anyway. So, no, missy, I don't miss being married. You young'ns think it's all pretty words and bouquets of flowers, but I'm here to tell you that it ain't.

RACHEL: Your husband's a good man. Become a good solid Shaker. Works hard.

POLLY: Being with a man's a natural thing.

RACHEL: For the world's people. Not for us.

JANE: Well, I don't miss it. *(Looks offstage.)* What am I going to do? That ole bull won't let me near the clothesline. Flies at the fence every time I try to take down a linen.

RACHEL: Comet wouldn't hurt a no-see-um flying in his face.

POLLY: But it's natural, wantin' to be with a man.

RACHEL: Mother Ann Lee teaches us to keep our eyes on heaven. Not on earthly wants.

POLLY: We eat and we sleep.

RACHEL: So we can do Mother Ann Lee's work.

JANE: Mother Ann lost four babies. Afore she stopped lying with her husband. Four babies.

RACHEL: *(To Polly.)* Fix your eyes on heaven. You won't think about earthly wants.

POLLY: If it's natural, like eating and sleeping . . .

RACHEL: Some people find a sweetheart and get married. We give our hearts to God. *(Rachel grabs some of the laundry and exits.)*

JANE: *(Looking off.)* That ole bull Comet sure don't like those linens on the line. The worst is the petticoats. He sees them a-wavin' at him and he goes crazy, just like a man. Goin' crazy over the petticoats on the other side of the fence.

(Izzy comes running in.)

IZZY: Mischief had kittens!

POLLY: Again?

(Jane keeps working.)

IZZY: She had kittens! Three, four of 'em! In the laundry basket. On the clean laundry! I don't think anyone'll mind, do you? She just popped one out and licked it and then another came out and another. One looks like Mischief and two look like Mr. Chickenhouse. But the last little one, all motley colored, was just lying there. Mischief didn't even lick that one. Just pushed it aside. *(Izzy looks at Polly, who doesn't speak. Izzy turns to Jane.)*

JANE: Cats are smarter than people sometimes. *(As she gets up to go.)* Know when to give up on a sickly child.

(Jane goes back to the side benches. Rachel, Betsy and Izzy carry off the laundry baskets as they exit to the side benches. Lights change.)

Scene Ten

Polly sings as she moves the benches. She stacks one on top of the other to make a table.

POLLY: *(Singing.)* My carnal life I will lay down
Because it is depraved.

I'm sure on any other ground
I never can be saved.
(Lights change.)

Scene Eleven

Polly finishes her song and begins to draw, standing at the "table." Betsy enters from one side and Peggy from the other. All three women use dowels for brushes and mime drawing.

BETSY: You have a beautiful script, Sister Polly. And look at that apple. That is a lovely apple. *(Betsy and Peggy begin to work.)*

POLLY: I like making pictures. Drawing the fruit.

PEGGY: Some Sisters couldn't tell the jelly jars apart. Before you started making pictures for them.

POLLY: Why not?

BETSY: Can't read. Some of the older Sisters are unable to read. And some of the younger ones if they're new.

PEGGY: Your fruit pictures are welcome.

POLLY: I try to make them pretty.

PEGGY: Just make them plain and simple.

BETSY: A little color is nice.

PEGGY: Just to tell what the fruit is. Don't embellish.

BETSY: Sister Polly is an artist.

PEGGY: *(To Betsy.)* Sister Polly is of service here. Her labels are clear. *(To Polly.)* We'll have you helping Sister Betsy with the seed packets next.

POLLY: Seed packets would be fun.

PEGGY: It's not for fun.

POLLY: Sister Betsy's seed packets are beautiful.

BETSY: They are useful. Sell the seeds to the world's people.

POLLY: They are beautiful. All the colors.

BETSY: I try to keep them simple.

POLLY: They look just like the vegetables. Not like my drawings.

PEGGY: Your fruit drawings are unmistakable. Plain. Simple.

POLLY: My trees.

PEGGY: *(Curious.)* What trees?

POLLY: Oh, if I were to draw a tree . . . On a seed packet.

PEGGY: *(Confused.)* There are no seed packets for trees.

POLLY: If there were.

PEGGY: There aren't. *(They work in silence.)* Are you drawing trees, Sister Polly?

BETSY: I must commence working on some herb pictures. Sister Polly, I simply can't seem to get the rosemary right. All those spiny little leaves. Tricky little leaves. Would you sketch it out for me?

(Polly just stares at her.)

PEGGY: Are you drawing trees, Sister Polly?

BETSY: It's the little details that escape me. I'm better at the vegetables.

PEGGY: Sister Polly?

POLLY: Yes, Sister Peggy?

BETSY: I like a good round radish. Or a tomato. Even a carrot. Something with color. Don't care for drawing potatoes or turnips. And those little herbs are tricky. Trying to tell them apart. Always have to ask Sister Phebe which is which. All those little leaves.

PEGGY: Perhaps Sister Polly can help you with the little leaves on the herbs. For the seed packets. Perhaps Sister Polly is accustomed to drawing leaves. Perhaps Sister Polly should direct her drawing talent toward useful service.

(Peggy exits. Betsy and Polly work in silence for a moment. Polly stops and looks at Betsy.)

POLLY: I have a gift to draw.

BETSY: You have a talent to draw.

POLLY: I have a gift to draw.

BETSY: What's your meaning, Sister Polly?

POLLY: I have a gift to draw. It just comes out of me. The strangest drawings. Trees and birds.

BETSY: Trees and birds aren't strange.

POLLY: Trees and birds like I've never seen. I have a gift to draw trees and birds, but I only see them in my head. Well, you understand. You have a talent.

BETSY: I have a talent to draw what I see so others can recognize it. Vegetables. Fruits.

POLLY: But you see it in your head.

BETSY: No. I have to look at what I'm drawing for anybody to be able to tell what it is. Can't just draw it without seeing it.

POLLY: But you see it in your head. Right now. You could draw a carrot. Right now if you wanted to.

BETSY: Might look like a long orange potato. No. I have to look at what I'm drawing. See it in front of me.

POLLY: Not in your head.

BETSY: On the table in front of me.

POLLY: Oh.

BETSY: Have to see it. *(A pause.)* Do you draw from your head, Sister Polly?

POLLY: I have a gift to draw.

BETSY: I would make certain it is not a false gift.

POLLY: I have a gift to draw. *(Polly pulls something from her pocket.)* This is for you, Sister Betsy.

(Polly hands her a colored heart with drawing and writing on it. Betsy just looks at Polly for a moment without speaking. Lights change. Betsy and Polly move the benches as the other women enter.)

Scene Twelve

The lights are suddenly bright, as if the sun is shining. The Sisters are chasing chickens, ad-libbing "chick, chick, chick."

RACHEL: Here, chick, chick, chick.

PEGGY: Some roosting in the trees.

BETSY: Chick, chick, chick.

RACHEL: Get the cats! The cats are chasing the chickens. Mr. Chickenhouse! Mr. Chickenhouse!

PEGGY: Got a chick in his mouth. He's under the coop. Here, kitty, kitty, kitty.

RACHEL: Mischief! Mischief!

BETSY: There she is. Yonder past the trees.

(Jane enters.)

RACHEL: Chickens are gone.

PEGGY: Chick, chick, chick.

RACHEL: Dogs chased the chickens into the woods.

FANNY: Chick, chick, chick.

BETSY: Mr. Chickenhouse better not come out, neither, if he knows what's good for him.

RACHEL: Wait'll the chickens get hungry.

IZZY: We'll get them back.

RACHEL: Catch 'em then.

POLLY: Chickens are stupid. *(Polly laughs.)*

PEGGY: So stupid you can't catch 'em.

POLLY: *(Laughing, as she looks for chickens.)* Chick, chick, chick.

RACHEL: Mr. Chickenhouse's got a baby chick. Under the coop.

POLLY: *(Suppressing a giggle.)* Chick, chick, chick.

IZZY: *(Horrified.)* No! *(Polly giggles more.)*

BETSY: You find that funny, Sister Polly?

FANNY: She has a laughing gift. *(Polly can't stop giggling.)*

POLLY: I have a laughing gift! *(Polly and Fanny laugh uproariously. Izzy looks at them.)*

FANNY: We have a laughing gift.

(They are falling down with laughter. Polly laughs hysterically and bumps into Izzy who catches the laughing gift. Rachel begins to laugh. Peggy watches in disbelief.)

RACHEL: We have a laughing gift.

(At this news, Fanny, Polly, and Izzy explode with laughter. Izzy falls into Jane, and she laughs. Fanny exits, looking for the chickens. Phebe enters.)

PHEBE: Who left the gate open? Who left the gate open? *(No one answers.)* It's not funny.

RACHEL: *(Laughing.)* Maybe it's the devil.

PHEBE: Who was feeding the chickens?

PEGGY: I sent Sister Polly out for some eggs.

POLLY: I saw Sister Fanny walking past the hen house.

PHEBE: I will have a word with Sister Fanny. You, too, Sister *Polly.* *(She sees a chicken and goes after it.)* Chick, chick, chick. *(The women howl. Maybe Polly imitates her.)* This is not funny. This is not funny. *(They look at her.)* What are you going to eat tomorrow? No eggs for breakfast. Or for bakin'. What are you going to feed the Brothers for breakfast tomorrow? Or the day after tomorrow?

(The women are subdued. Hannah enters.)

PHEBE: The chickens got loose.

HANNAH: Talking won't catch them. Here, chick, chick, chick.

(Hannah exits. Serious now, Rachel, Peggy, Phebe chase after the chickens. Betsy starts to exit, but Izzy stops her.)

IZZY: Sister Betsy. It was me. Left the gate open.

BETSY: In all my years of schooling you, I never knew you to tell a lie. Don't start now.

IZZY: I was feeding the chickens. Had a gift to go past the meadow. Went past the meadow. Must've left the gate open. Sister Betsy, what's out there past the meadow? Is the devil out there?

BETSY: No devil.

IZZY: Sister Rachel said the devil let the chickens out.

BETSY: We're living in heaven here. Remember your lessons? You have confessed your sins, so you are without them. Everything is perfect here. *(Betsy exits. Lights change.)*

Scene Thirteen

Peggy, Rachel, Polly, Izzy, Jane march into dinner moving the benches as they sing. Phebe, Betsy, Hannah go to their dinner on another part of the stage.

ALL: *(Singing.)* Come the feast is ready,
   While the table's loaded,
   With the choicest fruits from afar and near.
   While leaders and people, parents and children,
   Love, and affection, all are here.
   (Both groups kneel. Fanny enters, late, and kneels.)

HANNAH: Gracious God, we are your humble servants.

PEGGY: Mother God, Father God, we thank you for this food.

BETSY: We thank you for that which you have provided us.

RACHEL: May we serve you.

PHEBE: May we use this food in your everlasting service.

PEGGY: We eat in silence and respect. Amen.

ALL: Amen.

HANNAH, BETSY, PHEBE: Amen.

   (All sit. The Sisters eat in silence. Each has a small dowel as a prop. Hannah, Betsy, and Phebe are eating alone together. They are freely talking, in great contrast to the quiet dinner of the rest of the women.)

BETSY: This squash could do with some seasoning.

HANNAH: Sister Peggy cooks plain and simple.

BETSY: Mighty fine bread, though.

HANNAH: Sister Phebe . . .

PHEBE: Yes, Sister Hannah?

HANNAH: I'm concerned.

PHEBE: About what?

HANNAH: About the girls.

PHEBE: Yes?

HANNAH: Their hearts are to God, but their hands don't seem to want to work.

PHEBE: I'm not catching your meaning.

HANNAH: The girls are not attentive to their work.

PHEBE: The work is getting done.

HANNAH: Sister Polly has missed her kitchen duties. Sister Fanny takes long walks alone. The girls are not doing their share, are they?

PHEBE: No, they are not.

HANNAH: Ah.

(A beat.)

PHEBE: They are young. They drift off, return.

HANNAH: More than that.

PHEBE: Perhaps.

HANNAH: What do you think is happening?

PHEBE: I don't think they are lazy.

HANNAH: That is not what I am asking.

PHEBE: They are attentive at service. *(Hannah turns to Betsy.)*

HANNAH: Sister Betsy?

BETSY: These beans are good.

HANNAH: Sister Betsy, you are as inattentive as the girls. There is an oddness in the air, an expectancy even. Sister Polly keeps running with the younger girls.

BETSY: Sister Polly never had a childhood. Sister Polly was working on her back in a fancy house in Lexington when she was twelve.

HANNAH: I am well aware of Sister Polly's provenance. *(To Phebe.)* You must guide them better, Sister Phebe. You must tend to order.

PHEBE: Yes, Sister Hannah.

HANNAH: You must keep them better occupied. I see girls whispering in the corner. We have no secrets here.

BETSY: Sister Hannah — *(Pulls a heart-shaped gift drawing out of her pocket.)* One of the girls gave this to me.

HANNAH: They are not permitted to make such things.

BETSY: She said she was the instrument. She said it was from Mother Ann.

HANNAH: Mother Ann?

BETSY: She said that Mother Ann came to her from heaven and told her to make this for me. That this is a gift from Mother Ann to me.

HANNAH: And you believe her?

BETSY: There are strange things going on. What shall we do?

HANNAH: Sister Phebe, what do you think we should do?

PHEBE: I think we should wait.

HANNAH: That is good advice, Sister Phebe. We will wait . . . And we will watch.

BETSY: I wonder what we have for dessert today.

(Lights change as the next scene begins immediately. One of the benches stays in place for the following scene; the rest are placed on the sides. The women sit on them.)

Scene Fourteen

Fanny is seated on the end of a bench, in the special interrogation light. Hannah and Peggy stand on either side of her. The pace is quick.

HANNAH: *(To Peggy.)* What did you see?

PEGGY: Who was there with you?

HANNAH: What did you see?

FANNY: I saw angels.

HANNAH: *(To Fanny.)* Who was there?

FANNY: Angels. There were angels there.

HANNAH: You must tell us who was with you.

FANNY: I tell you. I tell you again and again. I saw angels.

PEGGY: *(To Hannah.)* Maybe she saw . . .

HANNAH: *(Overlapping.)* You must tell us what you saw.

FANNY: Angels —

HANNAH: *(Overlapping.)* There was another sister there?

FANNY: No.

HANNAH: Brethren? Who was there? *(A pause.)*

PEGGY: There are good reasons . . .

FANNY: I'm thinking.

PEGGY: We'll help you think.

HANNAH: There were Brothers there?

FANNY: I don't know their names.

HANNAH: Brothers from the North Family?

FANNY: Not Brothers.

PEGGY: Men from town?

HANNAH: Old men? Young men?

FANNY: Not men.

PEGGY: Boys?

FANNY: No.

HANNAH: Not men or boys?

FANNY: Angels! Gabriel, Michael. Peter. I don't know all their names.

PEGGY: Oh, Lordy.

FANNY: I'm telling you. There were angels. *(Lights change.)*

Scene Fifteen

Peggy begins to sing. Betsy hears her and enters.

PEGGY: *(Singing.)* Glory unto God we'll sing
> *(Betsy motions Peggy to stop. Betsy looks around to see if anyone is listening. She motions Peggy to continue. When Peggy begins to sing again, Betsy joins in.)*

PEGGY, BETSY: Praise to Christ the saviour
> *(Betsy begins to harmonize, much to Peggy's excitement.)*
> Who the joyful news did bring
> That we might conquer every sin
> And reign o'er death forever.
> *(They sing full out, joyfully.)*
> All the heavens praise his name
> Angels give him glory
> *(They become aware that they might be overheard.)*
> Saints on Earth come join the strain
> Let your chorus be the same
> Crying holy holy.
> *(As the song finishes, the women have returned to their seats. Lights change.)*

Scene Sixteen

During the song Polly and Izzy have entered upstage. When the lights change we see they are pulling weeds. They each have a basket beside them. Throughout the scene the women are very careful not to talk about what happened at the meadow. Various Sisters cross behind them, so that they are never alone and can't talk about the vision.

POLLY: I don't like pulling weeds.
IZZY: Nobody does.
POLLY: Sister Phebe does. She's always in the garden.
IZZY: She has a garden talent.
POLLY: 'T'aint fair. I have a kitchen talent.
IZZY: You'll be in the kitchen next month. *(A beat.)* Polly, what did you see out there past the meadow —

POLLY: *(Interrupting her.)* Hush. *(Rachel and Fanny enter; Fanny carries a basket. She puts it on the ground as Rachel exits.)*

FANNY: Got sent out here to help. Finished my baskets and they sent me out here.

IZZY: You been back past the meadow?

FANNY: You want to go with me?

POLLY: Weren't nothing there.

(Phebe and Betsy cross the stage. Polly stands up.)

POLLY: My knees hurt. Can't keep sitting on the ground.

BETSY: We're having a picnic tomorrow.

IZZY: A picnic!

PHEBE: Can't sit on the ground, can't go to the picnic.

(The Sisters exit. Fanny and Izzy keep pulling weeds. Polly sits.)

POLLY: My knees hurt.

FANNY: Poor, pitiful Polly.

IZZY: I got bit by a bug.

FANNY: Don't got no time for complaining. *(Fanny works harder.)*

POLLY: I'm hungry. *(Another Sister hurries past and exits.)*

IZZY: Why are you working so hard? There's always going to be more weeds.

POLLY: Proving.

IZZY: Proving what?

FANNY: She's saying that I'm a winter Shaker.

IZZY: But it's summer. You can't be a winter Shaker in the summer, can you?

FANNY: She thinks I'm just here to get a good meal and a warm bed.

POLLY: Didn't say that.

FANNY: Didn't have to say that. I know'd what you mean.

IZZY: You work harder than anybody.

FANNY: I'm used to work. Work's not hard. When your momma's dead, your daddy's a drunkard, and his new wife don't like the nose on your face, well, then you just keep working to stay out of their way.

POLLY: My daddy was a drunk, too. Izzy don't know much 'bout her daddy.

IZZY: Do, too.

POLLY: He dropped you off here when you was three.

IZZY: 'Cause my momma died. But I've seen my poppa twice since. I've seen him twice.

FANNY: Fortunate for you. Your daddy bringing you here. Learn to read. Always got shoes. Never hungry.

POLLY: I'm hungry now.

FANNY: You're going to be fed soon. Sisters making supper right now.

POLLY: Sister Peggy?

FANNY: Making your supper. Smelled it on my way over. Smells good.

POLLY: Won't taste like much o' anything. Always tastes the same. I'm hungry for something different.

FANNY: Being real hungry is when your stomach's growling and there's nothing to eat. And when you know there's not gonna be anythin' much to eat for days and days.

IZZY: I'm going to always stay here. I'm going to sign the covenant. I'll be old enough in three years.

FANNY: Might as well sign the covenant.

POLLY: You don't know any different. Never know'd anything else.

FANNY: No place better than this.

IZZY: I want to be a deaconess. Or an eldress.

POLLY: Then you won't have to pull weeds.

(They continue to pull weeds in silence. Lights change as Betsy unfurls a big cloth from the side of the stage. As she speaks, she places it on the ground to begin the picnic scene. The lights are bright and there is much movement on the stage.)

Scene Seventeen

Betsy, Rachel, Peggy, Jane, Izzy, Phebe, Polly, Hannah, Fanny at the picnic. Betsy, Rachel, Peggy lead the way, carrying cloths and baskets. Izzy, Polly, Phebe, Jane follow. Hannah and Fanny seem to both be keeping to themselves.

BETSY: Mighty fine day.

RACHEL: We thank God for this beautiful day.

PEGGY: Never a better one this year.

RACHEL: You bring the napkins?

JANE: Right here.

IZZY: What are we having?

BETSY: *(She flings out a blanket.)* It's a surprise!

JANE: Bet it's your favorite!

(The women lay blankets on the ground and sit, arranging their baskets, etc., during the following.)

PHEBE: Everything is her favorite.

IZZY: Is not.

PHEBE: Name a food you don't like.

RACHEL: She always cleans her plate.

IZZY: 'Cause we're supposed to!

POLLY: What if you didn't?

IZZY: Didn't what?

POLLY: What if you didn't have to clean your plate? What would you leave on it?

BETSY: Vegetables!

IZZY: Wouldn't!

RACHEL: Yes, you would.

JANE: Children never like vegetables. *(She hands something to Phebe.)* Here, Sister Phebe.

POLLY: What if you could eat whatever you want?

PHEBE: Thank you, Sister Jane.

IZZY: I like everything.

POLLY: If you had to choose.

IZZY: Sister Peggy's chicken and gravy. That's my favorite.

JANE: I'm sitting on a rock.

RACHEL: Trade with me then.

JANE: It's not a hard rock.

RACHEL: All rocks are hard. Sit over here.

IZZY: Sit by me! Teach me Jacob's Ladder.

JANE: Don't need to be knowing Jacob's Ladder.

BETSY: Every child learns that.

RACHEL: Hmm.

IZZY: Never did. Always got the string tangled.

RACHEL: Best not put you on a spinning wheel!

PEGGY: Or a loom. You'll be snapping beans in the kitchen from now on.

IZZY: I could learn to spin!

PEGGY: You are a bean-snapper!

BETSY: Or a whippersnapper!

IZZY: *(Holding out some string to Jane.)* Teach me Jacob's Ladder.

JANE: Got better things to do.

POLLY: I used to do Jacob's Ladder. And Cat's Cradle. I could do them.

IZZY: *(To Jane.)* You said you would teach me.

BETSY: We'll have you spinning wool this winter, Sister Polly! And weaving!

JANE: I said I knew how. Didn't say I would teach you.

RACHEL: Sister Polly, you never learned how to spin?

BETSY: Lots of things she never learned. We're here to help Sister Polly. She never lived on a farm before. Not like the city.

IZZY: Did you have servants?

POLLY: Where'd you get such an idea?

IZZY: Sister Betsy said you came from a fancy house.

RACHEL: Hmm.

BETSY: Izzy!

PHEBE: You're here with us now, Sister Polly.

RACHEL: *(To Polly.)* You have a new life now.

PEGGY: Sister Polly, would you like some cornbread?

POLLY: Had better food in Lexington! *(Polly walks away.)*

RACHEL: Hmm.

JANE: *(Indicates Izzy should come to her.)* Izzy.

IZZY: *(To Jane.)* Please, please teach me Jacob's Ladder?

JANE: Why you askin' me? Lots of other sisters could teach you. Polly could teach you.

IZZY: You take time to explain things. You'll teach me the right way and I'll remember it. *(After a beat.)*

JANE: I'll show you one, anyway. I'll do one quick for you to see. *(Jane creates the Jacob's Ladder with her string, explaining all the while.)* Over two, over one, over two. Put your fingers there and . . . Inside out . . . Jacob's Ladder. Up to heaven. *(Jane holds up the string figure.)*

IZZY: Oh!

JANE: *(Holding up the Jacob's Ladder.)* See the strings, top and bottom of the X?

IZZY: I see them.

JANE: Grab each one of them. No. Pinch your fingers. One hand on the top and the other on the bottom. Pinch the top and bottom of the X. That's it.

IZZY: Got it.

JANE: And pull.

(Izzy does and the string unravels perfectly.)

IZZY: Oh! Now teach me. Please?

JANE: It's not hard. Make certain the knot's tied right so it won't give way when you pull on it. Gotta start right if you're going to finish right.

(Jane begins to show Izzy. Fanny stands very still, looking off in the distance.)

BETSY: Storm a-brewin'?

RACHEL: No. Not a cloud in the sky.

PHEBE: Better not be a storm.

(Fanny continues to stand still and stare off. Her arms begin to raise, pointing outward.)

BETSY: What do you see, Sister Fanny?

PEGGY: Something off in the woods?

JANE: You see an animal? Where? Is it big?

PHEBE: Most likely a deer.

BETSY: Sister Fanny, would you like some chicken?

> *(Fanny just stands still. Polly watches her. Polly starts to sing. The women join in. After a moment, Fanny's reverie is broken and she watches the women.)*

POLLY: Hop up and hump up
And whirl 'round, whirl 'round

SISTERS: Gather love, here it is all 'round, all 'round.

> *(Polly makes a round begin. But as soon as the Sisters realize, they stop, one by one.)*

SISTERS: Here is love flowing 'round
Catch it as you whirl 'round
Reach up and reach down,
Here it is all 'round.

HANNAH: *(Interrupting.)* Sister Polly, we sing in unison. It is not permitted to embellish.

POLLY: Would be more fun if we did.

RACHEL: Sister Polly! *(Fanny stands up and continues to stare out.)*

PHEBE: Are you ill?

HANNAH: Are you ill, Sister Fanny? *(Fanny raises her arms slowly upward, as the women all watch in silence.)*

RACHEL: She's an instrument.

HANNAH: Sister Rachel, will you help Sister Peggy pack up our dinner?

PEGGY: Are we finished?

HANNAH: Yes.

IZZY: We just got here. I'll eat the vegetables. *(All the women begin to pick up the picnic items. Fanny slowly turns, arms heavenward.)*

HANNAH: Sister Fanny.

IZZY: You spoiled the picnic!

> *(We move immediately into the next scene. Lights change.)*

Scene Eighteen

> *The picnic clothes have turned into laundry. Rachel, Phebe, Peggy are doing laundry and ironing. Hannah and Betsy are folding the picnic blanket together.*

HANNAH: Sister Fanny will be moving into the East Family Dwelling. Next week.

RACHEL: She's very new.

PHEBE: Won't be signing the covenant anytime soon.

BETSY: Shouldn't she stay in the Gathering Order?

PEGGY: With the newcomers?

HANNAH: I see the men looking at her there.

PHEBE: Brother Harris'll be looking at her over here.

RACHEL: Hmm.

PHEBE: He likes to look at the young'uns.

BETSY: Just 'cause one eye a-wanders. His eyes don't look in the same direction. Cain't tell where he's lookin'.

PHEBE: He's got a wanderin' eye, all right.

PEGGY: Just 'cause he's afflicted in his eyes.

PHEBE: You don't know 'bout men and their lookin'. You were reared here. Don't know the ways of worldly men.

BETSY: Leastways he's not cross-eyed! Like that son of Brother Ethan. I declare, I don't know how he dances the circles without falling down dizzy.

RACHEL: Maybe that's why he's cross-eyed.

PHEBE: Poor thing. How do you think he drives those pegs so straight? With those crossed eyes a' his?

BETSY: He'd be good at basket making. Keep two sides going at once.

PEGGY: Or weaving.

PHEBE: Get the warp and woof weaving at the same time.

PEGGY: Couldn't match up his plaids, I bet.

BETSY: Makes a straight chair, though. Drives those pegs in straight. Even with crossed eyes.

PHEBE: If his eyes ever straightened out, he'd be driving pegs crooked.

(They all are twittering.)

HANNAH: Is everyone finished with their discussion of men's eyes?

BETSY: Beg pardon, Sister Hannah.

RACHEL: Beg pardon.

HANNAH: Sister Fanny will be moving to the East Family dwelling. In the room with Sister Rachel.

PHEBE: Sister Jane's in that room.

RACHEL: I'm with Sister Jane.

HANNAH: Sister Jane will move in with Sister Polly.

PHEBE: That'll be a teary room. Whiny little Sister Polly with sad Sister Jane. Best be assigning them some extra hankies. Puttin' those two together.

HANNAH: Are you suggesting that Sister Jane shares with you?

PEGGY: *(To Phebe.)* Sister Jane snores if she's been crying.

RACHEL: Her nose fills up and she snores.

HANNAH: Sister Jane and Sister Polly will share the room. The decision has been made. *(Hannah exits with Betsy.)*

PEGGY: Sister Jane won't be happy.

PHEBE: Sister Jane is never happy.

(Fanny, Polly, Jane enter.)

PHEBE: Sister Jane, would you bring the rest of the ironing off the line?

JANE: I don't mind ironing some.

PEGGY: There are kerchiefs on the line.

FANNY: I'll go.

PHEBE: I asked Sister Jane to go.

RACHEL: Let Sister Fanny go.

PHEBE: Sister Fanny will remain here.

RACHEL: Then let me go. I'll get the kerchiefs.

JANE: Please don't send me.

PEGGY: It's a beautiful day. Be nice to be outside.

JANE: *(Tearing up.)* I don't want to go out to the clothesline.

FANNY: *(Starting to go.)* I'll go.

PHEBE: You will not go. You will not go outside.

FANNY: But Sister Jane is afeerd.

JANE: Don't make me go.

RACHEL: Sister Jane, what are you afraid of?

JANE: It's outside.

PHEBE: What is? What is outside?

JANE: By the clothesline.

RACHEL: What's by the clothesline?

JANE: I don't like it!

PHEBE: Sister Jane —

FANNY: She's afeerd of —

PHEBE: Sister Fanny, you will be quiet.

JANE Comet!

POLLY: You're afraid of Comet?

RACHEL: That old bull?

JANE: He runs to the fence.

PEGGY: Fence'll keep him in.

JANE: I'm scared he'll jump the fence.

PHEBE: Sister Peggy will you go fetch the kerchiefs? Don't bother yourself any more, Sister Jane. Sister Peggy will fetch the kerchiefs.

PEGGY: I'll go fetch the kerchiefs. I'm not afraid. That ole bull knows not to pick a quarrel with me.

(Peggy exits. Polly and Fanny begin to fold a sheet. Izzy enters, carrying a basket.)

IZZY: I saw the kerchiefs on the line. They were scaring Comet.

(Polly and Fanny begin to play with their sheet.)

POLLY: Scaring Comet!

PHEBE: Sister Polly?

POLLY: I have a spinning gift. *(Polly and Fanny are now spinning playfully.)* I have a spinning gift!

FANNY: We have a spinning gift. *(Polly and Fanny wrap the sheet around Izzy's waist and spin her.)*

IZZY: I have a spinning gift. *(Izzy joins hands with Jane and starts to spin.)* We have a spinning gift.

JANE: We have a dizzy gift.

(Izzy and Jane let go. Jane is dizzy and begins to walk crookedly. Polly and Fanny are spinning around the stage.)

POLLY: *(Pointing to Jane.)* You have a drunk gift! You have a drunk gift!

JANE: I have a drunk gift!

(Fanny spins slowly upstage, her arms reaching upward.)

POLLY: I have a drunk gift.

FANNY: I have a spinning gift.

IZZY: I have a spinning gift!

JANE: I have a spinning gift.

(They all whisper "I have a spinning gift, I have a spinning gift," over and over and over while twirling slowly with their arms held high. Phebe looks on in amazement. Betsy enters.)

PHEBE: *(To Betsy.)* They have a spinning gift.

(Betsy looks at the girls. Lights change. As the next song begins, the Sisters clear the stage.)

Scene Nineteen

As the women move the benches back to the perimeter of the stage, Peggy begins singing, The others join in. We are at a Shaker worship service.

PEGGY: *(Singing.)* O sisters, ain't you happy.
O sisters, ain't you happy,
O sisters, ain't you happy,
Ye followers of the lamb.

Sing on, dance on,
Followers of Emmanuel.
Sing on, dance on,
Ye followers of the lamb.
(After the set has changed, the women line up in a formation to finish the dance.)

BETSY: *(Singing.)* I mean to be obedient

ALL: I mean to be obedient,
Ye followers of the lamb.
Sing on, dance on,
Followers of Emmanuel.
Sing on, dance on,
Ye followers of the lamb.

PHEBE: I'll cross my ugly nature

ALL: I'll cross my ugly nature,
I'll cross my ugly nature,
Ye followers of the lamb.
Sing on, dance on,
Followers of Emmanuel.
Sing on, dance on,
Ye followers of the lamb.

RACHEL: I love to attend to order

ALL: I love to attend to order,
I love to attend to order
Ye followers of the lamb.
Sing on, dance on,
Followers of Emmanuel.
Sing on, dance on,
Ye followers of the lamb.

IZZY: I'm glad I am a Shaker

ALL: I'm glad I am a Shaker,
I'm glad I am a Shaker,
Ye followers of the lamb.
Sing on, dance on,
Followers of Emmanuel.
Sing on, dance on,
Ye followers of the lamb.
(During the last chorus, Fanny suddenly begins to turn round and round with her arms stretched upward. The dance is disrupted.)

FANNY: Mother Ann is here. Mother Ann is with us.

(Polly and Izzy also begin to turn, arms high.)

POLLY: Yes.

IZZY: I hear heavenly music.

(Lights change. Some of the women exit to their benches at the side. We move immediately into the next scene, which begins while the benches are being set. The lines begin as the women move into place. We are in Hannah's office.)

Scene Twenty

PHEBE: They're not doing their chores.

RACHEL: A-screaming in the woods at midnight.

BETSY: They try to do their chores in the afternoon.

RACHEL: No. One of them always gets a gift and off they go. Whooping and hollerin'.

BETSY: They labor the entire day at their worship.

PHEBE: Well, I can't do all their chores for them.

BETSY: They have a gift to sing and dance.

RACHEL: They have a gift to sing separate from the others. If we're going to start singing in harmony, we might as well be Methodists.

BETSY: Perhaps they have a true gift to sing.

PHEBE: I don't have a gift to do their chores.

RACHEL: They're filled with the spirit.

PHEBE: I'll fill them with a spirit. Castor oil, maybe.

BETSY: You'll catch more flies with honey.

PHEBE: *(To Hannah.)* There is talk in town. There were world's people at the service. The Brothers are disturbed. Sister Izzy is telling them to give up meat.

BETSY: They will tire of this.

PHEBE: I'm tired of it. Sick and tired.

HANNAH: Sister Phebe.

PHEBE: Perhaps Sister Polly should leave. Sister Fanny, too.

BETSY: Sister Polly has no family but us. Sister Polly was a, a fallen woman before she came to us. We cannot desert her.

PHEBE: *(Sharply to Betsy.)* Something must be done.

RACHEL: Maybe it's the end of the world.

PHEBE: Maybe it is.

HANNAH: Listen to yourselves. This is not the way we talk to each other.

RACHEL: There is poison here.

HANNAH: Ten years ago this community was failing.

RACHEL: After my husband passed.

HANNAH: Ten years ago I was sent here from Union Village with Brother Eza-kiah to restore order. We are now prosperous. Are we to return to what was before? We must determine what is happening. The community is more important than one individual. We must tend to order. *(The three women all start to speak. Stopping them.)* We must send a report to Mount Lebanon. *(They all look at her.)* We will interrogate the girls. We will get testimonies from every woman in the village. We will send a report. *(Lights change. Hannah begins to speak her lines for the next scene as the women move the benches and get into place.)*

Scene Twenty-One

The three groups of women are onstage, three in each group, as in each of the previous interrogation scenes, except this time all together. Group One is Han-nah, Peggy, and Fanny. Group Two is Betsy, Jane, and Polly. Group Three is Phebe, Rachel, and Izzy. Fanny, Polly, and Izzy sit on the ends of the benches in their groups, with the other two women on each side and slightly behind them. The pace is rapid.

HANNAH: *(To Fanny.)* What did you see?

BETSY: *(To Polly.)* What did you see?

PHEBE: What did you see?

PEGGY: Who was there with you?

HANNAH: What did you see?

POLLY: I don't know.

BETSY: Must have been something powerful.

POLLY: Weren't much o' nothin'. Nothin' at'll.

HANNAH: What did you see?

FANNY: I saw angels.

IZZY: *(To Rachel.)* They were from heaven.

PHEBE: What were?

RACHEL: Everything comes from heaven.

HANNAH: *(To Fanny.)* Who was there?

FANNY: Angels. There were angels there.

IZZY: They were beautiful. They were the most beautiful —

PHEBE: *(Overlapping.)* Tell us everything you saw.

IZZY: Gold. Lots of gold. And I heard music.

JANE: We sometimes don't know what we see.

POLLY: Didn't see much of anything, I reckon.

BETSY: Well, then.

POLLY: You believe me?

JANE: No.

HANNAH: You must tell us who was with you.

FANNY: I tell you. I tell you again and again. I saw angels.

PEGGY: *(To Hannah.)* Maybe she saw . . .

HANNAH: *(Overlapping.)* You must tell us what you saw.

FANNY: Angels.

PHEBE: Maybe you were dreaming.

IZZY: It seemed like a dream. So beautiful.

PHEBE: What did it look like?

IZZY: Light. Beautiful light.

HANNAH: There was another sister there.

FANNY: No.

HANNAH: Brethren? Who was there?

BETSY: If you say you didn't see anything, then, yes, I believe you.

JANE: She didn't say that. Didn't say she didn't see anything.

PEGGY: There are good reasons . . .

FANNY: I'm thinking.

PHEBE: *(To Rachel.)* She was dreaming.

IZZY: Weren't no dream.

PHEBE: I wasn't talking to you.

PEGGY: We'll help you think.

BETSY: *(To Polly.)* Then what did you see?

POLLY: I don't know.

JANE: She don't know what she saw.

HANNAH: There were Brothers there?

FANNY: I don't know their names.

HANNAH: Brothers from the North Family?

FANNY: Not Brothers.

PEGGY: Men from town?

HANNAH: Old men? Young men?

FANNY: Not men.

PEGGY: Boys?

FANNY: No.

HANNAH: Not men or boys?

FANNY: Angels! Gabriel, Michael. Peter. I don't know all their names.

PEGGY: Oh, Lordy.

JANE: *(To Polly.)* You don't know what you saw.

POLLY: I don't know. It couldn't be —

BETSY: What couldn't it be?

FANNY: I'm telling you. There were angels.

IZZY: Weren't no dream. I thought it was. I thought I must be dreaming, so I pinched my hand. I pinched it hard. Look at the bruise. Weren't no dream.

PEGGY: Oh, Lordy, Lordy.

HANNAH: *(To Peggy.)* Sister Peggy.

RACHEL: Surely that must be heaven she seen.

PHEBE: Dreams show us heaven sometimes. You pinched yourself in your sleep.

IZZY: No! Fanny seen it, too.

JANE: We want to know what you saw.

POLLY: Fanny said it were angels.

FANNY: There were angels.

IZZY: I saw angels!

FANNY: Angels!

> *(Lights change. The benches are quickly cleared as we go right into the next scene. Or there could be an intermission here.)*

END OF ACT I

Act II

Scene One

Izzy, Polly and Fanny run onstage as the other women move the benches from the previous scene. Izzy is not wearing her cap but is holding her head as she runs, and she collapses to her knees on the stage. Betsy, Phebe, Rachel, Peggy quickly enter. Jane stands to one side, watching.

POLLY: We whooped 'em! We whooped 'em!

BETSY: Lay her down.

RACHEL: Did she fall? *(To Izzy.)* Did you fall?

FANNY: Who were they?

PHEBE: Look at me, Izzy.

POLLY: Boys from town.

JANE: What happened? What happened?

RACHEL: Is she bleeding?

PEGGY: Lordy.

IZZY: They threw rocks at us.

POLLY: I got one of them.

IZZY: They hit me with a rock.

PHEBE: Where?

FANNY: By the tannery.

PHEBE: Where'd the rock hit you?

FANNY: Hit her in the head.

POLLY: Just got hit in the head. That's all.

PHEBE: It's not bleeding.

JANE: All righty.

PHEBE: Goose egg of a knot, though.

IZZY: *(Feeling the back other head.)* I've got a goose egg!

RACHEL: *(To Polly.)* You get hit?

POLLY: I was throwing back at 'em.

PHEBE: You must not engage them.

BETSY: *(To Fanny.)* What happened?

FANNY: Just walking along the main road. Saw these boys and they started chasin' us and calling us names and throwing rocks.

PHEBE: Did you get hit?

FANNY: Arm and leg. Just bruised.

IZZY: They had so many rocks.

POLLY: I got the tall one!

PHEBE: *(Grabbing Polly.)* I tell you, you must not antagonize them.

POLLY: They started it.

PHEBE: We are a peaceful community.

POLLY: Can't even defend myself?

RACHEL: Mother Ann Lee will defend you.

POLLY: Mother Ann wasn't there. They coulda killed us.

PEGGY: Let's get her to her bed.

IZZY: Don't want to go to bed.

BETSY: You're going.

POLLY: There was four of 'em.

IZZY: There's pie for supper tonight.

PEGGY: I'll bring you some. You can eat your dinner in bed.

POLLY: I got hit, too.

PHEBE: Where? Where did you get hit?

POLLY: On my . . . on my foot.

PHEBE: Can you walk?

POLLY: Yes.

PHEBE: Good.

POLLY: I got hit on the foot. A big rock. I threw it back.

PHEBE: *(Losing her temper.)* We do not throw stones at our neighbors. You are never, never, never to do that again. You must go confess to Sister Hannah. You have been wicked. Wicked. Do you hear me? *(She grabs Polly by the shoulders.)* Do you understand me? We are a peaceful community. We do not throw stones.

POLLY: Yes, Sister Phebe.

RACHEL: *(To Phebe.)* She was just scared.

POLLY: Weren't scared.

BETSY: Let us go pray for our neighbors.

(Phebe exits. Betsy leads off Polly in a different direction.)

JANE: *(To Izzy.)* Your head hurt?

IZZY: Just a little.

JANE: Were you scared?

IZZY: They called us shaking devils. Said we were going to hell.

(Jane puts her arm around Izzy and leads her off.)

Scene Two

The lines begin as the scene is being set. Rachel, holding a dowel and paper, is sitting looking up at Hannah and Phebe, beside her.

RACHEL: Explain it to me again.

HANNAH: A testimony. Just write your testimony.

RACHEL: It's Fanny and the other girls should be writing testimonies.

PHEBE: We want your testimony. *(A beat.)*

RACHEL: My script's not what I'd like it to be. And I'm not a good speller.

PHEBE: Doesn't matter. Just write how you came here. Everything. From the beginning.

RACHEL: Not much different than anyone else's story. Came here by the grace of Mother Ann Lee. Don't know why you are asking me.

HANNAH: We're asking everyone. Everyone will have a written testimony.

RACHEL: I'll give you my testimony. I have been a good and steadfast Shaker. I have obeyed the laws. I have humbled myself in the spirit.

PHEBE: We are not accusing you, Sister Rachel.

RACHEL: Best not be. There's a devil in our midst. Either there's a devil in our midst or the end of the world is near.

(Lights change. The women exit during Peggy's song.)

Scene Three

Peggy brings on a bowl and resets the benches.

PEGGY: *(Singing.)* Our father who art in heaven
Hallowed by thy name
Thy kingdom come
Thy will be done
(Having set the benches one on top of another in the "table" position, Peggy begins to stir something in her bowl, still singing.)
On earth as it is done in heaven
Give us this day our daily bread
And forgive us our debts
As we forgive our debtors.
(Polly enters, interrupting Peggy.)

Scene Four

Peggy and Polly alone. Polly holds a piece of paper in her hand, shaped like a heart.

POLLY: It's a gift.

PEGGY: You have a gift to draw.

POLLY: I'm the deliverer. I'm the instrument.

PEGGY: It's beautiful.

POLLY: *(In a whisper.)* It's from Mother Ann.

PEGGY: You shouldn't be making drawings.

POLLY: Mother Ann made it. I'm delivering it to you. It's from Mother Ann to you.

PEGGY: How could Mother Ann make this for me?

POLLY: She came to me. Mother Ann came to me. I looked across the room. Mother Ann was standing there, pointing to the wall. And on the wall was a big picture, all painted with colors of light. I copied down what I saw on the wall. It's from Mother Ann. It's for you. Did you know Mother Ann?

PEGGY: *(Looking at the heart.)* Mother Ann sent this to me?

POLLY: It has words. I copied down the words I saw on the wall. They were shining. The words were on the wall, shining like a light.

PEGGY: *(Reading.)* "To help you through this world of strife and cheer your path to heaven. From Mother Ann."

POLLY: Mother Ann loves you, Sister Peggy.

(Polly exits. Peggy moves the benches, so they are lined up next to each other.)

PEGGY: *(Singing.)* Lead us not in temptation

But deliver us from evil

For thine is the kingdom

The glory and power forevermore

Amen.

(Lights change as Peggy moves the benches for the next scene. Jane, Phebe, and Betsy have entered during Peggy's song.)

Scene Five

Jane is dictating to Betsy as Phebe looks on. Betsy holds a paper and a dowel.

JANE: Seemed like after the little twins died there weren't much use a-livin'. I birthed five children and all of 'em died afore they was six. Everything on the farm seemed to be dying, too. Cow stopped givin' milk. Seemed like the cow didn't have to give milk anymore since there weren't any young'uns around. The well went dry, too. Dried up one day, just like the cow.

PHEBE: You only have to tell us why you came here.

JANE: I'm telling you. And everybody knows anyway, don't they? All my babies dead. What were we gonna do? No children to help tend the farm. Came 'cause my husband came here. Where else was I gonna go? Didn't have much choice, did I?

PHEBE: *(To Peggy.)* Will you read Sister Jane's testimony to her so she can sign it?

BETSY: *(Reading.)* "By the grace of Our Lord, I came here by my own will with my husband William. Through the bountiful goodness of Mother Ann Lee I have discovered the joy of a simple life. May I continue to strive to be a better Shaker and to be pure in heart and mind until the time has come that I go onward to greater rewards in heaven."

PHEBE: Is that your testimony, Sister Jane?

JANE: I reckon it's close enough.

BETSY: Make your mark on this page.

(Jane starts to sign as the lights change. The benches are moved as the next scene begins.)

Scene Six

Lights up on Hannah and Phebe entering. They go over to Izzy who looks at them and begins to sob. The rest of the Sisters slowly drift onstage. Peggy carries a small suitcase and a cloak.

HANNAH: Your father has come to fetch you.

IZZY: Won't go. Can't make me go.

HANNAH: Your father's here.

IZZY: Give me the covenant. I'll sign.

PHEBE: You're not old enough.

IZZY: I'll sign right now. Give me the covenant. I want to sign the covenant. You can't make me go.

BETSY: You can always come back.

RACHEL: *(To Betsy.)* He won't let her come back.

BETSY: Come back to us when you're twenty. You can come back. Sister Izzy, listen to me now. Hush. You just come back when you're old enough. See? We want you back.

IZZY: If I'm gonna come back, why do I have to leave? *(She sobs.)*

HANNAH: Where's her suitcase?

RACHEL: Right here.

PHEBE: Who's carrying her cloak?

PEGGY: I'm carrying it for her.

PHEBE: Got the warm winter one?

PEGGY: Yes.

FANNY: Where's she going?

PHEBE: Her daddy's come to fetch her.

POLLY: She don't even know her daddy.

IZZY: Didn't say good-bye to the chickens! I didn't say bye to the chickens!

PEGGY: That old rooster be in a pot soon. Won't know you're gone.

IZZY: And Mischief. And Mr. Chickenhouse!

BETSY: We'll tell'm bye for you. The cats'll all be here when you get back.

IZZY: I made Mr. Chickenhouse a bonnet.

BETSY: I'll put the bonnet on him. I'll take care of him.

IZZY: *(Howling.)* I didn't say bye to the lambs. The little baby lambs! I didn't kiss the kittens!

HANNAH: Honey, your daddy's waiting for you in the visitor's parlor.

IZZY: I want a kitten. I want one of Mischief's kittens! Let me have a kitten.

BETSY: Those kittens too young to leave their momma. They'll be waiting for you when you get back.

IZZY: They won't be kittens any more!

JANE: There'll be more kittens. There'll always be kittens.

IZZY: I love THOSE kittens. I want a kitten to take with me!

RACHEL: Honey, a kitten'd smother in your little suitcase.

POLLY: *(To Phebe.)* Her daddy left her here when she was a baby. He don't know her. He can't take her away. Not right.

PHEBE: Contract says he can come get her whenever he wants. Until she's of age.

BETSY: Your daddy has a farm. There'll be kittens there. Barn always has cats.

IZZY: I only seen him twice! I don't know what he's got. I don't want him. I want a kitten! *(She sobs.)*

HANNAH: You don't want your daddy to see you like this, do you?

BETSY: Want your daddy to be proud of you.

FANNY: Izzy, you don't have to go.

HANNAH: She has to go.

IZZY: What?

FANNY: You don't have to go. And if they make you go, just run away, Izzy, quick as you can.

POLLY: Just run away.

HANNAH: Sister Fanny, you are needed in the kitchen.

FANNY: Izzy, if your daddy don't treat you right, you just run away.

HANNAH: Sister Fanny.

PHEBE: Don't make it harder on her.

HANNAH: You can always come back and visit us.

FANNY: Just run away, quick as you can.

IZZY: I don't want to run away. I don't want to go!
    (Hannah stands, helpless. Jane moves to Izzy. Phebe goes to Fanny.)

JANE: You write to me.

IZZY: I'll write.

JANE: And I'll write to you.

IZZY: You can't write.

JANE: Someone'll write for me.

IZZY: Tell me about all the animals.

JANE: I'll tell you about all the animals.

IZZY: I want a kitten!

JANE: I'll write you. I'll learn how to write. I'll learn how to write, and I'll write you all about the kittens. Now say a proper good-bye to everyone.
    (Izzy turns and hugs the Sisters. Jane is last. She gives Izzy the Jacob's Ladder string. The Sisters walk her out to the benches, where she sits or exits.)

FANNY: *(Waving.)* Bye, Izzy.
    (Phebe turns from the other women back into the scene.)

PHEBE: This is a-cause a'you.

FANNY: How could this be 'cause of me? I don't know her daddy.

PHEBE: Her father heard.

FANNY: Her father heerd what?

PHEBE: Her father heard you girls were dancing up the ridge. With no clothes on. Her father heard that you girls were unclothed.

FANNY: Didn't go unclothed.

PHEBE: Too late to say you didn't. Strange things going on. Oughta thought about what you were doing.

FANNY: I didn't do nothin'.

PHEBE: *(Phebe starts to leave.)* All 'cause a' you. *(Phebe exits.)*

FANNY: I didn't do nothin'. I didn't do nothin'!

(Fanny begins to exit the opposite way of Phebe but is swept up with the arrival of the sisters coming to service. Lights change.)

Scene Seven

Lights up on a service. The women are marching in a prescribed circle. During the dance Polly hands a piece of paper to Jane.

ALL: *(Singing.)* If ye love not each other
   In daily communion,
   How can ye love God,
   Whom ye have not seen?
   If ye love not each other
   In daily communion,
   How can ye love God,
   Whom ye have not seen?
   (By the end of the song the benches are set for the next scene, Lights change. Hannah, Jane, and Phebe are sitting on two benches put together. Betsy stands.)

Scene Eight

HANNAH: *(Looking at a drawing.)* Where did this come from?

JANE: It was given to me.

HANNAH: By whom?

JANE: Says on the paper. Says it's for me. There's my name.

HANNAH: You are not permitted to have such things. *(To Phebe.)* We have no secrets here.

JANE: There's other words written on the paper, but I cain't read 'em.

BETSY: It's very beautiful.

HANNAH: *(To Jane.)* Who gave you this?

JANE: It was sent to me from Mother Ann. It's a picture of my children.

BETSY: Perhaps it's a gift drawing.

JANE: It's a picture of heaven. See, there are pictures of my children. There are all my children. Frederick, Susannah, Benjamin, Margaret, 'Lizbeth-Ann. It's a gift from Mother Ann to me. My children are in heaven. With Mother Ann. Mother Ann loves me. She sent me a picture of heaven.

HANNAH: It is a sin to create a picture of heaven.

JANE: Why?

HANNAH: How can we with our imperfections create a picture of something perfect? *(Phebe starts to interrupt.)* This is a picture of pride. This is a picture of sin.

JANE: My babies are innocent.

HANNAH: Your children have gone to live with their heavenly father and mother. You must accept the wisdom of our heavenly parents. You will find more comfort in prayerful contemplation. *(A pause.)* This is a not a gift. It is a work of pride from a confused, misguided young woman. We will no longer indulge these false gifts. *(Hannah tears up the drawing. Jane holds out her hand for the pieces. Hannah puts them in her own pocket.)*

BETSY: Come, Sister Jane. We must return to our chores. *(Betsy and Jane exit to the side benches.)*

PHEBE: You should apologize to her.

HANNAH: I should what?

PHEBE: You should apologize to her. That picture brought her comfort.

HANNAH: She will find more comfort in her labors. In her work.

PHEBE: She never has before.

HANNAH: Perhaps you should guide her better, Sister Phebe. Especially if you hope to become an eldress yourself some day.
(Hannah exits. Phebe moves a bench. Lights change.)

Scene Nine

The women all kneel in prayer.

PEGGY: *(Singing.)* I never did believe
    that I ever could be saved
    without giving up
    all to God.

HANNAH: Let all confess their sins.
    (No one speaks. Jane stands up and exits.) We will now confess our sins.
    (During the silence, Fanny rises.)

FANNY: Holy Mother Wisdom speaks to me. *(Fanny begins to shake.)* Holy Mother Wisdom speaks to me. Holy Mother Wisdom speaks to me. *(All the women are looking at Fanny.)*

HANNAH: *(Abruptly ending the service.)* May we go forth in the strength and the power of the gospel and labor for the spirit of conviction.

ALL: Amen.

(Lights change. All sit on the side benches except for Fanny and Hannah. We go immediately into the next scene.)

Scene Ten

HANNAH: I'm suggesting you leave the community.

FANNY: I'm a strong worker. You can't make me leave.

HANNAH: You haven't signed the covenant.

FANNY: When the time comes I'll be a-signin'.

HANNAH: You won't need to.

FANNY: Why wouldn't I? No place better than this. It's heaven on earth here. Learned that from you. Don't you believe that, Sister Hannah?

HANNAH: We are not here to talk about my beliefs, but yours.

FANNY: Is that what we are talking about?

HANNAH: You are insolent.

FANNY: Not meaning to be. Just tryin' to understand.

HANNAH: Then understand that it is time for you to depart.

FANNY: I want to understand the angels. I want to know what they say.

HANNAH: You are making this up.

FANNY: The others hear them. They send them songs. And pictures. I see the angels, but I mostly don't know what they're saying. I want to understand them. I want to know what they say.

HANNAH: Angels speak in heavenly tongues. *(Corrects herself.)* Would speak in heavenly tongues. If they were here.

FANNY: But what do they say? Please help me.

HANNAH: They are not here, I'm telling you.

FANNY: Polly hears them. Izzy hears them. *(She corrects herself.)* Heard them.

HANNAH: You have created this yourself.

FANNY: Why do they talk to me?

HANNAH: Indeed. Why would angels speak to you? *(A pause.)* You must go.

FANNY: Where do you want me to go? You can't just send me away with a little suitcase. No, you wouldn't do that. You care about people. You do,

Sister Hannah. You'd be thinking about me. You'd wonder what happened to me. Did my half-wit brother tear my clothes off me in the outhouse? Did I give birth to my father's next child on some snowy night all alone with the wind a-howlin' through the cracks in the winders?

HANNAH: That is enough.

FANNY: You gonna send me out in the cold and pray that I don't end up like Polly a-laying on my back in some fancy house in Lexington? Some travelin' men a-pawin' at me? Is that where you are sending me? You gonna pray for me there? You gonna pray me to a safe life, or pray that I go quickly up to heaven?

HANNAH: You cannot talk to me this way.

FANNY: Won't you even pray for me then? *(Possibly a pause.)*

HANNAH: I pray for you every day.

FANNY: But what do you pray? That I will disappear? Or that I'll show you where the angels are?

HANNAH: We know where you go. The men are clearing the place right now.

FANNY: No!

HANNAH: The land will be plowed and fenced. Perhaps your "angels" won't be there any more. Why don't you simply stop talking about spirits? The others will forget about it and we can all resume our lives here.

FANNY: You're telling me that if the angels go away I can stay.

HANNAH: I am giving you a chance.

FANNY: You're tellin' me that if the angels leave I don't have to.

HANNAH: Girl, think about what you have been doing! Think! Do you honestly believe that celestial manifestations would appear to you, an uneducated young woman who has not even signed the covenant? If Mother Ann were to visit us, don't you think it would be the elders who would see her first? You are not a stupid girl. Don't you think Mother Ann would have something to say to us? To me?

FANNY: Would you recognize her if you saw her?

HANNAH: You will leave tonight!

FANNY: *(With a sudden intake of breath, Fanny looks at something behind Hannah.)* You are not to send me away.

HANNAH: You have no choice.

FANNY: *(Fanny stares at something behind Hannah.)* I'll be good. I try to do . . . I try . . . I try . . .

HANNAH: You will not do this.

FANNY: Don't you see them?

HANNAH: See what? What do you see?

FANNY: They are so beautiful. So beautiful.

HANNAH: *(Hannah looks all around.)* There is nothing there.

FANNY: You can't see them, can you? You can't see them.

(Hannah holds Fanny by the shoulders and begins to shake her.)

HANNAH: There is nothing to see.

FANNY: I hear their voices. *(Hannah shakes Fanny.)*

HANNAH: Tell me you see nothing. *(Hannah shakes Fanny harder and harder.)* Tell me you see nothing. Tell me you see nothing! *(She lets go of Fanny and kneels.)* Please. Please. Holy Mother Wisdom, hear my prayer.

FANNY: They speak to me.

HANNAH: Grant me the vision to see from my eyes as well as my heart.

FANNY: *(To her spirits.)* What are you saying? *(Fanny shakes harder and harder and finally collapses on the floor sobbing joyfully.)*

HANNAH: *(Looking around the room.)* Holy Mother Wisdom, grant me this prayer. Let me see! Let me see! I will see. I will see. You will come to me. *(Betsy, Phebe, Rachel rush in.)*

BETSY: We heard shouting.

HANNAH: Sister Fanny is ill.

RACHEL: I'm scared.

HANNAH: There is nothing to be frightened of.

RACHEL: Sister Fanny's an instrument. I've seen her. I see the face of Holy Mother Wisdom. The end of the world is near.

BETSY: Calm yourself.

RACHEL: I am a hypocrite. I haven't always believed.

BETSY: Sister Rachel, you are a good Shaker.

RACHEL: The sky is darkening. I must confess my sins before it's too late.

HANNAH: Sister Rachel, you are free from sin. Have no fears. Sister Rachel, would you and Sister Phebe take Sister Fanny to her room? And pray for her salvation. Sister Fanny is ill.

(Rachel and Peggy assist Fanny. Hannah and Betsy move to another part of the stage. Lights change.)

Scene Eleven

PHEBE: Are we being visited by angels?

BETSY: The other villages report visits from spirits. The girls are seeing angels. At the other villages. Mount Lebanon. Hancock. Enfield. Tyringham. They all report visitations from the spirit world. Saint Peter, Saint Michael,

Mother Ann. *(A pause.) Sister* Hannah? *(A pause.)* Sister Hannah? What does this mean? *(A pause.)* All of the villages. Spirit manifestations. Songs, drawings. Visions. Gifts. Angels. *(A pause.)*

HANNAH: There are no angels.

PHEBE: There are reports from —

HANNAH: I know about the reports.

BETSY: Perhaps we are not acknowledging the gifts we receive.

HANNAH: The truth of a spiritual gift is tested over time.

BETSY: Sister Rachel believes the end of the world is coming.

HANNAH: Sister Rachel is mistaken.

PHEBE: It's spread throughout the entire community —

BETSY: The elders at Mt. Lebanon are preparing a Sacred Site. *(A pause.)*

HANNAH: Are the elders receiving gifts? At Hancock? Mount Lebanon? Are there reports of the elders receiving gifts?

PHEBE: No. Not the elders.

BETSY: Earthly vessels are sometimes unworthy of the spirits that fill them. *(A pause.)*

PHEBE: We must act upon this.

HANNAH: We must all get back to work. There is much work to do.

PHEBE: Sister Hannah, we can no longer ignore —

HANNAH: Who is ignoring this? I would like to ignore it. How can you ignore giggling girls awake at all hours of the night? Spinning when the mood strikes them. Shaking and trembling and saying that spirits are interrupting their chores.

BETSY: Sister Hannah . . . *(Hannah turns to her.)* Mother Ann had a shaking gift. Mother Ann saw spirits. Mother Ann had gifts. But she did not turn away from her gifts. Nor did she question the source.

(A long pause, as Hannah takes this in.)

HANNAH: I will have a gift. I will have a gift that we are to have a service at our own Sacred Site. You will report to the girls. You will report that we have had a gift that we are to make ready for a service. We will unite together in worship. *(Betsy and Phebe don't move.)* We are the leaders and we must lead. The girls are little lambs lost in the valley. They have forgotten their simplicity. It is our gift to return them to their mother.

(Betsy and Phebe stare at her.)

HANNAH: We must be the ones with vision. The men will prepare the Sacred Site. We'll lead our lost lambs to Mount Sinai's Holy Plain.

(Lights change. Hannah continues speaking as the scene changes.)

Scene Twelve

All the Sisters except for Izzy enter the scene. A bench is set on end, looking somewhat like a gravestone.

HANNAH: I have a gift.

PHEBE: I have a gift.

BETSY: I have a gift.

PHEBE: I have a gift to go past the meadow.

HANNAH: Beloved, our fountain stone is ready. We will go together in unity and harmony. Sister Peggy will lead us in two-part singing as we march to our Sacred Site.

(They lead the girls in a march to the Sacred Site.)

BETSY, HANNAH, PEGGY, PHEBE: *(Singing.)* Come to Zion,

Come to Zion

Sin sick souls in sorrow bound.

Lay your cares before the altar

Where true healing may be found.

(As a round, with all singing.)

Shout halleluia! Halleluia!

Praise resound o'er land and sea.

All who will may come and share

The glories of this jubilee.

(Lights change as they march to the Sacred Site. They march into place, forming two columns, winding up in a horseshoe formation.)

HANNAH: Beloved children. You stand on holy ground. *(Hannah cues Phebe.)*

PHEBE: Let us give thanks and say amen.

ALL: Amen. *(Hannah cues Betsy.)*

BETSY: Let us pray that we may free ourselves from sin.

HANNAH: Beloved, are ye prepared to cleanse your spirit at the fountain stone? Answer, Sisters.

ALL: Yea, God helping us.

HANNAH: We must wash with heavenly water. Let all who truly desire to be Shakers wash themselves at the fountain stone.

(This is clearly a challenge to Fanny and to Polly. Phebe and Betsy lead the women to the fountain stone. They splash water on themselves.)

HANNAH: Don't you sense the presence of Holy Mother Wisdom? I see above me fruit and flowers from our heavenly mother. Let us reach out and take fruit from the hands of the angels. *(Hannah demonstrates, The women are confused. There is an awkward silence.)* The spirit has sent us cups of silver. Hold out your goblets and receive holy wine. Let ye who are worthy drink their fill. *(Hannah looks pointedly at Fanny, who then mimes drinking.)*

PHEBE: Let us be lifted in mind and purpose from this world of sorrow and sin. The angels have brought us a heavenly feast.

RACHEL: I see them. *(Rachel points skyward. This is unexpected and Hannah tries to cover. She looks at Fanny, who has covered her eyes, trying to block out the vision.)*

HANNAH: The angels dance above us, hearing our prayers.

RACHEL: I see the angels. I hear music.

HANNAH: Is there music? Has Holy Mother Wisdom sent us heavenly music?

RACHEL: I hear singing.

JANE: *(Frightened.)* I hear music.

PEGGY: I hear the angels singing.

RACHEL: I hear the horn of Gabriel.

PEGGY: I see a cloud.

RACHEL: A host of angels.

PEGGY: I see a cloud of angel wings.

JANE: I see a cloud.

RACHEL: A host of angels. I hear the angel's voices.

HANNAH: Let us not hear false voices.

PEGGY: We are in the hollow of God's hand.

RACHEL: The angels are gathering.

PHEBE: This is Mother Ann's work. She comes to unite us.

RACHEL: I feel rain from heaven.

(All the women respond individually to the "rain.")

FANNY: Holy Mother Wisdom speaks to me!

HANNAH: We will fight the temptation of false gifts.

FANNY: *(To Hannah.)* Let not any think because they can't see into every gift that is, they will not believe it to be a gift.

HANNAH: Let us shake out our sins.

FANNY: We are without sin! God has made his second appearance on earth. Mother Ann has saved us. Let us rejoice! *(The Sisters begin to murmur and confess rapidly.)*

RACHEL: Forgive me my sins.

POLLY: Forgive my thoughts of lust.

PEGGY: Mother Ann, may I be meek in your eyes.

JANE: I confess that I have cursed God for taking my children.

BETSY: I confess that I have spoken when I should not have.

PHEBE: Forgive my arrogance and pride.

(Fanny holds out her arms and looks upwards. Some of the Sisters follow her gaze and look up.)

JANE: I see my children. I see my babies, and they have angel wings! I see my children! *(Jane is overcome with joy. The murmuring builds and the women begin to shake, their arms raised to heaven. The intensity mounts.)*

FANNY: *(Shaking and speaking in an unknown tongue.)* On-eak-la-to-menni-ska-pra-leh-sa-bah-nuj . . .

(The women continue their movement, but the sound retreats. They are holding their arms high and shaking. Hannah looks at Fanny and looks at the women.)

HANNAH: *(Looking up.)* Please. Please.

(Lights change. The women are shaking upstage, hiding the scene change happening as Jane and Betsy set a bench and sit.)

Scene Thirteen

Betsy is teaching Jane to read.

JANE: Blessed are the . . . poor . . . in spirit for the . . .

BETSY: Theirs . . .

JANE: . . . Theirs . . . is the . . . kingdom . . . of heaven. Blessed are the . . . they . . . that mourn . . . for the . . . they shall be comforted. Blessed are the . . .

BETSY: Meek.

JANE: Blessed are the meek: for they . . . shall . . . inherit . . . the earth. Blessed are they which do . . . hunger and thirst . . . after righteousness . . . for they shall be filled.

(Lights change. During the transition we hear . . .)

ALL: *(Singing.)* More love, more love,
The heavens are blessing,
The angels are calling,
O Zion, more love.

Scene Fourteen

Hannah sits, waiting with Betsy and Phebe. Fanny enters. There is silence for a moment.

HANNAH: Please sit.

FANNY: I have my bag packed.

PHEBE: You'll be tending the herb garden at South Union. They need a new gardener.

FANNY: I will be happy to serve.

HANNAH: They have need of your . . . gifts. At South Union.

FANNY: Oh.

(Hannah puts a bright copper bowl on the floor. She has a small cloth as well.)

BETSY: Some Brethren heading down there today. Brother James. Taking them some lambs. And some herb seeds. You'll be going with them. It's pretty down t' South Union.

FANNY: So I've been told.

PHEBE: Write to us.

FANNY: I will.

BETSY: Tell us all about South Union.

FANNY: I'll do that.

HANNAH: May I help prepare you for your journey?

(Fanny nods, unsure of what she means. Hannah kneels in front of Fanny. In silence she takes off Fanny's shoes and stockings and washes one of Fanny's feet. As she finishes the first foot, the other women come into the room. They fall silent as soon as they notice what Hannah is doing. She finishes and stands.)

HANNAH: You'll make deaconess someday. At South Union.

(Hannah moves the bowl away and the others descend on Fanny.)

RACHEL: Wouldn't been right you leaving without a sendoff.

PEGGY: We brought you some sweet cakes. Sister Jane, Sister Polly and I made them for you.

FANNY: Thank you. *(She looks at the Sisters.)* What long faces! I'm just going down to South Union! I'll come back and visit.

JANE: You come visit us.

FANNY: I'll do that.

RACHEL: We'll visit!

PEGGY: We'll come visit you!

POLLY: *(Starting to cry.)* I'll miss you!

FANNY: Best be on my way.

(Ad-lib hugs and good-byes. Fanny exits. Jane, Rachel, Betsy, and Polly follow her.)

PHEBE: They need a good gardener at South Union.

HANNAH: It has been requested that she instruct them in the new style of worship.

PHEBE: Indeed.

(Phebe looks at Hannah and exits. Betsy looks in the direction of Fanny's exit.)

BETSY: I will miss her.

(Betsy starts to exit. Hannah sits.)

HANNAH: Sister Betsy, did you see angels? Did you see angels at the Sacred Site?

BETSY: I saw . . . I saw . . . bright light. *(A pause.)*

HANNAH: Did you hear celestial singing?

BETSY: I heard singing like I'd never heard before.

HANNAH: Did you see angels?

BETSY: Did you?

HANNAH: When I looked at the Sisters' faces I almost thought they were angels.

BETSY: Maybe they were.

(Hannah doesn't say anything. Betsy exits. Hannah is alone on stage for a minute and then picks up her bench to move it back into place as lights shift and all the Sisters enter singing.)

Scene Fifteen

PEGGY: *(First begins to sing, turning slowly as the others dance around her.)*
    Come dance and sing around the ring
    Live in love and union

ALL: *(Joining in, skipping and singing.)* Dance and sing around the ring
    Live in sweet communion
    (One at a time the others join in singing and dancing in a circle.)
    Sing with life, live with life
    Sing with life and power
    Sing with life, live with life
    Sing with life and power
    (By now all are holding hands dancing in a circle.)
    Come dance and sing around the ring live
    In love and union dance and sing around

The ring live in sweet communion
(Polly breaks off and begins to twirl.)
Sing with life, live with life
Sing with life and power
Sing with life, live with life
Sing with life and power
(They begin twirling and clapping, singing faster.)
Sing with life, live with life
Sing with life and power
Sing with life, live with life '
Sing with life and power
(Clapping and dancing and twirling and singing faster and faster.)
Sing with life, live with life
Sing with life and power
Sing with life, live with life
Sing with life and power.
(They raise their arms to heaven. Blackout.)

END OF PLAY

Curtain Call

"Simple Gifts" may be sung in the curtain call.

ALL: 'Tis the gift to be simple,
'Tis the gift to be free,
'Tis the gift to come down
Where we ought to be;
And when we find ourselves
In the place just right
'Twill be in the valley
Of love and delight.
When true simplicity is gained;
To bow and to bend
We shan't be asham'd
To turn, turn will be our delight
'Til by turning, turning,
We come round right.
(The Sisters exit, possibly singing.)

Degas In New Orleans

By Rosary O'Neill

This play is dedicated to three brave and visionary men:
Aldon James, the president of the National Arts Club where
the play was perfected; Stephen C. Hartel, Jr. my dear brother
who provided support for its completion; and Bob Harzin-
ski, my best friend who motivated me to keep to the dream.

PLAYWRIGHT'S BIOGRAPHY

Rosary O'Neill's recent professional achievements include: *Degas in New Orleans,* which was invited to the New End Theatre (a heralded theater for contemporary plays) in London in January 2002 and featured in the Best New American Play Oktoberfest of the Ensemble Studio Theatre (a leading theater for new work) in New York City in October 2002.

She is the author of ten plays produced internationally by invitation of the American embassy in Paris, Bonn, Tibilisi, Georgia, Budapest, Hungary, and Moscow. Her play *Uncle Victor* was chosen Best New American Drama by the Cort Theatre, Hollywood, and *Blackjack* was selected for Alice's Fourth Floor Best New Play Series. She was founding artistic director at Southern Rep Theatre from 1987 to 2002. She has been playwright-in-residence at The Sorbonne University, Paris; Tulane University, New Orleans; Defiance College, Ohio, and the University of Bonn, Germany. Other fellowships include the Virginia Center for the Creative Arts (VCCA) Playwriting Fellowship to Wiepersdorf, Germany, and two fellowships to the Playwriting Center at Sewanee University. She also received a play invitation to The Actors Centre, London, as well as residences in playwriting at the VCCA, Ragdale, Dorset Arts Colony, Byrdcliff Arts Colony, and the Mary Anderson Center.

She was chosen outstanding artist in Paris and awarded a Fulbright to Paris for her play *Wishing Aces.* She was a finalist in the Faulkner Competition for New American Writers; a finalist for outstanding artist for the state of Louisiana 2002; and a finalist in the Ireland Tyrone Guthrie Residency in playwriting with the VCCA 2002. She was awarded a Senior Fulbright research specialist in drama to Europe, 2001–2006, and received first invitations to the Conservatoire Nationale du Drame (leading acting-training center in Paris) and the Conservatoire Nationale de la Danse (leading dance-training center outside Paris).

Scenes and monologues from her plays *Exposition Boulevard* and *Degas in New Orleans* were chosen for publication in three new anthologies by Smith and Kraus, Inc.: *Best New American Scenes 2002, Best Male Monologues from New American Plays 2002,* and *Best Female Monologues from New American Plays 2002.* A second edition of *The Actor's Checklist* was published by Wadsworth Publishers in March 2002, and a proposal for *The Director's Checklist* for Wadsworth Publishers is in progress. She is represented by Marta Praeger, Robert Freedman Dramatic Agency, New York and by M. T. Caen, California.

ACKNOWLEDGMENTS

Dale Edmonds, of Tulane University, assisted with research for the play, John Bullard produced the play at the New Orleans Museum of Art, David Villarrubia presented the play at the Degas House where it is set, and Susann Brinkley championed the play and sponsored it at the Oktoberfest of Great New American Plays at the Ensemble Studio Theater in New York. The National Arts Club furthered this project with a champagne reception in New York City. My agent in New York City, Marta Praeger of the Robert Freedman Dramatic Agency, continually offered the encouragement needed, as did my London agent, Bryan Drew.

Highly talented actors birthed the play in a Southern Rep production in New Orleans under the direction of Erica Szanto and in a workshop reading at the Ensemble Studio Theater spearheaded by director Linda Ames Key.

Those who believed in the play enough to sponsor its execution include patrons Bobby Monroe, Lois Hawkins, Paula Mayer, Freda Lupin, Ken Weiss, Nina Kelly, Frank Gonzalez, and David Schulingcamp. Friends who were at my side throughout the writing of the play include: Jose Rodriguez, Denise Gremillion, Rexanne Becnel, Jeanne Fayard, Marie Garon, Veleka Gray, Collette Cooley, and others. No acknowledgment would be complete without a thank you to the closest people in my world, my children: Dale, Rosary, Rachelle, and Barret, who applauded the project and urged me to complete it.

I am particularly grateful to my son Barret for his insights into the role of Rene, which he created for both the New Orleans and New York performances and to actress Soline McClaine. The Degas story was a legend waiting to be told but it needed the hands and the inspiration to bring life to the page. I thank all the champions who made *Degas in New Orleans* a reality.

INTRODUCTION

I come from a long line of women storytellers and have lived most of my life in New Orleans. With the exception of two books on theater, everything I have written has been about this city; a fascinating, lurid, passionate place where crime and love meet face to face on the same block, often fighting for the same soul. Because the city is surrounded by three bodies of water, Lake Ponchartrain, the Mississippi River, and the Gulf of Mexico, natives live in fear of being flooded and killed. Protection from hurricanes is prayed for weekly at church services during hurricane season. A rainy port city, New Orleans has a high share of crime, exoticism, insects, and pests from roaches to water rats. Along with its treacherous and intriguing natural environment, New Orleans boasts a kaleidoscope of unusual people.

Most of my plays have been based on fictional characters (who are actually real). *Degas in New Orleans* is the first based on real characters that have been fictionalized. I first came to the story when I toured the Degas House, the only house Edgar Degas lived in that remains in the United States or Europe. The house has been tastefully restored by its owner, David Villarrubia, and dedicated to his two brothers who died unexpectedly and young. The house has that combined feeling of mourning and celebration. It is surrounded by oak trees and the lush avenue of Esplanade, an avenue checkered with dilapidated buildings as well as beautifully restored mansions.

I came to the Degas House in search of materials for a one-man play on Degas. But because of the information I discovered on the eighteen members of the Degas family who eked out an existence there after the Civil War, I felt compelled to bring Edgar's family to life. So the play includes eight relatives who greatly impacted the painter during the five months in 1872 when he was in New Orleans. Edgar was suffering from a loss of eyesight, a mild depression over his middling artistic career, and loneliness, his two brothers having moved to New Orleans and many friends having died during the Commune in Paris.

In New Orleans, Edgar was confined, for the most part, to the Degas House where he developed a melodious, pensive style of portraiture. Edgar painted twenty-two pieces at the Degas house (all portraits of his family). He captured in light and shadow the haunted faces of his New Orleans cousins, the Mussons, after the Civil War. So devoted was he to this collection of his relatives that it remained with him in his studio until his death.

Degas in New Orleans is based on a true story in which Edgar and his younger brother Rene confront bankruptcy, forbidden love, and racism. The play exposes the scandalous confrontation over love and money that kept the brothers from speaking for ten years and led Edgar to return to Paris where he began a new direction for his work, soon known as Impressionism.

Telling this story was gratifying since it had been erased for a century. Edgar Degas was the only Impressionist painter who visited America. Still, because of scandals in the Degas/Musson family, the name Degas was changed and until recently no one knew the great painter came to New Orleans or that he has over thirty descendants (both black and white) in the city today.

It is my hope that the play will provide insight into the challenges of a great artist so that others who paint, write, perform in New Orleans, and around the world will celebrate themselves in Edgar's wake. Edgar Degas created a legacy in New Orleans that lives on in the Degas House, in the Museum of Art where his *Portrait of Estelle* is hung, and in all the museums around the world where his two thousand paintings bear witness to the fact that Edgar believed he was "almost Louisiana's son."

ORIGINAL PRODUCTION

Southern Rep Theatre production of *Degas in New Orleans:*

Director	Erica Szanto
EDGAR DEGAS	Ray Vrazel
RENE DEGAS	Barret O'Brien
MICHEL MUSSON	Ron Gural
DESIREE (DIDI) MUSSON	Ashley Nolan
MATHILDE MUSSON BELL	Maria Mason
ESTELLE (TELL) MUSSON BALFOUR DEGAS	Veronica Russell
JOSEPHINE (JO) BALFOUR	Lashley Schullingkamp
EMILY CUCKOW RILLIEUX	Deborah Lee Smith
AMERICA DURRIVE OLIVIER	Carolina Paiz
PLAYWRIGHT'S PROLOGUE	Nell Nolan

CHARACTERS

EDGAR DEGAS: Thirty-eight, painter.

RENE DEGAS: Twenty-seven, brother of Degas.

MICHEL MUSSON: Sixty, their uncle.

THREE SISTERS

> DESIREE (DIDI) MUSSON: Thirty-four, their unmarried cousin.
>
> MATHILDE MUSSON BELL: Thirty-one, their married cousin.
>
> ESTELLE (TELL) MUSSON BALFOUR DEGAS: Twenty-nine, their blind cousin, Rene's wife.

JOSEPHINE (JO) BALFOUR: Ten, Tell's little girl from her first marriage.

EMILY CUCKOW RILLIEUX: Forty-five, free woman of color, Degas' second cousin.

AMERICA DURRIVE OLIVIER: Twenty-four, Rene's mistress.

WILLIAM BELL: (Offstage), husband of Mathilde, never appears.

SETTING

We are in a two-story rental house on 2306 Esplanade Avenue, New Orleans, Louisiana. It is 1872. A double parlor with the remnants of grandeur: a glittering chandelier, an elegant tattered sofa, a mahogany desk, and a high-back chair. To the right, two floor-to-ceiling windows open onto a gallery; to the left, a door to the pantry. Upstage two matching parlor doors lead offstage to an unseen staircased grand hallway that connects the upstairs and the front and rear of the house. Outside we hear the clanging of a random mule-drawn streetcar. Throughout the play, Degas' paintings or the rapturous colors within them are projected onto the rear wall, lending their transparent blues, pinks, and violets to the bleak setting.

Degas in New Orleans

Prologue: Edgar

Edgar stands facing the audience. As he mentions his cousins and brother they enter the scene and pose in a tableau of beautiful young people in the countryside. Music playing softly.

EDGAR: I have a picture in my mind of the best painting I never painted: three women and two men in untouched expectation. It's October 1863. I'm in the French countryside with my cousins, unclaimed jewels from New Orleans riding out the Civil War in France. My brother Rene is there, the bloom of youth on his cheek. I'm twenty-nine. He is only eighteen. We're dining in the forest, our enthusiasm buoyed by the smell of red wine, fresh bread, and the lightness of each other. Mathilde with her husky voice talking at full speed about Italian plums and Van Dyke. Didi with her notes on Flaubert and Therese Raquin and Tell, beautiful Tell, just twenty and already a Civil War widow. And oh, the sunlight and the, God knows why, laughter. We were in our twenties and life seemed good, forever a future. *(Music fades out.)* That was before thirty thousand Parisians were killed in the Commune, six hundred thousand boys died in the American Civil War. I was copying Delacroix at the Louvre and hurrying to the French country to relax. Nine years later when I visited New Orleans, our worlds had changed.
(Slides — Degas' face and then the Degas house on Esplanade Avenue in New Orleans. Throughout the play we hear ragtime music like the compositions of Louis Moreau Gottschalk.)

ACT I

October 25, 1872, 5:30 A.M. Gottschalk music and slides of the Degas House at the same time. Jo Balfour, ten, is asleep on the floor, in a pink tutu and ballet slippers, her hair caught in a ribboned ponytail like Degas' statue of La Fille de Quartorze Ans. Jo rises dreamily and begins to dance. She lies back on the floor, returning to her sleeping state. Music fades, slides out, lights up. Tell Degas, twenty-nine, a blind woman, feels her way across the stage, counting the steps from the door to a sofa. She is exquisite, fragile with a porcelain beauty. Now and then she stumbles but stabilizes herself with a little moan and moves ahead with even more fervor.

TELL: One, two, three, four . . . *(Bumps into a table.)* Five, six, seven, eight. *(Stumbles on a suitcase.)* Who put that there? Whose suitcase? Edgar's? *(Smiles affectionately.)* Edgar's coat? What a wonderful smell. *(Her manner drifts to a shy girl as she wraps herself in it.)* It's far too long. I must look like a scarecrow. *(Feels another coat and flask with a worried look.)* Rene's coat. He'll sleep till noon. *(Turns, trips on her daughter's legs, and cries distraught.)* Jo, what are you doing on the floor? You're supposed to be on the sofa.

JO: *(Gets up restlessly.)* Oh, Mommy. I dreamed I was a bird and could fly high, but I flew into a clothesline and my wings got caught. What's that mean?

TELL: You're just excited because Uncle Edgar's coming to visit.

JO: I don't want you to love him more than me.

TELL: Don't be foolish, Josephine.

JO: Don't use that silly girl's name. I told you I want to be called Jo after Papa. *(Tell goes to fold the sheets, trips on a puppet, and cries disgustedly.)*

TELL: You can't leave these puppets out!

JO: I don't want to give my room to Uncle Edgar.

TELL: You must. This house is so crowded. If anything is out of place I'm going to fall.

JO: Use your cane.

TELL: I don't want Edgar to know I use it.

JO: Why? *(Turning, Tell stumbles into the table. She gives Jo a sharp warning look.)*

TELL: Lord, Jo, did you touch this table?

JO: I didn't.

TELL: You can't do that.

JO: Why do I have to give my room to Uncle Edgar?

TELL: Don't fret. Fold up your sheets.

JO: I need my own place.

TELL: Painters are sensitive to their environment.

JO: Maybe he'll be my friend. Then they'll never send me away.

TELL: Are you listening to me?

JO: *(She pauses, looking away — then with an undercurrent of lonely yearning.)* Buy me a little painting. Please.

(Tell turns to comfort her daughter, collides into the suitcase again, and cries with nervous exasperation.)

TELL: My God. I almost slipped again.

JO: *(Hugs her mother and her face lights up with a charming, shy embarrassment.)* I want Uncle to paint you, Mama. You're so beautiful. If he would have painted Papa, he'd have been with me always. I don't know what he looked like. If Uncle paints you, you'll be with me forever.

(Tell smiles, puts an arm around Jo's shoulder coaxingly.)

TELL: Come with me.

(A burst of laughter comes from the hallway. They hurry out. Mathilde, thirty-one, an elegant but frazzled woman, walks in through the pantry with a tray with a coffee pot and cups and saucers. Pours her coffee expectantly and sits on the sofa. Uncle Michel, sixty, dressed in a Confederate Army uniform, barges in from the front hallway followed by Didi, thirty-four, an intense pretty lady with soft features. All move quickly, full of eager anticipation to greet Edgar first.)

UNCLE MICHEL: No matter how early I get up, it's never early enough. *(Goes to the back parlor doorway and calls.)* Out, Jo, out.

DIDI: *(Shocked but giggling.)* Shush, Papa. Take off that uniform. Someone's going to shoot you.

UNCLE MICHEL: I need to greet my nephew in style.

MATHILDE: *(She comes to him, laughing, and pats his shoulder playfully.)* Go back to sleep, Papa.

UNCLE MICHEL: I just want to have a quiet cup of coffee alone.

DIDI: I just wanted to have a quiet cup of coffee alone.

UNCLE MICHEL: *(With indignant appeal.)* Jo, out. *(Grumbling.)* The dressing room is always occupied in this house. God, I've got a headache.

JO: *(From the rear hallway shouts.)* One minute.

MATHILDE: *(Gives him a sharp warning look, but he doesn't see it.)* You should stop drinking.

UNCLE MICHEL: Babies screaming through the night.

DIDI: Put some sherry on their lips.

UNCLE MICHEL: Or let me strangle one of them. *(Calls toward the back parlor doorway.)* Jo. Get out. *(Regards Didi with a shrug of his shoulders.)* Mathilde, I want you to help Didi fix up. Didi needs a husband. Edgar is her last chance. I wouldn't have picked him, but the pickings are slim. A girl's life is like a ship. When she's sixteen, you've got to launch her, deck her with flags and ribbons, sail her out. At twenty-three, the ship turns and starts back to port. Didi is at the dock.

MATHILDE: Good morning to you too.

UNCLE MICHEL: *(Turns to Didi, in a merry tone that is a bit forced.)* Who's going to care for you when I keel over? Your sisters' husbands? The church? Remember what your mother said about those spinsters who spied on their married neighbor. They'd snicker when they heard her husband beating her or when they saw bruises on her arm. One day, that wife charged out of her house and screamed, "You can laugh and you can hiss but on me tombstone won't be 'Miss.' On me tombstone won't be 'Miss.' "

MATHILDE: Just let us enjoy Edgar's company as we did in Paris.

UNCLE MICHEL: *(With humorous exaggeration.)* Keep away from Edgar. You've got a husband.

JO: *(Shouts from the hallway.)* Finished.
(Tell comes in from the back hallway.)

UNCLE MICHEL: Excuse me, girls. *(He leans over, kisses Tell's cheek impulsively, then turning back, adds with a constrained air.)* Mathilde, do Didi's hair like yours. She looks like a gargoyle.

TELL: *(Once her father has gone Tell speaks with girlish gravity.)* Will didn't come home last night? I didn't hear him.

DIDI: Oh, you were awake, you didn't come down. Mathilde, your husband was drunk as usual.

MATHILDE: Edgar can help Will turn his life around.

TELL: How did Edgar look?

MATHILDE: It was so late and they were exhausted so we just greeted each other. *(She chuckles — then with a pleased, relieved air.)* Uncertain, tentative, as if he had some secret. He was all dressed the part of the painter/poet — so kind and so subdued. You know how young bachelors do.

TELL: It's sad. They're not going to get drawn into matrimony, but they practice in case the real thing —
(From the hallway, Jo and Uncle Michel's voices are heard.)

DIDI: *(Hastily.)* Have you told your husband about the new item?

MATHILDE: Didi!

TELL: *(Too vehemently.)* Not yet. Don't say anything. Y'all promised.

(Uncle Michel and Jo dash in, enthusiastically fencing with canes. He laughs, and she laughs with him. There is an old boyish charm to his gestures.)

JO: Mommy.

TELL: Stop, Jo.

DIDI: Not with Tell's cane.

UNCLE MICHEL: En garde.

DIDI: It's not her, it's him.

UNCLE MICHEL: Move back the furniture.

TELL: You're messing things up.

MATHILDE: Stop him.

DIDI: *(Jokingly but with an undercurrent of resentment.)* It's not my turn to watch him.

(Uncle Michel and Jo go out into the front hallway, still fencing. Mathilde talks to Didi with nervous irritation.)

MATHILDE: Didi, take Tell, I'll straighten up.

TELL: Yes, but if the furniture is off —

MATHILDE: By an inch, I know.

(Didi hurries Tell off through the back parlor doorway. Mathilde gets some coffee, sits, and drinks contentedly. Edgar pokes through a gallery window. She stops abruptly, catching Edgar's eyes regarding her with an uneasy, probing look. She is overcome by a fit of acute self-consciousness.)

MATHILDE: Edgar? Oh Lord. You scared me. You mustn't glance about, till we're —

EDGAR: *(With an awkward tenderness.)* You look wonderful. I told you last night.

MATHILDE: I was tired. Why are you looking at me like that? I know I've changed. Will's business is doing poorly. I can't get rid of these dark circles. Once my husband talks to you . . .

EDGAR: *(A strange obstinacy to his face.)* I'm not here to do business.

MATHILDE: We're depending on you for prosperity.

(Edgar moves hastily to the desk; his eyes are drawn to a picture.)

Tell's wedding portrait. To Joe Balfour. She was sixteen.

EDGAR: She looks like a pouty child.

MATHILDE: Not with those breasts. She got the family collection. Look, Edgar's blushing. Tell always did that to him.

EDGAR: No, it's you — you're trying to embarrass me.

(He smiles now with teasing affection.)

MATHILDE: You have to know us to paint us.

(Uncle Michel's and Jo's voices are heard in the hallway. They enter in a flurry.)

UNCLE MICHEL: There you are. Welcome, Edgar.

JO: Oh, Uncle Edgar.

EDGAR: *(Takes her hands and gently lifts them up.)* Can't be Jo. Such a big girl.

JO: Will you stay with us forever —

(Didi comes in from the back parlor.)

DIDI: Edgar, oh no. Edgar. You're up already. I still can't believe you're here.

EDGAR: You've a different hair-do.

DIDI: You noticed.

(She smiles, her face lighting up, and hugs him gratefully. He turns, sees Tell standing quietly in the front parlor doorway. He speaks almost gently.)

EDGAR: Tell, is that you?

TELL: Hello, Edgar.

EDGAR: You're even more beautiful.

TELL: *(Embarrassed and pleased.)* You think so.

EDGAR: *(Catches himself.)* All the Musson sisters . . . beautiful.

(Didi, Mathilde and Jo surround Edgar.)

ALL GIRLS TOGETHER: Come talk to us. Tell us about Paris. Sit by me. No, me. Over here.

UNCLE MICHEL: Down, girls. Let's leave Didi with Edgar.

TELL: Fine.

(With a knowing nod to Didi, Uncle Michel, Mathilde, Jo, and Tell slip out. Didi paces, speaks quickly, unable to tame her excitement.)

DIDI: I made a list of things we can discuss. I jotted down novels you might like, and borrowed those I could. We can't always get the latest books, it's not Paris. But I did find *Madam Bovary,* some Dumas père and Baudelaire.

EDGAR: I haven't read poetry for a long time.

DIDI: I got Alfred de Musset and George Sand. Are you following . . . the controversy about her novel, *She and He?*

EDGAR: Not yet.

(He smiles, and she smiles with him. Then she changes to a brisk businesslike air.)

DIDI: The two principal figures are both artists . . . I suppose you've read the son of Titian, whose hero is endowed with his father's talent but is so overwhelmed in love that he renounces his art.

EDGAR: *(Impressed — mollifyingly.)* Are you still reading a book a week?

DIDI: *(With hearty confidence now.)* No, but now that you're here I'll do more. I'm going to copy you. Whenever you paint, I'll write. I'm writing a novel.

EDGAR: The three Musson sisters, always together. *(Hesitates.)* How's Tell?

DIDI: Fine. *(Her hands flutter up to her hair.)* Tell me, did you get my letters? You didn't respond much.

EDGAR: *(Evasively.)* Most painters aren't good with words. That is why we draw pictures.

DIDI: I don't like people who talk all the time but say nothing. I like your new signature. One word like Delacroix, not De la Croix. "Degas," not the two words "de Gas" that implies aristocracy. Your brothers were furious. They paid for that false coat of arms, and the name change. They don't want people to know the family goes back to a bunch of bakers. What I admire most about you is your awareness of the smallest element of art, even one so peripheral and personal as the signature. I've studied the signature and there are similarities between the *D* in Daumier, the *E* in Delacroix and the final *S* in Ingres. I need to find a distinctive professional signature for my writing and a male name like George Sand. With a woman's name you can't become successful. Don't you agree?

EDGAR: Sorry. I wouldn't know.

(He stiffens, looks at her awkwardly, but she flounders on.)

DIDI: I amuse myself with letter writing. I used to so look forward to sealing that envelope, placing a stamp on it, knowing your hand would touch it. I'd reread each letter several times before I sent it. Most were not up to my standards, a misspelling, a clumsy adjective. Some I rewrote four or five times to get them perfect. Want to see? *(Goes restlessly to the desk, takes out letters with a frightened, protective tenderness.)* These are the ones I never sent. Next to the ones I received. Silly, but I like to reread them both. My way of being in Paris with you. *(Compulsively, as if talking to herself.)* I love your stationery and bright blue ink. The paper is so smooth and every letter signed boldly. "'Degas." Just like your paintings. I've a special folder for each letter. You can count on me to guard every aspect of your history.

(Edgar is sleeping on the sofa. Didi tiptoes closer to him, baffled. Rebuffed and hurt, she minces toward the door, peers back at Edgar, then slips out. Tell enters, with practical authority. She is silent, keeping her chin up, her hands stretched delicately in front of her. She bumps into the sofa, with a tiny sigh recovers, moves forward. Carefully Edgar stirs. She turns her head that way. Her smile vanishes.)

TELL: Edgar? Edgar. *(Worriedly.)* Good. He's gone.

(Edgar stretches. She turns back, stops abruptly, then moves again, her hands reaching for the table top. Slowly Edgar wakes up. He watches Tell, shocked.

His expression becomes somber as he stares at her with a growing dread. Suddenly she is self-consciously aware that someone is staring fixedly at her.)

TELL: Edgar?

EDGAR: *(Hesitates, then bursts out guiltily.)* Tell, what's wrong? Can't you see me?

TELL: I wasn't paying attention.

EDGAR: I've been watching you. *(Gets up worriedly and touches her arm.)* I don't know what to say.

TELL: *(Quickly.)* Don't say anything. I'm so ashamed. I wanted to fool you completely.

EDGAR: You can't see me? *(A defensive uneasiness comes into his voice.)* God, you can't see me.

TELL: I see a little.

EDGAR: *(Strickenly.)* How long . . .

TELL: What?

EDGAR: Have you been this way?

TELL: A year now.

EDGAR: That long?

TELL: Yes.

EDGAR: What . . . happened?

TELL: An infection, an operation, another infection.

(Edgar stares at her, ignoring the explanations.)

EDGAR: Go on.

TELL: Another operation — Perfect sight for a day, then . . . blindness.

EDGAR: *(Takes her hand with deep seriousness.)* You don't have to be embarrassed.

TELL: *(Her voice is suddenly moved by deep feeling.)* I want you to remember me the way I was.

EDGAR: I do.

TELL: For instance?

EDGAR: You used to run with such splendor. *(Struggling for words.)* Always the first, way out in front of the others.

TELL: And what else?

EDGAR: In the country, how you loved to try out different paths, searching for new trees, flowers. *(Awkward pause where they smile at each other affectionately. Then a strange undercurrent of revengefulness comes into his voice.)* All those letters — Didi said nothing.

TELL: I made her promise not to.

EDGAR: Why didn't Rene tell me?

TELL: I made him swear, too.

EDGAR: I'd have come.

TELL: I'd have thrown you out . . .

EDGAR: I wouldn't let you.

TELL: You're insistent.

EDGAR: Yes. *(Genuinely concerned.)* Perhaps in Paris the specialists can help.

TELL: Don't give me false hope . . . for something that's not going to happen. I've seen specialists here . . . in Boston . . . New York.

EDGAR: But . . . What can I do?

TELL: Ask me what I need and I'll tell you. If I'm walking towards a chair and you bring it to me I'll probably trip.

EDGAR: You see nothing? *(Stares at her — then looks away — after a pause.)* Nothing at all?

TELL: I can see blurs.

EDGAR: How do you cope?

TELL: Badly, as you see. *(With a brave air of weary acceptance.)* You never get over it, you get used to it.

EDGAR: Do you?

TELL: I get by working with contrasts.

EDGAR: Is that so?

TELL: Analyzing the whole moving environment.

EDGAR: Oh.

TELL: Move and I'll find you. *(He hesitates.)* Go on.

EDGAR: *(Moved, his love for her coming out.)* I can't. . . I'm so . . . I just can't imagine . . .

TELL: Do it for me.

EDGAR: *(Reluctantly, he moves away.)* All right. Should I talk?

TELL: *(Laughs, a lilt comes into her voice.)* No, that would make it too easy. Go on.

(He moves away; she walks in the wrong direction; he steps into her path.)

TELL: There! I found you. See?

EDGAR: I should have come sooner. *(His voice grows husky and trembles a little.)* I could have helped you. If only you'd —

TELL: *(Changing the subject.)* Do you look different?

EDGAR: *(Jokingly but with an undercurrent of passion.)* I have a few gray hairs, but they say my shoulders are stronger.

TELL: Oh, my. I'm trying to imagine you — I'm so excited. I can't. *(Timidly.)* Can I touch your face? *(Her hands glide lovingly over his features. He squeezes her hands.)* You haven't changed much. What's this scar?

EDGAR: A ricochet wound. *(He is suddenly shamefaced.)* I went through some ugly things fighting in the Commune.

TELL: Did you?

EDGAR: I've staggered through blood baths, watched my friends dying. Anybody in any way connected to the Commune or in the wrong place at the time was shot.

TELL: But you survived.

EDGAR: *(Looks away guiltily.)* I escaped because I was mistaken for a corpse. All the friends I had in Paris are unhappy or dead. *(Grins at her provocatively.)* I'm here to make a new life in New Orleans.

RENE: *(Scowling from the front hallway.)* Tell, Tell.

EDGAR: *(Tactfully.)* There's your husband.

TELL: I'm in here.

(Rene saunters in, enthusiasm covering his hangover.)

RENE: Morning.

EDGAR: Morning.

(Edgar disappears to a chair on the gallery. Rene looks after him annoyed, then hugs Tell reprovingly.)

RENE: I reached for you in bed but you'd gone. I missed you.

TELL: I have a surprise for you. My heart is racing.

RENE: *(Putting an arm around her with a playful squeeze.)* If you're happy, that's all that counts.

TELL: I'm so distracted with the thrill of it. I don't want to disappoint you. I'm afraid I'm going to now.

RENE: *(Smiling, glances at mail.)* You can't hurt me, Sugar.

TELL: I know what I'm going to say has to be approached delicately so everything can start in the best way . . . I know I look the same but I'm not. I want you to appreciate my change. *(Walks to him, giddy, and bumps into sofa.)* I can get around well by myself. I'm prepared for spontaneity. The children are happy. They see me as this person who does things in this magical blind world. Oh, Rene, we're going to have a baby.

(Rene stops short — then smiles broadly, with a painful effort to be a good sport.)

RENE: You're serious? It's settled? Another child? Oh my God. *(Hugs her, unable to conceal an almost furtive uneasiness.)* You said you couldn't get pregnant . . . A . . . A third child. We agreed two were enough.

TELL: True, but a baby!

RENE: Last time someone had to walk you about.

(A look of contemptuous hostility flashes across his face.)

Didn't the doctor forbid this? The other children aren't even three. One a year. Don't you remember how we had to walk the floor! Always some infection, the earaches, sore throats, the colic.

TELL: *(Ashamed.)* You won't have to do anything.

RENE: Your father keeps prodding me about making money, about my place as head of the house. I turn around and you're having another baby. Can nothing be done? How did this occur? I thought you were nursing.

TELL: Yes . . . it's a miracle. God wants this for us, Rene. There are nights I feel something is happening inside me, despite me, I can't get over it. Please be happy for us.

RENE: The doctor says you're a high risk. Let's wait to tell the others till you're further along.

(Stung, Tell disappears out the front parlor. He watches her condemningly, swigging from the flask in his pocket. Mathilde comes through the pantry, her face worried. She is reassured to find Rene alone. Rene turns, adjusts his jacket.)

MATHILDE: Good morning.

RENE: Good morning.

MATHILDE: Coffee? It's wonderful to have you home. *(Winks with a kidding grin.)* Did you have a grand time with Edgar in Paris? Paris. I like your new suit.

RENE: *(Nervously buffing his sleeves.)* I've got to give the impression I'm successful, to make money in the future.

MATHILDE: You seem bitter.

RENE: That's what I sound like when I'm amused.

MATHILDE: Soon as you settle in we must talk about the loan I made you. *(She looks at him — lovingly.)* You promised to get Edgar to invest in Will's business.

RENE: Can this wait until later? I've such a headache.

MATHILDE: *(In a light tone that is a bit forced.)* Will's creditors won't wait.

(Uncle Michel and Jo explode through the back parlor door, fencing with canes.)

JO: Parry.

MATHILDE: We need Edgar's help.

UNCLE MICHEL: Out of my way.

MATHILDE: Papa, please . . .

(Uncle Michel and Jo go out the front parlor door. Rene turns on him reproachfully.)

RENE: The man doesn't see I'm here. He's my father-in-law.

MATHILDE: You said Edgar would repay us.

RENE: *(Yells, in Uncle Michel's direction.)* And he can't say hello. Why is that?

MATHILDE: Is that a yes for the money?

RENE: Yes, but not today.

(Mathilde lifts up the coffee tray with bitter resentment.)

RENE: Leave the coffee.

MATHILDE: *(Turns on him sharply, goes out through the pantry.)* This has to last the week.

(Light focus changes to gallery. Rene stares at his flask with fascinated disgust, slinks in a chair, drinks. Edgar goes to him with a stubborn, bitterly resentful look.)

EDGAR: She's blind. You couldn't tell me?

RENE: *(He flounders guiltily.)* The woman swore me to secrecy. She didn't want to see you. And now . . .

(He laughs, then scowls.)

EDGAR: What's wrong?

RENE: Tell's . . . pregnant . . . I never get sandbagged by men, just women. I've pretty much decided my life is over for the next few years . . .

EDGAR: She wasn't supposed to have children?

RENE: Right. *(Evading his eyes.)* We need money for — for doctors, medicines . . .

EDGAR: Here.

(Unfolding bills from a stack in his pocket.)

RENE: That's too much.

EDGAR: You're my favorite brother.

RENE: Soon as we go to the cotton office, you can help me collect on our accounts.

EDGAR: I'm not here for that. *(Stiffens.)* I've got to paint.

RENE: *(Jovially passes him the flask.)* Have some.

EDGAR: So early?

RENE: *(Puts an arm around Edgar, with false confidence, gives him a boyish hug and steers him back into the parlor.)* I'm celebrating your arrival New Orleans style. The thing about Louisiana is nobody's trying to get ahead. You meet amazing people who are not looking for money. They go to parties given by their best friends, that's all. I believe in New Orleans and her possibilities. No place has the flamboyance, the charm this city has. And I don't want us to sell cotton unless selling it makes our lives every day so much richer.

UNCLE MICHEL: *(Comes in from back parlor. He gives a quick suspicious glance from Rene to Edgar.)* Edgar . . . Welcome. Good you came. *(With a concerned tone.)* I need to talk to you about . . . Didi.

EDGAR: Why, is something wrong with her?

UNCLE MICHEL: No, no, she is fine. All right, we will talk about her later. *(His expression turns solemn.)* First things first . . . Business.

EDGAR: Rene is doing well in the cotton business.

UNCLE MICHEL: Hasn't Rene told you?

EDGAR: No.

UNCLE MICHEL: *(With a resentful glance at Rene.)* Rene is not in the cotton but in the manufacturing business. He manufactures unhappiness.

EDGAR: You are always joking.

UNCLE MICHEL: I won't talk about what it used to be like — when I ran things because that would involve adverse comparisons.

EDGAR: I know Rene is doing his . . .

UNCLE MICHEL: Don't defend him. The man gives his best energy to traveling and drinking, activities that are clearly not lucrative.

RENE: *(He flounders guiltily.)* That's not fair.

UNCLE MICHEL: Did you do any business in Paris or did you just have fun?

RENE: I negotiated business with my father and I met with Edgar and I spoke to . . .

UNCLE MICHEL: Rene never said the word I. Then he married Tell . . . that word became his new toy. He can say I want financing for a new venture. I want tickets to Europe. That's all right. I can afford another child.

RENE: *(Wincing — his lips quivering.)* I had my associates collate all my invoices and I will go over them personally . . .

UNCLE MICHEL: Now he pretends he handles things, but he runs off or takes a nap.

RENE: You misunderstand.

EDGAR: Can I help in some way?

UNCLE MICHEL: *(Miserably.)* See if Rene paid the rent, will you, and any of the bills? *(Yanks out some mail. Sourly, but with a trace of curiosity.)* Oh, Edgar, the mail came. You got a letter . . . From the wrong side of the blanket. Cousin Norbert. I hope you're not getting involved with him. You should avoid confusion with these gens de colour. Everyone is free now so free men of color like him, they are the same as other colored; no, they are worse, they are angry and they are a lot smarter. Am I right, Rene?

RENE: Yes.

EDGAR: *(Attempts a light, amused tone.)* He's a relative. I let him know I was coming. I'm very interested in his inventions.

UNCLE MICHEL: *(Ignoring this — spitefully.)* Keep your distance. We don't want a family hanging.

EDGAR: I want to meet with him and hear about his vision of the future. *(Abruptly turns to leave.)*

UNCLE MICHEL: Don't walk away while I am talking to you. *(Without conviction.)* I'm fond of Norbert. We played together as boys. It's him I'm protecting. He's the one liable to get lynched. Stay away from these gens de colour.

(Edgar is about to make a sneering remark to Uncle Michel, but he shrugs his shoulders and goes out on the gallery as America slips in from the pantry. She lingers by the doorway as Uncle Michel hands a bill to Rene and testily growls.)

UNCLE MICHEL: Invoices with no checks. Both used to come in one envelope.

(Uncle Michel sighs, goes out the front parlor. Once he is gone America lifts her head, laughs with a relieved air and runs and throws her arms around Rene. With a warning glance he breaks away and nervously checks the doors and windows for eavesdroppers. He hurries back to her and they kiss madly.)

AMERICA: Rene, finally we're alone. I missed you. Sixty days without you is so long. Every day I tell myself one more day without Rene.

RENE: I can't talk now.

AMERICA: Tonight, usual place?

RENE: We've got to postpone our plans.

AMERICA: *(Stares at him puzzledly.)* I don't want to wait any longer.

RENE: I can't leave Tell with the children alone.

AMERICA: *(She controls her anger defensively.)* I care about her children, about the whole household more than she does.

RENE: Tell's . . . pregnant.

AMERICA: She's . . . You got her pregnant? You . . . slept with her while I'm waiting?

RENE: She said she couldn't get . . .

AMERICA: *(Dumbfounded, her voice rising.)* You've . . . I thought you weren't intimate.

RENE: *(Moves to her restlessly, motioning for her to keep her voice down.)* Ah, sugar. I'm just as upset . . .

AMERICA: What does that mean? Ah, sugar. Don't touch me. My husband gets angrier every day, looking for that money I loaned you.

RENE: I know. I can't let our cotton business go under. Now Edgar's here we'll repay you.

(Takes her hands and gently wraps them around him. Kisses her.)
Can't we talk later?

AMERICA: My husband's going to kill me if I don't give him that money right away. When he discovered it was missing, he tore up the house looking for it. At night he rolls over and makes awful grunting sounds, cursing under his breath. We've got to leave tonight . . . run off as soon as we can. Money and retaliation, that's all the judge cares about. One nod from him and I'm in prison or a mental hospital. If he finds out I stole that money . . .

(A burst of laughter comes from the pantry. Jo, shouting "Surprise" offstage, comes in carrying a birthday cake, prodded by Mathilde. Edgar walks in from the gallery.)

JO: Surprise. It's a birthday surprise.

MATHILDE: *(Gathering them around the cake.)* Everybody get ready to sing to Didi when she arrives.

RENE: Edgar, come here. This is America Olivier.

AMERICA: *(Teasingly.)* My goal is to move to your exotic Paris.

RENE: She reads to Tell and helps the children with their music.

EDGAR: How kind.

AMERICA: *(With a touch of pride.)* Rene wants to move back, too. You must teach us how to do that.

(Happy voices in the hallway. Didi comes in the front parlor door coaxed by Tell, her face lit up expectantly.)

ALL: SURPRISE!!

DIDI: *(Worried, glancing at Edgar.)* I don't like surprises. I said I'm not celebrating.

JO: It's just three candles.

DIDI: *(Embarrassed.)* No.

MATHILDE: *(Lighting the candles with satisfaction.)* You are still on the sunny side of thirty.

UNCLE MICHEL: From now on you should freeze. Your mother was forty for years.

(Didi, half-reassured, blows out the candles. Jo lightens the mood by getting all to applaud, then chasing Didi around the table.)

JO: Round the table you must go. You must go. Must go . . . it's your birthday.

UNCLE MICHEL: *(He winks at Didi, with an encouraging glance at Edgar.)* Let's give Didi a kiss.

EDGAR: *(With awkward enthusiasm.)* I've missed you all.

(Uncle Michel sits boredly; behind him Jo crouches with her puppets, singing, putting warring puppets on his shoulders. Mathilde and Didi sit restlessly, sewing on the sofa, now and then glancing at Edgar painting Tell on the gallery.)

JO: "Frère Jacques, frère Jacques, dormez-vous? Dormez-vous? Sonnez le matines. Sonnez le matines. Ding. Dang. Dong. Ding. Dang. Dong."

MATHILDE: If I were single, I'd marry Edgar. I would surely. Yes indeed. Last night I dreamed I was by Will's casket. I whispered, "Thanks for freeing me." And off I went to Paris. Does that mean my husband will get shot? It's awful.

DIDI: *(Embroidering diligently.)* You've three children.

MATHILDE: I'm tired of living just for them.

UNCLE MICHEL: *(Affectionately reprimanding.)* Come watch our puppet show. Someone needs to give Jo attention. Call all the children out.

MATHILDE: No. Not now.

UNCLE MICHEL: *(A trifle acidly.)* You don't want to see your children?

MATHILDE: I need some time with Edgar. Desiree will later.

DIDI: *(Stung.)* No, I won't.

(With a baffled shrug of his shoulders Uncle Michel leaves through the rear parlor door with Jo. Didi puts her sewing down, takes her sister's hand with deep seriousness.)

DIDI: I'm waiting to read my writings to Edgar. Literature has always deeply interested him. There is the writer in him in addition to the artist. He quotes Racine and Saint-Simeon. We've much in common. Many of Edgar's paintings are based on his reading in Biblical, Classical, and Romantic literature. Did you know that?

MATHILDE: So he'll be proposing soon?

DIDI: Our discussions are purely intellectual.

MATHILDE: Really. How disappointing.

DIDI: *(Quickly.)* Who knows? He admires women writers and protagonists. He reads repeatedly *Madame Bovary,* no doubt discovering in it a solace for his loneliness.

(Focus swings to the gallery, Edgar painting Tell with an awkward uneasy tenderness. Ragtime music plays in the distance.)

EDGAR: It's amazing. You have these moments of terrific intensity and utter passiveness. I can't wrap my mind around it. I work better from memory rather than reality.

TELL: I used to watch you painting at the Louvre for hours.

EDGAR: I sensed you watching me.

TELL: You didn't.

EDGAR: That's where the extra red came in my *Daughters of Japheth*. I was blushing.

TELL: Really.

EDGAR: I wanted to paint your face on every female torso.

TELL: I never knew . . .

EDGAR: People are animals. We feel these things.

TELL: It was a crush.

EDGAR: More like an affliction. I was observing you even when you didn't know it.

TELL: I felt you, observing me.

EDGAR: I felt you . . . feeling me observing you. *(Laughs.)* That's what painters do. *(Hesitates — then slowly.)* Still there was something inexplicable — sacred in the way we connected.

TELL: *(Her hands flutter shyly to her face.)* You were lonely.

EDGAR: Don't diminish what I'm saying. You felt it.

TELL: Yes.

EDGAR: I wasn't prepared for how that would stay with me.

TELL: I wish I could see your painting.

EDGAR: You might not like it. *(Kiddingly.)* No. You probably would. You're a good liar. *(Music fades out.)* I always felt I had to paint but after you left I wasn't sure. *(Reluctantly.)* There was this hole in my heart and I didn't know what side it was on. I had to proceed unattached. What else could I do but wait? *(Ashamed.)* Even painting seemed senseless. I'd scattered interest in my art, but I had to face it. No one believed in me like you had. I was no young prodigy.

TELL: Says who?

EDGAR: What talent I have has come through merciless work, experiment, and deliberation.

TELL: You're a great painter.

EDGAR: That's not enough. *(With sudden tenseness.)* The problem is what kind of art to make and why.

TELL: It'll come to you.

EDGAR: When? Papa wants me to go to law school and follow a more solid profession.

TELL: Nothing's certain except your talent.

EDGAR: Maybe he's right. I admire my friends Edouard Manet, Henri Roualt. *(Dryly.)* They're working along more daring lines.

TELL: Listen to your heart and you will know.

EDGAR: I don't trust my heart. I'm thirty-eight. I've wasted too much time. *(Turns on her — resentfully.)* I didn't come this far to mince words. I'm not the man you knew. When you're in a crisis, there's no time to pretend. After you left, I volunteered for the National Guard hoping I'd get shot. Ran into shell fire, chose the scariest lot. Instead, I found myself searching for friends in mounds of blood, a rag to my nose so I could stand the smell. Something was going wrong with my eyes. I refused to admit it at first. I was weakly defiant. Then — *(He frowns and shakes his head mechanically.)* I promised myself if I made it through the war I'd see you once more. I dreamt about it . . .

TELL: We are not responsible for our dreams.

EDGAR: God was talking to me.

TELL: Warning you.

EDGAR: To confront reality . . . Turn. That's beautiful, Raphaelite. Hold it.

TELL: It's best not to eulogize distant friendships —

EDGAR: If you hadn't left, I wouldn't need to. *(He stares at her sheepishly, his voice drifting deeper and deeper into himself.)* When you touched my face earlier, I said nothing. But there's those intricacies of feeling even I can't understand.

(Rene walks in with nervous exasperation.)

RENE: Estelle. You think it's right to ignore the children?

(Babies' crying comes from the rear hallway. Tell turns her head, stung, jumps up, and starts out. He reaches for her arm guiltily, but she stiffens and keeps going past.)

RENE: Take the cane. You're going to kill yourself, swear to God. I can't raise these monsters alone. *(She stiffens. He stares after her with scared defiance. To Edgar, with amused dismay.)* My God, what's happening to me? I used to love children, but I can't stand the sight of them. *(Lights in the parlor rise as she enters. Rene calls out worriedly.)* Didi, help Tell with the . . .

(He stops abruptly, drinks nervously from his flask.)

EDGAR: You were the one with the vision of family life.

RENE: *(With a false heartiness.)* I've no vision. My creditors have it but I don't. *(Puts an arm around Edgar and hugs him appreciatively. They go inside the parlor.)* You've no idea of the hardship conditions here. You can't just go out and find clients. There is always someone who can get there before you. *(Taking a swig from his flask.)* Country traders bartering cotton. God knows who they are. Negotiating is getting ugly. Hell, I'd like nothing more than to get away from here as soon as possible. *(Drinking more.)* When are you coming to the office?

EDGAR: I'm here to paint.

RENE: You can do that at night . . .

EDGAR: Don't start.

RENE: Hey . . . I need you at the office . . .

EDGAR: I never promised that.

RENE: What business have you done?

EDGAR: Huh?

RENE: Well . . . Have you asked Papa for another loan?

EDGAR: I just gave you money . . . look . . . Cousin Norbert is here.

RENE: I can't work with him.

EDGAR: Why not? He could help you with his new inventions.

RENE: Its not that simple. He couldn't do it without facing threats.

EDGAR: From whom?

RENE: Members of the White League. *(Glances uneasily to the entranceways with a change of tone.)* They fight against the rising tide of colored people. Names like the Ku Klux Klan, the White Brotherhood, Camellias of Louisiana, mean anything to you? Uncle runs one white group. Our brother-in-law runs another.

EDGAR: *(His face hardens.)* And you?

RENE: *(He smiles strangely, his voice wavering.)* I'm involved also . . . I have to be.

EDGAR: This is what your Confederacy has given you?

RENE: You don't understand how it works here.

EDGAR: *(He turns on his brother accusingly.)* I fought for a dream. I joined the Commune because I believed all citizens were brothers.

RENE: *(Smiles cynically.)* Nice theory.

EDGAR: I still believe it. *(He walks away, his face darkening with rage.)* We admitted all foreigners to the honor of dying for our cause. The Commune numbered eighty-one members, mostly in their twenties. All lacked political experience. Each time a barricade fell the defenders were put up against a wall and shot. Three hundred died in La Madeleine Church, one hundred twenty women were massacred at one barricade. Citizens stabbing off the enemy with makeshift weapons. Bodies carried off. Pieces of men. You weren't there. The White League is the opposite of everything the Commune fought and died for . . .

RENE: *(Knows he is lying . . . vaguely.)* This is another world.

EDGAR: Then it's not mine.

(Edgar's face clouds over. He keeps his eyes averted from Rene, goes out the front parlor, and can be heard stamping noisily upstairs. America slumps

against the pantry doorway, then seeing she and Rene are alone rushes over and kisses Rene with excited desperation.)

AMERICA: Rene, when are you going to tell your wife?

RENE: *(Holding her in his arms, with quiet intensity.)* Right now, I can't. Tell is very fragile.

AMERICA: And me? What will happen to me?

(Rene grins at her provocatively and takes a ring from his pocket.)

AMERICA: *(Shocked but pleased.)* A silver ring? I want you, I want a future, not a silver ring.

RENE: This isn't silver. It's platinum. Handmade in France. The jeweler was so snobbish I could barely talk to him.

(Jo eavesdrops at the gallery window.)

RENE: Later. Believe me, we'll talk later.

(Rene looks at America with an understanding sympathy, kisses her, and then slips out into the front hallway. America goes to the window, looking at the ring in dismay. She hears Jo, looks up annoyed.)

AMERICA: What do you want, anything?

JO: No.

(The levee, some time later, street musicians play in the distance. Emily, a pretty middle-aged woman of color, sneaks in panting, nervous. She spots Edgar by a street lamp, touches his shoulder, and draws him into the shadows.)

EMILY: Edgar? You don't recognize me? Of course not. I am Norbert's wife, your cousin Emily.

EDGAR: *(Concerned.)* I didn't think you were coming. Where is he?

EMILY: He doesn't know I'm here. I'm out of breath. I took all the back routes. Who'd have thought I'd be sneaking about? Any Negro is a target. Don't matter if you are free.

(Music fades out.)

EDGAR: Why are people staring at me?

EMILY: Three reasons: your shirt, your hat — but the main reason is me. *(Whispers.)* There was a lynching last night. Mob sounded like thunder. You could smell the fear. Boy barely fourteen, they strung him up. He died slow and terrible because he was so young and strong. They dug a trench, tossed him in it.

EDGAR: My brother didn't say that you and Norbert were in danger. He's an important man in Louisiana. I was hoping he and Norbert could work together.

EMILY: *(Looks at him, aghast.)* Rene's like your uncle. Norbert's the best engineer in the South and his own cousins won't have him to the house. Don't matter he knows more. *(Shudders. Wraps her shawl tightly about her.)* My legs are so cold walking through that dampness. Don't look like New Orleans is ever going to dry out. Does it rain in Paris?

EDGAR: Nothing like here.

EMILY: Do Negroes keep apart there like here?

EDGAR: No. Negroes live next to whites.

EMILY: You kidding. Nobody try to lynch them there? My dream been always to go somewhere my skin isn't a source for punishment. To live in a safe place where I can walk the streets at night. *(Takes a deep breath.)* Norbert deals with it better. He spends time in thought. While he invent I worry. They're killing strangers here. *(Swallows hard.)* It's been seven years since the war and it seems like the hatred got worse. How long does it take? God knocked Paul from his horse, but how many men get thrown down and start to see. Norbert says, "Lift them up, lift them up." He says a new age coming with shining kind people. Then the inventions will multiply. Carriages gonna go by themselves. Streetcars gonna run on tracks. He sees the bright future. I don't. He closes his eyes, I can't. He wants to leave for Paris, I want to stay.

EDGAR: The French love scientific progress, intellectual achievement. He'd be better off there.

EMILY: I know; he knows also. Norbert says that once we cross that ocean we won't be coming back. *(With bitter stubborn persistence.)* I don't want to leave. I say Emily, you closing the book on one life to open the book on another. I'll sit by the river one last time, then I won't think. I'll just go. I fear I'll want something a woman can't have. But finally we are leaving. When are you going? I'll feel safer if we travel with you.

EDGAR: There are people I can't say good-bye to.

EMILY: Course you can. I know it's hard . . . Inside me I just want to scream. I got a sister, mother, all from here. When that ship pulls off and I hear that horn blow and see them waving, I know the tears going to burst me apart. I tell myself, serve as an example of a woman who got out. *(Holding back tears.)* What you think God want me to do?

EDGAR: I don't know.

EMILY: You should. You wrote us there was revolution there. What were y'all fighting for?

EDGAR: Freedom and equality.

EMILY: And what was the end?

EDGAR: Women and children massacred.

EMILY: That is always the end. *(Her face grows hard.)* Terrible thunder! Looks like Satan's afoot. Oh Lord. We being watched. By that fellow over there and there. I better go.

EDGAR: They can't harm you. I'll make Uncle receive you —

EMILY: Don't go getting yourself shot. You dealing with some mean men. Yanks and the Freedman Bureau can't stop their rally. *(With bitter irony.)* You haven't seen your Uncle's getup? He and Will are planning a battle. They are so mad they can't carry a gun and vote. *(Her voice trembling with rage.)* They'll kill any Negro that try to stand up, and any white man that help him.

EDGAR: Yes, I know. My brother also.

(He reaches out shamefaced and takes her hand, but she drops it immediately.)

EMILY: Colored politicians can't save no one. You watch out.

EDGAR: *(Impressed and at the same time disgusted.)* Christmas is coming and so much bloody news.

EMILY: Wars don't stop on a holiday. Run from here.

EDGAR: I'll escort you home.

EMILY: *(Glances about fearfully.)* No, it's best I go alone.

(She turns with dignity and disappears through the shadows. Inside, Rene sits at the desk, struggling with bills. Jo, lying on the sofa, makes one of her puppets beat another.)

PUPPET-JO: I've had enough of her. I'm going to do something to her. *(Rene shushes her.)* I'm not going to kill her but she's got to suffer.

AMERICA: *(From the pantry, calls out.)* Jo!

(Jo hides behind the sofa. Strolling in, a basket of clothes on her hip, speaks with mounting peevishness.)

AMERICA: Come practice piano. She is always hiding somewhere. *(In a detached, reminiscent tone.)* Oh Rene. I went looking for you upstairs.

RENE: This place is turning into a nursery. I had to come down. I'm going to pay for my children to grow up, then I'm going to Paris and stay drunk.

AMERICA: *(Inches behind him, puts her hand down his shirt, and kisses him deeply.)* How long can I be expected to take all this? Have you talked to Edgar about leaving for Paris?

RENE: *(Runs his fingers through her hair.)* I can't yet. Look . . . You're married too.

AMERICA: *(She laughs . . . a hopeless depressed laugh.)* What kind of marriage do I have? *(Coquettishly.)* At least before the war my husband never worried about money, because there was always more, more. Now he counts every penny. *(She gives a little nervous knowing chuckle.)* My grandma used to say what would you rather be, an old man's darling or a young man's bride? I settled for the old man's darling, but now I'm not even that. He thinks because I worked in the kitchen before, I should be grateful for any crumb I've got. *(Sits on Rene's lap, throws her arms around his neck, excitedly.)* I'm young. I want to travel. He never expected me to want that. I'm so bored. When he talks, it's only to repeat himself or say something ugly. He hates everybody I like and one day all his meanness will come out at me. When it does, I'm a dead woman. *(Passionately.)* We've got to leave. When will you talk to Edgar?

RENE: *(Placating.)* How can I leave when the pregnancy is in trouble?

AMERICA: Edgar can run the business! You've done your share here. I can't wait. My husband will put me in prison if —

RENE: *(Lowering his voice reassuringly.)* I'll pay you as soon as the first check comes in. Don't worry. I'm going to ask Edgar for another loan from Papa. Used to be we talked about . . . us. You could enjoy life. We are the same.

AMERICA: *(Sharply.)* No, you're worse. I'm taking the risk for you.

RENE: *(There is a silence in which Rene moves away awkwardly. A strange aloofness comes over him as if he were speaking impersonally of strangers.)* What time do the guests arrive?

AMERICA: They're not.

RENE: *(Goes on as if he hadn't heard.)* I'm supposed to introduce Edgar to . . . new clients.

AMERICA: I canceled the party.

RENE: *(He stares at her, stunned.)* What?

AMERICA: I won't be one of those big-bellied women carrying around the memory of a fiery night.

RENE: You were supposed to help me and Edgar. Use the judge?

AMERICA: His friends have no money. They're looking for money from you.

RENE: *(Exasperated.)* Everybody cannot be broke. Some people have inherited money.

AMERICA: Yeah, but the rich really love their money. They'll turn from you.

RENE: *(An undercurrent of rage comes into his voice.)* So you're calling off the Christmas party?

AMERICA: *(Her manner becoming more and more distant.)* To which I'm barely invited, although it's at my house. I'm the servant who happens to own the house. I don't act like one of y'all. But Tell's the angel mother. If I've to hear once more about her first husband being nephew to Jefferson Davis —

RENE: *(Jeeringly.)* You said the judge would lend money if Edgar approached him.

AMERICA: Yes, but we haven't had relations in eight months.

RENE: *(Stiffens defensively, his voice cracking.)* You think it's fair to punish me? You know I'd love to run off with you. Never look at this wanting house again. How can I act dishonorably? So many people are depending on me. Every night when I go to bed I imagine — you alongside me. Every other second I think of you. When I'm shaving, combing my hair, stepping off the gallery, hopping on the streetcar, opening the office door, picking up the mail. *(He gives a little despairing laugh.)* There's hardly an action I do without daydreaming about you. That's my personal torture. *(America avoids his eyes, folding clothes, rigid, unyielding. Jo sneaks out onto the gallery, frowning, leaving a puppet behind. America watches her, irritated, then picks up the puppet and throws it on the sofa, and walks out the front parlor. Outside it thunders, and rain begins to fall. Moments later, Mathilde and Jo come in from the gallery, Mathilde with a vase of red gladioli.)*

JO: *(Jo hides her face in Mathilde's skirt, sobbing.)* It's true, I did see Mr. Rene and America kissing here. They're gone but they were here, kissing.

MATHILDE: My. They are just good friends.

JO: Good friends don't kiss so long. *(Gives her aunt a glance of concern.)* Is she going to have a baby?

MATHILDE: *(Soothingly, arranging the flowers.)* Heavens no. It's Christmas time. People are drinking, full of friendliness. That kiss doesn't mean anything.

JO: *(Then worriedly.)* Why are Mr. Rene and America always kissing — if it doesn't mean anything? *(Jo tries to look in her aunt's eyes, but she keeps them averted, arranging the flowers.)*

MATHILDE: Some things you can't understand until you grow up. *(Trying to speak naturally.)* Now don't talk about this to your mama.

JO: Why not?

MATHILDE: Because —

JO: Because what?

MATHILDE: *(Protesting uneasily.)* Josephine, that's enough. Now let's get you dressed for the Christmas party.
(Mathilde coaxes Jo out to the front hallway as Tell comes in the rear parlor dressed in splendid velvet and satin, her pregnancy heightening her voluptuous sensuality. On hearing the rain and thunder, she adjusts her sleeves with a forlorn gentleness.)

JO: *(Turning at the doorway.)* Mama?
(Her curiosity recedes into helplessness and she leaves.)

TELL: Merry Christmas.

(Christmas music plays, something Like "Oh Holy Night," as Tell moves to the desk and smells the vase of red gladioli. Lights dim and a slide is displayed briefly. Edgar comes in from the back parlor. A pause. His expression becomes thoughtful, almost as if he's seeing the painting, Portrait of Estelle.*)*

TELL: *(Hesitantly.)* Edgar. I know it's you.

EDGAR: How's that?

TELL: I know very close friends by their footsteps.

EDGAR: Is that it?

TELL: Well, there's actually an energy.

EDGAR: That's better. *(He stops short, overcome by his acute attraction.)* Can you sense what I'm doing?

TELL: It feels like you're watching me. *(He observes her with growing pleasure.)* It's rude to stare.

EDGAR: *(With awkward uneasy tenderness.)* I'm taking in the whole picture.

TELL: Can I get you something?

EDGAR: Just your company.

TELL: *(A defensiveness comes into her voice.)* We should have champagne.

EDGAR: *(Fighting the effect of her beauty and trying to be flatly conversational.)* You're all dressed in a rose-colored gown.

TELL: I mostly wear black.

EDGAR: Let me see.

TELL: *(She adds smilingly.)* I've clothes I've never worn simply because I don't know what they look like anymore. *(She gives a little laugh of affectionate amusement.)* For tonight I tried on every gown in my armoire.

EDGAR: I love fine fabrics, the softness on the skin, like being touched.

TELL: *(She raises her hands flirtatiously.)* Don't muss me up.

EDGAR: Let's sit here.

TELL: *(Moves away automatically and bumps into the sofa, with a sigh. She recovers and sits.)* I'm so nervous.

(Edgar looks at her, impressed.)

EDGAR: Why?

TELL: I want to . . . please you.

EDGAR: And me you. I wish there was some way I could help. *(He pauses, struggling with himself. Outside it thunders and rain drops down.)* Could you tell me how the blindness first began?

TELL: I'd rather not . . .

EDGAR: I won't tell anyone.

TELL: I don't want people to know or remember. I began knocking glasses of water off the table. I couldn't tell where the ends of things were — tables, steps, and sidewalks. Two weeks ago, I lost a little more sight. Everything changed. Just that little fraction, I'm bumping into things. I've bruised my arms from walking about.

EDGAR: What did you do . . . at first?

TELL: I did what anybody would do. I denied it. I went to the Gulf Coast and knocked myself unconscious by walking into a tree.

EDGAR: Oh, my God. That's so awful, terrible.

TELL: No . . . Nothing is so good or so bad as you think it is going to be.

EDGAR: *(His face tenses.)* I've never spoken about this to anyone, afraid to acknowledge it and make it stronger. I've been plagued with headaches. At first, I thought it was an empathetic response. I was suffering with you. Then I blamed the weather. It's unusually hot. Temperatures in December, I thought you had in June. I've had a sudden drop in vision. The less light in the room, the less I can distinguish. Colors and detail blur. My right eye is mostly worthless. They say you don't know what you have unless you lose it. Well, painters know our eyes are important. There is always that fear, so when it happens it's traumatic.

TELL: Maybe you should see a doctor.

EDGAR: Doctors know everything and nothing. What if I can't paint anymore? What if — if I lose the other eye? My God, no. You just woke up one morning, blind? I couldn't face it.

TELL: After two operations, when they put a sharp object in the eye . . . well, the results can be . . .
(Her voice trembles.)

EDGAR: Weren't you angry?

TELL: In a rage . . . But then acceptance set in. Now . . . Sometimes I think I sense more than when I had my eyesight. *(He remains hopelessly silent. She adds sadly.)* You've two options: not paint or work with your limitations.

EDGAR: What choice is that?

TELL: A hard one, but I think you see from inside.

EDGAR: You would.

TELL: Painting comes from there.

EDGAR: But if my eyes go and I can't see the colors, the tones, what can I do?

TELL: You'll find out.

EDGAR: How?

TELL: *(She smiles strangely.)* You'll use all your senses, your hearing, your touch. I think I see you more clearly, now, than ever before.

EDGAR: That's what I miss the most — your optimistic attitude. After you left, I was dazed. I rode past places we used to haunt: parks, restaurants, and imagined you there. It was comforting trying to recall what you wore: the colors, the flowers on the table, the tone of the conversation. Sometimes I felt the places calling to me as if they missed you too. A silent partnership between me and an empty table. Other times I advised myself — don't think about her, imagine her dead. I counted off days in my journal, then weeks, months. I told myself my need for you would lessen as time passed, but the images of you got stronger, not vaguer. I said that wasn't the real you . . . You were harsh, conniving, cruel. There was a side of you I hadn't seen, a side that made you prefer a flashier life, a life with Rene, not me. I bargained with God. I'd give up drinking if you'd write me one letter. My painting suffered. I couldn't focus. I cursed your intelligence, humor, sensitivity. I lay in bed assuring myself God would send me someone better than you if I just concentrated on my work. I told myself: just do your work and get through the day. She's not thinking about you, remembering you. Then you had one baby, then two. And still despite all the evidence, my heart wouldn't let go of you . . .

(He reaches out and clasps her hands . . . sadly. Outside the rain intensifies. America comes in from the pantry, flounders guiltily.)

AMERICA: I'm sorry. Edgar, we must talk about that trip to Paris —

(From the hallway, we hear uncanny, gay singing. Mathilde, Didi, and Jo walk in through the front parlor doors, singing "Oh Holy Night," letting themselves go, now and then bellowing with delight.)

AMERICA: *(Looks at Tell with focused repulsion.)* The plan for a party won't work now — I've canceled it. *(Everyone freezes, shocked. Staring at America. She stammers.)* What with the rain, the heat . . . Every few seconds this nasty thunder.

DIDI: I counted on this evening. One night I wouldn't have to be the household nun.

MATHILDE: What about the guests?

AMERICA: *(Self-righteously.)* I told the servants to send them away.

DIDI: I guess I won't recite the Baudelaire I had planned.

MATHILDE: *(Encouragingly.)* No, recite it for the family.

DIDI: *(Minces a bit waveringly to the center of the room. Recites dully with flat, empty gestures.)* "Woman . . . for the artist . . . is the object of keenest admiration and curiosity that the picture of life can offer its contemplator. No doubt woman is sometimes a light, a glance, an invitation to happiness, sometimes just a word; but above all she is a general harmony, not only in her bearing and the way in which she moves and walks, but also in the muslin, the gauzes . . . in which she envelopes herself . . ."

(America rises, guiltily, avoiding their faces. She looks remotely in Rene's direction.)

AMERICA: Who will walk me home?

RENE: I'll walk you home. A terrible storm's coming. I didn't expect it. It hasn't rained in weeks. *(Pats Tell's cheek in dismissal, huskily, forcing a smile.)* Don't wait up. *(Follows America out.)*

JO: *(Trails and taunts them with her puppets.)* Kiss me, kiss me.

MATHILDE: Put those up. Come with me.

JO: No, I want to stay.

TELL: Let her stay.

MATHILDE: *(Attempts to catch her niece's eye.)* Where's Will with the little tree? He's promised to decorate it with Edgar. If only he can spark Will's confidence.
(Mathilde turns away with a tense laugh and goes out the rear parlor. Tell walks somberly to the sofa. Jo tiptoes behind her.)

JO: Can I comb your hair, Mama?

TELL: *(Her lips quiver and she keeps her head held high.)* Yes, there is a brush on the desk.

JO: Mama.
(Pauses, staring at the floor, her face set in a defensive expression.)

TELL: Yes?

JO: Never mind. *(With a probing look.)* What was Papa like?

TELL: I've told you this before, Jo. Your father was good-looking, dashing. I picked him from a circle of carefree southern boys, now mostly dead.

JO: Do you miss Papa now you've a second husband?

TELL: That was a long time ago. We were children then.

JO: What's it like being married? Do you kiss a lot?

TELL: *(Unable to hide a furtive uneasiness.)* Sometimes.

JO: Do you need to be married to kiss?

TELL: No.

JO: *(Losing all caution.)* Do married people kiss other people too?

TELL: *(A spasm of pain crosses her face.)* Sometimes. Yes, but differently. *(Injuredly.)* So many questions.

JO: Why did you have to marry again? Who do you love most? Papa or Mr. Rene?

TELL: I love you most, that's all you have to worry about.

JO: I miss my real Papa. I keep thinking about what it'd be like to have him here. I'd sit on his knee, play horsey. Why did you bring Mr. Rene into our lives and not Uncle Edgar?

TELL: Be thankful you have Mr. Rene.

JO: I want a real papa, not a pretend papa. *(She reaches out and grasps Tell's arm.)* Send Mr. Rene back to Paris and marry Uncle Edgar.

TELL: And the babies? Don't they need their real papa?

JO: I never thought about them. *(She gives a little sad sigh.)* Does it hurt having babies?

TELL: Sometimes. Babies don't care about their mama. They don't know where they're going so they kick and scream. You arrived fighting, your face red.

JO: My face was red?

TELL: Your uncle, Jefferson Davis, sent me a diamond pin, a swan with green eyes, but I hocked it way back when.

JO: Why did you marry Mr. Rene and not Uncle Edgar?

TELL: *(Smiles with ironic amusement.)* Rene played the part of the successful young banker. So handsome and so smart. He'd been to his tailor and bought the costume. Suntan suits in summer, a scarf thrown over his shoulder to give the impression he was rushing. He flitted around the edge of single ladies, not knowing he'd get caught in the web of a blind woman.

JO: That's not true. *(Stares at her, puzzled.)* You like being married?

TELL: The best part is anticipation. Hearing a man's footsteps at your door. *(Mathilde comes in from the rear parlor door, frowns admonishingly.),*

MATHILDE: This isn't talk for a child.

TELL: *(Pats Jo's cheek.)* She's mine. Besides, she understands everything.

JO: I do. *(Bell jingles.)* That's Uncle Will. *(Bursts out excitedly.)* He promised he'd bring the tree trim with Uncle Edgar. *(Jo runs off into the hallway.)*

MATHILDE: *(Trying to shake off her hopeless stupor.)* No party.

TELL: I feel so unhappy. *(Didi walks in with prim politeness through the front parlor, hands a note to Mathilde.)*

DIDI: A message for you. I didn't open it. *(She leaves curtly. A loose smile twists Mathilde's face as she reads.)*

MATHILDE: There'll be no tree.

TELL: Will won't be home tonight? Is he with . . .

MATHILDE: *(With a tough, tortured laugh.)* Don't mention her name. *(Walks toward the vase of gladioli on the desk, yanks off leaves.)* All men cheat. When Will went to the altar, instead of saying "I do," he should have said, "I'll try." Certain women become the strange attractors.

TELL: Why do men think they can get away with these heartless episodes?

MATHILDE: Because they can.

TELL: *(She smiles strangely.)* How do you handle it? How can you accept it?

MATHILDE: *(Sliding into intense detachment — quotes casually.)* There is a sense of relief when you know, but you never admit it. I light a candle, recall my licentious thoughts. It's good for wives to reflect in silence. If we can't save ourselves, perhaps we can save our children.

TELL: I couldn't cope . . .

MATHILDE: *(Brokenly.)* Men are hunters. They aren't capable of loving a woman, much less of telling her they do, or of doing anything about it.

TELL: *(She talks excitedly.)* That's not true. There are men who value how their actions affect others, men who listen.

MATHILDE: *(Disdainfully.)* Edgar, again?

TELL: I didn't say that.

MATHILDE: Aren't you tired of standing at the door, wringing your hands, asking your husband to talk to you till your voice sounds like thunder?

TELL: I'm just lonely.

MATHILDE: I've suffered loneliness for sure, but I've lots of tasks done for me so I can keep my shine. Wives have to look good, so as our husbands age, we can replace their mistresses and become their mothers, perfecting the technique of living with them while they're ignoring us. The home should be a wife's sanctuary. I try to shift the routine by putting breezy surprises into every day, a Christmas ornament. *(Her hands fly up nervously to fix her hair.)* An Easter bouquet. Nothing unpleasant. I dare not mention the loan to Rene.

TELL: *(With stubborn naiveté.)* He's repaid you, hasn't he?

MATHILDE: No, and now I find out . . . he hasn't paid the bills for six months, nor has he spoken to Edgar about a loan.

TELL: For God's sake . . . take this.

(Tell yanks off her ring.)

MATHILDE: Not your diamond. *(With bitter sadness.)* Anyway, it's nothing. A drop in the ocean.

(Mathilde goes out quickly through the pantry doors. Thunder intensifies. Moments later, Edgar enters, carefully watches Tell for a few moments. He walks slowly to where she sits. She looks tired, miserably sad.)

EDGAR: It's Edgar. Are you all right?

TELL: I'm fine. I'm in alone time. It's necessary, it's difficult, but it's here. See me in the morning, and I'll have a little repartee with you.

EDGAR: *(Moved in spite of himself.)* You're one of the solitaries of the world. *(With fond solicitude.)* We'll celebrate tomorrow.

TELL: *(Bluntly.)* Stop trying to make things right, to understand, to help so much!

EDGAR: Sorry.

TELL: *(Rebukingly.)* You should know better.

EDGAR: It's been a long time since I've had family.

TELL: Start one of your own.

EDGAR: Maybe I should.

TELL: *(With dull anger.)* You've got a ruined Christmas.

EDGAR: I can handle it.

TELL: Will's drunk and not coming with the tree.

EDGAR: That's all right.

TELL: The Christmas party is canceled.

EDGAR: There'll be others.

TELL: *(Cynically brutal.)* Why are you so . . . so complacent?

EDGAR: Because you . . . make me happy.

TELL: I don't know why.

EDGAR: I don't either.

TELL: You annoy me.

> *(She avoids looking in his direction. There is condemnation in her smile mixed with a new violent attraction.)*

EDGAR: *(He tries to copy her coolness but is unable to get over his heartsickness. There is a pause of icy silence. He goes to the window, watches the rain as if he were talking aloud to himself.)* Such a cold moon night. A brittle moon, stone blue. Like your wedding night. The hard darkness of the Cathedral almost gobbles up your bright gown as you come down the aisle. I imagine you are walking to me. I get there an hour before the others just so . . . I can be ready . . . for what I don't know.
> *(From the window, without turning around.)*
> Why'd you — marry Rene?

TELL: He made me . . . the right offer.

EDGAR: *(Turning abruptly.)* What is that nonsense!

TELL: I'd a small child . . . He was willing to live in America.

EDGAR: Off your papa's money . . . When Rene told me he'd marry you, I accepted it. I adored him, so why shouldn't he have you.

TELL: You were upset?

EDGAR: Crazed . . . Up to the last minute, I thought, prayed you might cancel.

TELL: You never came over.

EDGAR: Why bother? Rene was always there by you. I had to get through him to see you.

TELL: You acted aloof.

EDGAR: *(With a maudlin laugh.)* What in the hell did you expect? The most difficult thing was to say congratulations. Because till I said that you weren't really married.

TELL: You never spoke —

EDGAR: Hearing you say, "I do," I . . . I . . . My body felt like stone. I was cold quiet. But you knew. You knew. It was there all over me, in my eyes, my awkwardness.

TELL: People said you were ill.

EDGAR: *(Wincing his lips, quivering, pitifully.)* I blamed it on a fever, yes.

TELL: You left early.

EDGAR: I told myself I'd get through it if I didn't see you. To stay away at all costs. Don't write. Don't —

TELL: We thought you were off painting.

EDGAR: But I was so down, painting became unimportant. *(Shrugs his shoulders — thickly.)* And when I went back to painting, my perspectives were off. I've said about all I can say without —

TELL: *(Protests penitently.)* I thought your role was to paint, that's why I chose Rene. I was a widow tired of crying, hungry for life. *(With sharp irritation.)* You never proposed. I waited . . . and waited.

EDGAR: *(Wrathfully.)* Admit it. You preferred him.

TELL: *(With sudden tenderness.)* Rene was carefree with a childish grandiosity. True. *(Wryly.)* And you sat in the corner with your paintings, quiet, unpredictable, even defiant.

EDGAR: *(Breathes deeply and looks away.)* I couldn't look at you and speak at the same time. And after you left, I kept in motion, traveling about — Rome, London, Madrid — even their visual splendor couldn't keep my eyes from turning inward. Each day I wrote you a letter and each night I tore it up. And no word from you.

TELL: Didn't Didi write?

EDGAR: Yes, but she hardly mentioned you. I combed her letters for clues. Were you happy, sick . . . *(He takes her hand with deep caring.)* I wish I could have been there with you when you lost your sight.

TELL: Me too.

EDGAR: *(His voice grows husky and trembles.)* I would have been your eyes. You could have counted on me.

TELL: *(Half-reassured but frightened.)* How — with you somewhere off . . . Look. I'm married. I can't talk from my heart.

EDGAR: Oh, don't be prim. Not with me. We're two broken souls so . . . let's have one thing complete between us. An honesty "In to Me See."

TELL: *(Clutches her stomach in pain. Startled, Edgar looks about nervously and helps her to the sofa. She looks up at him, pleading frighteningly.)* All right, I'm going to the end of this . . . or as close to the truth as I can possibly stand.

(Stricken with a cramp, she stiffens, patting his hand, trying to act normal.)

EDGAR: Let me call someone.

TELL: No. Now that I've got you here alone, stay with me. Closer. Be with me. Bless me, Father, for I have sinned. For so long I've dreamed of having you here like this, your face by mine. Your hand here.

(A spasm of pain crosses her face. She squeezes his hand in hers.)

EDGAR: Let me call Mathilde.

TELL: No. And since you came, I can't sleep. I barely eat and I feel full. I sat before you while you painted, heard the brush on the canvas, smelled the oils, felt your voice all around me, and I was totally happy. I wanted to sit there forever, bask in your radiance, feel your eyes on me. That just having you in the same room could make me so delighted. I ordered my fingers to hold on to the chair for fear I'd lift off. You're here leaning over me.

EDGAR: Don't talk.

TELL: *(For the moment she loses all caution.)* I feel like I must have died and gone to heaven. That I could have you beside me to myself. And you could tell me you've been loving me all along. That it's your hand on mine, your eyes looking at me. Your body bending so close. I don't want to move or wake up for fear you'll be gone. I want to live here in this dream.

EDGAR: Let me call your sisters.

TELL: No. . . stay with me. One more moment. *(Another intense cramp.)* OH, MY GOD. OH, NO. OH, MY GOD.

(Blackout.)

END ACT I

ACT II

Slide up of the Degas house, then ragtime music like the composition of Louis Moreau Gottschalk and lights at the same time, slide out. Jo is on the floor dancing in her dreams, Rene sits wearily at his desk, rises, walks slowly out like an old man. Sounds of flooding rain. Jo crawls onto the sofa like a scared little girl. Didi and Mathilde come in from the rear hallway, Didi whispering roughly to hide her tense nerves.

DIDI: I can't sleep.

MATHILDE: *(Dully.)* Me neither. America's hatred level spikes at night. How did she take over the house?

DIDI: She runs Rene. The woman who runs the man runs the house. *(She stops, looking through the front parlor toward the window where the rain pours.)* If only Edgar would take me to Paris.

MATHILDE: Bring me and Will too. *(With a confused strange smile.)* How did everything go wrong? I was a joyful person. Remember? Then life turned sour. When did we take the wrong turn? Maybe Edgar can figure it out.

DIDI: You've been hit too many times. I'm so disappointed. If I could just understand. We were happy once. All of us in this house. How did we come to this? I can't talk to anyone anymore, and we used to chat into the night. Now if I say anything to Will or Papa it erupts into a fight.

MATHILDE: *(Weakly defiant.)* What happened to my marriage? My family? Edgar's the only nice one —

DIDI: You've got to stand up for yourself. Papa schooled us for a better life. We were raised in a family where men took care of women. Men were generally mean, but they took care of us. Now, they don't care for us and they're mean.

MATHILDE: *(With a bitter laugh.)* Who knows which way is better, with or without a husband.

DIDI: *(Lowering her voice, hurriedly.)* Come in my room when he's violent. You suffer more than Mama did.

MATHILDE: Papa didn't beat her.

DIDI: *(Pats her hand consolingly.)* No. But their marriage was based on her obedience. Show those bruises to Papa.

MATHILDE: *(Her vanity piqued, testily.)* Will would deny it or blame Edgar. He shames anyone who won't join the White League. *(She turns her head away.)* I keep hoping Will will get shot in a skirmish. Collapse with a heart attack. Bless me, Father, for I have sinned.

(America comes in with a irritated glance around the front parlor. A hard obstinent set to her face, she walks over to Jo, and yanks her sheets off.)

AMERICA: Jo, get up. Get up, I need your help.

JO: *(Her eyes half-open, she scrunches into the sofa.)* I'm sleepy.

AMERICA: *(Maliciously.)* We've got homeless all over the house. Your grandpa keeps letting them in because of the flood.

JO: Go away.

AMERICA: Get up, I'm telling you. We've got vagrants everywhere. There's a break in the levee. Can't you be useful while we're exhausting ourselves?

DIDI: *(With a quick calculating glance at America.)* She's just a child. She's —

AMERICA: *(Ignoring, Didi — resentfully.)* A bully. Bully, bully!

DIDI: Go away. I'll take over. *(Quickly.)* Shush. Tell needs her rest, she's still hemorrhaging.

AMERICA: Jo sleeps way too much. Nobody helps me. Jo's the one who should assist me. She waits for me to do everything. *(Turning to Didi.)* And you and Edgar encourage this laziness, when you should demand that she help out. Jo's so lazy, lazy, lazy!

JO: *(With sudden exasperation.)* I'm not!

AMERICA: The girl's totally spoilt, mentally unstable.

JO: *(Shouting.)* I'm not!

AMERICA: She should be off on her uncle's grand plantation, playing.

DIDI: *(She laughs — then scowls abruptly.)* Filled with war veterans, amputees, victims of malaria.

AMERICA: I'm trying to hold things together. Jo can't live in the nursery. Yesterday she threw a pair of scissors at Gaston, then she punched little Will.

JO: Little Will punched me and Gaston threw . . . my puppets out the window . . . Ask Uncle Edgar.

AMERICA: *(Stung to sneering jealousy.)* I've a headache, which she has given me. I've had one for two days now.

JO: Uncle Edgar says you should go home.

AMERICA: And leave this house unattended? Who can take care of it but me? Tell's health is precarious. Jo just irritates her. She should leave before things get worse. *(In a burst of resentful anger.)* I know what's best.

(Uncle Michel approaches — swaying in the front parlor doorway — in a loud voice.)

UNCLE MICHEL: What's going on here? Will's drunk and the children are running around. *(Chuckles tipsily to Didi.)* You should be with Edgar.

DIDI: Go to bed, Papa.

AMERICA: Mathilde's husband gambles and drinks. Edgar couldn't straighten him out.

(They watch Uncle Michel's wavering progress through the front parlor. He goes out.)

AMERICA: That old man's a drunk too.

DIDI: *(Her rage still smoldering.)* Please show my father some respect.

(Didi and Jo go out the front parlor door, and America stomps off through the rear parlor door. Rene, clutching a baby, enters from the gallery, turns, watching the rain. Sips from his flask. Moments later Mathilde slips in from the pantry with bassinet.)

MATHILDE: *(Whispers, alarmed.)* Did you get the doctor?

RENE: *(Sarcastically.)* In whose boat? There's six feet of water out there.

MATHILDE: You've been drinking.

RENE: I've got to have a few drinks to start the day. How's Tell?

MATHILDE: Her bleeding's slowed. But the baby is worse.

RENE: I know. *(Moved despite himself — helplessly.)* Doctor doesn't want Tell to get too attached, because it's a matter of time. They sent me here to get the baby.

MATHILDE: Take it quick before she comes back.

RENE: *(With a hurt, bitter look, blinking back tears.)* How tiny, how warm. Poor little creature can't survive long. Struggling to breathe. Oh, my God. I'd like to help it — comfort Tell, but — I never wanted this baby, and she knew it. Her name's Jeanne, but she's no fighter. She hardly opens her eyes. When I put my finger in her fist, she barely squeezes. I rub her stomach, but she hardly notices. *(A look of terror comes into his eyes.)* If only I'd acted enthusiastic, gotten more loans through Edgar, things would have turned out all right —

MATHILDE: *(Wisely.)* Maybe not.

RENE: *(He winces — all life seeming to drain from his face.)* They say with Jeanne's pneumonia it'll be a sweet painless end. It'll get harder for her to breathe until she stops. I hope I don't have to see it.

MATHILDE: Does Tell know?

RENE: *(He stammers wearily.)* No. I had to fake some slight hope for her.

MATHILDE: *(Her eyes are on him, condemningly.)* You gave her hope?

RENE: What else could I do? The woman keeps waiting for good news. *(Uneasy now — with alcoholic talkativeness.)* How did this happen? Yesterday I was a banker's son in Paris. Women sparkled about me, sent me perfumed notes, anonymous flowers. I thought I'd come to Louisiana and

Tell's father would make me a southern planter. Louisiana was the New World. Where you could be a success by age thirty. Yesterday I was a superficial dreamer. That was the real me.

MATHILDE: Let's prepare the baby.

RENE: *(He sighs gloomily and resentfully.)* I tried, swear to God. What did I find when I got here? Lazy people too lost to help me. Mosquitoes, moths, and caterpillars dropping from trees. A bitter humidity, thousand-leg spiders, termites gobbling all they see. Prehistoric roaches. A stifling heat. A river waiting to burst its banks full of alligators and moccasins, and water rats fleeing up the oak trees. Children dropping with yellow fever, scarlet fever, typhoid. Unnamed infections. Hurricanes, floods, and infants struggling to breathe.

MATHILDE: *(She puts her arm around him soothingly and gives him an affectionate hug.)* Go on, cry. Let your heart break like everyone else's. *(Firmly.)* But do what you have to do.

RENE: *(In a changed tone — repentantly.)* I suppose I'll order a little casket.

MATHILDE: Yes, you must.

RENE: *(Gulps from a flask, grins wryly.)* Thank God for alcohol. Things seem pinker, calmer. A strange quiet soothes your ears, making you able to hear anything, accept anything. Soon in a room of death you are peacefully alone.

MATHILDE: Is that what you want?

RENE: *(With drunken melancholy.)* In this house you can't be by yourself. People coming and going. I want to be alone.

MATHILDE: No, you don't. You want to be with someone else.

(Rene holds up a hand, then walks out heavily. She stares after him with mingled worry and irritated disapproval. Seconds later, Uncle Michel blusters into the room, his eyes glassy.)

UNCLE MICHEL: I can't sleep.

MATHILDE: My God, Papa, go back to bed.

UNCLE MICHEL: *(He starts as he hears heavy footsteps on the stairs — with suspicion.)* Where's Rene going? We have a White League meeting today. He's supposed to bring Edgar.

MATHILDE: Leave Rene alone.

UNCLE MICHEL: He's probably going back to sleep. He works from a part of his brain which is least developed. *(For a second he looks miserable and frightened.)* Oh well, maybe he's a good fighter, that's his last hope.

MATHILDE: *(Commanding.)* Leave him alone.

(Didi hurries in through the front parlor doors. She pauses, wrinkling her brow.)

DIDI: Where's Rene? Did he take the baby?

(Mathilde leaves discreetly with the baby through the pantry as Edgar enters quietly through the rear parlor doors. Didi spots him, lowering her voice to a delighted tone of whispered confidence.)

DIDI: There you are. Papa is already drinking this morning. Will has smoked up all the cigars . . . *(With intentional impertinence.)* I'll have to declare myself sick to get rest. Is it still raining?

EDGAR: Steadily. *(Smiles with detached tenderness.)* I'll be leaving soon.

DIDI: *(Alarmed.)* How soon is soon?

EDGAR: Next week.

DIDI: Couldn't you stay a little longer?

EDGAR: Its time.

DIDI: *(Coaxingly affectionate.)* Could I ask you something?

(Uncle Michel rises, fighting a tipsy drowsiness. With a remote amusing smile he goes to leave them alone.)

DIDI: It's about this novel that I am writing.

(Intrigued, Uncle Michel grins a bit drunkenly and sits again.)

DIDI: I want to check certain details. The story's about a woman who wants to be a writer, live in Paris. Is this possible, for a woman . . . to have her own Bohemian garret?

EDGAR: Yes, but artists' studios are small, unheated, with a horrifying amount of dust and dirt.

DIDI: *(She gives a little exalted, shy laugh.)* Yes, I know, I know. So she lives in this poor garret, but she joins the Paris café society and finds artist friends who are challenging and supportive.

EDGAR: Let's not forget jealous. That café crowd, everyone is in competition with everyone else.

DIDI: *(With stubborn blankness.)* Yes, I know. Despite the envy she causes, she enjoys evenings spent in the salon, musical soirees. She does public lectures sponsored by friends whose estate she visits in Normandy.

EDGAR: How did she learn to maneuver so well in a —

DIDI: *(Her tone has become more and more rapturous.)* She had a taste of this as a young girl. Exhilarating afternoons spent with her father at the Café Guerbois and the Nouvelle-Athenes where ideas for a new painting were debated. *(With an elaborately offhand casual manner.)* Well, it was here that she became stronger and stronger. Her sense of purpose became clearer and clearer. She met a man, a painter who fought in the Commune.

UNCLE MICHEL: *(Rises dazed as if this were something she shouldn't talk about.)* What nonsense, Didi!

(Uncle Michel goes out on the gallery. Suddenly Didi's whole manner changes. She becomes pathetically relieved and eager.)

DIDI: She falls in love with this man . . . and they marry.

EDGAR: *(With a feeble attempt at teasing.)* I was in love with all the Musson sisters.

DIDI: And we with you —

EDGAR: *(He doesn't appear to hear her. He adds pleasantly.)* I couldn't get enough of you all, Mathilde, you, and Tell. Beautiful Tell, so young, already a mother and war widow. I used to study her from afar.

DIDI: You studied her?

EDGAR: *(Obsessed with the memory.)* Such a stricken face, the tightness of her lips, the untidy strands of hair. Her eyes, deeply shadowed, downcast, always wet as if bleeding for that young captain sent to slaughter. I couldn't look at her without thinking that face filled the eyes of a dying man.

DIDI: *(Backs into a chair.)* You couldn't forget her face?

EDGAR: I had no concept of what loss could be till I saw this vision. No matter what I brought to captivate her, bon-bons, marroons, glacés, she found no consolation. No comfort. Even now weak and suffering.

DIDI: *(Stammering.)* So she's the one . . . Bravery?

EDGAR: You're right. She's the brave one. I'm the coward.

(Kneels by her, takes her hand in a comforting gesture.)

I made a mistake. I never should have let Rene have Tell. Although she's blind and sick, I'm still in love with her.

DIDI: *(Crestfallen.)* You're in love with her?

(Uncle Michel comes in through a gallery window. Edgar is on his knee in front of Didi. Triumphant, fighting the effect of his last drink, Uncle Michel blushes and bursts out.)

UNCLE MICHEL: Didi, why don't you get downstairs. Baby's screaming. I'd like to offer some sherry in celebration, but our liquor supply is shot.

EDGAR: We had wine in the cupboard.

UNCLE MICHEL: *(Joshing.)* No more, it's drunk up. I was commissioned as a lieutenant in the Army. I should have been an officer but I had enemies.

(Jo runs in from the gallery. She turns impulsively to her aunt, grabs her arm.)

JO: Aunt Didi. Gaston's thrown all my puppets out the window into the water. Aunt Didi . . . Gaston's . . .

DIDI: *(Drops her hands from her face, with a loose, twisted smile.)* All right. I'm coming.

(Jo pulls her off onto the gallery. Uncle Michel stares after them with bleary affection, looks suspiciously at Edgar, goes out the front parlor door, baffled. Moments later, with a growing dread, Tell rushes in from the pantry. She feels about the room. Tense with a hopeful, fearful expectancy.)

TELL: Edgar, is that you?

EDGAR: Yes.

TELL: Oh my God. I can't find my baby. Where is she? Did she die? Where did they put her?

EDGAR: Mathilde is watching her.

TELL: Why did they move her?

EDGAR: *(He stops her — gesturing upstairs — lowering his voice sincerely.)* Mathilde just took her to the sick room.

TELL: *(With frightened resentment.)* But she needs me to hold her. How can they take her from me without asking?

EDGAR: You were sleeping.

TELL: Jeanne needs me. If she misses me too much, she may lose heart. Has her fever gone up? *(She moves about worriedly, speaking with a tone of concern, burying her face in her hands miserably. He stares at her sheepishly and shakes his head.)*

EDGAR: They wanted to spare you. Come here.

TELL: Spare me. They've taken her off to die.

EDGAR: No one would do that.

TELL: Is her breathing worse? Did the doctor ever get here?

EDGAR: He's on his way.

TELL: Damn floods. No one can get in or out.

EDGAR: *(With awkward tenderness.)* Come. Sit. Get hold of yourself.

TELL: I don't want to. *(Hesitates, then blurts out guiltily.)* You're the only one who talks to me. Rene hasn't said a word since Jeanne was born. I don't think he's seen her. God, he can't visit me? Not for ten minutes? I can't face this alone.

EDGAR: Jeanne's . . . just in the sick room.

TELL: *(She stiffens, with a terrified defiance.)* Isolation, that's the first step. I've spoken to other mothers. She'll stop eating. Without me, she won't eat.

EDGAR: But you're weak.

TELL: I know. My milk is bad. I'm an unfit mother. I fed the others.

EDGAR: Nothing's wrong.

TELL: I cried without stopping since she was born. Now I can't even feed her. *(Her expression becomes somber.)* I called her Jeanne, after the Maid of Orleans, because I wanted her to be strong. But I've got to face it. She's not.

(She speaks quickly, with a superstitious dread.) What will I do if she passes? My babies keep me going, holding them, skin on skin.

EDGAR: She's a little better.

TELL: Don't lie. Not you too. Not you too.

EDGAR: *(He takes her hands and gently seats her by him. Puts his arm around her, he draws her against him.)* Here, sit back.

TELL: *(Her fear receding into resigned composure.)* I want my girlhood back. The Paris Opera, the ballet, the racetrack. I want to see dancers turning in white tutus . . . *(Wistfully.)* Arabian stallions, you drew so well. *(Light changes.)*

EDGAR: *(Touched, he leans in closer.)* If you move to Paris, I'd buy you a stallion and we'd ride it. *(Music and slides of Paris during his speech.)* I'd take you to the opera, the ballet, the popular theater, and the absurd Café Chantant, past the Rue de Rivoli, the Champs Elysees, the Arc de Triomphe.

(Music and slides out when she sits up.)

TELL: *(Grins, at her ease again.)* That's what I miss. Nonsense. Nonsense and seeing your work.

EDGAR: *(His manner becomes tenderly solicitous.)* I'll take you to my studio, show you my modeling in wax. I'd put each piece in your hands. Do you remember the "Walking Horse" I made once? You could feel the muscles, the shadows. I'd teach you. We could forget conformity, gentility, and even the need to remember. *(His voice is suddenly moved by profound feeling.)* I've been holding your words close. They've been driving me, whispering to me, filling my thoughts with hope. I've had to face a lot of emotions I've been painting about obliquely for a long time. I tell my mind to stop, but it goes to you anyway. I blink and you're in my thoughts. I'm fantasizing about you, fighting a slow idolatry. When I'm with you, I look for the silence unspoken — the nod in my direction.

TELL: Don't give me hope for something that's never going to happen.

EDGAR: It's hard to confess but I have to . . . And you?

TELL: I know what I feel is inconsequential. *(She looks away with a helpless far-off quality in her gaze.)* If I go away, I'll never see my children again. Rene's not the person you knew. He's confused. But he's my husband.

EDGAR: . . . and my little brother.

(Edgar goes slowly out the front parlor door, a blank hard expression on his face. Moments later, Didi comes in from the back parlor. Worried, she speaks in a placating tone.)

DIDI: Tell . . . are you all right?

TELL: Yes, I'm fine. *(She becomes restless, sensing Didi's devotion, and struggling to keep down her emotion.)* Didi, I've got to tell you something. I know it's wrong. There's no excusing it. But I always tell the truth, which endears me to no one.

DIDI: *(Cynically.)* It's about Edgar.

TELL: Yes. First I . . . *(Pauses, ashamed.)* I admired his persistence . . . His commitment to painting contemporary life. What ferments in his head is breathtaking. I'm scared of it and awed by it at the same time.

DIDI: *(With a wry sadness.)* Yes. I am too.

TELL: Then I loved his . . . his humility. *(She gives a little laugh of affectionate amusement.)* He's uncertain about the quality of his earlier works. Astonishing paintings of ballet rehearsals and horse races as I recall them. Then I appreciated his loneliness, assessing in middle age what he wants to do with his life. With him it's visceral — it goes beyond language — it's crazy, it's wonderful, that at my age, with my difficulties, Edgar loves me and I love him.

DIDI: *(Appalled.)* You've already had two husbands, it's not fair.

TELL: I . . . I never encouraged him. I'd forgotten what it's like to feel valued.

DIDI: *(Starts and stares at her sister with bitter hostility — thickly.)* So you have to steal Edgar. You . . . you seduced him. You know how to fix yourself up — how to flirt — There are no men left since the war . . . You knew I wanted Edgar. How could you?

TELL: I said I'm sorry.

DIDI: *(Her mood changes to arrogant disdain.)* Don't excuse it. Maybe it isn't your fault. I can't wash away the unwanted birthdays. Men say they want intelligent independent women, but they don't, not really. *(She puts a hand to her face, holding back a sob.)* Edgar and I are perfect for each other. The same artistic ambitions. Id be happy just living with him, writing my stories. But with you flaunting yourself, he doesn't see me.

TELL: *(Looks down, guiltily.)* Didi, calm down.

DIDI: I will not calm down, not this time. You're blind not only with your eyes but with your heart. *(In a burst of rage, she grabs her sister by the arm and twists it till Tell falls backwards.)* Your own husband's having an affair with America, and you don't see. Yesterday I walked in on them in the back hall. But no, no matter what Rene does, you won't see. You lie there, doing nothing, feeling sorry for this baby you should never have had. The doctors warned you, but no, you had to put us through this misery. *(Her voice trembling with suppressed fury.)* Where do you think that sickly baby is? In my room. I'm the one who's got to watch it die. You're a saint while I'm just a woman without a husband. No matter I sit up nights writing. Nobody ever asks to read my work. My eyes burn while you lie there in your lace and satin, flaunting those new nightgowns Rene bought you. And you know that he did it out of guilt because he's seeing America. I take care of a dying baby so that Rene can sleep with America and Edgar can drool over you. *(Emotion raging through her.)* I've been dreaming of him, prayed he'd come for me, but he never stopped loving you. *(Guilty with the shocked realization of what she's said.)* There is a bridge between our past and our present. Somehow when he arrived, like lightning you and he were connected all over again.

(Didi chokes huskily, sobs overcoming her, as she barrels out to the front hallway. Mathilde, who is coming in, shrinks back, then calls back to Didi uneasily.)

MATHILDE: Didi, what happened? *(Turns to Tell in a confused panic.)* Are you feeling worse again?

TELL: I don't want to talk about it.

MATHILDE: You can tell me.

TELL: *(Her face tensing.)* No, I don't want to talk about it. Leave me alone.

(Mathilde goes out into the hallway, yelling indignantly.)

MATHILDE: Desiree, Desiree?!

TELL: *(Tell stiffens, turns toward the doorway with frightened defiance, then hollers.)* Rene! Rene! Rene!

(Moments later, Rene dashes down the stairs, hurries to the front parlor door, anxious.)

RENE: Yeah. What's wrong, the baby's fine. She's with me. Sit, you all right?

TELL: *(Bursts out with a look of accusing hate.)* I've just had a terrible shock. I learned something that I . . . I can't believe.

RENE: From whom? Edgar.

TELL: No. Now tell me the truth. Don't lie to me.

RENE: *(With guilty vehemence.)* I won't. You all right?

TELL: Someone came to me.

RENE: Edgar?

TELL: *(Staring condemningly at him.)* And told me you're having relations with America. Is it true?

RENE: Who told you that?

TELL: Never mind.

RENE: Someone is talking behind my back?

(With vague exasperation, he forces a casual tone. He comes to her, embracing her with a quick measuring look. She breaks away.)

TELL: Is it true?

RENE: We're friends.

TELL: *(Hysterically.)* Did you make love to her?

RENE: How could you believe such . . . gossip.

TELL: Did you touch her?

RENE: America is . . . loyal.

TELL: Kiss her?

RENE: I would never do . . . *(Keeping his eyes averted.)* How can you think that? You're making up vicious stories.

TELL: *(Turns on him, wounded, broken.)* Liar! Liar! Liar!

(Mathilde runs in the front parlor door. She sees Rene moving to the rear parlor door and lingering there. She regards him with dislike, comes round in back of Tell, touches her shoulder tenderly.)

MATHILDE: Tell?

TELL: *(Shattered, her eyes fixed downward.)* I thought that America was a fine person . . . *(Strangely, as if talking aloud to herself.)* Sometimes I felt queasy when she was overly solicitous of Rene . . . Still, I told myself don't be small-minded because she is so good with the children. *(Pause of dead silence.)* Now I've got to accept the fact that while I was being nice, she was sleeping with my husband. Or so Didi says. Rene denies it?

(Rene scowls, signaling to Mathilde to lie for him. Without turning from Rene, Mathilde says sharply.)

MATHILDE: He's a coward.

(Rene looks after Mathilde angrily, shrugs, and goes and slouches by the rear parlor door.)

TELL: *(To Mathilde, disgustedly.)* You knew? You knew — and — you didn't tell me? You were protecting Rene. God. I'm your sister. You and Didi have been covering for him.

MATHILDE: For God's sake. Everyone knew about it but you . . . and maybe Edgar.

TELL: Tell him too! Inform the world.

UNCLE MICHEL: *(Comes in from the pantry, letting the door slam behind him.)* What is happening in my house? In the old days women knew how to behave.

MATHILDE: Papa, go to bed.

(Mathilde and Tell go out the front parlor doors, with Uncle Michel grumbling. Once they have gone, he strolls maliciously up to Rene as if he will hit him. Rene moves quickly away from the doorway, feigning concern about an envelope on the desk. Uncle Michel goes out, slamming the door behind him.

Seconds later Edgar comes in, reviewing some bills. He looks at Rene with a quick calculating glance. Walks over to Rene at the desk. Edgar's hands jerk nervously as he shows Rene a bill. He gives him a strained, almost contemptuous glance.)

EDGAR: Tell me if I'm wrong but it doesn't look like you've paid back any of Papa's loans.

RENE: I can't talk about anything else today.

EDGAR: I've got to make some sense out of these records.

RENE: *(Tensely, moves away toward the window.)* As I explained, Papa stopped keeping books for the planters. The old field hands are getting credit from shopkeepers. Railroads and the telegraph are diverting cotton to inland markets and drying up the power base on the river.

EDGAR: Still, we've been selling cotton without exacting a commission?

RENE: *(Ignoring this resentfully.)* I contacted our creditors. I did everything short of sending a drawing with a gun to my temple saying "Pay this or I'll kill myself." I didn't create the financial panic. I've had a short and sorry business life. I don't speak the language, I don't get the nuances of these cotton people. I just want to leave. *(Abruptly his tone changes to exasperated contrition.)* If it wasn't for Tell, I'd have left Louisiana. I don't know a single person who wouldn't leave if the means were at hand. The French Quarter is the end of New Orleans, which is the end of Louisiana, which is the end of the world. We're standing at the end of the end.

EDGAR: I'm trying to get some clarity.

RENE: So you can report to Papa what you did right and I've done wrong.
(Rene drinks restlessly, sensing Edgar's struggle to make sense of the invoices.)

EDGAR: I'm the one who influenced Papa and our sisters and brother to invest in cotton, but you've the control over all his property. That's what Papa wanted, I'm not questioning it.

RENE: Did I run away when Uncle went bankrupt, sold the big house, and moved into this wretched rental property? I'd to get Papa's power of attorney to keep us from starving.

EDGAR: *(Looking down, trying to ignore Rene's tirade.)* But self-dealing will put you in jail.

RENE: True, Papa loaned me too much money.
(Suddenly pointing a finger at Edgar, his voice trembling.)
But he also financed the girls' marriages, your never-ending studies, not to mention the Confederacy. *(Moving a step back, defensively, his face growing hard.)* Papa wanted to turn to you, but trusting me was all he had.

Our grandfathers were the geniuses, not him. They made the fortunes in Louisiana cotton and Italian investments. He just inherited their nest egg.

EDGAR: Poor fellow trusted you. You came home raving about Louisiana and telling us all we had to do was give you money for the shears and you'd cut the golden fleece. *(He stares at Rene with increasing enmity, removes a letter.)* Do you know what Papa wrote to me? "I was counting on Rene, who has sent me nothing. Is he going to let our bank, that was held up with so much effort, tumble down? If the creditors put my back against the wall, they'll take me to court."

(Rene crouches on the sofa, picks up his flask listlessly.)

RENE: Papa's been using the bank to loan himself money. That's why his bank is in trouble.

EDGAR: Fine. Even if I sell a painting a week, I can't make enough to stop them from —

RENE: *(He glances away, miserably dogged, drinks.)* American-style business wiped Papa out. I worked hard.

EDGAR: For which you charged us substantial fees. God, we can't have a conversation with you without getting billed. *(Confronting him with the charges.)* Look at this: conversations with Michel Musson, your own uncle, whose house you live in gratis, ten hours. And this, bank deposits for Uncle, conversations with Didi, Mathilde, and Tell Musson. My God, you even billed us for talking to your own wife.

(Rene shrinks down onto the floor, sitting sideways on an arm of the sofa, so he cannot meet Edgar's eyes.)

RENE: I charged you a reduced fee.

EDGAR: You knew the cotton business was failing and you gouged funds. You were my favorite brother. God, I trusted you. You had it all, and you took it all.

RENE: *(He jumps up, losing his temper, refusing to admit anything to his brother.)* I am appalled you think I'd do anything unethical. The authorization for my action was Papa's idea. In reference to your . . . accusation . . . about my fees. I and my assistants have spent many hours working . . .

EDGAR: *(Takes a threatening step toward him.)* Such as?

RENE: *(Jeeringly, shoving Edgar back.)* You have benefited . . . directly from the money you have received . . . your gallery openings, your studies, your trips as well as indirectly from Mama and Papa's generosity to you from moneys they've received. It's not my fault the cotton business is failing. I am deeply hurt by your actions as my brother. *(His rage smoldering, he pushes Edgar violently into a chair.)* If you chastised me for my relation-ship with America, that I could understand. I feel guilty about that.

EDGAR: *(Edgar's hand goes to his head in an aimless stunned way. He stabilizes himself, looking straight at Rene now. There is a tense pause.)* What is that you are saying? You are sleeping with America? I knew she was helping you with running the house, tending to the children, caring for Tell, but —

RENE: It's been more than that for some time.

EDGAR: You're not . . . You are. You're having relations with her. *(Sharply, letting his resentment come out.)* Here?

RENE: *(With a detached, impersonal tone.)* She understands me. Comforts me.

EDGAR: Your baby is dying, your wife is critically ill, and you're having an affair with her neighbor in her house?

RENE: It didn't start now. It started a year ago.

EDGAR: This is worse than the money. This is Biblical sin. *(Gives a hard, sneering little laugh.)* I can't believe I gave Tell to you. I let you have her, court her first. And you wasted this possibility. You knew how much I cared. She commanded my attention, and she did so for a long time. *(With threatening anger.)* You couldn't tell me about America all these months I've been here. We all have to deal with unbearable situations. But we don't bring our mistresses into our house.

RENE: I hate myself. But God, I'm bored. *(With broken weariness.)* There's no defending it. I've become the men I knew. I wake up and see, like Papa and Uncle, I've a mistress and a wife. *(Rene goes to the window, glad of an excuse to turn his back.)* I want it to end, but it's impossible. I'm too exhausted to break it off. Too disappointed. When we're alone, America's different. She lifts my spirits. *(From the window without turning around.)* No one believes in monogamy anymore. We only choose it when we have no appealing alternatives. Sex is everywhere in a city, except in a husband's relationship with his wife. I say I love my wife, but I'm cold below the neck. I feel nothing. She's attractive to many men, but to me she's not, so I put on a false face. My life is a total lie. Wives dream of other husbands, husbands dream of other wives, and we both shut our eyes.

(A pause. The brothers avoid looking at each other.)

EDGAR: Does Tell know about America?

RENE: I guess she suspects. *(Rene comes around in back of his brother, not looking at him, and grabs Edgar's shoulder.)* I don't want to lie, so I'm evasive. It takes so much energy. Believe me, being a liar is tiring.

(Slides in. Edgar and Emily walk cautiously down an alley. She pauses, a look of growing uneasiness comes over her face.)

EMILY: We leaving tomorrow morning. Four days on trains, three hours in New York, ten days at sea in an English ship. Good-bye, New Orleans. *(She stares before her, hopeless.)* We got no choice. Look out there. Soldiers marching up and down the streets. People running. Mean-eyed police. Now free people of color don't mean anything. The whole city is in silence. Men are fighting everywhere. It's madness. *(Turns impulsively, grabs his arm, lowers her voice.)* Last night four men in sheets broke in our house. They knocked Norbert down. Cause Norbert spoke out. Because we feed these poor souls that come to our door. You don't read the paper. Go out? Coloreds are hit for no reason. And the poverty. Homeless every corner. It's getting worse. There's going to be a fight. Too many hungry people, and ones who got nothing but hate.

EDGAR: *(He pats her arm with an awkward tenderness.)* I need to leave. But I have unfinished business.

EMILY: You best go before a battle break. You don't want to be a foreigner in gunfire. *(Her voice begins to tremble.)* I've seen things these past few days. Secret groups riding and killing more than ever now. Yanks pretend they want to help but they do nothing. Old masters want to stop coloreds from getting their rights. They watching people like Norbert. Next time it be worse.

EDGAR: *(He frowns and shakes his head mechanically.)* I can't leave Tell with no one to protect her. She can't count on Rene. He's never there.

EMILY: *(Suddenly it is too much for her and she breaks out and sobs.)* Take your luggage and get out. Before they send a pack of dogs and madmen to get you. You have a mission in life. *(She throws her arms around him, hides her face in his shoulder, then runs out.)* God bless you. Good-bye. *(Music and slide in as she is leaving.)*

(Tell sits on the porch. She has fallen deep into herself and finds relief for an instant in silence. Jo comes in, dressed in a traveling cape and bonnet. With forced gladness, she taps her mother on the shoulder. Tell hugs Jo to her breast; using remoteness to contain her sorrow.)

JO: I'm ready.

TELL: *(Squeezes her affectionately.)* Your whole life you have been with me. Now, different cities, different houses.

JO: I'll come back for the Carnival balls.

TELL: And Papa will present you. I can't take it.

JO: Don't cry, Mama, I'm not afraid anymore. I want to leave.

TELL: No, do you really?

JO: I'm grown-up. *(She pauses — then speaks in a flat, empty tone.)* I can travel alone. I'm leaving all my puppets. I placed them in a row for little Jeanne so she can play with them when she gets better. I'm too old for puppets.

TELL: Well, won't you miss them?

JO: I packed a baby one in my bag, but don't tell anyone.

TELL: *(Smiles as if she hasn't heard it.)* I won't. Are you sure you want to go, you don't have to if —

JO: Don't stop me.

TELL: *(With detached motherly solicitude.)* Oh, I can't stand it.

JO: I want your life to be easier, Mama, you worry so. Trying to make everyone happy. I know how hard it is, because I see.

TELL: Oh, shush. I just need another hug.

(Jo climbs on her lap, hides her face in her mother's shoulder.)

JO: I'm only going for a while. Then I'll be at the convent in Mobile. I'll come back a grown-up elegant lady. Everyone will like me. Now I just make trouble for you.

TELL: *(Her voice shifting far away.)* How can not having you be better for me?

JO: You'll see. Things will be easier.

TELL: Don't talk that way.

(Didi walks in wearily from the front hallway, sits tensely on the sofa staring before herself as if in a sad dream.)

JO: There are too many people here. When people are squished like that it's hard for everyone to be nice. It'll be better for you if I leave.

TELL: *(Rocking her like a baby.)* You don't know, you don't.

JO: *(Curling a finger through Tell's hair.)* Don't feel sad. I'm happy, Mama.

MATHILDE: *(Walks in briskly from the rear hallway. She looks at Didi matter-of-factly.)* You're in one of your depressive moods.

DIDI: Jo's been mine since she was three weeks old.

MATHILDE: I thought you were fine with her going.

DIDI: *(She sighs gloomily.)* I've enough other reasons to be bitter and sad.

MATHILDE: Oh, yes. Edgar is also leaving.

DIDI: *(Her face set in stubborn denial.)* Don't talk. I don't want to fall apart.

(Reluctantly, Jo leaves her mother and walks slowly to where her aunts stand waiting.)

JO: I'll go say good-bye.

DIDI: *(Grief-strickenly whispers to Mathilde.)* I won't survive this.

MATHILDE: Didi, I didn't think I'd survive the death of my baby boy. I made it, and you'll make it.

(Jo walks in, sees Didi crying. Jo looks at her aunts, bravely covering her helpless, hurt feelings. She feels their sad eyes on her and forces a smile.)

JO: I would like to say good-bye to you, Tante Didi and Tante Mathilde.

DIDI: *(Stubbornly fixing a hat on Jo's head.)* Oh, no.

(Uncle Michel comes in from the back hallway — summoning his soldier's heartiness. Takes Jo's hands, sits, and gives her a pony-back ride on his knee. Feigning a laugh, he clicks his heels and waves an imaginary whip.)

UNCLE MICHEL: I'm proud of you, Jo. I'm glad your grandmother didn't live to see this day. I'll go with Jo. Soon we'll be galloping horses on Pass Christian.

JO: You're too old, Grandpa.

UNCLE MICHEL: I never do things like old people. I feel like I'm three, I used to look around, and I was the youngest in the room, and now I'm the oldest. *(Another forced laugh.)* I should leave also. After the fall of New Orleans, I refused to take the oath of allegiance to the Union, so they're not going to tell me what to do.

MATHILDE: You'd only get in the way, Papa.

UNCLE MICHEL: *(Importantly.)* Jefferson Davis is writing a chronicle of the war. Now Jo's going, I can tell you for the past ten years I've been —

DIDI: Keeping a journal, we know.

UNCLE MICHEL: *(With painful effort to be jolly.)* But Jo doesn't know the extent of the collection. I've been writing down each dream I've had along with every daily event and political occurrence. About fifteen hundred pages a year. For my heirs so they can know everything about me.

JO: *(Enthusiastically.)* About me too?

UNCLE MICHEL: *(Glad for an excuse to keep talking.)* Yes, I'm showing how the dream relates to the event and the routine. *(Tries to get his appeal started.)* Well, what do y'all think? I've thousands of entries. Mr. Davis will find them interesting.

DIDI: Papa, she doesn't understand.

JO: Yes, I do!

MATHILDE: Shush. *(Mathilde is about to make a sneering remark to her father, but she shrugs her shoulders and embraces Jo.)* You're such a big girl, so grown-up, and you'll be even more so when you return from your papa's people.

JO: I want to go with Uncle Edgar.

MATHILDE: Will and I are moving to Ocean Springs — that's not far from you. I'll visit. I'm only sorry Aunt Didi won't be with us.

DIDI: *(Grumbling.)* Thank God I don't have to cope with Will anymore.

UNCLE MICHEL: One more hug. Rene can't make you go if I say no.

JO: Don't worry about me, Grandpa.

MATHILDE: Don't blame Rene, we all agreed.

UNCLE MICHEL: *(He growls.)* I never.

DIDI: Papa, please.

UNCLE MICHEL: Write me like you promised. A page a day.

JO: Yes, sir. Have Uncle Edgar send me a little sketch of the family.

MATHILDE: *(Distracted, sad.)* I almost forgot the lunch basket.

UNCLE MICHEL: *(Feigning a smile.)* We'll wait for you outside, Jo.

(Uncle Michel gives her a strange lost glance, disbelieving she can truly be leaving. Uncle Michel blows his nose and goes out to the gallery. Mathilde and Didi give way to a flurry of guilty business and leave swiftly. While Jo is silent, keeping a head turned toward their footsteps, Edgar comes in with gifts for her. He goes directly to Jo, his face set in an expression of kind sympathy.)

EDGAR: Where's the little lady? I have a gift for you.

JO: What is it?

EDGAR: *(Puts a hand affectionately on her shoulder.)* Open it.

JO: *(Embarrassed and pleased.)* Are all these pencils for me? Oh my.

EDGAR: That's not all.

JO: A miniature of Mama! Oh, she's so beautiful. Thanks, Uncle Edgar. *(She smiles, her face lighting up, and kisses him gratefully.)* Come with me to Mississippi. How will I learn to draw if you don't teach me?

EDGAR: Take my memorandum book.

JO: I couldn't.

EDGAR: All my life I've carried a notebook where I sketch images. *(With a touch of pride, he gives her a shiny binder.)* I took this one when boarding the Scotia, the last paddle steamer. See, I've sketches of the passengers. Here I've drawings of horses, a genre painting called *Pouting,* and the *Orchestra of the Opera.*

JO: I couldn't draw like that. I dance even in my dreams, but if I try to draw it I cannot.

EDGAR: Neither could I at first. *(She laughs and he laughs with her.)* You must practice. That's how you learn. Study and paint, then come to Paris. I'll get you permission to copy inside the Louvre. Show you Ingres and Delacroix.

JO: What are those?

EDGAR: Great painters. Let's find your mother.

JO: *(She opens the book, smiles with humorous exaggeration.)* Let me sign my name. Jo Balfour 1873. *(Reluctantly.)* Must we go?

EDGAR: Sometimes we must go away even though we'd like to stay.

JO: I don't want anyone to know about the miniature. They might take it.

EDGAR: *(He looks at her with understanding sympathy.)* It's our secret.

(Music fades in slowly. Edgar takes Jo's hand and they walk out bravely to the gallery. She smiles, controlling an impulse to cry, clutching the miniature. Mathilde comes out to the gallery — uneasily — with a plate of sandwiches. All feign smiles and hug Jo with elaborately casual airs and pathetic attempts at heartiness. Tell hugs her to herself — sobs brokenly. Jo leaves slowly and her mother rushes back inside, bumping into Rene. Huskily trying to force a smile, Rene walks on to the gallery just as Jo passes out of sight. He waves feebly. Mournful sounds of a carriage are heard. Moments later, America marches out onto the gallery. She attempts to catch Rene's eye, looking for sympathy, but he walks back inside, staring at the floor. There is a dead silence. America follows Rene inside with guilty talkativeness.)

AMERICA: Jo should have appreciated me more. She forgot to thank me. The girl's all right as people go, but one more child or less, in this house . . . what does it matter?

(Mathilde and Didi walk dully into the parlor. Mathilde's expression changes as if she were deliberately giving way to hunger and seeking to hide behind food. She attempts a light, amused tone, and passes sandwiches to Didi, Rene — loitering at the desk, and America.)

MATHILDE: These sandwiches look lovely on Mama's calendar plates with Monarch butterflies and roses.

DIDI: How can you talk of food when Jo's leaving?

MATHILDE: *(Gives her a quick apprehensive glance.)* Edgar's going.

(America glares at the sisters with a hard accusing antagonism. Her face is stony and her tone icy.)

AMERICA: Food shouldn't be eaten in the parlor. You want rats? Yesterday I saw one leap from the banana tree. We'll have to shave it back, replace that rosebush with a cement slab. We must economize if Rene's going to get back to Paris. Isn't that right, Rene?

(He doesn't respond and she leaves noisily through the pantry.)

MATHILDE: People usually behave better with food.

DIDI: *(Gloomily.)* When exactly are you leaving?

(Mathilde pauses — then lowers her voice to a tone of whispered confidence.)

MATHILDE: After Will's meeting at noon. Excuse me if I gloat. I woke up this morning and thought "praise God I'm finally leaving." I'll have my own big house and my own room, thick sheets and a satin quilt. Aren't you happy for me?

DIDI: I should be happy for you, but I'm not. Abandoning me with Tell and

Papa. He won't come in and she won't come out. *(She gives a little rebellious toss of the head.)* Don't you need someone to read to the children?

MATHILDE: We'll get a nurse in Ocean Springs.

(The front parlor doorway opens and Uncle Michel walks in, worriedly, with a quick sly glance at Rene. Children's voices are heard and Uncle Michel walks to Mathilde with a disconcerting laugh.)

UNCLE MICHEL: Mathilde, little Will needs you. He's bawling for Edgar.

MATHILDE: Thanks, Papa.

(Vaguely resentful, Mathilde goes out into the front hallway.)

UNCLE MICHEL: *(Moves over to Rene — irritably.)* It should be over by now.

DIDI: *(Looks about, tense.)* I have a feeling something bad's happened. What is it?

RENE: Will's been in a duel.

DIDI: What?

(He pats her shoulder. She gives him an uneasy, almost frightened glance, wondering if her father really means this.)

UNCLE MICHEL: Will was set on a challenge. They were shooting pistols at noon. Strange, since it's usually dawn.

DIDI: *(Looks at him sharply.)* We should warn Mathilde.

UNCLE MICHEL: *(His face hard — grimly.)* It's over by now. Anyway, it's not women's business.

DIDI: We should do something.

RENE: Calm down.

DIDI: *(She turns on her father accusingly.)* But Papa —

(America comes in from the pantry. She is terribly annoyed again as if the strain of the departure activities had been too much for her. She frowns at them suspiciously.)

AMERICA: Are you talking about me again? Every time I leave and return I see these caught faces. The devil's going to punish you for talking about me. I won't have it.

RENE: *(Turning away, wryly.)* We were discussing politics. A certain weariness in people getting their dream —

AMERICA: I know what I hear.

UNCLE MICHEL: *(He shrugs his shoulders — cynically.)* She'd be a good woman if someone held a gun to her head twenty-four hours a day.

AMERICA: How dare you insult me?

UNCLE MICHEL: I'll do what I want. I'm the head of this house. And the head doesn't take orders from the tail. *(He takes a threatening step toward her, raising his cane.)* Would you mind leaving?

AMERICA: Happily.

UNCLE MICHEL: I'm in a fighting mood. If I kill someone it might as well be her. Nobody would miss her.

(He stamps his foot, genuinely pleased and grateful for the explosion. He goes out the front parlor — roughly — grazing past Mathilde, who is coming back in. Mathilde adjusts her hair in an aimless anxious way and walks to Rene, seated at the desk. Her hands drop distractedly to her dress.)

MATHILDE: Somehow I'm so nervous today. We're all packed, Will has to run off. I don't get it. If he knows we're leaving, couldn't he stay home? What could be so important? *(With forced casualness.)* Sweet Jesus, don't let him get into trouble.

(America comes in through the front parlor, goes straight up to Mathilde, who avoids her eyes. There is a cracking silence.)

AMERICA: Mathilde, Mathilde, Mathilde. It's such a disgrace. *(There is a tense pause, then she speaks jeeringly.)* I just received word at the door, Will's been shot in a duel.

MATHILDE: Shot?

AMERICA: *(An undercurrent of vengefulness comes into her voice.)* He never made it to any meeting.

MATHILDE: Is he dead?

AMERICA: Wounded, slightly.

MATHILDE: *(With a despairing laugh.)* Will's always tilting against windmills.

AMERICA: This time he killed a police officer.

MATHILDE: *(Stunned.)* He did what?

AMERICA: They've posted a bond and thrown him in jail. You'll have to use your travel funds to bail him out.

MATHILDE: *(Hastily — gruff.)* Well, get my hat and coat!

(Her reaction has an automatic quality as if it did not penetrate to real emotion. Her face darkens — stung, and she goes out. With a scornful shrug of her shoulders, America snorts.)

AMERICA: Don't bring Will in the front door! We'll never outlive the humiliation. *(She starts for Rene and sighs grudgingly.)* I suppose I'll have to clean up by myself. I want you to tell Didi and Mathilde to help around the house. I don't intend to keep getting used. If you're curious about what you can do to help out, I've got some suggestions. *(Guiltily explosive.)* Are you listening to me?

RENE: *(Bored with her complaints.)* I'm trying not to.

(Rene takes out his flask and drinks. America gives him a quick biting look and disappears through the back parlor. Moments later, Edgar comes in the

rear parlor doors, suitcase in hand. His manner is nervously apprehensive. He stops abruptly, catching Rene's eyes, regarding him with an uneasy hopeless look.)

RENE: I can't believe you're going to leave when we've so much trouble. I've been counting on you, looking up to you for twenty-five years. You can't leave with the baby ill and the cotton business bankrupt. I depended on your partnership. You were coming here to help us. What happened to that? *(He is moved in spite of himself. His voice quivers.)* In six months the cotton business could turn around. I can't have this end with us not talking. I did the best I could.

EDGAR: It's better for everybody if I go. Better for me and Tell.

RENE: What about me? I need you. I'm drowning here. I've no one to turn to.

EDGAR: Talk to your wife.

RENE: *(He looks directly at Edgar, a note of pleading in his voice.)* You don't understand. I wanted to impress you. That's why I took this big chance. *(Putting on an eager heartiness.)* Oh, don't give up on me. Stay. How could it be better with you miles away?

EDGAR: I'm stepping back for the second time. It's not healthy for me to be so close to your family. I start being overprotective . . . thinking I'm the father. . . the husband —

RENE: *(With a cynically appraising glance.)* You're too fond of my wife?

EDGAR: *(Averting his eyes, suddenly overcome by guilty confusion — stammers.)* No . . . Yes. I must leave. Take this last chance and save your marriage. *(Uncle Michel comes in hastily from the back parlor. Goes worriedly to Edgar, puts his arm around him.)*

UNCLE MICHEL: This house is always in the middle of disaster. Now I have to get Will out of jail. *(A shadow of vague delight crosses his face as he hands Edgar a magazine.)* Something to amuse you on the ship. I think it's a sin to read these magazines. I read them anyway. So what. The problem with heaven is some awful people are going to be there so I'd just as soon be in hell.

EDGAR: Well . . . Thanks . . . Uncle Michel.

UNCLE MICHEL: *(With a flash of apprehension.)* It bothers my ears to hear my name. My name embarrasses me. Before I was Michel Musson. Now I don't know who I was five minutes ago, let alone next week. I'm sixty and I don't know who I am anymore.

EDGAR: The whole world is changing. People want to breathe freely . . . Negroes, whites — everyone just wants to breathe.

UNCLE MICHEL: *(Edgar goes to Uncle Michel, but he cannot face him.)* I don't understand your ideas about a New World. I want my old one back. You're leaving, Jo's gone, Mathilde's in trouble. Suppose I should be happy. Fewer mouths to feed, more room. *(Heroically covering his grief.)* Still — I've to bludgeon myself to fake a smile, to put one foot before the other. My God, can't you stay? Your brother needs you. You're the strong one. We never got along, but I respect you. I don't know anything about painting, but I know people.

EDGAR: I'll miss you. I'll miss you all.

UNCLE MICHEL: Is that a fact? You're the strange one that's hard to tell. Money was what you came here for, wasn't it?

(Edgar looks away, shrinking into himself.)

UNCLE MICHEL: You and Rene, prospecting in the New World. Take this for your trip.

(He pulls out a small roll of bills from his pants pocket and carefully selects one. Edgar refuses it.)

EDGAR: I'm fine.

UNCLE MICHEL: I'd liked to have given you more. Twenty years ago, I could have. It was a damn comfortable life. I hoped we'd have something in common . . . that you'd take an interest in the White League.

(Edgar turns sharply, seized by guilt, fumbling with his pocket watch.)

UNCLE MICHEL: What's that frown for?

EDGAR: Shame overcomes me when you talk about this. I'm not from here. But oppressing the Negroes cannot be justified. People must learn to live together.

UNCLE MICHEL: Everyone oppresses someone! Right, Rene?

(Rene shrinks in the doorway, Edgar stares at his watch without seeing it.)

UNCLE MICHEL: The Negroes are angry . . . there are conspiracies among them to murder the whites and outrage our women. The White League was formed to protect our rights. You want to see your cousins raped?

(Edgar looks up with a start.)

EDGAR: This is the old ghostly fear.

UNCLE MICHEL: *(With rising anger.)* I don't know what I did to offend you . . . I don't understand you. I welcomed you into my home. I treated you like the son I never had. *(Removes a gun from the desk, cocks it, calls distractedly to Rene.)* Rene, we have a meeting to attend.

(Edgar stops Rene with a punitive glance. For a second he seems to have broken through to him. Rene shrugs guiltily and skulks out the rear parlor door after his uncle. Didi enters, breathless from the gallery. Seeing Edgar, she blushes. Her voice flutters.)

DIDI: So, you're leaving. Can't you wait till summer? You haven't experienced anything till you've spent a day out in the boiling air and open sun. It's really refreshing. The heat just hangs there between the oak trees. I picked you a boutonniere.

(She pulls out a flower she's been hiding behind her skirt, touches his lapel gently. He draws away, smiling uncomfortably.)

EDGAR: *(His hands jerk nervously to his lapel.)* I'll do it.

DIDI: *(With an excited obstinacy to her face.)* Mama used to have a flower lady who came every week and taught me what to do. Hold still a minute.

EDGAR: I don't know if I can. *(Hesitates.)* They like you to board early. I'll be returning on a French ship, traveling via Havana. Where did I put the ticket?

DIDI: Your jacket? Check the front pocket. Where? Oh.

EDGAR: I hope I didn't pack it.

DIDI: *(Soothingly.)* There it is.

EDGAR: *(Grateful, steps back.)* You're so observant.

DIDI: That's what you said when I first visited Italy. You said I found more subtleties in your painting than anyone you knew. That's because I saw the suffering.

EDGAR: I don't have much time.

(Didi gives a quick suspicious glance to the entranceways, then kisses him passionately. He backs off and turns her away from him with genuine concern.)

EDGAR: Wait. Forgive me if I've done anything to mislead you. You're like a sister to me.

DIDI: *(Mumbles, a trifle acidly.)* Like a sister.

(She stiffens, with resigned helplessness, and backs out onto the gallery from the room. Tell comes in cautiously through the rear parlor doors with a hopeful, fearful expectancy of finding Edgar.)

TELL: Edgar, are we alone? Good. I want to remember the feeling of you alone in the room with me.

EDGAR: It doesn't have to be a memory. *(With awkward tenderness.)* I've said little in lots of time. Now I feel I must say lots in little time.

TELL: All this time I saw myself going with you. *(She smiles rigidly, her voice beginning to tremble.)* My life wasn't touched by you, it was scalded. I, who had ruled out happiness in my life, suddenly had access to it. And now you're leaving. I didn't know it'd be this hard.

EDGAR: *(He walks her to the sofa, regarding her from somewhere far within himself, a place of bitter sadness.)* There were a lot of things I didn't know. The brutality of your sun. Can I tell you a secret? Before I go to sleep I imagine you beside me, a hairsbreadth away. Like in a painting, I imagine your neck, your body caressed by thick sheets, the quicksilver light falling on your thigh. I'm terminally romantic. I close my eyes and imagine you touching me on a wild and melancholy night.

TELL: *(With strange coquetry.)* I know.

EDGAR: How many times when my soul fell into solemnness have I lain with you? Bodies merging, two wrongs becoming a right. *(Then with a teasing boyish laugh.)* Now what use is my fantasy? I'll have my pencils, papers, paints. But here, I've been surrounded by little ones.

TELL: You're dancing with something bigger than family, your talent. There's an involuntary glory in that. You must hurry. Paint the paintings only you can paint. *(She seems not to notice the tears in her eyes.)* One day you may lose your sight. Painting will be your legacy. Other artists your family.

EDGAR: I'm wistful for a home of my own. *(Moved in spite of himself.)* Come to Paris with me.

TELL: Nonsense.

EDGAR: Let nonsense become sense.

TELL: I'd be a burden.

EDGAR: You'd inspire me.

TELL: And the children?

EDGAR: More subjects to paint.

TELL: Rene would never let them go —

EDGAR: He'd have America.

TELL: You're brutal.

EDGAR: Honest.

TELL: Three children and a blind wife.

EDGAR: Finally, a family.

(She lets him take in the fantasy, hiding deep within herself. Her face looks amazingly youthful and innocent. Then she gives a forlorn toss of her head.)

TELL: You're crazy.

EDGAR: In love.

TELL: Go before you —

EDGAR: Do something impulsive: jump the fence, strip naked, swim the Mississippi. *(He stares at her with the quality of a bewildered boy.)* I can't bear the thought of life without you. Drifting into the day, meaninglessness setting in. You make me believe in myself, in my deep judgment.

TELL: *(She pauses with a bitter laugh.)* I'm the latest in a long line of people who believe in you.

EDGAR: Not true. I can give myself to you without being consumed. After you left, I shut down my heart. My wounds were so deep I thought I might die if I made my heart vulnerable. I joined the ranks of the dispossessed. Became another mad soldier. I've let you reenter my heart and know my deep self. And now I can't leave without you. Return to that cynical place.

TELL: *(She smiles hopelessly.)* You know if you really need me, I'm there for you. *(Her voice quivering.)* Who knows, maybe we'll be together in another life.

EDGAR: I want you now, today. *(Bell chimes.)* Run off with me. Leave. My best art was done like that, in a flash. A release of spirit, a concession to a greater power.

TELL: If I went . . . your paintings would suffer.

EDGAR: *(A trusting smile on his lips.)* I have to step back and take care of bigger things than my painting, things that painting didn't take care of. There is an illusion with art that feels like it can save us. Dreams do not go away. They go to the grave with you. As you move toward a dream, the dream moves toward you. It meets you.

TELL: *(She winces — her lips quivering pitifully.)* But how can we . . . I can't leave my children.

EDGAR: I'll take your arm, wrap it around mine, and we'll walk out of hell together. *(Sound of carriage bells.)* God, it's time to go.

TELL: No, no, no.

(He draws her to her feet, he touches her face and she his forehead, eyes, mouth. She buries her face in his neck. He draws her away, but she gets up and throws her arms around him — hiding her face in his shoulders sobbingly.)

EDGAR: *(Suddenly it is too much for him and he breaks out.)* I don't think we were meant never to see each other. I don't think I was never meant to hear your voice or the ripple of your laugh, or to see the dimple when you smile.

TELL: Don't forget.

(Edgar breaks away and leaves quickly out the front parlor door. She does not respond at first, her hands fluttering to her eyes to wipe back the tears. Her two sisters join her, coming in hastily from the rear parlor. The three sisters rush after him, moving to the gallery window to wave farewell. Didi, forcing a laugh, inches in front and waves the most. Rene walks in from the pantry with awkward, heavy steps. He goes somberly to the window. He nods in Edgar's direction. Once Edgar has gone, Rene steps back into the parlor and busies himself at the desk and speaks with a sad bitterness to Tell, who comes into the parlor, shaking her head helplessly.)

RENE: Tell, I wish there were something I could say. This is embarrassing, sugar.

I won't ask any questions and you shouldn't ask any questions. Maybe this way we can live together.

(His eyes stare at the floor, his face set in an expression of defensive cynicism.)

TELL: *(Rebuffed and hurt, shrugs her shoulders.)* I hope so.

(Mathilde comes in and walks Tell to the gallery for fresh air. They look in Edgar's direction. Mathilde sits on the arm of Tell's chair, her arm around her. Didi joins them from the front parlor, standing behind Tell's chair.)

DIDI: *(With finality.)* He's gone.

TELL: *(Wistfully.)* Paris took him back. I wonder if anyone will know that Edgar came to New Orleans?

EDGAR: *(Music plays softly. Walks slowly to the ship's railing, slipping into reverie.)* I stood on the deck watching New Orleans fade into light. It felt like peering through a looking glass, hallucinatory, the vast wild sky expanding into mirrorlike water. I'd come to find the people to whom I belonged, to close up this hole in my soul. *(A blank, far-off quality in his voice.)* The long way back made me face my own lie. I'd come for Tell. If only I'd captured her beauty in that painting in 1863. I recalled her home on Esplanade, the half-exposed body, the bare shiny arms, the wonderful warmness of the profanity of life. Broadly stated limbs, outstretched arms with a vaguely underwater feeling, gossamer torsos caught up in light and shade. *(He pauses — then longingly.)* I'd found a raw reality for my paintings. A new direction I'd been avoiding in life and on canvas.

And I would struggle to feel it deeper and deeper in explosions of color, people, soon called Impressionism. *(Nostalgically.)* Years would pass. Great stretches of time, and like New Orleans, my cousins would fade in memory. Little Jo, Didi, Mathilde, and Tell. Sweet beautiful Tell. *(With strange, sad detachment.)* And all the paintings in the world would never bring them back. *(He leaves abruptly, three slides appear in incandescent blues, violets, and scarlet, ending with something like the* Portrait of Estelle.*)* *(Jo's ballet movement across the stage. She twirls bravely, with a voracious delicacy reminding us of Degas'* Fille de Quatorze Ans. *There is an uncanny, gay freedom in her manner as if in spirit she were released to live again.)*

END OF PLAY

Epilogue:
What Happened to the Degas Family

1878   Jeanne, Rene and Estelle's baby, dies of yellow fever.

1878   Mathilde dies in childbirth, as does her baby.

1878   Rene runs off with America. They obtain false divorce papers in Chicago, marry bigamously in Ohio, move to New York City, and a year later to Paris. They later have three children (plus the two children by her first marriage).

1879   Estelle gets a divorce via her father's efforts and lives in New Orleans until her death in 1909.

1881   Jo, age nineteen, dies of scarlet fever at the Convent of the Visitation in Mobile, Alabama.

1882   Norbert and Emily Rillieux self-exile to Paris where he continues to invent.

1883   Michel Musson legally adopts Estelle and Rene's children.

1884   William Bell dies.

1885   Michel Musson suffers a breakdown and dies.

1902   Desiree, after caring for Estelle and their father, dies.

1917   Edgar dies. Half of his estate goes to Rene, who oversees the sale of works in Edgar's studio.

1921   Rene dies. Estelle and Rene's children, when contacting the French court regarding their father's estate, learn of their half-siblings.

1961   A descendant of William and Mathilde Bell, Judge John Minor Wisdom, begins dismantling segregation through his judicial opinions in the fifth circuit court of appeals. He is now regarded as a Civil Rights hero.

Golden Ladder

By Donna Spector

For my father, Sidney Spector (1905–1980), with love

PLAYWRIGHT'S BIOGRAPHY

Donna Spector's play *Golden Ladder* (finalist in the Herbert Mark Newman Theatre Competition) was produced Off Broadway at the Players Theatre in 2002. Her first play, *Another Paradise*, was produced by Donald Goldman at the Player's Theatre in 1986 after productions at the Open Space Theatre and the Chinook Theatre in Edmonton, Canada. Other plays and theaters where they appeared include: *Hanging Women*, University of California, Hayward; *These Are My Adults* (finalist in the Beverly Hills/Julie Harris and Mill Mountain Theatre contests), Playwrights Theatre of New Jersey; *Manhattan Transits* (semifinalist in the Beverly Hills/Julie Harris contest and the Chesterfield Writers Film Project), Medicine Show, Trenton's Passage Theatre, and Contemporary Theatre of Syracuse; *Strip Talk on the Boulevard*, Lark Theatre Company and Waterfront Ensemble; *Not For the Ferryman*, produced through a grant from the Geraldine R. Dodge Foundation, also staged readings at Buffalo Ensemble Theatre and Princeton University Theatre; *Missing Families* (semifinalist in the Mill Mountain Theatre Competition), Bloomfield College Theatre; *Dancing with Strangers* (semifinalist in the Chesterfield Writer's Film Project), Playwrights Theatre of New Jersey and Wings Theatre in New York; *A Sense of Movement* produced through a grant from the New York State Council on the Arts; and *Seductions*, Lark Theatre, Playwrights Theatre of New Jersey, and William Mount–Burke Theatre. A member of Dramatists Guild, Harbor Theatre Company, Women Playwrights International, and the International Conference of Women Playwrights and Poets & Writers. She received two National Endowment for the Humanities grants to study in Greece, where she attended the latest International Women Playwrights Conference. Her poems, short stories, and monologues have been published in many literary magazines and anthologies.

INTRODUCTION

My father was Russian Jewish from Chicago and my mother vaguely Protestant Irish from Paradise, Kentucky. After encountering anti-Semitism early in their marriage, my mother denied for the rest of her life that my father was Jewish. My father never contradicted my mother, except in his behavior when we visited his Jewish family. My sister and I were raised Presbyterian because that was socially acceptable in our neighborhood. Knowing that this sort of experience is not uncommon in our society, I have attempted in this semi-autobiographical memory play to explore the confusion a young person experiences growing up in a family divided by different religions and cultures.

In *Golden Ladder* my heroine Catherine tries to come to some understanding of her identity by recalling her bewildering childhood and adolescence stemming from her mother's denial of her father's background and her father's struggle to give up his spiritual heritage to please his wife.

ORIGINAL PRODUCTION

Golden Ladder was developed in workshop by the Harbor Theatre Company and opened Off Broadway at the Players Theatre in February 2002. It was produced by Donald H. Goldman and directed by Thomas G. Waites. Set design and lighting were by Barry Arnold, costumes by Laura Frecon, sound design by David A. Gilman. The production stage manager was Terri Mintz and the assistant stage manager and understudy for Carole and Mary was Julia Motyka. The cast (in order of appearance) was as follows:

CATHERINE BRONSON . . . . Amy Redford
AARON FELDMAN . . . . Michael Anderson
CAROLE HAVENS . . . . Christi Kelsey
BERNARD BRONSON . . . . Neal Lerner
LAURA BRONSON . . . . Annie McGovern
MARY SCACCIA . . . . Marjan Neschat
HOTEL CLERK . . . . Christi Kelsey

CHARACTERS

CATHERINE BRONSON: Plays both a young girl seven to fifteen, and a woman, thirty, daughter of Bernard and Laura, intelligent, introspective, also a writer, wishes to discover the truth about her family.

BERNARD BRONSON: Young, twenty-one, and older, forties, Catherine's father, Jewish, a writer and storyteller, idealistic and romantic.

LAURA BRONSON: Young, eighteen, and older, forties, Bernard's wife, Irish Protestant, a great beauty, vain and controlling.

AARON FELDMAN: Fifteen to sixteen, and at the end, thirty-one. Catherine's first boyfriend, a nerdy but charming intellectual.

MARY SCACCIA: Thirteen to sixteen, Catherine's girlfriend, energetic, naive and honest.

CAROLE HAVENS: Fifteen to sixteen, Catherine's girlfriend, preppy, conventional.

HOTEL CLERK: May be played by same actress who plays Carole Havens.

TIME

Moves back and forth to various times between 1943 and 1980. Catherine's adolescent scenes take place in the early 1960s.

PLACE

Pasadena, California, and in the memory scenes between Bernard and Laura, Evansville, Indiana. The setting, however, is a bare stage.

Golden Ladder

ACT I

Scene One

Lights up on Catherine, standing with Aaron. Both in their thirties, Catherine wears a coat and a shawl over her head, holds a baby in her arms. Aaron wears a yarmulke.

CATHERINE: Ye-hei she-la-ma ra-ba min she-ma-ya ve-cha-yim a-lei-nu ve-al kol Yis-ra-eil, ve-i-meru: a-mein. O-she sha-lom bi-me-ro-mav, hu ya-a-seh sha-lom a-lei-nu ve-al kol Yis-raeil, ve-i-me-ru: a-mein. *(She looks down at baby.)* That was the Kaddish, Leah. The Jewish prayer for the dead. And look where your grandfather lies — in a Christian graveyard.
(Aaron exits with baby, coat, and shawl.)

CAROLE: *(Enters. fifteen, dressed in a pink cashmere sweater and silk skirt, pearl necklace.)* Catherine, we need to know. Just tell us.

CATHERINE: *(Now fifteen, she turns to Carole.)* I don't even know why you're asking me this.

CAROLE: Because I'm your friend, and that's why the girls have sent me.

CATHERINE: Oh, Carole, please. If you were my friend . . .

CAROLE: You're making this very unpleasant for me, Catherine. For all of us. If you'd just tell us clearly yes or no . . .

CATHERINE: Why does it matter?

CAROLE: Don't be ridiculous! This is a Christian club.

CATHERINE: I know that.

CAROLE: Yes, you know that. *(Beat.)* So. Are you Jewish?

CATHERINE: No. *(To audience, as Carole leaves.)* There are times in your life when you do something so against your conscience you don't want to look at it. You begin to change the story, to justify your actions. You could almost convince yourself, except for your dreams.

BERNARD: *(Enters, in his forties.)* Oh, Catherine.
(He crosses down left and sits.)

CATHERINE: My father. When I was little, I thought he was wiser than God, In my earliest memories he sits by my bed and tells me stories.

BERNARD: Once upon a time there was a golden ladder, that reached from earth all the way to heaven. The ladder wasn't always visible to people on the earth, but sometimes, when they were walking along the road or standing in a field listening to the ducks and geese, or lying in bed half-asleep, the golden ladder would appear . . .

CATHERINE: *(Age seven. Crosses to him, sits.)* Like a rainbow?

BERNARD: Almost like a rainbow, but not red, green, blue and violet that stain the sky after rain. Just the color of gold people believe waits where the rainbow touches down.

CATHERINE: Did anyone ever find the gold?

BERNARD: Probably not, because the rainbow always ends just a bit farther from where you are.

CATHERINE: Daddy, can people climb the golden ladder?

BERNARD: It could happen. Once, there was a man who began to understand life on earth, which is a place so wonderful and terrible it is truly absurd, and this man began to laugh. And as he laughed, he grew lighter, as though the force of gravity couldn't hold him anymore. Then, just as his feet began to leave the ground, he saw the golden ladder shimmering on its way into the clouds. And, people say, he climbed the ladder, laughing until he disappeared.

CATHERINE: I've heard him laughing, Daddy. Did you ever climb the golden ladder?

BERNARD: No, I'm not wise enough.

CATHERINE: I think you are. I *know* it.

BERNARD: That's because you're seven years old. Maybe when you're older . . . But now it's time for you to sleep.
(He withdraws into shadows.)

CATHERINE: *(She stands. To audience.)* He thinks he can leave, but I've got him now, the way you can never have anyone in real life.

LAURA: *(Voice Over.)* Kathleen!

CATHERINE: Ah, yes. My names: To my mother I was Kathleen. A nice Irish girl. I was Catherine to my father, who believed the name was Russian. Who performed the Cossack dance at parties when he'd had a couple of drinks, so everyone would think he was Russian. Perhaps an émigré from the Tsarist regime. But he wasn't Russian, not in that sense, and the name Catherine comes from the Greek word *katharos,* which means pure, clean as a cloudless sky. So I am, you might say, a misconception. Or to put it more kindly, a romantic notion.

BERNARD: *(Enters, as his younger self.)* Where is she? That girl with the incredible eyes.

LAURA: *(Enters from opposite side, as her younger self. She runs past Bernard, calling out to a friend.)* Maude! Wait for me!

CATHERINE: My father meets my mother at a college in Indiana. A romantic notion which may be true. It is, at least, a story both my parents told. A mutual mythology. *(She withdraws but watches.)*

BERNARD: *(Chasing after Laura.)* Excuse me!

LAURA: *(Stops and turns to him.)* What?

BERNARD: I need to ask you something.

LAURA: Who are you?

BERNARD: I'm the editor of *The Sentinel.*

LAURA: The who?

BERNARD: *The Sentinel.* Our college newspaper?

LAURA: Oh.

BERNARD: You haven't been reading it?

LAURA: No, I haven't. But I *will,* once I get settled in. And you're the . . . ?

BERNARD: Editor. Yes. I'm looking for some freshman reporters, and I thought . . .

LAURA: You thought of me? Why?

CATHERINE: He wanted to say, Because you are the most beautiful woman I've ever seen. But he said . . .

BERNARD: You seem so intelligent.

LAURA: I do? Well. Thank you.

BERNARD: So alert, and . . . sensitive.

LAURA: Really? That's so . . . nice of you. I mean, you don't know me.

BERNARD: But I'd like to.

LAURA: Oh. Well, I have to go right now, but maybe tomorrow . . .
(She turns to leave.)

BERNARD: Wait, Laura.

LAURA: You know my name?

BERNARD: I've asked about you.

LAURA: *(Suddenly shy.)* What's your name?

BERNARD: Bernard.
(They look into each other's eyes, transfixed.)

LAURA: What would I have to do, Bernard?

BERNARD: I would give you assignments. You would go to theater events, club meetings . . .

LAURA: That might be interesting.

BERNARD: And athletic events.

LAURA: Sports? Oh, I don't think I could . . .

BERNARD: Let's say no sports. But clubs would be all right with you? You could take notes, write a small report . . .

LAURA: I could do that.

BERNARD: Sure. You just begin with a strong lead . . .

LAURA: A strong lead.

BERNARD: You know. The five W's.

LAURA: Oh. The five W's.

BERNARD: You'd get your own byline . . .

LAURA: My own byline?

BERNARD: Sure. You'll become famous. On campus, at least. Everyone'll know who you are.

LAURA: Oh, no, I don't think so.

BERNARD: What do you mean?

LAURA: I want . . . to be like everyone else. Here, at college.

BERNARD: Hunh. *(Beat.)* OK. You can write anonymously. *(Beat.)* Say, what're you studying?

LAURA: Literature.

BERNARD: You are? *(Beat.)* Do you know Wordsworth's poetry?

LAURA: No, but he's on our reading list.

BERNARD: She was a Phantom of delight
When first she gleamed upon my sight,
A lovely Apparition, sent
To be a moment's ornament.
A dancing Shape, an Image gay,
To haunt, to startle, and way-lay.

LAURA: That's so beautiful!

BERNARD: *(Shyly.)* So are you. *(Then, embarrassed at his boldness.)* So, tomorrow? You could come to my office? Just over there, by the bulletin board.

LAURA: I'll come after lunch.

BERNARD: You know, if you came at lunch time, I could buy you a sandwich. And a soda? Then we'd have more time for me to tell you . . .

LAURA: I'd love to.

CATHERINE: The only way my father could buy my mother lunch was if he went without dinner. But he clutched his heart, knowing this love was a sickness from which he would never recover.

BERNARD: *(Clutching his heart.)* I need an aspirin. *(Stepping into the edge of the light.)* I worshipped her like an icon, Catherine.

CATHERINE: I know that, Daddy.

BERNARD: Remember the way you played with your mother's jewelry? I tried to build a house for her of colored glass and jewels, a place so lovely she would always be happy.

CATHERINE: But she wasn't always happy.

BERNARD: Whatever she wanted. I would do anything.

(Fading into the shadows.)

CATHERINE: You would give up anything. *(Sighs. Then, to audience.)* Until I was nine I thought my mother was perfect. She was much prettier than other mothers. She had a closet full of silky dresses and fancy shoes. I would try them on, spraying myself with her My Sin perfume. Then I would sit at her dressing table and play with her shiny rings and necklaces. I smeared her red lipstick and rouge on my face, trying to look just like her.

LAURA: *(Enters.)* Look at your hair, Kathleen!

CATHERINE: *(To audience.)* Then everything changed. *(To Laura.)* What's wrong with it?

LAURA: You look like an Italian immigrant. Take this clip and pull that hair out of your eyes.

CATHERINE: No.

LAURA: I won't take you to church looking like you just stepped off the boat.

CATHERINE: Fine.

LAURA: *(Fixing Catherine's hair.)* That's a good girl. Now go get dressed. I put your pink skirt and blouse on your bed.

CATHERINE: I don't like pink.

LAURA: Don't be silly, Kathleen. You and I chose that outfit last month, you remember? We'd just had lunch in Bullock's Tea Room, and we went down to the Junior Dresses . . .

CATHERINE: I wanted that black dress, but you wouldn't pay for it.

LAURA: Why are you always contradicting me? No nine-year-old girl wears black. I buy what looks good on you.

CATHERINE: You buy what you like. I'm just your little doll to dress in cute clothes.

LAURA: If we're late for church, Kathleen, I'm going to have a hemorrhage. Then you'll be sorry.

CATHERINE: I'll wear that pink stuff if Daddy comes to church with us.

LAURA: Your father is too busy to come to church. You know that.

CATHERINE: But he never comes.

LAURA: That's because he's writing his novel, darling. He always writes on weekends.

CATHERINE: *(To audience.)* Ultimately, I gave in, just as my father did.

BERNARD: *(From the shadows.)* Make nice, Catherine, that's a good girl. Don't upset your mother.

CATHERINE: All right, Daddy.

LAURA: You look so much prettier in pink, darling, that's a good girl. And don't forget, when we visit Gram, leave the picture of Jesus in the car.

CATHERINE: Why, Mommy?

LAURA: Because Gram doesn't like Jesus.

CATHERINE: Daddy? Do you know why she doesn't like Jesus?

BERNARD: She's old, sweetheart. Old people get ideas in their heads.

LAURA: But you just remember: you're Presbyterian. No matter what anyone says.

CATHERINE: What would they say? Would they talk about Jesus?

BERNARD: Not at Gram's.

LAURA: Kathleen, you're baptized now. And confirmed. So no one can say anything.

CATHERINE: When we went to Gram's house in Altadena we ate strange food, called latkes and gifiltefish. We drank sweet wine. Gram lit candles and said prayers in another language. It was a strange and secret world I didn't understand. Because no one named that world. No one told its stories. But I loved Gram. She had a soft voice and long white hair she brushed with a silver brush.

BERNARD: You were good, honey. Gram loves you.

CATHERINE: Because I didn't talk about Jesus?

BERNARD: No, she loves you because you're *you.*

CATHERINE: She doesn't love Mommy, does she?

BERNARD: Oh, they have their difficulties.

CATHERINE: Why? Mommy didn't talk about Jesus.

BERNARD: You know how women are,

CATHERINE: I do? *(To audience.)* Finally I figured it out: Gram had *met* Jesus somewhere and didn't like him. Maybe he said something like, You've got to leave your family and follow me. He said those things. I learned it in Sunday School. *(To Bernard.)* Daddy, is Gram going to Hell?

BERNARD: Of course not, sweetheart. Why would you say that? Gram is a good woman.

CATHERINE: Because in Sunday school they told us if you don't love Jesus, you'll go to Hell.

BERNARD: If they say that, it's not true.

CATHERINE: What was I to believe? I kept seeing Gram burning in flames, and

I was very worried. That night I heard Mother and Daddy fighting in their bedroom.

BERNARD: I don't want Catherine to go to Sunday school any more.

LAURA: Bernard! You promised me!

BERNARD: I've changed my mind.

LAURA: You can't do that.

BERNARD: They're telling Catherine my mother will go to Hell.

LAURA: Not your *mother*, Bernard. They don't say that.

BERNARD: Catherine told me . . .

LAURA: *Kathleen* is just a child. She doesn't understand.

BERNARD: She understands enough to say my mother . . .

LAURA: You agreed I could raise her Presbyterian.

BERNARD: For god's sake, Laura, even you weren't raised Presbyterian!

LAURA: I was raised Southern Baptist, and there's nothing worse than that!

BERNARD: Not even Jewish?

CATHERINE: Jewish? What was that?

LAURA: You're not Jewish. Not anymore.

BERNARD: All right. I'm not Jewish anymore. But my mother is, and I won't have any Christian preacher telling Catherine my mother is going to Hell.

LAURA: Darling, let's not talk about this now. Let's just . . . go to bed.

(Laura smiles and exits.)

CATHERINE: *(To audience.)* I couldn't wait to talk to my father. The next morning I found him alone, working on ads for his newspaper. *(To Bernard.)* Daddy, what's Jewish?

BERNARD: Jewish? Why do you want to know that?

CATHERINE: I heard some people talking about it, and I just wondered.

BERNARD: Well, Judaism is a religion.

CATHERINE: What kind of religion?

BERNARD: One of the world's major religions. There are Jews, Christians, Buddhists, Muslims, and . . .

CATHERINE: Presbyterians.

BERNARD: Presbyterians are Christians. There are many forms of Christianity. But Christians believe Jesus was the son of God, and Jews do not believe God would ever assume the form of man. Any representation of God by an image is forbidden.

CATHERINE: Are you Jewish?

BERNARD: I was. Not anymore.

CATHERINE: Oh. But why were you Jewish and Mother and I are Presbyterian?

BERNARD: Because I was born that way.

CATHERINE: And I was born Presbyterian?

BERNARD: No. Your mother decided you both would be Presbyterian.

CATHERINE: Why?

BERNARD: Because it's more socially acceptable. In certain parts of the world. Like our neighborhood.

CATHERINE: Why?

BERNARD: Some people don't like Jews.

CATHERINE: And that's why you're not Jewish anymore?

BERNARD: No, I wouldn't say that.

LAURA: *(Enters, smiling.)* What are you two talking about?

CATHERINE: Why Daddy isn't Jewish anymore.

LAURA: Oh, for heaven's sake! Your father isn't Jewish because Jewish is a religion that your father doesn't believe in.

CATHERINE: But Daddy was born that way. He said.

LAURA: Kathleen. Can we end this discussion now?

CATHERINE: Why?

LAURA: Nice people don't talk about religion, sex, or politics.
    (She exits.)

CATHERINE: So what are you, Daddy?

BERNARD: I'm an atheist.
    (He exits.)

CATHERINE: Oh, no. I knew from Sunday school that atheists were as bad as Catholics. Now I had two people to worry about: Daddy and Gram, blazing in the flames of Hell.

MARY: *(Enters, chewing gum.)* Hey, Cathy. Wanna go over to the park and watch the boys?

CATHERINE: *(To audience.)* My best friend Mary Scaccia, when I was thirteen. We did everything together. *(To Mary.)* Sure. *(She links arms with Mary.)*

MARY: I'm getting braces next week. *(As they walk along.)*

CATHERINE: What for?

MARY: My teeth are crooked. See? *(She flashes her teeth.)*

CATHERINE: They don't look so bad.

MARY: Everyone's gonna call me metal mouth. *(They sit together, facing audience.)* I brought some peanut butter and jelly sandwiches. Y'know, it's one of the last times I'm gonna eat peanut butter for the next few years.
    (She pulls them out of her bag, gives one to Catherine. They eat and talk.)

CATHERINE: I shouldn't eat peanut butter. I've got fat legs.

MARY: They're not fat.

CATHERINE: They're not thin like your legs.

MARY: Mine are skinny. Nobody likes skinny legs.

CATHERINE: I do.

MARY: I'm skinny all over. I don't even have to like wear a bra. Not like you, y'know.

CATHERINE: I hate my bra. It feels like I can't breathe when I wear it. Remember how Joe Arnold used to come up behind me in the cafeteria and snap my strap?

MARY: He's a jerk.

CATHERINE: He's *popular.*

MARY: Most popular guys are jerks. Would you kiss a guy like Joe Arnold?

CATHERINE: Oh, gross!

MARY: Y'know, I heard he French-kissed Francine Shacklin.

CATHERINE: Francine? She wouldn't.

MARY: I don't know. She's Jewish.

CATHERINE: What do you mean?

MARY: You know what they say about Jewish girls.

CATHERINE: What?

MARY: They're all fast. By the time they're fourteen they usually go all the way.

CATHERINE: No, they don't! That's terrible to say.

MARY: They can't help it. They've got like extra hormones or something.

CATHERINE: This sandwich tastes terrible.

MARY: What's the matter with it?

CATHERINE: There's too much jelly. It's making me sick.

MARY: I'll finish it. Hey, look at those Ramsey boys. Would you believe they're twins?

CATHERINE: No.

MARY: They're so *cute!* They're looking at you. I wish I had, y'know . . . *(Looking at Catherine's breasts.)* . . . what you have. It's gonna take *years* for boys to look at *me.*

CATHERINE: Do Jewish girls really have extra hormones?

MARY: Yeah. I read it in *Seventeen,* I think.

CATHERINE: What if you're sort of Jewish, but not really Jewish?

MARY: You can't be sort of Jewish.

CATHERINE: Well, I knew this girl once who had one parent who was *born* Jewish, but he quit because he became an atheist.

MARY: Boy, is that screwed up! Do I know this girl?

CATHERINE: No, I met her when we went to Lake Tahoe for vacation. But now, y'know, it makes me think. Did *she* have extra hormones?

MARY: Sure. Maybe not as *many*. I mean, maybe she wouldn't go all the way till she was fifteen. But you never know.

CATHERINE: What about Jewish boys?

MARY: Oh, they're the worst. They go all the way by the time they're ten. Like Aaron Feldman?

CATHERINE: Who's he?

MARY: That tall, thin kid in tenth grade who wears glasses and has really green eyes? He made a speech last year in assembly about some Jewish holiday.

CATHERINE: Yeah, I remember him.

MARY: Lisa Clark told me he slept with ten girls already.

CATHERINE: *Ten?* That's more than, uh, two a year. If he started when he was ten.

MARY: Yeah. And he looks so boring. I heard he's so smart he takes math at Cal Tech. So you never know. *(Beat.)* Hey, maybe we should go swimming in the high school pool? There might be more boys over there.

CATHERINE: I don't feel like it. Boys bore me.

MARY: Hunh. Well, OK. I'm gonna go anyway. See you later.

CATHERINE: *(To audience, as Mary walks off.)* That night I dreamed about hormones. They were naked women with huge breasts and bright red lips, and they were dancing all around me in high heels. *(Beat.)* When I woke up, I took a piece of cloth and bound my breasts so tight I looked like a boy. And I went on my own special diet: no more than ten bites of food at each meal. I was thirteen, so I had just one year to make myself so skinny I wouldn't be sexy.

LAURA: Kathleen, you're not eating.

CATHERINE: Can't you just call me Cathy? Both of you? It's very confusing to have two names.

LAURA: I made lamb chops, mashed potatoes, and peas, your favorite meal, and you refuse to eat more than a few bites of anything.

CATHERINE: I'd rather have latkes, the way we do at Gram's.

BERNARD: Your mother hasn't learned yet, honey, She's trying, but she doesn't have it down.

LAURA: I am not trying, Bernard. I just pretended to *try* to please your mother.

BERNARD: It would please me too.

CATHERINE: At school, y'know, everyone calls me Cathy.

BERNARD: Catherine's right, Laura. We should just call her Cathy. It's ridiculous the way we . . .

LAURA: Fine. She can be Cathy. *(To Catherine.)*
You can be Cathy. Now will you please eat?

CATHERINE: I eat.

LAURA: Not enough. You eat like a straw.

BERNARD: How can a person eat like a straw, Laura? You mean she looks like a straw?

LAURA: I mean what I say. Whenever I say it.

CATHERINE: My stomach shrank when I started taking ballet. It's because you make me practice all the time.

LAURA: One hour out of twenty-four isn't all the time. Are you on a diet? Because if you are, I won't have it. You're thin enough. *(Angry stare at Bernard.)* Like a straw.

CATHERINE: I'm not on a diet. I'm just not very hungry.

LAURA: Why not? Are you sick?

BERNARD: You know, Laura, sometimes that happens during puberty. Young girls' bodies change.

LAURA: You're always taking her side, Bernard. I can't even have an opinion around here.

CATHERINE: *(Sudden terror.)* How do they change, Daddy?

BERNARD: Oh, they . . . Well, sometimes they . . . *(Beat.)* Did I ever tell you about the chubby little girl who grew up in a witch's house? She knew the witch was going to cook her one day, so she got thinner and thinner . . .

CATHERINE: Daddy. Do Jewish girls have more hormones?

BERNARD: What? More hormones than who?

CATHERINE: Than girls who aren't Jewish.

BERNARD: I think everyone has the same hormones. No, that's not right. Hormones change when you . . . But Jewish girls are no different . . .

LAURA: Why are we talking about Jewish girls?

CATHERINE: I just wondered.

LAURA: Do you know any Jewish girls?

CATHERINE: Well, sure. There are some in my class. There's Francine Shacklin . . .

LAURA: That girl is not your type, Kathleen.

CATHERINE: Cathy. You said Cathy was OK.

LAURA: Cathy. I met the Shacklins at Back to School Night, and they're definitely not the sort of people we associate with.

BERNARD: Laura.

CATHERINE: Why not?

LAURA: Well, they're Jewish, and we're not. They go to a different church . . .

BERNARD: Synagogue.

LAURA: And they eat different food . . .

CATHERINE: Like Gram. And Daddy must've eaten Jewish food when he was little. Didn't you, Daddy?

BERNARD: Of course. What else was there?

LAURA: Just stop it, you two! I won't be ganged up on!

CATHERINE: But Mother, if Daddy's mother is Jewish, and he was *born* Jewish, then I must be . . .

LAURA: No. You are not. We're Presbyterians! We go to church every Sunday.

CATHERINE: Daddy doesn't.

LAURA: Look around you. Do you see any Jewish families in our neighborhood? In my women's club? Not that there's anything *wrong* with being Jewish, but . . .

CATHERINE: So what do you mean?

LAURA: It means we're not talking about this anymore! Now go to your room and do your homework.

CATHERINE: *(Getting up, in tears.)* All right, don't tell me if I have any extra hormones. See if I care! *(She walks away.)*

LAURA: See what you've done, Bernard?

BERNARD: I did it? Laura, if you'd let go of this prejudice of yours . . .

LAURA: Prejudice? That's so unfair! This is the way the world is. I'm trying to protect her.

BERNARD: No, you're not.

LAURA: You hate me!

BERNARD: I could never hate you.

LAURA: 1 gave up my family to be with you, and now . . .

BERNARD: Come here. *(He takes her in his arms.)* Imagine a beautiful princess who lives in a land where everyone tries to look the same, denying any differences because they're all afraid . . .

LAURA: Bernard, this is not the time to tell me stories.

BERNARD: Sometimes stories explain better than . . .

LAURA: Not now! I'm telling you . . .

BERNARD: All right. Tell me.

LAURA: I'm trying to do what's best for us.

BERNARD: So am I. But please. Don't talk about Jews the way you do.

LAURA: Me? Remember what your mother said to me when she found out . . .

BERNARD: Shhhh. She didn't mean it.

LAURA: She did. Sometimes she won't even speak to me. I could be invisible, and then she criticizes everything I do. Why don't you tell her to be nice to *me?*

BERNARD: I've tried. Believe me. And she's changing, I'm sure she'll . . .

LAURA: She is not! She's terrible! No matter what I do . . .

BERNARD: Please. She's my mother! And now she invites us over . . .

LAURA: Because of Kathleen. I'm still an outsider. So don't ask me to make Jewish food again to please your mother! She wouldn't come here to eat it anyway.

BERNARD: I won't.

LAURA: I'm not going to your mother's anymore. You and Kathleen can go by yourselves.

BERNARD: Oh, Laura. If you could only . . .

LAURA: And don't talk to Kathleen about being Jewish again! You know what can happen to her.

(They exit.)

CATHERINE: *(To audience.)* When I heard that, I understood: I was doomed. That's why we couldn't talk about it. And on my fourteenth birthday . . .

MARY: *(Comes running in, breathless.)* Cathy! Aaron Feldman wants to meet you.

CATHERINE: Oh, no! Why?

MARY: He's been asking about you. And when I told him today was your fourteenth birthday, he just begged me, I don't know.

CATHERINE: *(To audience.)* He knew. He saw it in me: my hormones must have kicked in. So I resigned myself. If I had to do it, at least it would be with one of the smartest and cutest boys in the tenth grade. *(To Mary.)* OK. Introduce me.

MARY: He's waiting over there by the live oak trees. Just a sec.

(She runs off.)

CATHERINE: *(To audience.)* My heart was doing gymnastics in my chest. I couldn't breathe, and my breasts hurt so much I turned around, reached under my T-shirt, and ripped away the cloth that bound them.

MARY: *(Entering with Aaron.)* Hi, Cathy, this is Aaron, Aaron, this is Cathy, it's her birthday, oh, I told you that, god, I don't know where my brains are. *(Beat.)* So. Here he is.

AARON: Hi.

CATHERINE: Oh. Hi.

MARY: Well, I'll be running along. See you.

(She exits.)

AARON: I hear it's your birthday.

CATHERINE: Y'know, maybe you've got the wrong idea.

AARON: It's not your birthday?

CATHERINE: Well, it is, but . . .

AARON: Your fourteenth?

CATHERINE: I don't know what you've heard about me, y'know, but . . .

AARON: Well, I heard you're very smart. Y'know. Best grades in your class. And, uh, well . . . You write poems. No, I didn't *hear* that, really. I read them. They're good.

CATHERINE: How do you know?

AARON: I guess it's just my opinion. I'm not a poet.

CATHERINE: You're a math person.

AARON: Yeah. Well. Uh, that's not all I am.

CATHERINE: Oh, I *know.*

AARON: there is no canopy
    for hiding, my love
    I have prepared
    a horse for riding
    time is open now
    let your body glisten
    in the sun

CATHERINE: That's my poem!

AARON: Yes.

CATHERINE: How did you remember it?

AARON: *(He continues to quote.)* who sings his song
    in our heart
    let him sing
    to the sun
    for we have chased
    the horses of the moon away
    and we hold the light
    in our hands

CATHERINE: I can't believe you know it. *(Beat.)* So, uh . . . How old are you?

AARON: Fifteen.

CATHERINE: That means at least two more. Maybe two and a half.

AARON: What?

CATHERINE: So, where do we, y'know, *go?*

AARON: What do you mean? *(Stares at her breasts.)* You look different. From when I saw you yesterday.

CATHERINE: *(Crossing her arms over her chest.)* You think so?

AARON: Yes. *(Beat.)* You want to *go* somewhere?

CATHERINE: Well, sure. I mean. We can't just stay *here.*

AARON: We can't?

CATHERINE: Well, I *mean. (Beat.)* Maybe it's not really true, what they say.

AARON: What do they say?

CATHERINE: You know.

AARON: I don't. *(Beat.)* You're really pretty up close.

CATHERINE: I'm not pretty.

AARON: Yes, you are. You're very pretty. *(Beat.)* Want to go swimming?

CATHERINE: In the *pool?*

AARON: You know anywhere else we could go swimming?

CATHERINE: No, I meant . . . I don't know very much, even though I'm fourteen. But the *pool? (Beat.)* How'd you find out about me?

AARON: Well, I . . . Y'know, I . . . Oh, maybe . . . *(Deep breath.)* I just saw you, and I knew.

CATHERINE: I figured.

AARON: Y'know, I . . . Well . . . I'd been watching you a long time.

CATHERINE: Waiting.

AARON: Well, sort of. I mean, it's hard, y'know.

CATHERINE: Is it? OK. I guess I have to know. You just can't escape your destiny.

AARON: Are you my destiny? Is that what you think? I mean . . .

CATHERINE: It looks like it.

AARON: Can I . . . ? What do you think? Could I . . . kiss you then?

CATHERINE: I suppose.

(They kiss tentatively.)

AARON: You're Jewish, aren't you?

CATHERINE: *(To audience.)* Then I knew. It showed. *(To Aaron.)* Not really.

AARON: What do you mean?

CATHERINE: Well, my mother's not Jewish, and my father was *born* Jewish, but . . .

AARON: Oh, I see what you mean. It's like a maternal lineage.

CATHERINE: What?

AARON: You know. Jews say you have to have a Jewish mother to be really Jewish.

CATHERINE: Really? Then I'm not Jewish?

AARON: Why? You don't want to be Jewish?

CATHERINE: No, it's not that. *(Beat.)* I just worry about the Jewish hormones.

AARON: Jewish hormones?

CATHERINE: Hormones are in the blood, aren't they?

AARON: Are they?

CATHERINE: So if my father was born Jewish, then he has Jewish blood, and I have some too, so I must have Jewish hormones.

AARON: This is the weirdest conversation.

CATHERINE: In which case, I'll probably end up doing it.

AARON: What?

CATHERINE: Going all the way.

AARON: I beg your pardon?

CATHERINE: But if my father quit being Jewish to be an atheist and my mother says being Jewish is a religion, not, y'know, something cultural . . .

AARON: It's both.

CATHERINE: Oh. Hell. Then I guess I'll have to do it. With you.

AARON: Oh. *(Beat.)* You . . . I mean . . . You're not the person I thought you were.

CATHERINE: What did you think?

AARON: Uh, y'know . . . You're really fast.

CATHERINE: I guess I am. I tried not to be, but . . .

AARON: I mean, most girls don't start talking about going all the way with a boy they just met.

CATHERINE: I've had no experience talking to boys. I didn't know.

AARON: You mean you just do it and don't talk?

CATHERINE: I never did, but . . .

AARON: Wow. Maybe we should go over to my house. There's nobody home.

CATHERINE: OK.

AARON: *(Takes her hand as they start walking off.)* Total silence. Hunh.

CATHERINE: *(Stops and speaks to audience.)* We went to his house and we tried to do it. We fumbled around a while, very embarrassed but not speaking. *(To Aaron.)* You don't know *anything.*

AARON: Gee, thanks. You don't know anything either.

CATHERINE: Well, I don't have to. I just turned fourteen.

AARON: So what was all this about going all the way?

CATHERINE: You ought to know. Didn't you start when you were ten?

AARON: Sex? When I was ten?

CATHERINE: I thought you'd done it with like twelve or so girls by now.

AARON: Shit! You did?

CATHERINE: Sure. What about your hormones?

AARON: What is this crap about hormones?

CATHERINE: Mary told me if you're Jewish, you've got more hormones, and you've got to go all the way with girls by the time you're fourteen.

AARON: I can't believe she said that.

CATHERINE: And she said you'd gone all the way with ten girls by last year.

AARON: Cathy. Don't you ever question things your friends say?

CATHERINE: She said she read it in *Seventeen.*

AARON: *Seventeen.* The ultimate medical and scientific authority. *(He starts laughing.)* That is so funny! Y'know, you ought to write a story about this.

CATHERINE: I don't think it's very funny.

AARON: Well, it is. Extra hormones.

(Aaron laughs even harder.)

CATHERINE: I'm going home.

AARON: Wait. I'm sorry. I'm not really laughing at you. Well, I am, sort of, but not in a mean way.

CATHERINE: I'm grateful to you for enlightening me. But I'd like to leave now.

AARON: Oh, Cathy. Couldn't we be friends?

CATHERINE: I don't think so. You make me feel stupid.

AARON: You're not stupid. Maybe, y'know, a little naive, but that's OK.

CATHERINE: It's not OK.

AARON: It's OK with me. Could I kiss you?

CATHERINE: No.

AARON: Just a friendly kiss. *(Beat.)* I'll tell you the truth. You're the first girl I've ever kissed.

CATHERINE: Not even a kiss?

AARON: Not even one. Till you.

CATHERINE: You're the first boy I ever kissed.

AARON: I know.

CATHERINE: OK, then. *(She raises her face. He bends down to meet her. They kiss, carefully, then more prolonged.)* Oh. I think that's probably enough.

AARON: Why?

CATHERINE: *(She backs away from him. Both are breathless.)* Because I feel you down there, and it makes me nervous.

AARON: OK. OK. I don't want to make you nervous.

CATHERINE: I'll be your friend, Aaron. Even if we don't have extra hormones.

(They both start laughing uncontrollably.)

MARY: *(Comes in, pulls Catherine aside.)* So, what? Are you his girlfriend now?

CATHERINE: No.

MARY: He didn't try to get you to go all the way? Because you'd be like his *thirteenth.*

CATHERINE: No, he didn't. *(She looks over at Aaron.)* He has enough experience. We decided to wait till I was older.

LAURA: *(Enters as Aaron and Mary leave.)* Aaron Feldman? What sort of name is that?

CATHERINE: Why do you want to know?

LAURA: Well, it sounds rather . . . I don't mean to say that he . . . But your father and I think . . .

CATHERINE: *(To audience.)* I should have seen this coming. *(To Laura.)* Daddy and you?

LAURA: Yes. Your father and I have discussed this sort of thing and . . .

CATHERINE: What sort of thing?

LAURA: The people you choose as friends. You're young, so we feel we should guide you in your friendships.

CATHERINE: Daddy doesn't care who my friends are.

LAURA: He certainly does.

CATHERINE: He cares whether my friends are Christians?

LAURA: Well, now that you put it that way, yes, he really does.

CATHERINE: Oh, come on, Mother. Daddy's a Jewish atheist.

LAURA: *(Slaps Catherine's face.)* Don't you ever say that again!

CATHERINE: You hit me.

LAURA: I won't have you talking about your father that way.

CATHERINE: *(Backing away.)* What way? Telling the truth? You won't have me telling the truth?

LAURA: Come back here, young lady. We're not through discussing this.

CATHERINE: Yes, we are. I'm going to tell Daddy you hit me.

LAURA: I'm sorry, Kathleen. I didn't mean . . .

CATHERINE: CATHY! And you're not sorry. You did mean it! DADDY!

BERNARD: *(Enters as Laura exits.)* What's the matter, honey?

CATHERINE: Mother hit me!

BERNARD: She did? *(Beat.)* What did you do?

CATHERINE: Nothing.

BERNARD: You must have done or said something that upset her.

CATHERINE: I called you a Jewish atheist.

BERNARD: Oh.

CATHERINE: Isn't that what you are, Daddy?

BERNARD: Yes. I think that's a pretty accurate label. Although I would say Jewish-atheist-writer-father-husband is even more accurate.

CATHERINE: Well, OK, but . . .

BERNARD: And what we have here is what I'd call the father-husband problem.

CATHERINE: She still shouldn't have hit me. Because I told the truth.

BERNARD: No. As a father I can tell you it was not a good thing to hit you for telling what we understand is the truth.

CATHERINE: I hate her.

BERNARD: Don't hate, Cathy. Hate corrodes the soul. As a husband I understand that for your mother the truth is different.

CATHERINE: She tells lies.

BERNARD: No, for her the truth is I'm a Christian.

CATHERINE: But you're not.

BERNARD: We all have ways of creating the world in our own image.

CATHERINE: God did that.

BERNARD: Did he? Well, tell him for me sometime that human beings have learned a lot from him.

CATHERINE: OK. *(They both smile.)* I have a Jewish boyfriend.

BERNARD: Do you? That's nice.

CATHERINE: Mother says you both don't want me to have Jewish friends.

BERNARD: Oh. *(Beat.)* Cathy, sometimes living in your mother's world is difficult, I know, but try not to upset her. Where she grew up, in Kentucky, there were only Protestants.

CATHERINE: Really?

BERNARD: Yes, and when we began dating each other . . .

(Catherine moves up left.)

LAURA: *(Enters. She is eighteen.)* Where do you want to go tonight, Bernard?

BERNARD: *(Now twenty-one years old.)* Laura, before we go out, could we talk?

LAURA: We always talk.

BERNARD: I think I ought to tell you something.

LAURA: OK.

BERNARD: I'm a Jew.

LAURA: A what?

BERNARD: A Jew.

LAURA: What's that?

BERNARD: A person who's Jewish.

LAURA: What does that mean?

BERNARD: You're kidding me, right?

LAURA: No. Am I smiling or something?

BERNARD: You really don't know what I'm talking about?

LAURA: I'm getting irritated, Bernard. What is this Jewish thing?

BERNARD: A Jew is a person who believes in Judaism, which is a religion. Like Christianity.

LAURA: Oh, that's nice.

BERNARD: But there's an important difference. You see, Jews believe . . .

LAURA: Can we go to the movies? I don't really care about religion. I just care about you.

BERNARD: *(To Catherine, as Laura exits.)* So I believed if I married her, everything would be fine.

CATHERINE: Well, I still don't see why she . . .

BERNARD: It was later, after we were married, that she began to have a hard time.

CATHERINE: What do you mean?

BERNARD: Certain things happened that made her close down.

CATHERINE: What things?

BERNARD: I'll tell you about it, but I need to talk to your mother right now. *(Beat.)* Sometimes people hold on tighter to their illusions than to the truth.

CATHERINE: Why?

BERNARD: Fear, I think. But it's hard work to create a dream world and believe in it.

CATHERINE: I'm confused.

BERNARD: That's the human condition.

CATHERINE: It is?

BERNARD: So, please, honey, let her believe what she wants. I need her to be happy.

CATHERINE: OK, Daddy. I'll try. *(To audience.)* And from then on, what I really tried to do was protect my father.

AARON: *(Enters as Bernard exits.)* Hey, Cathy.

CATHERINE: Oh, hi.

AARON: You said you wanted to talk to me.

CATHERINE: Oh. Yeah. *(Beat.)* Uh, how's your math class going?

AARON: You mean Cal Tech? It's great, y'know, even though I'm the youngest kid in the . . . *(Beat.)* Is that why you called me?

CATHERINE: Well, sure, I mean . . . Yes! I want to know how you like it, y'know, math, I mean.

AARON: Oh. Well, I like math a lot.

CATHERINE: Great! That's terrific.

AARON: Yeah.

CATHERINE: Yeah.

AARON: So. I'm glad we had this talk about how much I like math. Uh, how's your poetry . . . coming?

CATHERINE: Good! I just wrote this poem, y'know, about the ocean.

AARON: Oh. *(Beat.)* Great!

CATHERINE: Well, it's not exactly just the ocean, y'know, it's more about the way the light, in the late afternoon, y'know, when you're sitting on the beach, and it looks like a path of gold sometimes on the waves, and you could just follow it . . . y'know?

AARON: Hunh. *(Beat.)* That's great. Can I read it?

CATHERINE: Sure. Uh, listen, Aaron, I need to talk to you about something.

AARON: Didn't we just talk?

CATHERINE: Well, yes, but . . . There's this other thing. See, I . . . Well . . . *(Beat. Then in a fast mumble.)* My mother doesn't want me to be friends with you.

AARON: What?

CATHERINE: Didn't you hear me?

AARON: No.

CATHERINE: I can't say it again.

AARON: Come on.

CATHERINE: Uh. Well. *(Beat.)* My mother doesn't want me to be friends with you.

AARON: Why not? She doesn't want you to like anybody as smart as you?

CATHERINE: I'm not kidding, Aaron.

AARON: Oh. So what do you mean?

CATHERINE: Well, y'know, I mean . . . *(Beat. She closes her eyes and grits her teeth.)* It's because you're Jewish.

AARON: What?

CATHERINE: She doesn't like Jewish people.

AARON: Didn't she marry one?

CATHERINE: Well, yes, but she says . . .

AARON: I know: your dad isn't Jewish anymore because he's an atheist and . . .

CATHERINE: She says my father's a Christian.

AARON: Oh, man, that's seriously crazy.

CATHERINE: Stop it, Aaron. This isn't funny.

AARON: I wasn't being funny.

CATHERINE: So I'm not saying we should stop being friends, y'know, but . . .

AARON: Cathy. You're getting weird. Cut it out.

CATHERINE: Well, y'know, uh . . . *(Beat.)* Maybe we should be a little more careful about letting people see us together.

AARON: *You're* ashamed of being seen with a Jew, aren't you?

CATHERINE: No!

AARON: You're getting just like your mother, y'know. You don't want people to know your father is Jewish.

CATHERINE: It's not that. It's . . . Well, it's just that my father doesn't want me to upset my mother.

AARON: Did he tell you not to be friends with me?

CATHERINE: Not exactly, but being friends with you would upset my mother, and I'd *like* to upset her really, because I *hate* her sometimes, like now, but I don't hate my father, I . . . . really love him, Aaron, and he said he needs my mother to be happy.

AARON: He's a *grown-up,* Cathy. You don't have to . . . I mean, I thought you liked me.

CATHERINE: I do, Aaron, really, but . . .

AARON: *(On the verge of tears.)* You're the first girl I ever . . . I thought I could . . . I mean, we . . . Well, you and I were . . . y'know, so I . . .

CATHERINE: I'm sorry, Aaron, but . . . Listen, I mean, what if . . . Well, like, what if . . . we didn't walk around together all the time, and maybe, y'know, met each other sometimes in a private place, like your house? Just for a while.

AARON: No.

CATHERINE: It might be fun, y'know, like our own secret?

AARON: It's not fun, Cathy. It's sick.

CATHERINE: Aaron, please.

AARON: Forget it. I don't even want to know you.

MARY: *(Enters as Aaron exits, holding his head.)* How come I never see you with Aaron anymore?

CATHERINE: I don't know. He won't talk to me.

MARY: How come?

CATHERINE: He's just being weird.

MARY: Did he want you to go all the way and you said no?

CATHERINE: Something like that.

MARY: I told you Jewish boys have more hormones, y'know, but you wouldn't listen to me.

CATHERINE: I guess you're right.

MARY: So, wanna go over to the high school and watch football practice?

CATHERINE: No, I guess not.

MARY: The guys look really good in their shorts.

CATHERINE: I'll go some other time.

MARY: All those tan muscles.

CATHERINE: They look dumb running around in their shorts, shoving each other and kicking balls.

MARY: Hunh. *(Beat.)* Are you missing Aaron?

CATHERINE: No. *(Beat.)* Yes.

MARY: Well, look, Cathy, maybe you should just go all the way with him.

CATHERINE: I can't.

MARY: Why not? Then you can tell me what it's like. I hear you move.

CATHERINE: What do you mean?

MARY: The boy puts his thing inside the girl and they move around.

CATHERINE: I don't care.

MARY: I think it's weird. I mean, like do they move up and down or around the room?

CATHERINE: Don't talk about it.

MARY: So if you'd just do it with Aaron, we'd know for sure.

CATHERINE: I can't do it with Aaron, stupid! Not if he won't talk to me, and he looks the other way when I pass him in the hall, and yesterday he ate lunch with Francine Shacklin, and they were laughing, and . . . *(She starts to cry.)* I hate him!

MARY: I'm sorry, Cathy. I wish you wouldn't call me stupid though.

CATHERINE: I didn't mean to, but don't talk about Aaron ever again, OK? When I see him in the hall, I'm going to look the other way too, because I don't even want to know he exists, OK?

And if he goes all the way with Francine Shacklin, I hope he dies!

MARY: Yeah, because she's got all those hormones.

CATHERINE: Oh, shut up!

MARY: What did I say? I didn't mention you-know-who's name,

CATHERINE: Jewish hormones. You're really something, Mary.

MARY: I read it in *Seventeen.*

CATHERINE: *Seventeen.* The ultimate scientific and medical authority.

MARY: I'm going over to the high school now.

CATHERINE: Oh, do. Go watch the dumb boys do pushups in the mud.

MARY: I don't like you anymore.

CATHERINE: Who cares? *(To audience, as Mary exits.)* I didn't like myself either. As Aaron walked through the halls holding hands with Francine Shacklin, waited for her after classes, took her to dances, I'd roll my eyes and make anti-Semitic remarks like, "Oh, those Jews." I became the perfect WASP. *(She addresses an unseen church group.)* As president of the Presbyterian youth group, I want to talk to you about predestination and the damnation of unbelievers. As you know, we are all in the hands of God, who decides who is going to be saved and who, y'know, will be sent to Hell. Now, even though God has already made His decision and there isn't much we can do about it, I mean, actually, not *anything* we can do about it, we still try to be good and follow Jesus's teachings, because we *know* — I mean, it's only *logical* — that God isn't going to save anyone who isn't a Christian, y'know, preferably a *Presbyterian*. And although I do feel sorry for the unbelievers who are going to burn in the flames of Hell, it is their decision, isn't it? I mean.

LAURA: *(Enters.)* Cathy, don't you think that speech you made in church today was too negative?

CATHERINE: No.

LAURA: You made everyone very uncomfortable.

CATHERINE: Why? It's Presbyterian doctrine. I learned it in Sunday School.

LAURA: Yes, but most Presbyterians are more modern in California. They try to look on the bright side of things.

CATHERINE: Then they ought to quit teaching the darker side in Sunday School. I mean, either they believe it or they don't.

LAURA: What about your father? Having his very own daughter saying such things in public.

CATHERINE: Mother! How many millions of times have you told me Daddy's not, y'know, *Jewish* anymore?

LAURA: Yes, but suppose someone realized Bronson might be a Jewish name? It isn't anymore, but what if someone *thought*. . . And there you are, talking about damnation.

CATHERINE: Listen. You're saved or you're not. Right?

LAURA: I suppose. And your father *is* a Christian.

CATHERINE: Right. Daddy's a Christian, so, y'know, he's OK. *(Beat.)* Actually, maybe it really doesn't matter what he is, does it?

LAURA: It certainly does!

CATHERINE: No, I mean, if predestination is true, then I could be wrong about the unbelievers, y'know. I mean, God *is* God.

LAURA: But you have to be a Christian.

CATHERINE: Of course, you certainly do. *(Beat.)* So it's a good thing, y'know, Daddy's a Christian. *(Beat.)* What makes you think he's a Christian if he says he's an atheist?

LAURA: He never tells *me* that. He promised me he'd be buried next to me in a Christian graveyard.

CATHERINE: Right. And anyway, y'know, we don't care what other people think.

LAURA: Yes, we do. It's important if you want to succeed in life. Look at me.

I came from . . . .a very poor area, as you know. And what did I do? I went to college and married a writer! And look what we have now: One of the nicest houses in our neighborhood. We have money. We're respectable! No one can ever call us white trash.

CATHERINE: White trash?

LAURA: Never mind.

CATHERINE: Did people say that about your family?

LAURA: We're not talking about this.

CATHERINE: Why not? Why don't we ever see your family? My grandmother and grandfather? I must have aunts and uncles and cousins . . . Every time I ask anything, you brush me off. Is it some dark, dirty secret?

LAURA: All right. I'll tell you. But you must never repeat this to anyone,

CATHERINE: Even Daddy?

LAURA: He knows. *(Beat.)* About six months after we were married, we decided to move to California to start a new life. We left Evansville and, with the few things we owned piled into our Packard, we drove across the country and stopped in Kentucky to see my family. Your grandmother and grandfather were sitting in their new farmhouse kitchen reading the Bible. I said, "Momma? Daddy? I brought my new husband for you to meet." Well, they were surprised, because . . . I hadn't been able to get in touch with them about the wedding.

CATHERINE: Why not?

LAURA: Oh, they were . . . away.

BERNARD: *(From the shadows.)* No. They had no telephone.

LAURA: And their feelings were hurt, I think, and that made my father less polite than he could have been . . .

BERNARD: For a long time they didn't say a word, just stared at me.

LAURA: Naturally, they wanted to know about my new husband, so they asked a few questions . . .

CATHERINE: About what?

LAURA: About . . . religion. They were very serious about that, especially my father.

BERNARD: He said, "Are you a believer, young man?" And I said, "Yes, sir."

LAURA: My father was . . . abrupt.

BERNARD: He said, "You believe in the Lord Jesus Christ as your personal savior?" And I said, "No, sir. I'm Jewish, not Christian."

LAURA: Your father's answers didn't please him.

BERNARD: Your grandfather said, "I heard about Jewish people. They don't believe." And I said, "I believe in your daughter. I believe in our love."

LAURA: And I think they were disappointed in me.

BERNARD: Her father said, "Laura, you made your choice. You denied your family. Now, don't ever come back."

LAURA: So we've never spoken to each other since then.

CATHERINE: Oh, Mother. I'm so sorry.

LAURA: Don't be sorry for me. I have a good husband and a daughter I am going to be proud of all my life, because she will be a perfect young lady.

CATHERINE: No! I don't want to be a perfect young lady.

LAURA: But you will be, darling.

CATHERINE: Did you tell Daddy about my speech?

LAURA: Don't you think I care about his feelings? I wouldn't dream of it.

CATHERINE: Well, don't, OK? Just in case, y'know, he still *thinks* he's an atheist. *(To audience.)* It was a schizophrenic period.

BERNARD: *(Enters.)* Cathy, I just received a very disturbing visit while you and your mother were at church.

CATHERINE: You did? Who was it?

BERNARD: Aaron Feldman.

CATHERINE: Aaron came over? To see you? *(Beat.)* Why? What did he say?
(Catherine moves to the side and watches as Aaron appears down left.)

AARON: Hello, Mr. Bronson?

BERNARD: Yes?

AARON: Uh, hi. I'm Aaron Feldman, y'know, Cathy's friend?

BERNARD: Oh. Come in, Aaron.

AARON: *(As he follows Bernard into house.)* Actually, I'm Cathy's *former* friend.

BERNARD: Her *former* friend? Why is that, Aaron?

AARON: Well . . . She didn't tell you we weren't friends anymore?

BERNARD: No. She . . . doesn't talk to me much lately.

AARON: Listen, Mr. Bronson, uh, y'know . . . Uh, I think you ought to sit down.

BERNARD: That bad, is it? I'm all right standing up.

AARON: Well, uh . . . *(Beat.)* Your daughter's an anti-Semite.

BERNARD: Impossible.

AARON: No, really, I mean, it's true.

BERNARD: You have proof?

AARON: Uh, here's the thing of it . . . She's been calling me a Jew behind my back.

BERNARD: Well, you are Jewish, aren't you?

AARON: But, y'know? She says it in a really negative way, like, "Oh, those Jews."

BERNARD: You've heard this?

AARON: Her friend Mary told me. And, y'know, uh . . . I heard some kids say she made a speech in her church about how everybody who's not a Christian is going to be damned.

BERNARD: She didn't!

AARON: I'm telling you. Y'know, it kills me, Mr. Bronson. I mean, it seemed like . . . well, I thought we . . .

BERNARD: This is difficult to believe.

AARON: She's been telling people you're a Christian.

BERNARD: She told you that?

AARON: No, I heard it from some friends.

BERNARD: But Cathy understands this is something her mother needs to believe.

AARON: How do you know, I mean, she really understands?

BERNARD: We've discussed it. Privately.

AARON: Recently?

BERNARD: No.

AARON: Well. Y'know, if you'd just talk to her, now that you know what's going on?

BERNARD: I will. And thank you, Aaron.

AARON: *(Brokenhearted.)* Thank you, Mr. Bronson.

BERNARD: I'm sorry, Aaron. *(Beat.)* You were very brave to come here.

AARON: You think so? I always feel, y'know, my basic mode is cowardice.

CATHERINE: *(To audience.)* When your whole view of the world is based on unworkable oxymorons, if someone challenges you, you have to get angry. There's no other choice.

BERNARD: *(As Aaron exits left.)* Cathy. Have you become an anti-Semite?

CATHERINE: That's a stupid thing to say. Y'know, who the hell does he think he is, saying stuff like that?

BERNARD: I think he's someone who's very concerned about you.

CATHERINE: Right. He's so concerned he won't speak to me or even look at me.

BERNARD: When he says you've been making negative comments about Jews . . .

CATHERINE: I didn't!

BERNARD: And that speech of yours in church about the damnation of unbelievers . . .

CATHERINE: Oh, come on, Daddy, it's just church doctrine.

BERNARD: But you believe it?

CATHERINE: I learned it in Sunday School.

BERNARD: That's no answer.

CATHERINE: Y'know, I hate being questioned like this!

BERNARD: So you think I'm damned? I'm heading for some kind of Christian Hell? Or is it true you tell people I'm a Christian?

CATHERINE: No, I'm not saying . . . Look, Daddy, I was elected president of our youth group, and I have certain responsibilities . . . I have to seem . . . I mean, I have to be . . .

BERNARD: A bigot? You have to be a bigot to be accepted by these friends?

CATHERINE: You're calling me . . . your own daughter . . . Didn't you and Mother want me to be a Presbyterian? First she gets on my case, and now you. What the hell do you both want from me?

BERNARD: I want you to be an honest, decent, loving human being. Someone who accepts people as they are.

CATHERINE: Then you should have given me a different mother. Our family is so screwed up . . . I'm sick of this! Just don't talk to me about it any-more, OK? *(As Bernard exits, to audience.)* Having hurt the person in the world I adored most, I had to go for the next person I cared about.

AARON: *(Enters.)* You want to talk to me?

CATHERINE: You had no right to call my father. Y'know? Now he's very upset.

AARON: Well . . . I didn't know what else to do.

CATHERINE: What about me? You could have come to talk to me, but oh, no, you couldn't bring yourself to speak to me in person, just like you can't even look at me for *months,* y'know, while you prance around with Francine Shacklin . . .

AARON: Y'know, it's really hard to be Jewish and talk to an anti-Semite.

CATHERINE: Anti-Semite! Shit! Is that what you really think?

AARON: Yeah, and y'know, I think you're really defensive about it, because you never used to swear, and I know what you said in your church about the damnation of unbelievers and what you said about Jews, and, y'know, it all adds up.

CATHERINE: I see.

AARON: Yeah, I bet you do. *(Beat.)* Look, uh . . . I'm sorry about the way I've been acting toward you, y'know, I mean, ignoring you and sort of *flaunt-ing* my thing with Francine . . .

CATHERINE: I don't care about you and Francine!

AARON: I'd be jealous too, y'know, if it was you and some guy.

CATHERINE: Jealous? Of you and Francine? You're crazy! I never even liked you, if you want to know the truth.

AARON: You didn't?

CATHERINE: How could I like some scrawny Jewish nerd who takes math at Cal Tech? I was embarrassed to be around a jerk like you.

AARON: Oh. A scrawny Jewish nerd. *(Beat.)* Well, screw you, Cathy. Have a nice life with all your uptight little WASP friends.

(He exits.)

CATHERINE: The end of the school year passed in a haze of unhappiness. Aaron was right: I was so defensive I'd squeezed my heart into a rock that hurt my chest whenever I breathed. I was tired of swearing and talking tough. I didn't want to be a Presbyterian anymore. But I didn't want to be an atheist, because if there was a Hell I'd probably go there. And I didn't know how to be Jewish.

I kept dreaming about the golden ladder Daddy talked about when I was little. I knew that was the name of the novel he'd been writing for years, and I wanted to read it. I thought maybe there were secret instructions for becoming wise, so I could climb that golden ladder right up to Heaven. But he wouldn't let me read it till it was finished. So I had no hope of figuring things out.

Then one morning in the middle of summer I woke up and I knew what I had to do. The answer was so clear I started laughing, so I knew I was on the first step up that golden ladder. I had to become a *Catholic!*

END OF ACT I

ACT II

Catherine appears alone on stage. She is dressed in summer clothes.

CATHERINE: The idea to become a Catholic was so revolutionary I didn't want to tell anyone but Mary, who was a Catholic and could tell me how to do it. Unfortunately, there was one small problem: Mary hated me.

MARY: *(Enters, in shorts, very sullen.)* What do you want?

CATHERINE: Mary, listen, I'm sorry I was so mean to you last year, but now we're fifteen and . . .

MARY: Don't bother apologizing. I don't like you, Cathy.

CATHERINE: I don't blame you. Really.

MARY: You're a snot.

CATHERINE: A snot? Oh. I'm sorry. Here, I brought you a present.

(Hands her a wrapped present.)

MARY: What is it?

CATHERINE: Open it.

MARY: *(Unwrapping it.)* It's a book. *(Looks inside.)* The pages are all blank.

CATHERINE: It's for you to write in. Like your thoughts.

MARY: I don't write. *(Beat.)* But it's OK, I don't read much either. *(Beat.)* Thanks.

CATHERINE: It wasn't just you, you know. I was so flipped out over Aaron I was mean to everybody.

MARY: You weren't mean to those kids at the Presbyterian church.

CATHERINE: Well, I don't want to be a Presbyterian anymore.

MARY: You're pretty screwed up.

CATHERINE: Oh, I probably am. But guess what? I want to become a Catholic.

MARY: What?

CATHERINE: Promise you won't tell anybody? It's a secret.

MARY: Why?

CATHERINE: Well, I'm not sure how my parents would feel. *(Beat.)* Actually, I *know* how my parents would feel, but I thought if I talked to a minister . . .

MARY: A *priest.* Catholics don't have ministers.

CATHERINE: Oh? Well, right. If I talked to a *priest* . . .

MARY: Boy, you think you're so smart, but you don't know anything.

CATHERINE: I know. That's why I have to talk to a priest.

MARY: So what do you want to be a Catholic for?

CATHERINE: Well, I believe in God, at least, I think I do, so I . . .

MARY: You have to believe in God to be a Catholic.

CATHERINE: Right. But, you know, there were things Presbyterians believe that were a problem. And I like things about the Catholics, like you have these saints, don't you?

MARY: Of course. We have lots of saints.

CATHERINE: Well, I think that's pretty terrific, like all those saints you can pray to for different things. I mean, in the Presbyterian church you just have God.

MARY: Yeah, I heard that about non-Catholics.

CATHERINE: Well, they do have Jesus. And the Holy Ghost, but he's not really a person, I guess.

MARY: He's a flame.

CATHERINE: A flame?

MARY: Yeah, you know, over the heads of the disciples? In paintings. People saw those flames.

CATHERINE: Oh. *(Beat.)* And you've got the mother of God too, Mary.

MARY: I'm named after her. Mary, The Holy Mother. I'm not a mother yet, but someday . . .

CATHERINE: Wow, what a great idea. I'm really impressed that you're named after Jesus's mother. Do you pray to her?

MARY: Sure.

CATHERINE: Does she answer your prayers?

MARY: I guess so. Yeah. Usually. If I don't ask for a new bicycle.

CATHERINE: I really need a mother I can pray to and get answers. I mean, someone who's not always telling me I can't wear black and I shouldn't be negative and I shouldn't tell people certain things, but who just listens and smiles. She does sort of smile, doesn't she?

MARY: Yeah, it's a small smile.

CATHERINE: A small smile is OK. *(Beat.)* And you've got confession, right?

MARY: Of course we do.

CATHERINE: Where you go in this little dark room and tell the *priest* all your sins, and he says it's OK . . .

MARY: You have to do penance before it's totally OK.

CATHERINE: Like what?

MARY: You say some Hail Marys. On your rosary.

(She pulls a rosary out of her bra.)

See? I keep mine near my heart. They're blessed.

CATHERINE: Oh, that's so pretty! I know I'm going to like being a Catholic.

MARY: Here, you can have my rosary.

CATHERINE: That's so nice of you, Mary, but I couldn't.

MARY: I can get another one. You'll need to practice with it so you don't sound too stupid when you talk to a priest.

CATHERINE: I will. And could you take me to your church so I can meet the priest?

MARY: OK.

CATHERINE: I'm so happy we're friends again.

MARY: Me too.

LAURA: A Catholic?

> *(Enters, upstage, with Bernard.)*

MARY: See you later. *(She exits.)*

LAURA: This is the limit, Kathleen, the absolute limit! You're a disgrace to our family.

CATHERINE: Cathy. And I'm not a disgrace.

BERNARD: Why do you want to be a Catholic?

CATHERINE: Well, I don't know, I was thinking maybe some of the things Presbyterians believe aren't really true, and anyway, they teach you one thing and then when you talk about it, people get upset.

LAURA: It's your Italian friend, Mary, isn't it? Why do you let her influence you?

CATHERINE: Why do you have to mention that she's Italian?

BERNARD: Is she Italian? Oh, of course. Scaccia. That sounds Italian.

LAURA: You're ganging up on me again.

BERNARD: No, I'm just pointing out a simple fact.

CATHERINE: And anyway, the priest I talked to is Irish, like your family, Mother.

LAURA: You've already talked to a priest?

CATHERINE: I have. He was a nice man.

BERNARD: And what did he say when you told him you want to be a Catholic?

LAURA: I hope you realize Catholics are idol-worshippers.

CATHERINE: You mean the saints, Mother? You think the saints are idols?

LAURA: Certainly they are. What do you think happened when the Catholic Church converted pagan cultures? Their gods became saints. Which Catholics still pray to in the form of statues.

CATHERINE: Well, I don't know much about the history yet . . .

LAURA: And all the incense they use to cover up their body odor.

CATHERINE: Body odor? The saints?

LAURA: It's a well-known fact that Catholics seldom take baths.

CATHERINE: That's not true! Mary takes baths all the time, Or showers. Every time I go over there, I have to sit around and wait till she gets out of the shower.

BERNARD: Where did you get that idea, Laura?

LAURA: My grandmother told me stories about Catholics in Ireland, and even my mother remembered the way the Catholics were so dirty they . . .

BERNARD: Many Catholics were poor where your family came from in Ireland.

LAURA: I'm telling you both, those Catholics . . .

BERNARD: Please. Don't generalize. You shouldn't say "those people" . . .

LAURA: You mean I can't refer to a group of people as "those"? Those teachers who went on strike? Those lawyers who lost their case?

BERNARD: Of course, in those instances . . .

LAURA: So I'm not prejudiced. I just see things clearly. People come from different backgrounds, and sometimes it's difficult to relate to someone who is . . .

CATHERINE: A Catholic or a Jew? That's what you were going to say, isn't it?

BERNARD: Shhhh. Be quiet, Cathy.

CATHERINE: But all she really cares about is what other people think.

LAURA: No, I just think it's helpful to be with people who have similar tastes, interests and, yes, religion. Not that we shouldn't *associate* with them . . .

CATHERINE: But we shouldn't be intimate with them, right? Like marry them?

BERNARD: Laura, Cathy. Surely we can have a reasonable discussion.

CATHERINE: Never! This happens every time.

LAURA: You think you know everything, miss. But if you think you can become a Catholic and reek of fish every Friday, you've got another think coming! *(She exits in a fury.)*

CATHERINE: *(To Bernard.)* Reek of fish?

BERNARD: Catholics eat fish on Fridays. *(Beat.)* Every religion has its rules and rituals.

CATHERINE: Even the Jewish religion?

BERNARD: Oh, yes. There are many laws and rituals.

CATHERINE: What did you think was most important?

BERNARD: I think what Rabbi Hillel said, "What is hateful to you, do not do to others."

CATHERINE: Daddy, are you sure you're an atheist? I mean, sometimes when you talk about being Jewish, I think . . .

BERNARD: I'm not Jewish anymore, Cathy. I made a choice when I married your mother.

CATHERINE: You didn't have to do that.

BERNARD: *(An agonized outburst.)* Do you think it's been easy? Denying my family? How do you suppose my mother feels?

CATHERINE: Oh. I didn't realize. Gram seems so . . . well, around *you* she . . .

BERNARD: *(Pulling himself together.)* She knows why I made my choice. Now what I really am is an agnostic.

CATHERINE: What's an agnostic?

BERNARD: One who admits he doesn't know. But saying I'm an atheist feels more wholehearted. *(Beat.)* Now, what did the priest say?

CATHERINE: He said becoming a Catholic is a very serious decision.

BERNARD: Are you sure it's what you want to do?

CATHERINE: Yes.

BERNARD: Well, then I suppose you'll have to do it.

CATHERINE: Even if Mother hates me?

BERNARD: She could never hate you. I'll talk to her about it. Don't worry. And if you try being a Catholic and you find it's not what you want . . .

CATHERINE: Oh, it is. I know it.

BERNARD: I wish I could be so sure about anything. Even for five minutes.

CATHERINE: You're sure you love me, aren't you? And Gram and mother?

BERNARD: Oh, yes. That is one thing I'm sure about.

CATHERINE: Daddy, do people always become like their families?

BERNARD: What do you mean?

CATHERINE: Oh, y'know, Mother's family was prejudiced, so she . . .

BERNARD: Many things influence us, Cathy. The first time your mother realized what it meant to marry a Jew was on our wedding night.

CATHERINE: Your wedding night?

BERNARD: We got married in the morning, at a justice of the peace, with two of our friends as witnesses . . .

CATHERINE: What about your families?

BERNARD: I didn't want to tell my family because I was afraid they'd be upset if I married a shiksa.

CATHERINE: A what?

BERNARD: Never mind.

CATHERINE: Shiksa.

BERNARD: And your mother's family was poor, with so many children, and her father working in the mines . . . They were still living in that railroad car the company had abandoned . . .

CATHERINE: What railroad car? Mother never told me that.

BERNARD: She doesn't like to remember those things. We sent them a letter, but they never responded. *(Beat.)* Anyway, I wanted to take her to a fancy hotel in Chicago for our honeymoon, so we took a train to Chicago and went to the Whitehall Hotel . . .

CATHERINE: Was that fancy?

BERNARD: Very elegant. And I was so naive I didn't realize I should have tried to make a reservation. We just showed up at the desk and . . .

(Hotel Clerk enters with a reservation book, followed by Laura as her younger self.)

HOTEL CLERK: Good afternoon.

BERNARD: We'd like to reserve a room for two nights. Your bridal suite, if it's available.

(He smiles at Laura proudly.)

HOTEL CLERK: For which two nights?

BERNARD: Tonight and tomorrow.

HOTEL CLERK: *(Checking her book.)* Yes, it's available. You're newlyweds?

(She smiles warmly.)

LAURA: We just got married this morning. In Indiana. And we took a train here.

HOTEL CLERK: How nice, Is this your first time in Chicago?

LAURA: Yes. I can't wait to see the city. It looks so beautiful.

HOTEL CLERK: You'll find many wonderful places to see here. It's a good choice for a honeymoon.

BERNARD: *(To Laura.)* You see, honey? What did I tell you?

HOTEL CLERK: So. Your names, please?

BERNARD: Mr. and Mrs. Bernard Bronson.

(He and Laura smile radiantly at each other.)

HOTEL CLERK: Bernard Bronson?

BERNARD: Yes.

HOTEL CLERK: *(Looking at her book.)* How careless of me! I'm sorry, but the bridal suite is taken.

LAURA: Oh, that's too bad.

BERNARD: We'll take another room. Do you have any with a nice view of the city?

HOTEL CLERK: I must have been looking at the wrong dates. We are entirely booked for this weekend.

LAURA: No rooms at all?

HOTEL CLERK: None. I'm sorry.

BERNARD: I bet you are.

HOTEL CLERK: I beg your pardon?

BERNARD: Never mind. We'll take our Jewish name somewhere else. Come on, honey.

(He takes Laura's hand and they walk a few steps downstage as the Hotel Clerk exits.)

LAURA: What happened, Bernard? What did you mean about our Jewish name?

BERNARD: Never mind, honey. We'll find a nice room somewhere.

LAURA: OK, but tell me, Bernard. Jewish name?

BERNARD: OK. *(Beat.)* Some people think Jews are different.

LAURA: You're not different.

BERNARD: Some people think I am. Because I'm Jewish and they're not.

LAURA: I'm not Jewish.

BERNARD: But you married one. You've got my last name.

LAURA: Oh.

BERNARD: *(To Catherine, as Laura exits slowly.)* That night we went to one fancy hotel after another and no one would take us.

CATHERINE: That's awful. What did you do?

BERNARD: We finally found a small hotel on the outskirts of town. Your mother cried the whole night.

CATHERINE: Oh, Daddy.

BERNARD: And then my family would have nothing to do with us for years. Until you were born. And even then, my mother treated your mother very badly.

CATHERINE: That's why Mother won't go with us to Gram's anymore, isn't it?

BERNARD: I'm afraid so.

CATHERINE: I think I understand. *(Beat.)* Daddy, should I be a Catholic?

BERNARD: It's not my decision, sweetheart.

CATHERINE: You don't care. *(Beat.)* I think I'll do it then.

MARY: *(Enters as Bernard exits.)* I'm so glad you're becoming a Catholic.

CATHERINE: Me, too. Listen. *(She pulls rosary out of her bra.)* Hail, Mary, full of grace, the Lord is with Thee. Blessed art Thou among women, and blessed is the fruit of thy womb, Jesus. *(Beat.)* Don't you just love saying *thee* and *thou* and *art?*

MARY: Hunh?

CATHERINE: Those old words people don't say anymore.

MARY: We say them.

CATHERINE: In church. But, like, what if I said, Hey, Mary, how art thou?

MARY: Why would you say something like that?

CATHERINE: I wouldn't.

MARY: So why'd you ask me?

CATHERINE: Because . . . I mean, I was talking about *language.*

MARY: Why?

CATHERINE: Well, because . . . Oh, never mind. Hey, do you want to hear a poem I'm writing about Mary?

MARY: You wrote a poem about me?

CATHERINE: Not *you.* Mary, the mother of God.

MARY: Oh. Why don't you write a poem about me?

CATHERINE: I will sometime. I promise. But listen:

She waits for me in a blue-white silence,
opens her arms to receive my sins
like children she'll never have,
and suddenly candles everywhere are glowing . . .

MARY: I don't get it.

CATHERINE: It's about telling the Virgin Mother all my sins.

MARY: Why don't you tell the priest? In confession?

CATHERINE: I like the idea of telling this really understanding mother the bad things I do.

MARY: That's what you tell the *priest.* You *pray* to the Holy Mother.

CATHERINE: Well, I have these questions, like, about what prayer really is.

MARY: Boy, I used to think you were smart! You just ask for things, like not a bicycle but maybe lasagna for dinner or could I be happy.

CATHERINE: Father Flanaghan says prayer is more complicated than that.

MARY: He does? He never told me.

CATHERINE: And he knows I have trouble with confession because I don't really know what a sin is.

MARY: Boy! Everybody knows what a sin is.

CATHERINE: But is it like you hit a kid or you swear or you hate your mother . . .

MARY: Nobody hates their mother.

CATHERINE: Some kids do. Even when they know they shouldn't.

MARY: All that stuff is a sin.

CATHERINE: That's what Father Flanaghan says. But what if you're mean to someone and then you feel sorry right after? It's not a sin anymore, right? Or you think about kicking someone like Francine Shacklin in the ankle but you don't do it because it would be a crumby thing to do or maybe because you don't want some person you used to know to think you cared. Is that a sin?

MARY: You're giving me a pain in my eyeballs.

CATHERINE: But you can see how I have all these questions, and Father Flanaghan says . . .

MARY: You're sure you want to be Catholic?

CATHERINE: Oh, yes!. I just have a lot of problems. You know, with life. *(To audience.)* I kept thinking: if I just *did* it, just became a total Catholic in spite of all my unanswered questions, my family would become like a Catholic version of a Norman Rockwell painting.

(Bernard and Laura enter, smiling and holding hands. They kneel, down center, and Catherine joins them. All face front.)

BERNARD, LAURA, CATHERINE: Hail Mary, full of grace, the Lord is with thee. Blessed art thou among women, and blessed is the fruit of thy womb, Jesus. Holy Mary, Mother of God, pray for us sinners, now and at the hour of our death. Amen.

(They rise, smiling.)

LAURA: Isn't it wonderful that we're all the same religion at last?

BERNARD: It certainly is. My, I feel so cleansed and whole after a good mass!

CATHERINE: Mommy and Daddy, isn't life simple, when you come down to it?

LAURA: Oh, yes! And look, Catherine darling, there's your sweet friend Mary.

MARY: Hi, Mr. and Mrs. Bronson. I'm so glad you like me now.

LAURA: Oh, but we always did, dear. It just took becoming Catholics for us to realize it.

BERNARD: I always liked you, Mary.

LAURA: How true! My husband was much more accepting than I was. But now my mind has been opened.

MARY: That's really cool.

LAURA: *(She sniffs the air around Mary.)* And now I can smell how wrong I was. You *do* take baths.

MARY: Showers. I take showers.

LAURA: Showers are good too. I'm so glad you're a friend of our sweet Catherine. *(She takes out her wallet.)* Here. Take my Bullocks card, Catherine. Buy yourselves a couple of black dresses.

CATHERINE: *(To audience.)* My fantasies could get so far-fetched even I couldn't believe them.

AARON: *(Enters as Mary, Laura, and Bernard exit.)* I hear you're becoming a Catholic.

CATHERINE: Who told you?

AARON: Word gets around.

CATHERINE: So why do you care?

AARON: It's not a big deal. I'm just curious.

CATHERINE: If it's not a big deal, why should I tell you? I mean, you don't talk to me for centuries and suddenly you want me to tell you something personal. Not that you really *care*.

AARON: OK, I *do* care. About you and . . . What do your parents think?

CATHERINE: They think it's just terrific. They love having me be a Catholic.

AARON: C'mon, Cathy. This is your old friend Aaron talking to you.

CATHERINE: You're not my old friend, Aaron. You just show up sometimes to interfere in my life. Why don't you visit my father again if you want to know how he feels.

AARON: So maybe I shouldn't have visited your father. I don't know. He's such a nice guy that I thought . . .

CATHERINE: Don't think about me, OK? Or my father.

AARON: Listen, I try not to. I really do.

CATHERINE: Catholicism is a wonderful religion. Very satisfying for the soul.

AARON: The soul. Hunh. What do you think the soul is?

CATHERINE: It's a flame, for heaven's sake! *(Beat.)* No, that's the Holy Ghost. Well, the soul is . . . .what's inside the body that goes on after the body dies.

AARON: Ah. It goes on. *(Beat.)* Do you have to not have sex till you get married?

CATHERINE: Who says that?

AARON: Well, you can't use birth control, right? So I guess you could have sex, but if you got pregnant, you'd have to have the baby. So if I was a Catholic girl, I just wouldn't have sex. Unless I wanted a baby.

CATHERINE: We didn't get that far in catechism class. But if I want to go all the way, I'll do it.

AARON: Really.

CATHERINE: Yes, really, Mr. Know-It-All. Because that's why Catholics have confession. So they can do whatever they want and go to confession and do penance and their sins get wiped away. So there!

AARON: What a cool system. You could rob a bank or kill someone, then you just . . .

CATHERINE: Are you crazy? You can't do stuff like that.

AARON: But you just said . . .

CATHERINE: Some sins just don't get wiped away. Not that easily. I mean, there are big sins and little ones, I don't know their names yet — they have these *classifications* I haven't learned. And anyway, you'd go to jail.

AARON: Right. And sex is a little sin.

CATHERINE: It *might* be. I'll ask Father Flanaghan.

AARON: Hey, if it turns out to be a small sin, do you want to go all the way with me?

CATHERINE: Take a long walk off a short pier, Aaron.

AARON: I wasn't being flippant, Cathy.

CATHERINE: Oh, right. How about your girlfriend Francine?

AARON: We broke up. *(Beat.)* I told her I was still in love with you.

CATHERINE: You're what?

AARON: You heard me. *(Beat.)* Listen, we're a year older now. Could we try kissing again?

CATHERINE: I don't think so.

(But she's mesmerized by him.)

AARON: *(Moving closer.)* I'll tell you what. Let's do a game. I'll kiss you and you try to resist. I mean, don't kiss me back. It's very good for Catholic girls to try this kind of thing.

CATHERINE: *(Unable to move.)* Why?

AARON: *(Putting his arms around her.)* It's practice. For resisting temptation. *(He kisses her. She just stands there but can't resist more than a few moments. Suddenly they're kissing passionately.)* Come to my house. There's nobody home.

CATHERINE: You want to sleep with me?

AARON: Not exactly. Come on. I can't wait.

(He pulls her by the hand.)

CATHERINE: *(Holding back, although she's breathless.)* No, I've got to talk to Father Flanaghan. What if this is a big sin?

AARON: It feels too good to be a big sin.

CATHERINE: I don't want to have a baby.

AARON: *(Kisses her again.)* You won't get pregnant.

CATHERINE: How do you know?

AARON: I've got protection.

(He pulls condoms out of his pocket,.)

CATHERINE: *(Stops cold.)* Why do you have . . . those things?

AARON: Well, I'm sixteen and . . .

CATHERINE: Did you have sex with Francine?

AARON: *(Reluctantly honest.)* Yes. *(Sees her horrified look.)* Cathy, I needed life experience! I needed to be ready for you!

CATHY: *(Pushes him away.)* That is so disgusting! I hate you, Aaron! Go away and don't ever come near me again. *(As he backs away, she turns to audience.)* I needed to talk to someone. So I turned to the one person whose understanding seemed to be limitless.

(Bernard enters.)

CATHY: Daddy, do you have a few minutes?

BERNARD: I hope I have more than that.

CATHERINE: Well, I want to talk to you about being a Catholic and, uh, getting physical with, uh, boys.

BERNARD: This is a requirement for being a Catholic?

CATHERINE: I'm serious, Daddy. *(Beat.)* I like being a Catholic. I think. I mean, I like being in the church all by myself with the candles and saints and it's sort of gloomy except when sun lights up the stained glass windows, you know? And it smells like stones and incense, and you can feel all these prayers hanging around.

BERNARD: Makes me want to be a Catholic.

CATHERINE: You see? And mass is cool too, with everybody standing and sitting and kneeling and mumbling and Father Flanaghan speaks in Latin, which I really love . . .

BERNARD: Ah, yes. You and I are committed aesthetes.

CATHERINE: Aesthetes?

BERNARD: People who are highly sensitive to art and beauty.

CATHERINE: Oh. Maybe that's why I don't want to *think* about being a Catholic, I just want to *be* one. Like Mary. She just *knows.*

BERNARD: Remember what Confucius says? Confusion is the beginning of wisdom.

CATHERINE: Well, it sure doesn't feel like it. And then . . . remember my old boyfriend Aaron? *(Bernard nods.)* He came back and told me he loved me and wanted to . . . y'know?

BERNARD: Oh.

CATHERINE: But I said no.

BERNARD: That's good.

CATHERINE: Because he told me he already went all the way with Francine Shacklin.

BERNARD: Hmmm. *(Beat.)* Well . . .

CATHERINE: And he did it for *me.* He said.

BERNARD: We often do things and then interpret them in a way that makes us look good,

CATHERINE: I *know.*

BERNARD: But he seems like a decent young man who tries to be honest.

CATHERINE: Before he said that I was worrying was it enough just to go to confession and do penance. But just wanting to do it was probably a sin, like of omission or something.

BERNARD: Very confusing. I wish the road to wisdom wasn't so difficult. The Assyro-Babylonian hero Gilgamesh even went down into the land of death in his search for knowledge.

CATHERINE: Oh. *(Beat.)* So what should I do, Daddy?

BERNARD: You'll have to decide, darling.

CATHERINE: If I don't become a Catholic, Mary will be very disappointed.

BERNARD: That will be unfortunate. But as they say on TV, this is your life. *(He exits.)*

CATHERINE: *(To audience.)* When you're in the throes of a difficult decision, it's always helpful if someone can come along and make it for you.

CAROLE: *(Enters.)* Hi, Cathy. Where've you been all summer?

CATHERINE: *(To audience.)* Carole Havens, the most popular girl in high school. Talking to *me*. I couldn't believe it. *(To Carole.)* Oh, just around, I guess.

CAROLE: We were wondering if you'd like to come to a party.

CATHERINE: Me? A party? Sure.

CAROLE: We thought, here Cathy is the top student in our class and we don't even know her.

CATHERINE: I know what you mean. I don't even know myself.

CAROLE: What?

CATHERINE: Just a joke. So tell me about the party.

CAROLE: Well, it's pretty exclusive, really. We have this club we call Renaissance, which means rebirth . . .

CATHERINE: I know.

CAROLE: You do?

CATHERINE: Sure. Shakespeare and the metaphysical poets? And, of course, in Italy the Renaissance came earlier, when . . .

CAROLE: Right. But this is a different kind of renaissance. We're born again.

CATHERINE: What do you mean?

CAROLE: Have you accepted Jesus into your heart?

CATHERINE: Gosh, I don't know. I don't remember doing anything like . . . How do you do that?

CAROLE: You just open the door and let Him in.

CATHERINE: What door?

CAROLE: The door in your heart. Haven't you heard Him knocking?

CATHERINE: *(To audience.)* A door in my heart? I didn't want to ask. *(To Carole.)*
Uh, I guess not.

CAROLE: Don't worry about it, you'll find out.

CATHERINE: Who's in the club?

CAROLE: Jane Kelly, Nancy Allen, Cherry Snow, Kerry Christie . . . uh, well, you'll see. All the girls in my crowd.

CATHERINE: *(To audience.)* The list read like a *Who's Who* of my high school, all the girls who never seemed to know I existed. And suddenly I could be one of them.

CAROLE: So, this Saturday, OK? 7 P.M. *(Beat.)* By the way, somebody told me you were becoming a Catholic, but I said I doubt it. You're not, are you?

CATHERINE: No. Who told you?

CAROLE: Oh, it doesn't matter. See you Saturday.

CATHERINE: *(To audience.)* I was becoming an expert at betrayals. And I wasn't finished yet.

MARY: *(Enters.)* Cathy, guess what? Father Flanaghan told me we're having a special guitar mass before the dance Saturday night.

CATHERINE: Saturday night?

MARY: Yeah, remember? You and I are the greeters. We've got to get there a little early because we give people numbers and after the dance there's a drawing.

CATHERINE: Oh, Mary, I can't go.

MARY: What're you talking about? You know this is a special dance, all those kids from Holy Cross coming.

CATHERINE: But I forgot, and I told someone I'd . . .

MARY: Cathy! You made a commitment. And Holy Cross has tons of boys.

CATHERINE: Mary, I have to tell you something.

MARY: What?

CATHERINE: This is really difficult, I . . . I'm not going to become a Catholic. I think.

MARY: WHAT?

CATHERINE: I think it's too complicated for me, the kinds of sins and rules and . . . what if I want to make love with somebody. For example.

MARY: Just do it.

CATHERINE: But I'd have to use birth control and we're not supposed to do that.

MARY: Do you have some guy in mind?

CATHERINE: No, but, I mean, I might. Sometime. And then what?

MARY: You do it, then you go to confession. What's the problem?

CATHERINE: I don't know, it seems hypocritical, like deliberately misinterpreting something the church really believes in.

MARY: Boy, are you messed up! Somebody must've crossed your brain wires.

CATHERINE: And then tied them in knots.

MARY: Yeah, knots. Did you tell Father Flanaghan?

CATHERINE: No, but I will.

MARY: So what're you going to be now?

CATHERINE: Uh, I don't know. I'll tell you when it happens. *(To audience.)* But I knew I wouldn't, because I knew Mary would suspect my motives. She'd say:

MARY: You're just trying to be popular.

CATHERINE: Which was true, although I did hope something real would happen if I could find this door in my heart and open it. Maybe this was what I was looking for.

MARY: *(As she exits.)* Right. You just want to find some guy and get laid.

CATHERINE: *(Calling after her.)* They're all girls! *(To audience.)* Which was pretty much the way our conversation went when Mary found out. And then we weren't friends anymore. *(Beat.)* But the party was interesting, although a little odd. There were all the Renaissance girls welcoming me like I was a hot fudge sundae they couldn't wait to devour.

CAROLE: *(Enters.)* Oh, Cathy, everybody thinks you're so neat!

CATHERINE: I wonder why.

CAROLE: Because you're *special,* silly! Because Jesus loves you, and He's waiting for you.

CATHERINE: *(To audience.)* Suddenly I heard this ominous music they always play in movies when the killer is waiting around the corner. But I tried to ignore it, because I'd never been so completely *adored.* Especially by the popular boys. *(To Carole.)* So, how come all these boys are here? I thought it was just a girls' club.

CAROLE: Oh, they're the boys' version of us. Their club is called Good News.

CATHERINE: Good News versus the Renaissance. We definitely have a classier tone.

CAROLE: What?

CATHERINE: Just kidding. So who's the blond guy who keeps staring at me?

CAROLE: You don't know Tim Hutchins? God! Excuse me, I should never take the Lord's name in vain. He's a senior, president of the student council, and captain of the football team.

CATHERINE: Guys like that never stare at me. Maybe he thinks I'm someone else.

CAROLE: He knows who you are. *(Beat.)* So. Are you coming to church tomorrow?

CATHERINE: Sure, I guess so.

CAROLE: Great! It's time for you to be born again. *(She exits.)*

CATHERINE: *(To audience.)* That night I had a dream of going through the birth canal and getting stuck.

BERNARD: *(Enters.)* Cathy, are you all right? Wake up, sweetheart.

CATHERINE: Oh, Daddy! I was caught in the birth canal.

BERNARD: Well, I'm glad I got you out of that. *(Beat.)* Sounds pretty Freudian.

CATHERINE: Maybe, but I think it's directly related to tomorrow.

BERNARD: What's tomorrow?

CATHERINE: I'm going to be born again.

BERNARD: Really? Once wasn't enough?

CATHERINE: It's at this church where I went to the party. They want me to accept Jesus into my heart tomorrow.

BERNARD: Ah, ha! So you were rehearsing.

CATHERINE: Daddy.

BERNARD: I'm running late on all this, aren't I? Last time we talked you were trying to become a Catholic.

CATHERINE: Oh, this might be easier. All these cool kids did it and they seem really happy.

BERNARD: My daughter becomes a Fundamentalist Christian. Ah, the turns life takes!

CATHERINE: Are you angry with me? Do you wish I wouldn't do it?

BERNARD: I suppose it's all exploration. But it is a little funny that you're going back to your mother's roots.

CATHERINE: What roots?

BERNARD: Her Southern Baptist church in Kentucky.

CATHERINE: Really? They were born again?

BERNARD: I think that's the effort they were making. *(Beat.)* So. Tell me how it goes tomorrow. Maybe we'll have a birthday party.

CATHERINE: Daddy, please. *(To audience, as Bernard exits.)* Here's how it went: There was a huge crowd, everybody singing enthusiastically, songs like "What A Friend We Have in Jesus" and "Jesus Loves Me." Then this minister who looked like a movie star told us Jesus is waiting for us to open our hearts to him. People kept smiling at me, and I was nervous because I thought I might have to do something right then and I wasn't sure what it was. Then the minister said, "All those who wish to be born again, come forward."

CAROLE: *(Enters, grabs Catherine's hand.)* Come on, Cathy, it's time.

CATHERINE: *(A panicked whisper.)* Carole! I don't know what to do!

CAROLE: Relax. Just open your heart. *(She pulls Catherine forward.)* Kneel down. *(They both kneel.)* Let's pray.

(Carole closes her eyes, but Catherine stares ahead.)

CATHERINE: *(To audience.)* The minister prayed over us, asking Jesus to come, and there was this intense feeling everywhere, like *expectation,* the whole room sort of vibrating, and I was trying so hard to be open I passed out. When I came to, I was lying on the floor and everybody was saying "Hallelujah!" and "Praise the Lord!" so I knew something must've happened.

CAROLE: Oh, Catherine, I'm so happy for you! *(Helping Catherine to her feet.)*

CATHERINE: Is that all there is to it?

CAROLE: Yes! Don't you feel different now? Complete?

CATHERINE: Uh, sure. *(To audience.)* I really felt dizzy but also happy because nothing painful had happened and everyone was delighted with me.

CAROLE: You look radiant!

CATHERINE: Really?

CAROLE: Yes! You have this inner glow.

CATHERINE: *(To audience.)* Such conviction is hard to resist. Suddenly I felt glowing and happy. I let the minister baptize me — not total immersion, just a little water on my head — and then we were all hugging and Tim Hutchins asked me out.

CAROLE: You are so lucky!

CATHERINE: *(As Carole leaves, to audience.)* That night I talked to Jesus. *(She kneels, facing audience.)* Listen, Jesus, I really hope you're in my heart now, because I don't want to be a hypocrite, OK? Maybe you could give me a sign that you're really there? *(To audience.)* I opened my eyes and everything in my room was shining, like a halo everywhere, and even though I realized as I got into bed that it was a full moon, I believed I'd gotten an answer. Or I wanted to believe.

(She stands, as Aaron and Mary enter.)

AARON: Hey, there's the girl who keeps changing religions.

CATHERINE: Very funny.

AARON: We hear you're born again. Was it painful?

CATHERINE: No, it was terrific.

MARY: We saw you at the movies with Tim Hutchins. Is he one of the born-agains?

CATHERINE: Yes.

MARY: *(To Aaron.)* I told you that's why she's doing this.

CATHERINE: It is not! *(Beat.)* Since when did you two become friends?

AARON: *(Putting his arm around Mary's waist.)* Recently. *(Beat.)* Come on, Mary. Cathy doesn't want to associate with low-lifes like us.

MARY: *(As they walk off.)* She used to be my best friend. How come, do you think?

AARON: She was real then.

CATHERINE: *(Calling after them.)* I'm real now!

(To audience.)

Or I hoped I was. Without Aaron and Mary, it was hard, but I took deep breaths and tried to fit in with my WASP friends.

CAROLE: Hey, Cathy! Are you going to the church tonight for the barbecue?

CATHERINE: Sure. I'm bringing the hot dogs.

CAROLE: What are you going to wear?

(Turns, showing off her sundress.)

Don't you just love pink?

CATHERINE: Uh, sure. *(Beat.)* I saw this cool black dress with thin straps in Bullocks'window, but . . .

CAROLE: Oh, don't wear black, it's so intellectual.

(Aaron walks past them. Carole whispers.)

CAROLE: There's that Jewish nerd, Aaron. Didn't you used to be friends with him?

CATHERINE: No.

CAROLE: That's funny, I thought . . . Well, anyway. Jews aren't like us, are they?

CATHERINE: I guess not. *(Beat.)* Why aren't they like us?

CAROLE: Well, for one thing, they didn't believe in Jesus.

CATHERINE: But Jesus was Jewish. Remember how he taught in the temple when he was twelve?

CAROLE: Maybe he was Jewish then, but he gave it up. He was the first Christian. *(She exits.)*

CATHERINE: *(To audience.)* For a while I was sort of happy. The minister said:

OFFSTAGE VOICE: *(Very stentorian.)* YOU MUST LOVE EVERYONE.

CATHERINE: Which seemed easy, when I was with my new friends. But then the minister said:

OFFSTAGE VOICE: YOU MUST SHARE THE LOVE OF JESUS WITH EVERYONE, EVEN YOUR FAMILY.

CATHERINE: *(To Voice.)* Do you mean my mother?

OFFSTAGE VOICE: ESPECIALLY YOUR MOTHER.

CATHERINE: OK, I'll try. It's not going to be easy.

OFFSTAGE VOICE: YOU THINK JESUS'S LIFE WAS EASY?

CATHERINE: No, I didn't mean . . .

OFFSTAGE VOICE: JUST FOLLOW HIM. HE'LL HELP YOU. *(Beat.)* I NOTICE YOU DIDN'T MENTION YOUR FATHER.

CATHERINE: Oh, I already love my father.

OFFSTAGE VOICE: DOES HE LOVE JESUS?

CATHERINE: No. He's a Jewish atheist.

OFFSTAGE VOICE: WOW! WHAT AN OPPORTUNITY FOR YOU!

CATHERINE: What do you mean?

OFFSTAGE VOICE: BRING HIM INTO THE FOLD, CATHY! GO!

(We hear a brief flare of the "Hallelujah Chorus.")

LAURA: (To Bernard, as they enter.) I've been looking over my checkbook, Bernard, and I . . .

CATHERINE: (As Bernard and Laura enter.) Hi, Daddy. Hi, Mother. I'm going to a barbeque tonight. With Carole.

LAURA: That sounds lovely, Cathy. I'm glad you've found a friend who is more like you. That little Mary is not your type.

CATHERINE: What a stupid thing to say!

BERNARD: Now, Catherine, please don't . . .

LAURA: She called me stupid, Bernard!

CATHERINE: I didn't call you stupid; I called your prejudice stupid. Which it is.

OFFSTAGE VOICE: REMEMBER WHAT JESUS SAYS? LOVE YOUR MOTHER!

CATHERINE: Oh, right. Uh, listen, Mother, Daddy. How would you like to let Jesus into your hearts?

LAURA: What is she talking about?

BERNARD: It's her most recent venture into religion. (To Catherine.) No, thanks, Sweetheart. My heart is full enough already.

CATHERINE: It's not like your heart is a building where you've rented out all the apartments, Daddy. There's always room for Jesus.

BERNARD: I'm afraid I'm not that expansive.

CATHERINE: Oh, but you are!

BERNARD: In the area of religion I can't pull off a willing suspension of disbelief.

LAURA: Would you two please explain this conversation?

CATHERINE: Mother, I think you need Jesus.

LAURA: What?

BERNARD: Cathy has given up Catholicism. She is now into . . .

CATHERINE: Daddy, don't explain me!

LAURA: Given up Catholicism? That's wonderful! Why didn't you tell me?

CATHERINE: I tried to. Sort of. Not exactly. I wanted to be sure.

LAURA: Of course you did, darling. And what are you into now?

CATHERINE: Jesus. I'm born again.

BERNARD: Did you know that in every culture the hero has a virgin birth? The Irish hero Cucuchlainn was born from a glass of wine. I think it was wine. Although in those days it was probably mead.

CATHERINE: Daddy.

LAURA: Born again? They used to say things like that in our church back in Kentucky.

BERNARD: Cathy's returning to her roots.

CATHERINE: This is not anthropological research or the activity of some damn homing pigeon, Daddy! This is *real.* It's happening to me *now.*

LAURA: What's happening to you, darling? Are you all right? Is she all right, Bernard? No one ever tells me anything.

CATHERINE: Just open your heart to Jesus!

BERNARD: Ah, well. Do you have any other suggestions?

CATHERINE: Jesus will save you!

LAURA: From what? Do I have a problem? Oh, my God, I do, I'm overdrawn, Bernard, I forgot to tell you. I need a hundred dollars.

CATHERINE: I'm talking God, not money! Jesus says render unto Caesar that which is Caesar's . . .

BERNARD: In these days it's Bank of America.

CATHERINE: Just look at me! See how radiant I am?

LAURA: I think she has a fever, Bernard.

CATHERINE: No! I'm glowing with Jesus's love!

LAURA: She looks flushed.

CATHERINE: You've got to do it! It's very important not to die in the throes of materialism or being a Jewish atheist!

BERNARD: Cathy, you're going too far. This is enough.

CATHERINE: No, I want you to accept Jesus because you'll be so happy!

BERNARD: I would *not* be happy. Don't you know who I am?

CATHERINE: But just look. See how happy I am?

LAURA: You look frantic, darling. I'll tell you what. Bernard will give me two hundred dollars, and I'll give you my I Magnin's credit card so you can buy a dress for tonight.

CATHERINE: No, I'm talking God, not clothes! *(Beat.)* What kind of dress?

LAURA: All right, you can buy a black one. As long as you pick up a pastel short-sleeved sweater to wear over it.

CATHERINE: Really? A black dress? *(To audience.)* It was a hard year. I converted no one, which was a great disappointment to Carole and her friends. But I was their prize convert nonetheless, and I carried a Bible everywhere.

(Carole enters, hands Catherine a Bible and exits. Catherine sits and begins reading the Bible and praying as Laura and Bernard enter.)

LAURA: What's that sound, Bernard?

BERNARD: I think it's our daughter, praying.

LAURA: But it's 6 A.M.! Why is she praying at this hour?

BERNARD: She's a diligent young woman.

LAURA: I don't like it. This is excessive. I didn't raise a daughter to be excessive. She's waking me up. And it's right over our heads. Why is it right over our heads?

BERNARD: She's on the roof.

LAURA: On the roof? Why is she on the roof?

BERNARD: I suppose she feels closer to her god. Remember that folktale about a man who lived in a tree to be near God, and all the villagers . . .

LAURA: *(Calling.)* KATHLEEN! COME DOWN HERE THIS INSTANT!

CATHERINE: What do you want, Mother?

LAURA: I want you off the roof. RIGHT NOW.

CATHERINE: OK. I was just praying for you and Daddy.

LAURA: Don't pray for me, young lady. I need sleep.

CATHERINE: But the Bible says . . .

LAURA: Don't Bible me, either. Go to bed.

CATHERINE: I have to get ready for school.

LAURA: Fine. Put down that Bible and take a shower. Get dressed. And for God's sake, put on some makeup. Paint your toenails.

CATHERINE: Jesus doesn't care what I look like.

LAURA: I care. What does Jesus know about makeup? I'm your mother, and I won't have you looking like a nun at your age.

BERNARD: Why would you encourage your daughter to wear makeup?

LAURA: You're a man, Bernard, What do men know?

(Bernard and Laura exit.)

CATHERINE: *(To audience.)* Then I had a fateful run-in with Mary.

MARY: *(Enters.)* Oh, hi, it's you. The kid I don't know anymore.

(Tries to walk past Catherine.)

CATHERINE: Mary, wait! You know me. I'm the same person, really.

MARY: Oh, that's a big laugh.

CATHERINE: Please. I just want to ask you something.

MARY: I'm not talking about Aaron.

CATHERINE: Aaron? I don't want to talk about him. *(Beat.)* Are you going out with him?

MARY: You and your fancy friends. You've got Tim Hutchins, for heaven's sake. We're just nothings. What do you care?

CATHERINE: I do care. About you. I mean, I don't care about you and Aaron.

MARY: Good. So, bye.

CATHERINE: Listen, Mary, I miss you. And Aaron. *(Beat.)* Separately.

MARY: Right.

CATHERINE: No, really. And I was thinking . . . if we had something that could bring us together again, like Jesus, for instance . . .

MARY: Who?

CATHERINE: Jesus. I mean, if we all had Jesus in our hearts, we could pray together and . . .

MARY: Are you talking that born-again stuff at me? Because I'm a Catholic, remember?

CATHERINE: But Catholics have priests and saints and all, and we've found a more direct way to God. You just open the door of your heart and . . .

MARY: Yeah, "we found . . . " Cut it out, Cathy. You found a way to be popular. And now you think you found a way to get Aaron back too. But you can't. Because he's Jewish, just like you, only you can't admit it and still be in with those kids who run the school.

CATHERINE: *(Calling, as Mary walks off.)* I'm not ashamed of my background, Mary!

MARY: *(Over her shoulder.)* Oh, yeah?

CATHERINE: I can admit it!

MARY: We'll see.

CAROLE: *(Enters.)* Catherine, we need to know. Just tell us the truth.

CATHERINE: Why does it matter?

CAROLE: Don't be ridiculous! This is a Christian club. Are you Jewish?

CATHERINE: No.

(Carole exits and Aaron enters.)

AARON: What's the matter? You look like you sold out your best friend.

CATHERINE: No. I didn't sell out my best friend.

AARON: So what happened?

CATHERINE: I sold out me. And I'm not my best friend, I'm my worst . . .
(She starts to cry.)

AARON: Hey. *(He takes her in his arms.)* Come on. It can't be that bad.

CATHERINE: *(Still sobbing.)* Yes, it can.

AARON: So, tell me. Is it that guy you're going out with?

CATHERINE: No, I don't care about him.

AARON: *(Trying to lift her head from his chest, but she won't look at him.)* One of those girls you hang out with now?

CATHERINE: Oh, Aaron! Mary told them I was Jewish.

AARON: Oh, I get it. And you said . . .

CATHERINE: *(Really wailing.)* I said NO! Because I'm a coward! I wanted them to like me, and I don't even know why. I've become just like my mother! *(Beat.)* I got snot on your shirt.

AARON: That's OK. *(Beat.)* But doesn't this have something to do with what you believe? Like in Jesus and all that stuff?

CATHERINE: I don't know.

AARON: I mean, maybe you believe Judaism is a religion, not a culture or tradition, so you said . . .

CATHERINE: Don't justify me, Aaron.

AARON: Isn't that what your mother believes?

CATHERINE: I don't know *what* my mother believes. All I know is I'm Jewish, and I said . . .

AARON: Hey, don't worry. You didn't lie. You're not really Jewish.

CATHERINE: What are you talking about?

AARON: I told you once. You need to have a Jewish mother.

CATHERINE: I have a Jewish grandmother.

AARON: It's not the same.

CATHERINE: That's not fair! Oh, Aaron. I WANT MY FATHER!

AARON: Come on, I'll walk you home. But you have to stop crying just a little, because my shirt's getting pretty funny-looking.

CATHERINE: *(As they walk, still sniffling.)* Are you in love with Mary?

AARON: No.

CATHERINE: She thinks you are.

AARON: She knows I'm in love with you.

CATHERINE: *(Stops.)* You are?

AARON: I guess I'll always be.

(He kisses her lightly, and wipes her tears with his fingers. They cross to Bernard, who enters down right.)

AARON: Hello, Mr. Bronson.

BERNARD: *(Sees Catherine's face.)* What did you do to my girl, Aaron?

AARON: I just told her I love her.

BERNARD: Is that all? I've heard worse. *(Beat.)* Sweetheart, what's the matter?

CATHERINE: Oh, Daddy! *(Starts crying again.)* I just told Carole I wasn't Jewish!

BERNARD: Who's Carole?

AARON: That blonde friend of hers? Who looks like a Barbie doll?

BERNARD: Oh, I know who you mean.

CATHERINE: She said her friends have to know.

BERNARD: They do?

CATHERINE: Because it's a Christian club and they can't have Jews in it . . .

BERNARD: There's a law?

CATHERINE: Oh, Daddy. And I don't even know if I believe what they do anymore.

BERNARD: I think I understand. How about you, Aaron?

AARON: Yeah. She has doubts, and that makes her nervous, because for the first time in her life she was in with the popular kids who believe all this born-again stuff.

BERNARD: I couldn't have said it better.

CATHERINE: And now Aaron's telling me I'm not really Jewish because my mother isn't Jewish, but you're the one who understands me . . .

BERNARD: Catherine.

CATHERINE: It's true! And you know what's worse? What's really awful? Now I think I'm an Existentialist.

AARON: No kidding? That's far-out.

CATHERINE: *(Starts crying again.)* No, it's not. It's very confusing.

AARON: What made you think you're an Existentialist?

CATHERINE: *(Sobbing.)* I read *The Stranger* and that's how I felt. Like a stranger.

BERNARD: That's certainly one aspect of Existentialism.

LAURA: *(Enters.)* Cathy? Is my daughter upset?

CATHERINE: Yes.

LAURA: *(Sees Aaron.)* Oh. Hello.

BERNARD: Laura, this is Aaron Feldman.

AARON: Hello, Mrs. Bronson. I just brought your daughter . . .

CATHERINE: And maybe I'm an Existentialist because of what I believe but that doesn't mean I'm not Jewish . . .

LAURA: Who's Jewish?

AARON: I am.

LAURA: Yes, I know. I was speaking about . . .

CATHERINE: And Daddy is.

LAURA: Are we back to that again? How many times do I have to tell you . . .

CATHERINE: I know, I KNOW! Judaism is a religion, according to you.

AARON: But isn't it cultural as well? I mean, how can you separate . . .

LAURA: Be quiet, young man!

CATHERINE: Don't tell Aaron to be quiet! He's my friend.

BERNARD: Now, Cathy, Laura, please. Let's just . . .

CATHERINE: No! We won't just "make nice." That's what you've been doing all your life, isn't it?

BERNARD: I just want your mother to be happy.

CATHERINE: Is that why you gave up your religion? Why you became an atheist?

LAURA: Your father is a Christian! We own two plots in the Presbyterian graveyard.

AARON: *(Sotto voce.)* What a definition of Christianity.

CATHERINE: You were Jewish because it was your religion and your traditions and at Gram's you say the prayers and all, now that Mother stays home — so if you'd been willing to teach me, then I could have been — I know it! — in spite of my mother.

BERNARD: Oh, Catherine, there was no possible way . . .

CATHERINE: I hate that!

BERNARD: I'm sorry.

CATHERINE: You know what? I think you care just as much as she does about being "respectable." That's why you go along with her, isn't it?

BERNARD: No! It's your mother, I . . .

CATHERINE: Remember how upset you both were when I made that speech in the Presbyterian Church? You were afraid someone might know you're Jewish.

BERNARD: No. I was afraid you were becoming an anti-Semite.

CATHERINE: Like Mother?

LAURA: I am not an anti-Semite! I was protecting your father.

CATHERINE: Did you need protecting, Daddy?

BERNARD: No.

LAURA: Bernard . . .

CATHERINE: Yes! You didn't want people to know . . .

BERNARD: I have NEVER been ashamed of being Jewish!

CATHERINE: Oh? Then tell her, Daddy. Make her hear it.

BERNARD: Hear what?

CATHERINE: You're not a Christian. You're a Jew.

BERNARD: I am . . . whatever Laura wants me to be. If she says I'm a Christian . . .

LAURA: *(To Catherine.)* You see?

CATHERINE: *(To Bernard.)* You can't do it, can you?

BERNARD: *(Very softly, with pain.)* No. And I never will.

AARON: *(Quietly, to himself.)* Wow. *(He exits.)*

CATHERINE: *(As the others freeze.)* Oh, Daddy, I wish you could have been brave while you were alive, but you loved Mother more than the truth, didn't you? You know why I married Aaron? Because he had the courage to stand up for his beliefs, the way you almost did when your mother died. You came out of the closet in black overcoat and yarmulke, with nine candles in your eyes. And Mother, I wish you could have allowed him to be what he was, in spite of the pain your families and other people caused you.

(Aaron, wearing yarmulke, returns with baby and a shawl. He hands baby to Catherine and drapes shawl over her head.)

CATHERINE AND AARON: Ye-hei she-la-ma ra-ba min she-ma-ya ve-cha-yim a-lei-nu ve-al kol Yis-ra-eil, ve-l-meru: a-mein. O-she sha-lom bi-me-ro-mav, hu ya-a-seh sha-lom a-lei-nu ve-al kol Yis-raeil, ve-i-me-ru: a-mein.

BERNARD: *(Very softly.)* Once upon a time there was a golden ladder that reached all the way from earth to heaven. The ladder wasn't always visible to people on earth, but sometimes . . .

CATHERINE: Daddy? I've become Jewish now because in Judaism I've found an inner stillness and joy I was searching for all my life.

BERNARD: Once there was a man who began to understand life on earth, which is a place so wonderful and terrible it is truly absurd . . .

CATHERINE: And, Daddy? Over the years since you died I've read and reread your novel. And I know you thought you were writing about the pathway to wisdom, but I think all your novels were really about love.

BERNARD: And this man began to laugh. And as he laughed, he grew lighter, as though the force of gravity couldn't hold him anymore.

CATHERINE: This is our daughter, Leah. I'll tell her your stories.

BERNARD: Then, just as his feet began to leave the ground . . .

CATHERINE: Mother is still alive, but she doesn't know us anymore. She's gone completely into her dream world. But I'll tell Leah the truth: her grandmother was Presbyterian and her grandfather Jewish. And I'll say, "Grandaddy was a man who sacrificed his religion for love, and this caused him great inner suffering. But he knew he was doing it. And yet, I'd like to believe that one day he finally . . .

BERNARD AND CATHERINE: ". . . saw the golden ladder shimmering on its way into the clouds. And, people say, he climbed the ladder, laughing until he disappeared."

 END OF PLAY

Homecoming

By Lauren Weedman

To my mother. Both of them.

PLAYWRIGHT'S BIOGRAPHY

Lauren Weedman was born in Terre Haute, Indiana, in 1969. She, too, like her main character in *Homecoming,* was adopted. She, too, like the main character in the play, is named Lauren, almost as if she'd forgotten to change the names and details of the play to protect the innocent.

Ms. Weedman is not overly formally educated: one year at DePaul Theatre School in Chicago, a year at Indiana University studying film, and then off to Amsterdam for the next five years. It was during her "coming down" years in Seattle that she began to write and perform solo theater.

Besides *Homecoming,* her solo work includes: *If Ornaments Had Lips,* a Christmas musical with music by James Palmer originally produced at On the Boards; *Hun* at A Contemporary Theater (ACT); *Amsterdam,* a play with music, also by James Palmer at the Empty Space Theatre, and in the fall of 2002, the Empty Space Theatre premiered her latest solo work, *RASH,* with music by David Russell, which is scheduled to go Off Broadway in the fall of 2003.

Ms. Weedman is a regular on NPR's *Rewind with Bill Radke* and is a correspondent on Comedy Central's *The Daily Show with Jon Stewart.*

INTRODUCTION

When you are in New York or Los Angeles and you tell a fellow actor/writer that you do solo theater — he or she usually says "me too." Even when I invited people to come see my first solo shows, the reaction was usually, "Oh, God . . . a solo show. Let me guess what it's about — YOU." But *Homecoming* is a play. The themes of identity and family and the deep wish to be black or Jewish, though not universal themes, are ones that many of us can relate to.

The play is performed with no costume changes and with rapid character transitions and loud music.

Homecoming

Open Freedom Dance

Music blasts in. Aretha Franklin's "Think." Lauren dances and it's all about funk, with her back to the audience. Music fades out as she turns to the audience and transitions into Grandma Irene, a widowed eight-two-year-old woman living in a retirement community. She is anxious and waiting.

Scene One. 1969. The Arrival

Grandma Irene's — Merrillville, Indiana.

IRENE: *(She waves at the approaching car and notices that it has stopped in front of her driveway.)* Sid! Sid! I don't want you to park there, Sid! Well roll down the window! *(Groans and motions to roll down the window.)* Sharon! Tell Sid that I don't want him to park there! 'Cause he's blocking my mailbox. Hi, Lisa! Hi, sweetheart! Come see your grandma.
(Five-year-old Lisa runs right past Irene, almost knocking her over.)
Lisa, sweetheart, Grandma don't like the way you run. Slow down! Sharon, listen, eh, you don't have to bring her all the way inside. Just, I'll come out there and, eh, look at her through the car window. Well, because I just — ah fine then . . . do what you want. Bring her in.
(Sharon walks up the driveway, passing Irene and into the house. Irene walks into the house.)
Well, you've got a big bundle there, don't you? Yeah, you do. Yeah, you do. Well, she looks like she's real heavy. Is she real heavy? Is she? Yeah, well that's going to give you muscles, lugging that around, huh. Yeah, sure . . . oh no, I'm getting tired just looking at her. Well, so how much does she weigh? Oh! Isn't that too much? Oh well, I don't remember about that. Yeah, that was a long time ago for old Grandma. What are you doing, Sharon? No, no. She doesn't need to go on the couch — does she? No she doesn't. Just hold on a second.

Lisa! Here comes Lisa. Lisa, can you do Grandma a favor? You go get Grandma one of her old towels out of the linen closet. Can you do that for me? Can you? Well thank you, Lisa. Thank you, sweetheart! Yeah, well I know you are. I see that you're helping me. OK!

(Lisa runs off.)

She has such a nice disposition. Doesn't she?

(Putting her hands up to her ears and pointing to the baby.)

Well, she's . . . she's noisy, Sharon. Yeah! Well, was she that noisy in the car? Was she? Uh-oh.

Well, what . . . what are you gonna call her? Laura! Laura — oh, well . . . that's like my soap, Sharon! Yeah, that's like my soap! I didn't realize that . . . huh? Laurie? Oh . . . OK. Well, I like that better. Laurie . . . What?! Huh? Well, stop flubbing your words, so I can try to . . . ! Laur-EN?! Laur-EN! I don't know anybody called LaurEN — how am I ever gonna remember that? Did you ever think about that?

(Lisa runs back in.)

Well, there comes Lisa! Here she comes. Lisa, you were so quick I didn't even know you were gone. Go ahead and spread the towel out on the floor for Grandma. Can you do that for me? Well wait a minute, show me which one you got first. Oh, that's a dog towel. That's fine. Sharon, just put her down there, OK. She doesn't need to be up on the furniture, does she? No, she's fine down there.

Thank you, Lisa. Thank you, honey.

(Whispering.)

Does Lisa know? That she's got a new little, eh, adopted sister? Oh, does she! Is that the plan? You're just gonna tell everybody whenever they ask you? Is that what you're going to do? Well, no, no, I don't care what you do, Sharon. You can go ahead and tell everybody! That's your own business, isn't it? That's your own business. Sure it is.

Well, she's real pretty. Real pretty little girl. Oh! What happened to her eye there? What's that? Is she gonna need glasses? Well, did you ask them about that? Now, how old was the, eh, eh, ya know, the eh, the natural-eh — the nature . . . ya know, I don't know, the eh . . . birther? Well, because Sharon, because if she was too old the baby could have Down syndrome. And that could be why they didn't want her. Because they didn't want to have to pay for all them special schools.

Did they tell you anything about her when they gave her to you? No! Oh my goodness! Oh my — ! Are you kidding me? Well no, Sharon! I, eh, jeez . . . they could have dropped her or something, right before they brought her out to you. Yeah! They could've dropped her . . . ya know, woops! And then hurried and picked her back up, dusted her off, and then there ya go . . . bye-bye, good luck with her. Sure . . . Well, they do it at the grocery store all the time. You'll find out eventually. You'll find out eventually.

Do you know what race she is? Is she white?!?

OK! All right! OK, listen! If I'd known you were gonna act like that — I would've never asked you. No, I would've kept my mouth shut.

Now what are you doing? Huh? No. No. I don't want to hold her. Because Sharon, I couldn't hold her if I wanted to. You know that, because my wrist is so sore I can barely do anything. Just doing that little thing hurts me. *(Bends her wrist slightly.)* Ow. Ow. I'm gonna go defrost some meat for dinner. I don't know what you're gonna feed Laura. Laur-EN! Laur-EN! Jeez, you gonna yell at me in my house. Is that the plan? No, OK, just checking. OK . . .

(Transition into Sharon.)

Scene Two

Weedman House in Indianapolis, Indiana. Sharon has just returned from shopping and is holding a Halloween decoration in her hands. It is a ghost, one of those that when you clap or make a loud noise it begins to shake and make a "ghostly" noise. The ghost is performed as a character — shaking and howling.

SHARON: Lisa and Lauren, come down here, please! OK Lisa, hold on, wait for Lauren! Lauren, take him. I'm going to show you, all right. Just a second, hold on. *(Clap — nothing.)*

In the store he wouldn't shut up — ya know, you get him home and he, OK . . . he wasn't on.

(Turns him on.)

Shhhhh.

(Clap — the ghost goes off, "oooooooouuuuuooooo,")

Hah, hah. No, he's a Halloween decoration. Oh, my God. No, I just fell in love in the store. I almost bought two. No, I was just laughin' and laughin'.

(She claps her hands as she's laughing at him, setting him off: "oooouuuuooouuuoouu.") Hah, hah. You've got to be careful, because any little sound just sets . . .

(She slaps her legs — "ooouuuooouuuuoooouu.")

OK, OK. That's enough! All right! We get the idea. All right. Well, turn him off. Rip his batteries out of there, OK! OK, well, that got old fast, didn't it?! Put him back in the box, all right. You know what? Set him out in the hallway for me, would you.

All right. But wait a second. Stay here. Lauren, don't go away. Come in here. What was I doing? I wanted to show you the Halloween decorations . . . I wanted to scoop out the kitty litter, defrost the lamb patties for dinner, and oh, that's right . . . I want to ask you about my will. That's right. Come here, please.

(Sharon sits down.)

Lisa, this won't take too much of your time. Are you real busy? OK now, girls, I know that you know that your father and I are going on a cruise next month. Well, I don't know if you realize this or not but . . . we will be going through the Bermuda Triangle. *(Pause.)* It's not funny, Lauren — no it is not. Listen . . . My point is, that I have asked my lawyer if he would add a clause in my will that says if something were to happen to me, that it would be OK with you two if I come back and visit you after I'm gone. OK? Lisa, what do you think about that?

(Transition into Lisa. Lisa is seventeen years old and very emotional. She takes a moment to consider her possibilities.)

LISA: Um, well, if something, were to happen to you, um, I don't . . . well, um. I don't want my mom to die. *(Begins sobbing.)* NO! I DON'T WANT MY MOM TO DIE!!! NO, NO, NO, NO, NO, NO!!! PLEASE DON'T DIE. PLEASE DON'T GO . . .

SHARON: Lisa, my God! Nobody wants to die, all right. That wasn't the question. Ok, this is exactly why I'm asking you now because if all you're gonna do is collapse and cry then forget it. I won't come back. I'll save my energy. Lauren, what about you? What do you think about that?

LAUREN: You want to know if you can come back and visit us — as a ghost?

SHARON: No, Lauren, as a zombie. Yes, a ghost. Girls, I don't understand this. No, your father was so excited when I asked him. We shared such a, such a, special evening. You know what Lisa? If you can't handle it, go in the hallway. OK? Well, then keep it down, please. I can't hear myself think. Girls, what if I forget to tell you something? Ya know, like were the lockbox key is —

LAUREN: It's under your desk. On the right side. You taped it there. You've showed us a million times, Mom.

SHARON: Well I may move it, Lauren! And if I move it, I'd like to know that I can come back and tell you that I moved it! Or maybe, I'd like to come back just to say hello or good-bye.

LISA: . . . good-bye. Don't say that!!!! *(Sobbing.)*

SHARON: OK, Lauren, yes or no? Huh?

LAUREN: OK. You can come back. But . . . it has to be in the middle of the day. OK? Um, with a bunch of people around — like at a festival or something like that. Or, no . . . this is it. This is it. OK, mom. Write this down. Put this in your will. It has to be on a Saturday in the mall, in the Limited Express — but not when I'm changing my clothes OK. Wait until I'm out among everybody else.

Yes . . . I do. I want you to come back. Especially if you're dead. I just don't want you, ya know, hovering and spinning over my bed in the middle of the night!

SHARON: If I could do that, I would think that you'd be pretty impressed. OK. You know what? We can talk about this later. All right? Lisa, are you going to be OK?

LISA: *(Sob sob.)*

SHARON: Thank you, Lisa. I'm flattered.

(Sharon exits. Lauren stands alone in shock.)

LAUREN: I don't want her to come back and visit us as a ghost. I didn't know what to say, I didn't want to be rude. I mean, I don't understand. Since when are carnival cruises so dangerous that people are making out wills and stuff. Maybe if it's so dangerous, maybe they shouldn't go.

LISA: *(Sob, sob, sob.)* OK, Lauren . . . you may not care if something horrible happens to mother, but I do. Well, you've got your adopt, your, ah, birth, the, the people who, I DON'T KNOW WHAT YOU CALL THEM! OK? I'm upset right now. But, I don't have a plan B, Mom. OK?! She's the only one I've got. God.

Scene Three. The Inquiry

SHARON: Sid? What are you doing? Are you sleeping? OK, when you wake up I need you to come in here and help Lisa and I unload the groceries. *(To Lisa as she breezes past her.)* Lisa, leave that and unload the dishwasher. *(Yelling upstairs to Lauren.)* Lauren! We're home! *(To Lisa.)* Because it's nice to help your mother, that's why.

(Lauren enters.)

There she is — *(Singing.)* "Miss America"! Oh she hates that. Oh poor Lauren. Oh, I'm so mean to ya — mean old mom. Listen, Lauren, you had something you wanted to ask me about? OK, you need to ask me now because I gotta whole bunch of stuff I need to do. *(Sharon begins to breeze right on to her next task but is interrupted by a transition into Lauren.)*

LAUREN: Well, it's sort of important. So, I'd rather wait because you seem busy. *(Transition into Sharon.)*

SHARON: I'm not busy. Just ask me now because I'm getting ready to . . . Hello Lisa. Hi. Could you do me a favor and stack those neatly. So I don't open the cupboard and have them all come falling out at me. *(Transition into Lauren.)*

LAUREN: I wanted to ask you about my *real mom.* *(Transition into Sharon.)*

SHARON: I am your real mom. *(Sharon gives a nervous laugh.)* There! That was easy! *(Sharon tries to leave the room. Transition into Lauren.)*

LAUREN: No, you know what I'm talking about. And, I'm not asking because it's some like, big huge, like trauma for me or something. It's not that. Because if anything, mom . . . I'm proud of it. You know, like in school, when we come back from summer vacation . . . and the teacher asks everybody, "So, what'd you do over your vacation?" I'm always like, "I'm adopted." And everyone goes "oh, my God, adopted girl." "Can I borrow your pencil, adopted girl?" So, it's not that it's some big . . . it's just that um, it's just that I um . . . I don't know what I look like. Ya know what I mean? Its like every time I see a picture of myself I look like this big white squish. And, well, people at school keep asking me about it. Like, like, like Wendy and Grandma.

Grandma said you tried to get my medical records for me because you were scared I was inbred or something like that. So, ya know, have you found those? Or maybe a picture of my birth mother somewhere. Um, that you hadn't given me. And Mom . . . Mom . . . if you did have a picture somewhere — I wouldn't obsess on it or anything. If that's what you're scared about. I won't always be walking around, all the time, thinking like, oh, my God, there she is. Or building a shrine around her or something . . . I'd just like to have it to have in a drawer someplace, just to look at once in a while. It'd be no big deal. I just think that whatever information you have, I'd, I'd, I'd like to know it. OK? So whatever you know, I think I'm ready. *(Transition into Sharon.)*

SHARON: I guess we were gone longer than I thought. Huh, Lisa? She's been home thinking, thinking. So, um Lauren, what brought this on all of a sudden? It's not like we found you in a dumpster . . . or something like that. Is that what you're scared about?

(Transition into Lauren.)

LAUREN: Grandma said that —

(Transition into Sharon.)

SHARON: You know what Lauren? Your grandma can't even remember what she had for lunch — OK? I don't know why you're pumping her for information. You know, if you've got questions about where you came from, you should ask the agency where we got you from. Well, we got you, at um . . . God, I can see the building, I can't think of what they're called. Isn't that horrible? You'd think I'd remember a thing like that, wouldn't you?

Hey Sid! What's that agency we got Lauren from, do you remember? Oh forget it. He's sleeping.

Is this why you've been going to Hebrew School, Lauren? Is it? Do you think you're Jewish? Do ya? Is that what Wendy Schenburg told you, that you're Jewish? Well, no . . . no you're not Jewish. OK? Yes actually, I do know that for a fact. Because they don't give away Jewish babies like that — you have to go through the . . . *(Struggling for the answer.)* Jewish Community Center. It takes a very long time. It's a very long process. You have to sing a series of songs, and you know what? You don't need to go to Hebrew school, OK? No, you don't. I know you want to do it all. I know you do. But you just can't. You do too much and you get sick and then you can't do anything at all, and that's no fun. Is it?

Lisa, did you see what you just about did? No, you just about shut the kitty in the cabinet.

(To kitty.) She's trying to kill you. Why is she trying to kill you like that? I don't know why she is.

(To Lisa) Just be careful. Watch what you're doing, please.

(To Lauren) All right . . . OK . . . Lauren . . . Do you want to know what you are? Do you want to know what you are? OK, I'm going to tell you what you are. You are what we are! Isn't she, Lisa?

(Sharon gives Lisa a punch on the arm.)

Help me out here, Lisa. And, let's see . . . my side of the family are the Huntingtons, and we are very proper English. Oh, yes *(With an English accent.)*. And your Father's side are the Weedmans. Weed-man — its probably German or something like that . . .

(Runs to the family room.)

Hey Sid! Is Weedman a German . . . Well Excuse me!!! When you wake up I'd like to know whether you're German or not!!! *(Runs back to the kitchen.)* You're German-English! That's exactly what you are! German-English! Go on upstairs and look it up on your map! Oh, it's so fun to see where you come from. It's perfectly natural.

(Sharon's festive mood suddenly drops.)

You do too have an identity. Yes you do! Ya know what? You're being a little dramatic. Yeah, you are! You know . . . we're not gonna do this right now. OK, no! Lauren, go upstairs and, and go think about something else. OK? Lauren, go upstairs and go put your head someplace else.

(Transition into Lauren walking into her room. She is absorbing her new information.)

Scene Four. German Hip Hop and Sister Love

Lauren's bedroom.

LAUREN: OK. I'll try. I'm German-English. OK. I can live with that. German.

(Thick German accent.)

I'm German, Ja, bitter glochin —

(Thick English accent.)

Oh, but I'm English. Oh, yes of course — delightful.

(Thick German accent.)

Nah! But I'm German. Oom Pa Pa, Oom Pa Pa.

(Thick English accent.)

Oh, but I'm English. Yes, here we go. Tea? Tea? Tea? Tea for everybody! *(From an English accent into a rap rhythm. Music blasts in — "Arrested Development." She begins dancing, much like the funk of the opening dance. Lauren notices that her sister, Lisa, has entered the room. Lauren shuts the music off. Transition into Lisa.)*

LAUREN: Lisa! Yeah, well, you're supposed to knock first. I have an assembly for Black Student Union tomorrow, I'm just trying to get ready.

LISA: Lauren, how did you get into Black Student Union? Don't you have to be black? Well, do they know you go to Hebrew school? And they don't care? Listen, I just wanted to tell you that if you decide that you're going to search for your real, um your, um birth — biological — whatever — I don't know what you call them. OK! I just hope you're not doing this because what Grandma says. Because she's crazy, Lauren! Yes she is. She tied mom to a tree.

I don't know if I ever told you this or not, but for a long time I thought you were like a foster child that was just staying with us for a while until your family came and got you? And when I found out that you were really my sister, and you were staying, I was so happy. OK? And that's always how I felt about you. So whatever you decide . . .
(Long pause as Lisa registers what Lauren is wearing. Her mood abruptly changes.)
Is that my sweater? Is it?!! You're not to wear my things. No, you are not! Will you take that off, please, fold it and put it outside my door. And fold it nicely. Arms crossing, like this. *(Begins to weep.)* I love you. OK? And that's what I wanted to tell you. So, you need to hurry up and change your clothes, because Mom's waiting downstairs to take you to Weight Watchers.

Scene Five. Sam's Visit

Sharon responds to the doorbell. Peering through the curtains to check who it is before answering. She is startled by who she sees. There is a pause before she is able to open the door. When she does open it — she doesn't open it entirely. Just a crack.

SHARON: Hello. Listen, if you're having car trouble or something why don't you go ahead and give me the number you want to call and I'll call it for you, OK. Because we don't let people use our phones.

Oh — oh — yes. OK, sure. I think she may be here. All right, well, you're going to have to let me check all right. I'm going to ask you to wait outside. Yeah, well, we have dogs. OK. All right. I appreciate that. I'm closing. *(Slams door shut and yells in a loud whisper to upstairs.)* Lauren! Lauren! There is a young black gentleman out there to see you. He was very tall. I told him to wait outside, OK. Because we have dogs. *(Transition into Lauren.)*

LAUREN: What?! You told him to wait outside because we have dogs! Are you joking? Well, no, he's not dumb, Mom! He can hear that there's no dogs barking — what are you thinking?

Yeah, well, I don't like the looks of some of your friends, but I still have to let them in the house! I don't have this luxury to decide who gets to come in and who doesn't get to come in like that. So, is . . . is Sam still out there? You didn't let him in when he said that he knew me? Oh my . . . oh, you don't even know who Sam is, do you? You have no idea. OK. Well, I'm gonna tell you who Sam is. OK? Sam is the fine looking man who is standing outside your door. OK! I am going downtown with the man. We are going to church!

(Lauren goes to open the door. Sharon grabs the handle —)

SHARON: Lauren! Until I'm done talking to you, you're not . . .

LAUREN: I'm letting him in, Mother.

SHARON: No, this is my house, all right! And when I say you can let him in . . .

LAUREN: I'm letting him in, Mom.

(The door is opened.)

SAM: She is here. How you doing, Lauren? Yeah, I'm good man, all right. I didn't get a chance to introduce myself before. I'm Sam. I'm a friend of Lauren's from school.

Whoa, whoa. Lets chill on the boyfriend stuff, OK. I'm trying to talk to your mother.

So is it cool? Are the dogs all put away? Yeah. I mean, I'm good with dogs and everything. Yeah know, as long as they're not trained to attack black folks or something like that.

SHARON: Oh, well, certainly not, Sam. My goodness. Listen, I'll, um, I'll tell you what . . . our cleaning lady hasn't been for the past month, and my God does it show. It looks like a cyclone hit us. I hate to let anybody see it when it, it's looking like this. She's been sick now for about a month. So, we're really behind in our, um, um . . . It's not anything serious, but, eh . . . You know, she's actually got the skin disease where you lose the color in your skin. Yeah, so, I'm not even sure what you call that. But, um . . . well, what do you call that? When you start to loose the color in your skin?

SAM: Ah, I don't know. I couldn't tell you. Yeah, well you know, it's hard for me to keep up with all the black folk diseases.

SHARON: Oh, well, I'm sure it is. That's not what I meant . . . but . . . well, we certainly do miss her. She's not dead or anything. But, hey! This is interesting . . . actually, Lauren, I don't even think I told you this. The last time she was here we were waiting for her ride in the library. We're looking out the window and up the driveway pulls a black Jaguar. I thought, now who is that? I don't know anybody who drives a car like that. Well, it turns out it is her son's car. He is a doctor. And he went to Yale or Harvard — I don't remember which, but very prestigious school. So, yeah! I thought that was real interesting. Ya know, we get to laughing because she has to wear real heavy pancake makeup to cover up where she's lost some of her color. We don't laugh about that, certainly! Um, eh, well, she gets it all over our phones and I'm always joking that she ends up leaving the house dirtier than when she got here!

SAM: Are you ready to go? Are you ready? Yeah, lets go! You're not her natural mother, right? You know what my mother's always telling Lauren? Well, she's got a feeling Lauren's got some African roots. Yeah, yeah! Ya know she's got a great grandmother somewhere that's gonna surprise you when you find out!

SHARON: That certainly would be a surprise. I don't think so, but we'll definitely keep that in mind. Well, it was such a pleasure to have met you, Sam. I hope you can come back some other time when our house isn't such a, you know, such a, ah, shamble . . . Lauren is that what you are wearing to church? Is it? OK, no, you are not. I didn't realize that'd be leaving the house, you know what? I'm going to get you a little sweater or something to to cover up. I'll be back. Pardon me for one second.

(Sharon exits to quickly retrieve the jacket. Lauren and Sam immediately start making out. They stop when Sharon re-enters. Lauren grabs her jacket.)

LAUREN: Thanks, Mom. Bye.

(Lauren turns and exits. Transition into Sharon. She has been stunned into a moment of silence. In her trance she slowly walks over to the family room.)

SHARON: Sid, on your way home from work tomorrow would you stop by the lock box and find out the name of the agency we got Lauren from? Thank you.

(Pause. Music: Track 3 "Run DMC Christmas Music" blasts in.)

Scene Six. Christmas at the Weedmans

Attempting to yell over the music and still keep the holiday spirit.

SHARON: I'm doing final table check everybody — So I need Lisa . . . Lisa! Lisa! Come in here! We need some toothpicks for the oysters and cocktail napkins for next to — I can't hear myself think. Hold on . . . LAUREN!!! ENOUGH!!! ENOUGH LAUREN! ENOUGH!

(Music out.)

OK, I'm losing my mind. We're just about ready to — *(Sharon begins laughing so hard that it's hard for her to speak.)* Oh my God! What do you have on your head? What is that? Well no, don't take it off! Don't take it off. It looks like a big glove or something stuck to the top of your head. Oh my, it's a stitch. Where did you find that? Was that in our closet? What made you think to put it on your head? You've got to go in and show your father. OK? No, No, just go in there and show him — it's a stitch — just — Lauren! *(Stops laughing.)* LAUREN, GO IN AND SHOW YOUR FATHER! *(Resumes laughing.)* Turn around so he can see the front of you. Sid! Sid! Look what she's got on her head. Oh no . . . she's joining a gang, Sid. We're gonna have to do an intervention. *(Runs to get Lisa.)*

Lisa! Come look at what your sister's got on her head. Get the camera. No, I got it, I got it. Remember Easter when she had that thing tied around her face?

Hold on . . . Merry Christmas! This is the Weedmans.

(All laughter completely leaves her body.)

Oh hi, Mom. Yeah, OK. No, we're just having some nibbles and then we're gonna open up some presents. OK?! And you're not missing . . . no, you're not missing anything, all right. Now, no you're not. Listen, I don't want to keep you. I know everybody really wants to say Merry Christmas to you. Here's Lisa, OK. She wants to say Merry Christmas to you so I'm gonna pass the phone.

(Whispering to Lisa as she hands the phone off. Transition into Lisa.)

She's crying.

LISA: Hi, Grandma, this is Lisa. Grandma, are you having a white Christmas? Is it snowing? Grandma, I can't understand you when you're crying. Can you try to stop? Can you try? Grandma, if you can't stop crying I'll just have to say Merry Merry and thank you for my presents. OK? Merry Merry Grandma, and thank you for my presents. Bye-bye.

I couldn't understand a word she was saying . . .

(Transition into Lauren.)

LAUREN: You hung up on Grandma. Why did you hang up on Grandma? No, I was waiting to talk to her. I was standing in line. I was right behind you. You were supposed to pass the phone to me. I just wanted to see if she got my presents or not.

LISA: We sent presents to Grandma! Did we? Well did someone put my name on a present to her? Why didn't you tell me. I could've asked her if she'd gotten it.

LAUREN: I don't see what the big deal is about having her here. I mean, once she gets here, she's fine, right?! Yeah, she's a little emotional and stuff, but you know, she doesn't bother me like she bothers you people. I'm calling her back . . .

SHARON: No Lauren! Please don't! She probably just got calmed down, and we don't want to get her all upset again. And you know, that I would love to have her here. Absolutely. But once she got here, nothing would please her. She'd complain about the food, she'd complain we weren't paying enough attention to her. And I can't fit more than seven people around my table. Not comfortably.

LISA: Grandma is crazy. She tied Mom to a tree. Twice.

LAUREN: You keep saying that! What does that mean? Maybe it was harder to find babysitters back then or something. I don't know. I'm just saying that's your blood . . .

SHARON: It's very sweet that you're defending your grandmother. OK! And I hope when I'm old and senile that you'll defend me too. But what I need from you right now is to go upstairs . . .

(Sharon grabs at Lauren's arm.)

LAUREN: Get off of me with your claws, OK. Oh, my God. Lisa! All right listen, I'm just trying to say to you, that old woman is your blood. *(Pause.)* Oh, OK! Grandma told me that Mom wouldn't let her hold me. All right?! So, fuck you!

(Transition into Sharon.)

SHARON: LAUREN!!! *(Pause.)* I have done final table check and we are about ready to eat! I want you to go upstairs, please, and go run a comb through your hair. And don't come back downstairs until you are in a better mood!! *(She watches Lauren exit. Notices the table.)* Get me some cocktail sauce. Put it by the shrimp, please. Boy, she's really got no respect for Christmas. Does she? Maybe she is Jewish.

(Transition into Tammy.)

Scene Seven. The Adoption Agency

Front desk of Indianapolis Adoption Agency. Tammy is an overly sincere, overly tall, state worker.

TAMMY: Mrs. Weedman? OK, Mrs. Weedman . . . you want to come away from those files, please? Yeah, you're not supposed to be looking at those files like that. Those are state files. OK. Well, now you know. That's all right. Come on in. Have a seat. I'm Tammy. I spoke to you on the phone. It's a pleasure to meet you as well. OK, I'm gonna ask you to have a seat there. And I'm going to ask you to stay in your seat during the duration of your visit? All right? OK. Get all that official stuff outta the way.

You realize that Lauren is a state baby. I know, I know. It's been illegal to search in the state of Indiana since 1952. Her files are sealed. That's difficult. Absolutely. But, you know what I would like to do for you? I'd love to steer you toward some adoption support groups. They're sponsored by the state. Most of those are made up of adoptees and birth mothers, but I can tell you right now, that I think an adoptive mother would be a very welcome aspect to a group. Yeah. You certainly may ask me, but I can't guarantee I'll have an answer. No, but it don't hurt to ask.

Uh-huh. OK. You know what, Mrs. Weedman? I think that if Lauren had suffered any sort of head trauma as a baby — we would have been obligated to tell you about something like that. Yeah, I think so. I think so. Is Lauren a teenager? Is she? No, no . . . I've got three! Not a day goes by that I don't wonder if somebody was beating their heads in the womb with a brick! I know, I know! Nooo, I'm afraid medical files are a part of that sealed file. Yeah, that's all right. There's no harm in asking. You know what? You know what I do want to do for you? I do have some notes that were written on the outside of Lauren's file. You may already know most of this stuff but I'd love to share it with you.

All right now, basically. You know what? I can read this to you. I've got it covered. OK, well, I appreciate your help. OK, she was born in Terre Haute, Indiana. Yes, Terre Haute — that's real pretty there. Real green. Lots of parks and stuff. My husband and I enjoy it. Her birth mother was fifteen years old. And her birth father was sixteen years old. Yeah, so they were real young. Yeah, yeah, I don't think they were drug addicts or anything. I know, I just don't think they were quite ready for the responsibility of a baby. That's all. Uh, huh. No, certainly, you understand . . .

(As she laughs at her own joke, she takes a quick look into the file and registers a piece of information that causes her to stop her laughter — realize her behavior and try to cover.)

That's all I have for you. I don't want to send you away empty-handed though. I'd like to give you, a letter, um, I'd like to . . . OK, now I'm gonna turn my back for one second and I'm gonna trust you're going to stay in your seat. OK! I'm back!

This is a copy of a letter that was in "Dear Abby," a while back. And basically it's from a birth mother's perspective. No, it's the second one down there. It's the one titled, "Don't Search For Me." Basically it's just saying, there's a reason I gave you up. Please respect that reason. You coming back in my life, just bring backs all the pain . . .

Here, I'll walk out with you . . . I just think that sometimes we get so caught up in what we want, we forget there's a whole other life out there we could be possibly . . . destroying. I think that if you give this to Lauren, it just may give her a sense of peace.

(Transition into Lauren.)

Scene Eight. Dear Abby Seizure

LAUREN: Where did you go? The place where you, you got me from? You did? What'd they say?

Well, I don't read "Dear Abby," Mom. I don't want it.

Mom! Mother! I put it on the floor.

(From this point until the end of this scene — Lauren is struggling to breathe.) You can pick it up and put it on the refrigerator. I'll read it later. *(Struggling to breathe.)* Gasp, gasp . . . mother . . . Sharon . . . gasp . . . Mom, come in here. I don't know. I don't know. I can't get my breath. Punching at my — I can't — I don't — It's like the wind is being knocked out of me. Wind out of —

(Lauren moves to the chair) I can't breath. It's like the feeling — remember the time when — remember when . . . when I fell off the swing set and I landed really hard —

Remember how . . . Remember . . .

Don't you remember? How could you not remember that? You were right there!

(Lauren is now huddled over trying desperately to catch her breath. Lights slowly begin to fade to black as Lauren continues to struggle to breathe.)

Scene Nine. A Support Group

Basement of church in Browsburg, Indiana. A group of people ranging in age and sex are sitting in a circle. Dan, the facilitator, is a middle-aged pot-bellied working-class man, a tough exterior and battling acid reflux.

DAN: Circle up. *(He sits.)* Welcome. *(He stands.)* Leslie, get in here. The group starts at eight o'clock, not 8:05. You realize that? You gotta hug for me? *(Hugs her. Starts to close the door.)* All right. Have a seat. *(Opens the door again.)* Tim, get your late butt in here. What are you doing? You going to shake my hand? Tim, it don't mean diddly to me if you're gay, straight, or half pig, you know I'm gonna hug you. Get over here. *(Hugs him. Sits back down.)* Welcome. If you're here because you have an addiction to pornography, that's down the hall, in the nursery. If you're here because your life's been touched by adoption, you stay put. You're in the right room. I'm Dan. I'm a facilitator. I'm not a leader. I'm not a doctor, I just play one on TV! *(Smirks at his own joke.)* We're gonna have a lot of laughs in here. And we're gonna have a lot of tears. It takes both to heal. We're gonna do a roundabout. I'll start and we'll take it on this way. Adoptee, January 6, 1942. Go ahead.

ANGRY WOMAN: Adoptee. May 19, 1984.

HOUSEWIFE: Birth mother. June 11, 1974.

TIM: Adoptee. August. 16ish.. 17ish.. 1965ish . . . 66ish . . . 64ish. OK. They don't know for sure. So, lucky me.

SHARON: OK. I'm Sharon Weedman. I was born May 26th . . . Oh, OK. I'm already breaking the rules. I have an adopted daughter. We have an adopted daughter. My husband couldn't be here today. Her name is Lauren. She was born March 5, 1969. So, we're not looking for her. We know where she is. We know her. Well, it's stretching it a bit to say we know her. I'm just here for a little insight.

DAN: All right Sharon, welcome. Go ahead and finish up the circle. *(Listens as the circle is finished.)* OK. Let's get wet. Let's dive in.

TIM: I'll be Esther Williams. I don't have my cap on, but . . . ! Well, I found out where my birth mother is living. And I thought the minute I had more information I'd act on it immediately, but people, she's living in Kentucky. OK! And I'm just not quite sure that I'm ready to haul myself down there and meet my uncle daddy. Yah know, to go all the way down to the land of "get off me paw, your crushing my smokes." OK? So, I'm just envisioning my birth mother right now and it's so much fun.

I can imagine her being like 400 pounds, like no teeth, living under a rock, with chili stains down her moomoo. I may just end up, sort of settling for a photo. I don't know. I hope none of you are from Kentucky. That's all. I'm done.

SHY WOMAN: Yeah, I, had a reunion, last month. I have some pictures. This is a picture of my birth father and his two children. And this is a picture of my birth mother and her three children. They're not together, any longer. Um, there's so much that I could go into. But I guess one of the things that has struck me, that I wasn't really prepared for, was that I all of a sudden have all these half brothers and sisters, that I didn't know I had. And one thing I thought that was interesting was that my birth father took his two and sat them down, and told them that a long time ago he'd made a mistake and that this mistake was back. And, so when I met them for the first time, they were scared of me. But my birth mother took her three kids out to dinner. And they went out, and they were having pizza and there were balloons tied to the chairs and then a big cake came. And she said, "Guess what we're celebrating? You have a big sister and she's coming back. On Wednesday." And so even though they had no idea about me, they were like, oh, balloons, cake, sister, good.

So, when I met them for the first time I was at my birth mother's house and I was looking out the window and a school bus pulled up. And they were running so hard to try to get to the house to see me that they were dropping all of their school papers as they were running. Then they brought groups of little neighborhood kids over to just watch me for the next week, you know, to watch me brush my teeth . . . and to look at my toes, because, we . . . have the same toes. So. I've had an interesting couple of months.

SHARON: I'm sorry . . . can I ask . . . how do you do something like that. I mean, how do you even begin the search . . . or . . .

DAN: Sharon, we don't discuss searching here. We're just a support group only. OK?

SHARON: Oh, OK. So, I'm breaking the rules again. I'm sorry . . . I didn't get the list of what not to do when I came in. Well, now I know. Now I know. I apologize. I'm sorry, OK . . . I'm sorry. I just have to ask, I mean, you were a state baby, right? So how do you even take the first step? If you were adopted through Indiana . . . then you . . .

TIM: Sharon! Sharon! You look thirsty. You look parched. Let me show you where the water fountain is. OK? Come with me. We'll be right back. *(Whispering.)* I want you to meet me at Corner of 71st and Meridian at

the Pizza Hut. You'll go into the third booth. You tell the waitress you want breadsticks, no sauce. BREADSTICKS, NO SAUCE!
(Sharon reacts with silent confusion.)

Scene Ten

Back at the Weedman household.

SHARON: Lauren, come down here, please. I'm undercover! I want you to stand right over there. You can watch me. This is my HQ. Headquarters. Today, we're going to be calling a Miss Rhonda Mayhew of Terre Haute, Indiana. This is my script.
(Yelling upstairs.)
Nobody talk to me — I'm making an undercover call!
(Back to the phone.)
Yes, hello. Is this miss Rhonda Mayhew?
(Reading from her script.)
Oh hello, Rhonda. My name is Ruth Robinson. I'm calling from the Terre Haute Alumni Association. We're calling all of our alumni to see how they enjoyed their education with us. How did you enjoy your education with us, Rhonda? Oh. OK. Well, I gotta cut you off 'cause we've gotta lot of stuff to get to, Rhonda. Now, do you remember, sometime during your junior, your senior year, one of your female classmates being absent six to nine months of the year — perhaps due to an illness or a PREGNANCY?! Oh! Could you hold on one moment, Rhonda, I've got another phone call. Hold on a second. *(Puts hand over receiver.)* Sid! I've got another phone call. What do I do again? *(Back to Rhonda.)* OK, all right Rhonda, Rhonda, I'm clicking you over. Hold on. *(Clicks over.)* Hello? Yeah, he's here, he's napping. Call back later. I'm undercover. *(Clicks over.)*
Hello? Hello? I got disconnected. Oh well, it doesn't matter because she didn't sound a bit like you. But did you see that, Lauren? That's what I've been doing all day long!
(Transition into Lauren.)
LAUREN: What are you doing? Why are you wearing a wig, Mom?
(Transition into Sharon.)
SHARON: I'm undercover, Lauren. I told you that.
(Transition into Lauren.)

LAUREN: You're on the phone. What difference could it make? Where did you get those from? Are those mine or something? What are you doing?

(Transition into Sharon.)

SHARON: I needed a disguise. Because I went to Terre Haute High School today and I stole fifteen yearbooks! I just walked right by the lady with two big stacks like this! She didn't say a thing to me. And I've been sitting here all day long, going through these yearbooks. So what I do is I circle anybody's picture that looks even remotely like you. And there's a lot of them, Lauren. OK! There's a lot of them! Then I look them up in information. That's what I've been doing all day long.

(Transition into Lauren.)

LAUREN: Why are you doing this? "Did Dear Abby" tell you to do this or something?

(Transition into Sharon.)

SHARON: You wanted a picture, didn't you? Didn't you want a picture? OK, well, I'm gonna get you a picture. Now listen, my A.D. and I have a feeling — my Assistant Detective, OK. I met him at my adoption support group meeting . . .

(Transition into Lauren.)

LAUREN: You're going to adoption support group meetings too?! Shouldn't I be going? I'm the one who's adopted, Mom. Don't they ask you where I am? How do you get in?

(Transition into Sharon.)

SHARON: Lauren! A lot of things are going to be happening in the next week or so that I won't be able to be discussing with you. Because I'm going undercover! I just told you that! Now listen, my A.D. and I feel that by the end of the week we are going to have a picture of your B.M. Your birth mother! I call her your B.M.! Isn't that funny? I came up with that all . . .

(Transition into Lauren.)

LAUREN: No, Mom! That's not funny. Don't call her that.

(Transition into Sharon.)

SHARON: Laurennn! By the end of this week I'm gonna have a picture of your BM!

(Transition into Lauren.)

Scene Eleven. Mother Montage

In Lauren's bedroom.

LAUREN: By the end of this week I'm gonna have a picture of my B.M. Mother. Yeah, I do have something I'd like to say. How could you do that to me? How could you forget about me like that? Didn't you realize that they'd make me go to Weight Watchers? How could you do that? How could you forget about a baby like that?
(Helen Reddy's "You and Me Against the World" begins to play. Lauren is confronted by the first in a series of mother images. All, which is led and fed by music.)
Why no, Mother. I'm not angry with you, why would I be angry with you? You're too pretty to be mad at. Oh, my gosh, Mom look at your hair flip! I got so much I want to tell you about I don't know where to start. You're so pretty, I knew you would be. What's that smell, Mom? Is that cookies? Now how do you go smelling like cookies? Is that in a jar or something? Me too! I know! Sometimes I just start laughing and I don't know why! Me too!
(Heavy grunge music.)
What are you doing, Mother? Yeah, you better come back here. You gotta take responsibility for what you did, man. You can't leave a baby in a dumpster and think that shit's all right. You gotta take a look at yourself, Mom! Where you going? What do you think you're doing? You can't walk away from me — don't you dare try to walk away from me! Well, I don't feel like looking at your face either but you can't walk away from your responsibility. Come back here! I'm talking to you! Come back!
(Italian music.)
Hey, Momma — its me — I'ma back, Momma! Feed your baby, huh? Mozzarella . . . . hey, Giovanni, I slap you like — a this . . .
(New Age music.)
Mother, I had this dream about you, and in this dream, you were this blue vapor, and you went swirling into my center, and then I went swirling into your center, and then you were in me, and I was in you, and you were in me, and I was in you, and you were back in me, and then you went out the top of my head like a beautiful fountain of love.
(Runway model music.)
I knew you'd be tall, Mother, and I knew you'd be gorgeous, but this is creepy. It's like a mirror.

(Irish music.)

Yeah. I know who you are. I recognize ya. No, I don't feel like doin' a jig right now. Jeez!

(Tribal music. Lauren does a tribal birthing dance. Spanish music.)

Mi madre — Mi corazon — Mi madre. They call me Laurita, madre. Yo no se. Laurita.

(Aretha Franklin's "Chain of Fools" comes in. The dream has been realized.)

No, no, no, I had a feeling. I always had a feeling. Yeah, I'm coming in. Shoot, why would I wanna wait outside? Go ahead, girl.

(She begins her celebration dance to and with Aretha.)

Scene Twelve. Tour Guide, The Weedman Household

LAUREN: Wendy, do you want something to drink? We have Coke, Diet Coke, Diet Mountain Dew, Diet Cherry 7-Up, regular 7-Up, Squirt, Sprite, raspberry seltzer, and like, lemon-lime stuff. You don't want this. No you don't. It's probably like Mountain Dew, Dr. Pepper, and Diet Coke or something. You don't . . . OK, listen. My mom takes all the half-drunk coke cans I leave around the house, and she condenses them into this handy tumbler for me and I'm not allowed to open up another can of Coke until I finish drinking this, OK? So you want some? You don't want any? You don't want to drink my backwash? It's not just my backwash, either, it's the whole family's backwash. I'm not the only one who leaves coke cans around. Yeah, of course I'm gonna drink it. Because I would never disrespect my mother's rules like that, I'm not like you!

(Pretends to drink and then pours it out.)

No I'm not going to drink it, shut up! Please! OK, well just don't ever tell me your mother's crazy, OK? What, because she makes you do sit-ups? That is not crazy. Oh, OK, well then, have I shown you my list of house rules? Have you seen that? I haven't shown you that? Oh, OK, you gotta look at this.

(She opens a new can of soda. Takes a sip.)

Ewe. I didn't want that.

(Opens a new one. Goes to list. Reads from it.)

OK, Lauren's house rules. Number one, no shoes on the steps, which is like, a big thing with her. Number two, if you open a can of coke, be sure to, OK, you already know about that. Number three, stay out of the pantry unless accompanied by an adult . . . OK, this one. The other night, we were watching TV, and my mom comes in and she goes, "Well I was going to make cookies for everyone, but SOMEBODY ate my bag of brown sugar." She thinks I ate a bag of brown sugar. Like I'm sitting in a closet somewhere with a bag of brown sugar and stick of butter sitting there eating it like that. No, I have been at the doctor, when she says, in front of me, she's like, "I don't know why Lauren keeps getting fatter. I'm feeding her the same food everyone else's eating. No one else is getting fat from it."

What? What is what? What are you talking about? No, that's not brown sugar! That's, um, that's flour from before you came over. I was really hungry so I ate a bag before you came over.

That's the whole thing with this, like, list of house rules . . . so, so like I don't forget what I'm not supposed to do. So I'm in my room one day, if I'm like cleaning my gun and I go, "Wait a minute. Am I allowed to have a gun?" I can run over and check the list. "Gun . . . gun . . . gun . . . nope, not on the list! Guess it's OK!" I don't know. Oh please! No, no, OK, listen . . . did I show you what my dad did? OK.

Follow me. Do you see that? That's the living room. I'm not allowed to sit in there unless I'm with a guest. And you don't count. Wait a second. So that's my parent's room, that's Lisa's room and my room. Notice anything a little different? Yeah! My parents' room and Lisa's room both have chains and combination locks on them! My room has no locks. From the outside, inside, nothing . . . I can't lock it. I don't know. Because they don't want me going in touching their stuff I guess. It's really nice at night when everybody's coming home and they're all trying to guard their combinations so I can't see.

But I take a screwdriver and take all the screws out, and the whole thing comes off and I go right in. I don't know. I just go in and look at stuff, ya know.

If I find my birth mother? I'm, I'm still gonna call my mom my mom. What are you talking about? I'm not gonna stop . . . that's Lisa's. OK, she doesn't like it when I'm looking at her door. Come on.

Scene Thirteen. Grandma's Death

Lisa is deeply yet not deeply sobbing throughout.

LISA: Hi, Wendy. Um, Lauren, you need to ask your friend to come home right now because we have some family business that we need to take care of. OK? I'm sorry, Wendy.

Lauren, Grandma's dead. Grandma died. I miss her sooo much. Already. I just keep thinking about how, um, you know how we don't have a grandpa, and everything. Well now, now we don't have a grandma either! *(Stops crying.)*

I'm in charge of flowers, OK. Mom says. I'm thinking a lot about pink, 'cause Grandma really liked that color. So, you need to get yourself packed and bring two nice outfits. There's one for the visitation and one for the funeral. It's just like Grandpa's funeral — but don't wear the same clothes because a lot of the same people will probably be there. Oh my God . . . *(Sobbing.)*

LAUREN: *(Seizure begins.)* Gasp, gasp, gasp. Oh, Gram, Gram . . .

"Wade in the water. Wade in the water children."

What am I doing? Why am I singing the slave song?

"Amazing grace. How sweet . . . "

(She ends singing as soulfully and deeply as she can until she suddenly stops. She notices Sharon in the room. Gets up off the floor.)

SHARON: What are you doing? OK, you know what? I wouldn't put my face so close to the carpet here. Not until I vacuumed. Did Lisa come talk to you? OK, we have a very busy couple of days ahead of us. I need you to get yourself a little organized if you would. And start thinking . . .

No! No Lauren! No, Sam can't come. No. Because we're not bringing dates, OK. Because we're not bringing boyfriends. It's not the prom! Not this time. Maybe next time. OK? Yeah! No, it is not because he's black! Oh my God! Don't start. Listen, I need you to be thinking about some music, that you think, that Grandma . . . What was that? Hold on a sec. *(Yells down the steps.)*

Sid! What is that? Well, it sounds like one of the kitties is up on the table. Would you check, please? Just get the spritzer bottle and spritz them down. All right! *(Back to Lauren.)*

Listen, I want you to think of maybe some music you think that she would enjoy. That, that, you could . . .

(Back to Sid.)
What is he doing? Sid, what are you doing? You don't have to get up! Just show him the bottle. He knows what it means . . . I can't do two things at one time. Forget it. I'll do it myself. Thanks for your help, Sid. I appreciate it.
(Back to Lauren.)
Lauren, get yourself packed. We're leaving in four hours.
(Transition into Lisa.)

Scene Fourteen. At Grandma's House

LISA: It's so weird. Being at grandma's house. She's just — not here. It's like she's dead.
(Lisa begins to sob. Transition into Lauren.)
LAUREN: Lisa, when's the last time you saw Grandma?
(Transition into Lisa.)
LISA: Lauren, she was my Grandma. OK? She was my only grandma. you may end up with two or five or six or something, if Mom ever finds your real — your biologi — your — I don't know what you call them! OK! I am upset right now. God! Mom, can I have this lamp in here? Thank you. I miss Grandma.
(Lisa's energy abruptly changes and she speeds through the following instructions.)
OK, listen, Lauren . . . listen, you need to pay attention. Greet people at the door and take their dish from them. And bring it over to the table. If it's a hot dish make sure you put a hot pad so we don't ruin Grandma's table. You know how she liked to keep her things nice. And if it's a cold dish then put it right in the freezer. Have everyone sign their name, what they brought, and their address.
　　So we can write thank yous. I'm writing them. Yes I am. Because mother asked me to, and my handwriting's nicer. Here comes Mom. Here comes Mom. Hi, Mom! How you holding up? You OK?
(Transition into Sharon.)
SHARON: I found Grandmother's diary. And I wasn't ever aware she kept one. I thought maybe I could share this with you girls.
(She opens it and begins to read.)
OK, here we go. "September first . . . I have been cooking since eight o'-clock. It is so hot in the kitchen that I ended up opening both the front

and the back window. Even then, it's not enough of a draft to really cool off the house." OK, kinda boring. . . . Oh boy, more weather reports. Never mind. Sorry. Oh! That's interesting, "Omaha couple adopts Russian baby. Welcome Home Vladimir!" "Adoption — the Loving Choice — a Christian Perspective." Oh, Lauren, look. We've got this one. Look at this, "Don't Search For Me." Yeah, we've got this one. Look at this. Oh, um, "My Two Mommies." Oh gosh. Well, she thought of you. That must be nice to know. You know what? I'm just gonna set this here and we can look at it at our leisure. We need to get ready to go. We need to be at the home in about ten minutes . . .

LAUREN: Before we go could I share some music that I wrote for Grandma, real quick?
(She takes a long pause and then busts out in a beat-box beat and begins to rap.)
Going away and never coming back
Let me tell you all about thing called Black —
If I'm ever gonna say good-bye
Listen to my spirit when you hear it cry
Grandma's gone but the rhyme lives on
They're busting it in heaven. Ding dong live long.
(Transition into Lisa. Lisa is standing and screaming with all her midwest might.)
LISA: Ahhh, ahhhh. Stop it! Stop it! Mother! Lauren! That is so inconsiderate. Grandma didn't even know any black people! God!
(Transition into Sharon outside the funeral home.)

Scene Fifteen. The Calling, Gospel Seizure, Funeral Home

SHARON: Weedmans. Could I get the Weedmans, please? We're going to go in, and, we're gonna go see Grandma in her casket. I just want us all to go in as a family. Here we go. Oh, well, it's not as, um, stuffy as it was this afternoon. I was hoping they'd open up a window or something.
(Sharon makes a slow walk to the casket, deeply struggling with her grief.)
There she is. Oh, Mother. Oh my. Doesn't she look nice, Sid? Doesn't she? Yeah she does. Yes she does. Can you all see down there? Lauren, don't lean on there. It's not a table.

Yeah, that's the ah, that's the suit that she wore for her church photo.

Because she thought she looked so pretty in it. And she really does, doesn't she. Yeah she does. Absolutely. Yeah, she really knew her color. Yeah, yeah. I would've chosen that myself. The, the, um, Sid . . . can you excuse me for one second? So I can try to . . .

(Sharon notices flowers.)

Excuse me, Lisa. OK. Do you see that? No. Well, no. It's my lily plants. Do you see where they are? No, well, I wanted them elevated beside the casket. That was the whole point of ordering two. All right, so what is the mortician's name again? Bob? That doesn't sound right . . .

(Sharon yells for Bob down every hallway she can find.)

Bob! There he is. OK. Hello. Hi. Hi Bob! Hi. Yes, well, I'm Sharon Weedman. I spoke to you on the phone. Irene was my mother. That's right. So, so, did you know her in life? Did you? Yeah. Well, no, I thought you did! You got her mouth just right, Bob. She looks like she looked when she was angry. Which she was much of the time! Absolutely. Well, we'll certainly miss her.

Anyway, listen. I'm a bit concerned about the flowers, right now, this lily plant right behind you . . . Yes, thank you. But actually wanted them elevated beside the casket. Oh, perfect! No, that'll be fine. That was exactly . . . Oh, OK . . . well that was easy, huh. OK. That's fine. All right.

(Her social demeanor stays intact until Bob is clearly out of sight.)

Listen, Lisa, when people come in with the flowers I want you to greet them. And if you don't recognize their name, I want you to put them on this side of the church. OK? Now if you do recognize the names I want you to put them over here.

(Transition into Lauren.)

LAUREN: Mom. Are you OK? Why are you obsessing on the flowers?

(Transition into Sharon.)

SHARON: I can do what I want! All right?! I just lost my mother! *(Pause.)* Now I lost my train of thought. Where was I? Flowers, right. Thank you, Lisa . . . .Thank you.

So if you don't recognize their names it's probably her bridge or her church friends. Just, put them over there. That way, Sid, 'cause you remember at Daddy's funeral when the Snodgrasses said they sent the flowers and never did see those. And that way we can keep track. Well, I think its fair for both parts. So they can know they got there, and we can also tell them what it looked like if they didn't have a chance to come by . . . and, you know what, Lisa? Go ahead and spread the flowers out all along the side of the wall. You know so that way, it won't get all sort of cramped in, like, I think that's always nice. People can see what the arrangements looked like. And we can see the tags better. And, um, lets use the back wall for potted plants! The back wall for potted plants! OK! I think that's nice to bring in potted plants, and we can bring them home with us . . . or something sure, sure . . . .

(Sharon continues obsessing. Music: track 5 "Gospel" rises on Sharon's babbling "potted plants.")

Scene Sixteen. Six Months Later, The Eagle Has Landed

Back at the Weedman household the phone rings.

LAUREN: I got it! Weedmans. Sorry, HQ. Yeah, she's here. Oh, is that right. No, that's great. No, no . . . hold on, I'll ask her. Mom! Your A.D. is on the phone and he's got a B.M. update. You want it?

OK, well, it looks like for 500 dollars you can get the name of my birth mother just like that, because he bribed some guy in the hospital to type my name in the computer and her name came right up.

So do you want to do it? Do you really? No, I don't care what you do. Do what you want, it's your money. Hold on. How can I care, Mom? My God. In the last nine months you've had three leads, OK. And none of them were her. One of them was Asian. I'm not Asian. OK! We don't want to rule that possibility out. We don't know for sure. I don't think so! Yes! Absolutely. When you find her, and you KNOW it's her, you bring her to me. I want to meet her. But until then, I can't take it anymore. So just do what you want.

This is so clearly not about me. Mom, you want to know what this is about? This is about *Murder She Wrote.* Yeah it is. Denial just ain't a river in Egypt my friend. Yeah, check yourself.

Hey, Tim? She's good for the 500 man. It's a go. No, you can just tell me. "Diane. Diane McQuillen." Oh, boy. She likes that. Yeah, that sounds English. That makes her happy. Uh huh. Is that 317 area code? OK. She knows. She's been doing it for the last . . . OK, OK, I'll reminder her. Thank you. You too. Bye. *(Lauren hangs up.)*

OK, Mom. Here ya go. Here's your name and everything. Now remember, don't call her directly. Get someone from your adoption support group to call her, or whatever. It's the same thing you've been doing, so . . .

(Transition into Sharon. She grabs the paper out of Lauren's hands.)

SHARON: Give it to me. OK. I'm calling her right now! Yes I am. I'm skipping the group. I've been waiting on this one. Where are you going? No, no, now I want you to stay right there! I want you to watch me call. OK? Oh my God!

(Sharon runs to the family room.) Sid! Sid! *The eagle has landed, Sid!* The eagle has landed! I got her!! We got her.

(Sharon runs to the staircase.) Lisa!! Lisa! Landed Lisa!! Landed!!

(Sharon runs back to the phone.) OK. I gotta have my notes with me. No, I just going to have to wing it, I'm just going to have to wing it. AHHH! AHHH! Look at that! Look at that! Sid's in the kitchen. Sid's in the kitchen. Make him feel welcome. Make him feel welcome everybody . . . of course you're welcome Sid! Come on in. Look at that . . . it's your father.

OK everyone.

(Dials the phone.)

Diane McQuillen. Diane. Oh my God. It's so funny. It was such a popular name a while back. I knew four or five Dianes growing up just in my neighborhood. Did you as well Sid? Yes you did. Oh it was a very popular name. Oh, I'm going to have a heart attack. Can you imagine? Right before I call her? I'm like oh, ah, choke . . . I'm dead.

(Suddenly sober.)

Hello? Ah yes, is this Diane McQuillen? Um, Diane my name is . . . Sharon Weedman and . . . does the birth date March 5th, 1969 mean anything to you? Ah huh. OK.

(There is pause as Sharon listens to the voice on the other end of the phone. Then very quietly she informs the family.)

It's her. It's her.

(Back to Diane.)

Oh, my God. Oh, my God, Diane. You have no idea how long we've been looking for you! You have no idea. Oh, my God . . . I can't believe it.

No, my name is Sharon Weedman. Uh huh. And I'm her mother. I mean, you're her mother! You're her mother. Oh OK . . . she gets it. She gets it! She's all right! No, I've been looking for the last nine months. I've been writing a book. It's called, *I searched. I found.* And I did, didn't I? Yes I did. Yes I did. Final chapter, huh Diane. Final chapter. Yeah, absolutely. What? No, no, Lauren. She's right here. She's in the kitchen with me. Yeah Diane, she's in the kitchen all the time. Yeah, 'cause she loves to eat. Do you love to eat? Do ya? *(To the rest of the family.)* OK! It's her. We got her for sure! *(Back to Diane.)* Oh Diane. Thank you so much for her. We've just had so much fun with her. She has just been great. OK, listen, I've got a bunch of stuff I wanna ask you about because I gotta start working on my book, but I can't hear you cause my husband's yelling at me. Yeah, hold on.

Sid, what do you want? Oh yeah! Lauren, wanna to talk to her? Go upstairs and pick up the phone in your room!

OK, OK, so now tell me, are you married? Oh you're divorced. *(Aside.)* She's divorced! Any kids? Oh my goodness, you surely do have kids. Absolutely. OK, so now, now, when's your birthday? Oh you're a Pisces! Lauren's a Pisces too! Oh, but I guess you know that. I'm telling things you already know, huh.

(Transition into Lauren. She slowly crosses to her phone in her room.)

Scene Seventeen. Final Scene

Lauren listens to Sharon talking and talking to Diane on the phone.

LAUREN: Mom? Mother! Hey, could you hang up the phone? Just for one second, please? So I have a chance to . . . OK, OK. Thank you. Thanks. *(Pause.)*
Hi.
(Aretha Franklin's "Think" swells as Lauren listens to the voice on the other end finally dropping the phone and moving to the music, which dances her offstage. Music: track 6 "Closing" begins to rise as Lauren looks up. Lights fade to dance lights as Lauren stands. Celebration Dance.)

END OF PLAY

Lapis Blue Blood Red

By Cathy Caplan

For Cas and Caswell

PLAYWRIGHT'S BIOGRAPHY

Cathy Caplan's plays include *Lapis Blue Blood Red,* about the seventeenth-century painter Artemisia Gentileschi, and *Photographing Women,* which recreates photographs from 1930s Berlin and received new play commissions from the New York State Council on the Arts and the National Foundation for Jewish Culture. She coauthored *hair, blood, vinyl* with Rinde Eckert and the Juggernaut Theatre Company for the 1997 New York International Fringe Festival. She has explored alternate narrative structures in dramatic scripts for Grahame Weinbren's interactive cinema installations, *Sonata* and *March.* She was a Juilliard playwriting fellow in 1992–1993, a Mabou Mines artist-in-residence in 2000, and one of the three-member team that codirected and edited the Academy Award–winning documentary film, *American Dream,* produced by Barbara Kopple.

INTRODUCTION

In 1990, I finished working on the documentary *American Dream,* which went on to win the 1991 Academy Award for best documentary. For seven years I had been one of the three member team that codirected and edited the film. From his crib in the editing room, my infant son Cas watched me look at hundreds of hours of footage, finding moments of conflict and suggestive interactions that could be woven together into a narrative. When *American Dream* was released, Cas was four and I was ready to apply what I had learned from film editing to another area. I came across Mary Garrard's *Artemisia Gentileschi: The Image of the Female Hero in Italian Baroque Art,* the first monograph on the seventeenth-century Baroque woman painter, published in 1989. The appendix included a transcript of the 1612 trial, where Artemisia's father accused his business partner of raping his daughter, and I realized that this transcript could form the basis of a play. The record of the trial was a window into the lives of Baroque artists; though not a completely accurate picture, since most of the testimony was contradictory, and it is apparent that many of the protaganists lied, exaggerated, or obfuscated the facts — for a variety of reasons.

In an attempt to comprehend the texture of Artemisia's day-to-day existence, I attended a Renaissance life-drawing class at the New York Academy of Art taught by Randy Melick. The class began with a short lecture, such as how to draw a figure using only circles. All the other art students listened carefully to his lecture and then proceeded to ignore his assignment. The teacher expected this. I was the only one, the nonartist, who ploddingly tried to follow his technique. I continued my research posing for the artists Jacob Collins and Kate Shephard. Standing cold and stiff for hours, I began to understand the psychological connection of model and painter.

I went to Rome and visited the prison where Artemisia's alleged rapist Agostino Tassi was eventually incarcerated. Because it was a Sunday, the jail, now a museum, was closed. The guard agreed to let me in, on condition that my son and husband wait outside. He closed the heavy wooden door and took me upstairs to show me the jail cells and various instruments of torture. While alone in one of the cells, he pressed me up against the wall. I quickly pushed him aside and made my way back downstairs (I was nearly twice his height) and started banging on the heavy wooden door. For a moment the past and present had collided. I was happy to see the faces of my son and husband waiting in the street.

While writing the play, I was called for jury duty. Every day I'd report in and then I'd move around to the different floors, looking for rape cases in progress. Usually there were one or two. The sex crimes officer is the modern equivalent of the notary in Artemisia's time. He takes the victim's testimony in private and then presents her often disturbing, personal, and graphic description in the public courtroom, which he reads in a monotone, expressionless voice. I realized most date rapes have no witnesses, both now and four hundred years ago. The victim's case rests on character and credible narrative. Just as the lawyers have to create a believable story with very little evidence to convince the jury, I had to sift through contradictory testimonies to create a plausible story of Artemisia's entanglement with Agostino.

In many ways, *Lapis Blue Blood Red* has stylistic elements in common with cinema. I had in mind two actresses of different ages playing Artemisia at two stages of her life, with transitions between scenes very tight and possibly overlapping. Most scenes revolve around a particular painting, making that painting as important an element in the scene as any of the spoken words.

Lapis Blue Blood Red was developed in many stages, through many versions, over many years. It began in a director/writer/actor workshop run by Bob Moss; it was greatly enhanced under the influence of Tina Howe at the Sewanee Writers Conference. It was the basis for my acceptance at the Juilliard Playwrights-in-Residence program. Through the influence of Gwynn MacDonald, it was produced in Baltimore by the Splitting Image Theatre Company with the artistic guidance of Lori Kranz, James Magruder, and Charlotte Stoudt. The play developed and grew from readings at Naked Angels, the Robert Maxwell Playwriting Series, Guild Hall, and the Feigen Gallery. In 2002 it was presented by the Juggernaut Theatre Company at the HERE Arts Center in New York City.

I met Mary Garrard early in the process. She most generously recognized that the goal of the writer is different from that of the art historian. This play, like a number of other recent projects based on Artemisia's life, could not have been written without Mary Garrard's groundbreaking work.

ORIGINAL PRODUCTION

Lapis Blue Blood Red was presented by the Juggernaut Theatre Company at the HERE Arts Center in New York City, opening on February 11, 2002. The director was Paul Smithyman. The sets were by David Barber; the lighting was by Tyler Micoleau; the costumes were by Loren Bevans; the sound was by Eben Bull. The cast, in order of appearance, was as follows:

NAPLES (1638)

FRANCESCO/NOTARY .... Dustin Smith

PRUDENZA .... Natalie Arkus

ARTEMISIA (1638) .... Meg Gibson

ROME (1612)

ARTEMISIA (1612) .... Erica Berg

ORAZIO .... Scott Sowers

TUZIA .... Chandler Vinton

COSIMO .... Peter Blomquist

AGOSTINO TASSI .... C. J. Wilson

NOTARY .... Dustin Smith

CHARACTERS

1638

ARTEMISIA GENTILESCHI: Forty-two years old, painter.

PRUDENZA: Twenty-two years old, Artemisia's daughter.

FRANCESCO: Twenty-seven years old, Artemisia's brother.

1612

ARTEMISIA GENTILESCHI: Sixteen years old, painter-in-training.

ORAZIO GENTILESCHI: Forty-five years old, painter, Artemisia's father.

AGOSTINO TASSI: Thirty-three years old, painter.

COSIMO QUORLI: Forty-five years old, orderly and agent.

TUZIA: Thirty-three years old, upstairs tenant.

NOTARY

SETTING

The action of the play alternates between a painting studio in Rome, 1612, and a painting studio in Naples, 1638.

In the Renaissance, portable collapsible furnishings such as clothing trunks, folding easels, trestle tables, screens, and bathtubs on wheels were common, and each room served a variety of functions — painting, cooking, sleeping, conversation, bathing, dressing, and eating. The play replicates these aspects of seventeenth-century life — the actors set and clear furniture in full view of the audience as the requirements of the different scene changes.

Lapis Blue Blood Red

Act I

Scene One: Naples 1638. Painting Studio

Prudenza is posing nude as Bathsheba. Her right arm is hanging behind the chair and resting on a writing table not in the painting. She is taking dictation while she poses. Artemisia is sitting at an easel in front of almost completed David and Bathsheba. *Unfinished* Judith Slaying Holofernes *is off to the side.*

ARTEMISIA: When I started painting the background, I realized the central figure was all wrong for the painting. I have had to start again from the beginning. I must caution your most illustrious lordship that when I ask a price, I don't follow the custom in Naples, where they ask thirty and then give it for four. I am Roman, and therefore I shall act always in the Roman manner. Already I am losing money. I gave you an excellent price. What happened? You moved.

PRUDENZA: That is what happens when I am taking dictation and posing at the same time. I move.

ARTEMISIA: You can write and pose at the same time. I'm only working on your left arm. Write with the other one.

PRUDENZA: Stop painting. Finish dictating the letter. Then you can finish the painting.

ARTEMISIA: I gave you an excellent price.

PRUDENZA: I've got that. I wrote that already.

ARTEMISIA: If you were here with me, you would never ask me to lower my price. I have to watch fifty women undressing before I find one that has good enough proportions for me to use.

PRUDENZA: Your daughter.

ARTEMISIA: And then, if I find a good one, I have to sit with her all day and suffer her pettiness, her achiness, her whining . . .

PRUDENZA: Whining . . . yes.

ARTEMISIA: All of this, I suffer with the patience of Job. That one goes to Antonio Ruffo in care of his brother.

PRUDENZA: Patience of Job.

ARTEMISIA: Next. The viceroy. Most illustrious sir and respected master, I have almost finished *Judith Slaying Holofernes*. The painting could be completed immediately upon receipt of fifty ducats so that I can purchase the Lapis Lazuli needed to execute Judith's dazzling blue dress.

PRUDENZA: We haven't run out of lapis lazuli.

ARTEMISIA: I have painted the subject with the utmost care, placing the figures in the midst of pitch blackness with a bright light on their foreheads and forearms. I have painted Judith so that she bears a resemblance to myself. If the painting gives you no pleasure at all, then it is worthless to me. And if that alone doesn't satisfy you, you may lash the image of the artist, who is still aching from the cold endured while doing this work. I depend on your kindness while I remain sole provider for my household, including my daughter, who until I get her married, is a great burden to me.

PRUDENZA: Burden.

ARTEMISIA: Are you writing?

PRUDENZA: Yes.

ARTEMISIA: I kiss your hands in anticipation of your bounty. I think your lordship will not suffer any loss with me, and that you will find the spirit of Caesar in this soul of a woman. Look down.

PRUDENZA: I am.

ARTEMISIA: And I will show your most illustrious lordship what a woman can do, in striving to give you the greatest pleasure. Your most devoted and grateful servant, Artemisia Gentileschi. And pull your tongue in. I can't paint you with your tongue hanging out.

Scene Two: Rome 1612. Painting Studio

Artemisia is seated at one easel, copying a Judith and Holofernes *painting. Next to her is her father, Orazio, working on the painting* Woman Playing a Lute. *Tuzia is posing, seated, holding the lute.*

ORAZIO: *(To Artemisia.)* Artemisia, pull your tongue in. It's hanging out of your mouth like an idiot.

ARTEMISIA: You're bothering me.

ORAZIO: Or a malfunctioning person. Pull it in.

ARTEMISIA: Stop bothering me.

ORAZIO: Pull it in.

ARTEMISIA: I can look however I want to when I paint.

ORAZIO: Did you change something in my painting?

ARTEMISIA: Nothing.

ORAZIO: Yes you did. Stronger. More powerful. What is it?

ARTEMISIA: Look.

ORAZIO: What?

ARTEMISIA: Look.

ORAZIO: The earrings?

ARTEMISIA: Yes.

ORAZIO: You gave her earrings? I didn't tell you to give her earrings.

ARTEMISIA: Earrings. Earrings. I gave her earrings.

ORAZIO: That was very smart of you. How did you think of it? White in the middle of black. Draws the eye to her face. What else did you change?

ARTEMISIA: I made her fatter. Leonardo says if you are ugly, you will paint faces that are ugly. If you are fat, you will paint bodies that are fatter. Fat. Fatter. I made her fatter.

ORAZIO: Stop. That's enough.

ARTEMISIA: And braided her hair.

ORAZIO: Your hair is a mess. And stand up when you paint. You're crunched over like a hunchback.

ARTEMISIA: Now you did it. You made me. Dripped some paint on the bottom of her skirt. Because of you.

ORAZIO: How can you paint if you're all stooped over?

ARTEMISIA: But I like it. It looks like a trickle of blood dripping down her sleeve.

ORAZIO: Move the painting up. Move the easel up. Move the painting up.

ARTEMISIA: There. I'm finished.

ORAZIO: And how can you do any work in here at all? With all these things around. Piles of old clothes. Who will wear them? Throw them out.

ARTEMISIA: We need them for our models.

ORAZIO: How long has this piece of cloth been sitting here?

ARTEMISIA: I don't know. I don't remember.

ORAZIO: Throw it out. Five years. Ten years. Throw it out.

ARTEMISIA: Give it to me. I love that dress.

ORAZIO: In my old age, I'll be surrounded by old rags, broken things, things that are worn out, useless . . .(Picking up broken Cupid.) Can we get rid of this?

ARTEMISIA: We need that.

ORAZIO: How about these candlesticks?

ARTEMISIA: No.

ORAZIO: You're like a rat. Piles of clothes over there. Boxes of broken glass. If you have to keep those old ugly candlesticks, can't you at least use them sometimes? Never any light in here. And clean yourself up. Your dress looks like it has the last five paintings on it. Painted right there on the front. Is that how you plan to sell your wares? Paintings for sale. Paintings. Right here on the front of your dress. Can't you even wash that dress once in a while? Not every day.

(Artemisia puts hands over ears and makes droning sounds.)

ORAZIO: I know that would be too much to ask. We're not looking for perfection around here, not perfection.

ARTEMISIA: I'm not listening. I'm not listening.

ORAZIO: I don't think you'll be like honey to the bees if that's what you are worried about. You're safe there. *(To Tuzia.)* Play some music. What are you standing there for? I need your expression. What do you think I am painting, the lute, the way you hold the lute? No, the way you frown when you concentrate on music. Mouth turned downwards. Play something.

TUZIA: *(Playing the tune and then singing the English folk song "Bluebird Song.")*

When I was a young thing once on a day
Dreaming under my apple tree
A great flock of bluebirds sailing through the sky
Espied my tree as they passed by,
And oh, it was a wonderful sight to see
When they settled down to rest in my apple tree.
Count them said my mother. How? Said I.
Out of the window came this reply:
One you'll have sorrow,
Two you'll have joy,
Three get a present,
Four get a boy,
Five receive silver,
Six receive gold,
Seven's a secret that's never been told,
Eight a love letter with promises three,
Nine means your true love's as true as can be.

Scene Three: Naples 1638. Painting Studio

Prudenza has her robe on; she is still taking dictation. Francesco is standing in the middle of the room holding a travel bag. Artemisia is sitting at the easel in front of almost completed David and Bathsheba.

PRUDENZA: Tenth of June. 1638. Your most devoted and grateful servant Artemisia Gentileschi.

FRANCESCO: Where should I put my bag?

PRUDENZA: You can sign it.

FRANCESCO: Is anyone going to stop what they are doing —

PRUDENZA: Yes. I have to get ready for Mass.

FRANCESCO: — to talk to me?

(Prudentia brings letter over for Artemisia to sign.)

ARTEMISIA: Here. Kiss me on the cheek. I am on the verge of . . . I didn't say to break pose.

PRUDENZA: I finished the letter.

FRANCESCO: I have been on a boat for two weeks.

ARTEMISIA: Not the letter. The elbow.

FRANCESCO: I did come all the way from England to see you. Sleeping on a slab of wood.

PRUDENZA: We'll be back in an hour or so. Have a nap.

(To Artemisia, while Francesco lies down.)

Can I borrow one of your blouses?

PRUDENZA: *(Holding up blouse.)* The embroidered one?

ARTEMISIA: Yes. Francesco!

FRANCESCO: What?

ARTEMISIA: On the stool. I have an elbow to finish.

FRANCESCO: What about Prudenza?

PRUDENZA: I have to get ready for Mass. *(To Artemisia.)* You have ten minutes. Then we are leaving.

(Prudenza exits.)

ARTEMISIA: Francesco!

FRANCESCO: What?

ARTEMISIA: On the stool.

FRANCESCO: *(Goes over to his bag to get letter.)* I did come for important business. Not just to pose for you.

ARTEMISIA: Hands on the chalk marks.

FRANCESCO: And I have a letter I'm supposed to give to you. From father. *(Fish-*

ing around in bag, giving it to Artemisia.) He did pay my fare so that I would read this letter to you in person.

ARTEMISIA: Read it to me. From the stool.

FRANCESCO: I almost left it behind, in London. Luckily I opened my eyes before we left and saw my bag lying in the street. I said to the driver, "Is that my bag lying outside in the street?" It was. They weren't even sorry.

ARTEMISIA: Twist to the left.

FRANCESCO: Are you listening?

ARTEMISIA: Yes.

FRANCESCO: *(Reading.)* "I hesitate to write this letter for fear that you will tear it up. I have instructed Francesco to read it to you himself if you should show any resistance. Though I cannot trust him in most things, I feel he is capable of carrying out this simple task." *(To Artemisia.)* He knew I would hear this letter.

ARTEMISIA: Elbow up.

FRANCESCO: "The Queen has requested that I paint the ceiling at her house in Greenwich. Your brother advised me not to accept the commission, but as I assessed the project, it came into my head that this is the ceiling I will paint with Artemisia. Gentileschi and Gentileschi. Father and daughter." *(To Artemisia.)* I have to move my arm to get to the next sheet.

ARTEMISIA: Move your arm.

FRANCESCO: He never helps you, does he? He only asks for help. *(Taking ring out of letter.)* What is this?

ARTEMISIA: Give it to me. It was addressed to me.

FRANCESCO: *(Holding ring.)* Heavy. There's a lot of gold in this ring.

ARTEMISIA: *(Walking over to Francesco.)* It has my name on the envelope. Give me the ring.

FRANCESCO: Why does he want to give you a wedding ring?

ARTEMISIA: Give me the ring. Read the letter.

(Francesco gives Artemisia the ring and she walks back to her easel.)

FRANCESCO: He should find his granddaughter a husband. You can't be expected to.

ARTEMISIA: Elbow up. Neck turned.

FRANCESCO: *(Reading.)* "In England they will be in awe of your talents."

ARTEMISIA: *(Interrupting.)* Why can't you work with him? He trained you to paint, didn't he? In the same way he trained me. Why can't you assist him?

FRANCESCO: "When Van Dyck complimented my figures to father, he wasn't interested. He said: you should see the way his older sister paints, then you will be impressed. Lighting like Caravaggio. Figures like Michelangelo."

ARTEMISIA: He is still saying that? Keep reading.

FRANCESCO: *(Reading.)* "The subject matter is more suitable to a woman of your stature. I have been assigned to paint the muses: architecture, geometry, music, the liberal arts. When the King saw an Artemisia Gentileschi Judith, he called it a dreadful picture, proof of your genius and its misdirection."

ARTEMISIA: He turned me into an outcast. Then, I'll make my fortune by being an outcast.

FRANCESCO: "Come to England. Paint the ceiling at the Queen's house with me. Let's share the commission."

ARTEMISIA: I will not. Don't read any more.

FRANCESCO: "Better a bird in hand than two flying, and in our business, better a bird in hand than ten flying. I can see the face of Van Dyck when you are on the ladders, painting those strong muscular figures of yours. I know you won't be able to resist when you hear the dimensions of the ceiling: two rectangles twenty feet by fifteen feet, two rectangles twenty feet by ten feet, four corner roundels each twelve and a half feet in diameter, one central roundel twenty feet in diameter . . ."

Scene Four: Rome 1612. Painting Studio

Orazio's painting of Judith and Her Maidservant *and Artemisia's copy are next to each other. Artemisia is preparing a preliminary sketch of* Susanna and the Elders *on a large blank canvas. Orazio, Cosimo, and Agostino are looking at drawings while eating lunch, served by Tuzia.*

AGOSTINO: *(Sketching with red chalk on back of used canvas.)* Thirty-six feet wide, divided into three arches. Center arch fifteen feet wide. Flanking arches each ten feet. Painted loggia mimicking the architectural loggia below . . .

TUZIA: Did everyone like the lunch? What did you think of the omelette?

ORAZIO: Good. Nineteen figures, full architectural surround. What are they paying per figure?

COSIMO: Twenty-five a figure, roughly twenty figures, times twenty-five, five hundred. I think I could get five hundred for you.

TUZIA: Currants, marigold flowers, cinnamon, ginger. All cooked in yolks of egg. I would never use the whites.

ORAZIO: Good. Minus your cut, of course.

COSIMO: Minus my cut. I don't see you getting many jobs without me. The

Jesuits hired Baglione. The pope thinks you're crazy, that no one can work with you. He likes Reni.

ORAZIO: There is no one easier to work with than me.

AGOSTINO: *(Sketching and talking to himself.)* Cornice divides into three sections, center balustrade juts out from the side balustrade . . .

ORAZIO: What do you think you can get for him? For Agostino over here? Do you think you could get something for this surround idea he has?

COSIMO: Whatever you get, I'll get the same for him.

ORAZIO: Five hundred? Five hundred for an architectural surround. Don't you think you should get a little bit more for the figures?

COSIMO: Agostino is the best.

AGOSTINO: Vouet is paying me half of what he's getting. He's splitting it down the middle.

ORAZIO: I was thinking more like six hundred, four hundred. If you really think you can get that.

ARTEMISIA: If you get hired, they hire me too, right?

ORAZIO: *(Tuzia begins clearing dishes.)* Did you get her to eat something?

ARTEMISIA: I'm working. Can you see? Do you have eyes?

TUZIA: I'm putting the food away. I will not bring it out again.
(Tuzia exits.)

ARTEMISIA: If you get hired, I get to work on it too, right?
(Cosimo wanders over to watch Artemisia work. The following two conversations continue simultaneously.)

COSIMO: By looking at you I know what job is perfect for you.

ARTEMISIA: What?

COSIMO: Nude model. *(Silence.)* Do you ever pose nude for your father?

ARTEMISIA: No.

COSIMO: If I were a painter, I'd like to have you pose for me. Naked. No clothes. You. Au natural. I'd do justice to your figure.

AGOSTINO: It looks easy. But it is very difficult. I apprenticed in Mantua ten years. Ten years of education in mathematics, the science of light, perspective . . .

ORAZIO: Ten years. I've been painting twenty-five. And before that I worked in my father's goldsmith shop.

AGOSTINO: I've trained for ten years and I have so much respect for you. When I was living in the north, everyone admired what you and Caravaggio were doing down here.

ORAZIO: *(To Artemisia.)* No. You don't get to work on it. You get to work here, at home.

(Tuzia reappears to get more dishes, Cosimo follows her downstairs.)

COSIMO: *(While exiting behind Tuzia.)* Tuzia, feel my head, do I have a fever today?

ARTEMISIA: You never. You never let me. You never let me come to work with you.

ORAZIO: *(To Agostino.)* You didn't know I had a sixteen-year-old daughter?

AGOSTINO: No. Who can paint.

ORAZIO: Yes.

AGOSTINO: And design the compositions herself?

ORAZIO: Yes. I taught her. But she is probably a better painter than the two of us.

AGOSTINO: Better than you?

ORAZIO: On the subject of lighting, better than Caravaggio.

AGOSTINO: You've taught a girl how to paint.

ORAZIO: And on the human figure, the equal of Michelangelo.

AGOSTINO: I didn't think it was possible.

ORAZIO: And she's what? Sixteen. By the time she's finished her education . . . *(Pause.)* In fact . . . she's the one who could use the education. Fool-the-eye illusions. *(Pause.)* Five hundred scudi. I don't understand, but anyway. Work side by side with you. Learn those illusionist tricks you do. How long would it take to teach someone your tricks?

AGOSTINO: My work is based on nature, on laws of perspective. Not tricks.

ORAZIO: Right, right, how long do you think it would take?

AGOSTINO: To teach someone to paint like I do? I don't know. There are certain concepts of mathematics and science she would have to know. Has she studied Leonardo? Have you included his writings in her studies?

ORAZIO: I'll tell you what. You teach her architectural perspective, whatever you call it, I'll let you go in with me fifty/fifty on the ceiling project. We finish the palace and then *(To Artemisia.)* we move right next door to the Casino of the Muses scaffolding, ladders, everything — move it right next door. *(Pause.)* Gentileschi and Gentileschi. Father and daughter. Figures, lighting, perspective.

ARTEMISIA: I don't want a teacher. I don't want a teacher. You're my teacher. I don't want a teacher.

ORAZIO: Not bad for her to have someone else she can argue with.

AGOSTINO: Sixteen. That's a good age to learn. I learned most of what I know around that age. Why don't you let me take a look at what you're working on?

ARTEMISIA: Only my father. Only Orazio. No one else is allowed to look.

ORAZIO: You can let him take one look at it, go ahead, take a look. See what you think . . .

AGOSTINO: She can keep working. Why don't you show me when you're ready?

ORAZIO: Argument all the time. What do they say in Naples? Harder to run a family than a country. Maybe she needs someone else as her teacher. A little distance. Someone else to get her to paint better — someone else to do the fighting — let me be the loving father. I don't have to be the only teacher she ever had.

AGOSTINO: Even in a short time. You'll see the difference. I'll teach her the theory of the art of painting, and the philosophy of perspective, the rules that apply to light and to the eye . . .

ORAZIO: Do me a favor, don't argue with me all the time.

ARTEMISIA: And do me a favor, don't talk to me.

(Tuzia and Cosimo return.)

AGOSTINO: Material that I can work with, that I can mold.

ORAZIO: She's already been molded. She has the foundation.

ARTEMISIA: I don't want him. I don't want him for a teacher. You're my teacher. I don't want him.

TUZIA: You can let someone else teach you besides your father.

ORAZIO: You say blue, she says red, you say up, she says down.

(Sound of baby crying from upstairs.)

COSIMO: *(To Artemisia.)* Look at my arm swollen straight. Go ahead. Squeeze.

ARTEMISIA: No.

(Sound of baby crying from upstairs.)

ORAZIO: Tuzia! What is your job around here? Does any one else hear the baby crying or is it only me?

TUZIA: I will not be rushed.

(Loud sound of baby crying from upstairs. Tuzia exits.)

COSIMO: *(To Artemisia.)* Squeeze. *(Pause.)* I go around all day squeezing my arm. It feels like a large breast. I have to get a little pleasure out of this sickness.

ORAZIO: Cosimo, walk out with me. We'll talk about this casino deal. Agostino, why don't you stay around. See if you can teach her your rules of perspective, your methods of fool-the-eye.

(Orazio and Cosimo exit.)

AGOSTINO: *(Looking over Artemisia's shoulder.)* Susanna and the Elders. Two men together. Woman alone. Solid triangular composition. Very strong. Michelangelo twist. Bare flesh on the cold stone. Very expressive. "It was hot and she was desirous of washing herself in the garden." *(Waving wooden yardstick in air.)* It's too symmetrical.

ARTEMISIA: Too symmetrical?

AGOSTINO: What is the only thing that can tell you with exactitude the true relative size of one object to another?

ARTEMISIA: Charting points.

AGOSTINO: Charting points. Yes. Drawing lines. What else?

ARTEMISIA: What?

AGOSTINO: Mathematics. Mathematics. All terms of perspective are made clear by the five aspects of mathematics: Point . . . line . . . angle . . . surface . . . and solids.

ARTEMISIA: I know that. Point . . . line . . .

AGOSTINO: *(Interrupting.)* Perspective comes in where judgment fails.
(Agostino picks up lute and starts to pluck.)

ARTEMISIA: Put it down. It belonged to my mother.

AGOSTINO: Where is she?

ARTEMISIA: Died last year. *(Pause, then calling.)* Tuzia. *(To Agostino.)* We need Tuzia. She's posing as Susanna.

AGOSTINO: *(Singing to Artemisia.)* "Who can express what sweetness I taste? In gazing on that proud light of my lady." Is this how your mother sang to you?

ARTEMISIA: No. Yes. A little bit like that.

AGOSTINO: *(Laying it down.)* It's out of tune. If you put a mirror on the easel, I'll be able to see the pose and watch you paint.

ARTEMISIA: We don't have a mirror.

AGOSTINO: Doesn't your father check his paintings in a mirror?

ARTEMISIA: No.

AGOSTINO: Leonardo says that you should always look at your work in a flat mirror. In reverse it will look like it was painted by someone else. And you will be able to see its flaws.

TUZIA: *(Entering, overhears last part.)* I have a mirror for painting my face. I'll get it for you.

ARTEMISIA: I'll come with you.

TUZIA: Stay here.
(Awkward silence.)

ARTEMISIA: *(Shouting up stairwell.)* Did you find it? *(No reply.)* Do you have one?

TUZIA: *(Entering, carrying a mirror.)* I could never live in such a mess as you do. How shall I pose for you?
(Tuzia hands Artemisia the mirror and walks over to podium. Agostino takes it out of her hands and places it on the easel.)

ARTEMISIA: On the top step.

TUZIA: *(To Agostino.)* How do you want me? I would never trust her to set up a pose of seduction.

AGOSTINO: How she had you before. Shoulders to the left. Head bent down to the right. An excellent pose.

TUZIA: And is it flattering to my thighs?

(Cosimo enters.)

AGOSTINO: Yes. Cosimo, you stand behind the wall. Looking at Susanna. "There was nobody in the garden except the two elders that hid themselves and watched her."

COSIMO: *(Ignoring Agostino, looking around studio.)* I could sell these two Orazio's.

ARTEMISIA: *(Still working on Tuzia's pose, to Cosimo.)* One is Orazio's, one is my copy. See if you can tell the difference.

COSIMO: You look different to me. I'd rather look at you.

ARTEMISIA: *(To Tuzia.)* Cosimo sees no difference, thinks they're the same painting.

(Agostino leads Artemisia by the hand to the paintings against the wall.)

AGOSTINO: Let me look at the paintings. I'll be able to tell.

ARTEMISIA: Then look.

AGOSTINO: Judith. Judith. Very similar. Dress: the same. Face: the same. No. A little different. What did you change?

ARTEMISIA: Look.

AGOSTINO: Both sleeves are the same. Bare arms, the way your arms are bare . . .

ARTEMISIA: But you still didn't guess.

AGOSTINO: Forearms the same. Wait. How could I miss it? Now the paintings look completely different. You added an earring.

COSIMO: To my eyes, it is indistinguishable from an Orazio Gentileschi.

AGOSTINO: He's half blind. He can't see anything.

COSIMO: One hundred and fifty, maybe two hundred, I can get for it.

ARTEMISIA: Are you posing or not?

AGOSTINO: Get behind the wall.

TUZIA: *(To Cosimo.)* What do you think of this pose they have twisted me into.

COSIMO: Isn't Susanna supposed to be naked?

AGOSTINO: Once you notice the earring you cannot take your eyes away from it. The whole painting begins to decompose.

ARTEMISIA: What did you say? What does it do to the composition?

AGOSTINO: Destroys the composition. Splits the painting apart. Black is a broken vessel deprived of the capacity to contain anything.

ARTEMISIA: I know. Leonardo. You don't like it. Splits the painting apart.

AGOSTINO: That one spot of light.

TUZIA: Isn't the passage "they watched jealously for a sight of her?" Shouldn't the two of you be looking at me?

ARTEMISIA: Destroys the composition. I'll rub it out. Paint over it. Don't talk about it. I'll paint over it.

AGOSTINO: That might save the painting.

COSIMO: Don't do that. Give me the painting. I'll sell it and then we'll see how much anyone cares about that earring.

AGOSTINO: Let me spend some time with Judith. Take her home with me.

ARTEMISIA: I never give away my paintings.

AGOSTINO: I'm not asking you to give it to me. Your father hired me to teach you. I'm asking you to lend it to me. I need this painting. To study. Think about your strengths and weaknesses.

TUZIA: May I be released from my pose?

ARTEMISIA: I'm still working.

COSIMO: Don't give it to him. Give it to me. The pope relies on my artistic judgment. He asks my opinion first, before anyone else. Trust me . . .

AGOSTINO: Let me take home your painting.

COSIMO: Give me the painting. I'll sell it as an Artemisia.

ARTEMISIA: As an Artemisia?

AGOSTINO: Let me study the copy. I need time to analyze its errors. Then I will know best how to teach you.

ARTEMISIA: *(To Agostino.)* Then take it. To borrow. Not to have. To borrow.

COSIMO: I have a piece of information our young painter might be interested in.

ARTEMISIA: What?

COSIMO: *(To Artemisia.)* Why do you think Michelangelo chose to portray his large men with tiny penises? *(Pause.)* Do you know why?

TUZIA: I don't think she is the one to answer that question.

ARTEMISIA: Larger than a nose and it competes with the proportions of the legs.

COSIMO: Your father taught you well. I could never have modeled for Michelangelo. I have pleased a lot of women.

TUZIA: I'm getting up.

AGOSTINO: Cosimo, you're coming with me.

(Agostino exits with painting.)

COSIMO: Women more virginal than you. The pope asks my opinion first. He trusts my artistic judgment. You should've given me the painting. I would've sold it as an Artemisia.

Scene 5: Naples 1638. Painting Studio

Artemisia Gentileschi is working on David and Bathsheba. *Off to the side is the almost completed* Judith Slaying Holofernes. *Francesco is posing as Bathsheba.*

FRANCESCO: If you decide not to go to London, why don't you let me take some of the paintings back for you. I'd probably get more in London then you get here. The King is very intrigued by you, he always asks me what happened, what actually happened. I told him I know nothing.
(Prudenza enters.)

PRUDENZA: Where did you put the rosewater and oil of clove?

FRANCESCO: . . . that I was a baby at the time.

ARTEMISIA: *(To Francesco.)* That's enough. You're moving.

PRUDENZA: Where did you put it?

ARTEMISIA: Rosewater. Oil of clove. We don't have that.

PRUDENZA: You didn't buy it for me?

ARTEMISIA: No.

PRUDENZA: You didn't get the oils for me?

ARTEMISIA: No.

PRUDENZA: It was a small thing. I ask you for so little.

ARTEMISIA: Everything is little, but it adds up. I can't afford to spend money on fancy oils.

PRUDENZA: It would have cost a quarter of one ducat.

ARTEMISIA: That we don't have.

PRUDENZA: I should never have said I wanted anything.

ARTEMISIA: Linseed oil. Walnut oil. Balsamic turpentine. Venice turpentine. Take your pick, whatever you want. They are all here. We have them all.

PRUDENZA: Maybe I don't want to walk around smelling like one of your paintings.

ARTEMISIA: Venice turpentine. Wear that. More expensive than clove.

PRUDENZA: I know. I'm the one who orders it. You don't look ready.

ARTEMISIA: I'll stay here with my brother. You can go to Mass by yourself.

PRUDENZA: Not by myself.

FRANCESCO: Go with her. I'll take a sleep.

PRUDENZA: We made this plan a week ago.

ARTEMISIA: Before I knew my brother would be here.

PRUDENZA: No. I can't go. I can't go without you. Not this time. You promised me.

ARTEMISIA: He came all the way from London to see me.

PRUDENZA: Finish your elbow. Codazzi was right.

(Prudenza exits.)

FRANCESCO: (To himself.) Codazzi?

ARTEMISIA: (To Francesco.) After I finish the elbow, you can deliver the painting to Ruffo. I also have a letter that needs to be delivered to the viceroy.

FRANCESCO: I don't think Orazio knows how strong your business is. I'll tell him when I get back to London.

ARTEMISIA: . . . but make sure you do it in that order. First, the painting to Ruffo. Then the letter. I don't want the viceroy to see the Bathsheba that I painted for Ruffo.

Scene 6: Rome 1612. Agostino's Room

Agostino asleep in a simple bed in a cell like room. Artemisia's copy of Judith and Holofernes *is hanging above his bed. Cosimo walks into room, climbs onto bed, takes painting off the wall, and as he is about to get down he steps on the sleeping Agostino.*

AGOSTINO: (Asleep.) Humph?

COSIMO: Go back to sleep.

AGOSTINO: (Asleep.) All right.

COSIMO: It's Cosimo.

AGOSTINO: (Asleep.) What?

COSIMO: Your guardian angel. Watching over you.

AGOSTINO: Hmmmmm.

COSIMO: She told me to take it.

AGOSTINO: (Asleep.) Whatever you want.

COSIMO: Shall I read you the letter? Dear Agostino, Please give my copy of the Judith to Cosimo.

AGOSTINO: Hmmmm.

COSIMO: Dear Agostino . . .

AGOSTINO: (Still sleeping.) What?

COSIMO: You were licking your fingers thinking about what she was going to give you, instead she decided to give it to me.

AGOSTINO: (Waking up with a start and grabbing Cosimo.) What are you doing?

COSIMO: Reading her letter. (Reading.) Please give my copy of the Judith to Cosimo. I would like Cosimo to think about my painting style. I would like Cosimo to assess my strengths and weaknesses. I am sorry you didn't have the chance to enjoy it, but I would like Cosimo to have it.

AGOSTINO: She gave it to me.

COSIMO: Forgive a young girl a change of heart.

AGOSTINO: Let go of the painting.

COSIMO: When she looked at you and turned red as a pepper, you thought that was for you.

AGOSTINO: Put the painting back on the wall.

COSIMO: Her blushing wasn't for you.

AGOSTINO: Let go of the painting.

COSIMO: It was for me. Don't get jealous. She has come to the wisdom of her senses. She has seen me for the superior man I am. Shall I read you the letter again?

AGOSTINO: No.

COSIMO: *(Reading.)* I am sorry you didn't have the chance to enjoy it, but I would like Cosimo to have it. I like to spread my generosity around. Signed Artemisia. *(Waving it in front of Agostino's face.)* Would you like to see the signature?

AGOSTINO: Get out of my room.

COSIMO: Move to the side. I don't want to step on you.

(Cosimo exits with the painting.)

Scene 7: Rome 1612. Painting Studio

A few days later. Artemisia is painting Tuzia posing nude as Susanna in the almost completed Susanna and the Elders.

TUZIA: I am freezing, sitting here naked as a worm.

ARTEMISIA: Do you want to make me ruin it? You made me . . . Good . . . I did it . . . one more thing . . .

TUZIA: I am counting to one hundred, then I am counting to one hundred again, and then I am getting up. One . . . two . . . three . . . four . . .

ARTEMISIA: I'm working on your wrist. Let me finish the wrist then you can go upstairs.

TUZIA: Let me go now and I'll sit all day tomorrow.

ARTEMISIA: He stayed much longer last time. I wonder if anyone noticed he was late.

TUZIA: I doubt it. And who would care? He has to do the work.

ARTEMISIA: Didn't you see him looking at me? The whole time. Very strong. Staring. I don't know why he was staring at me.

TUZIA: You don't?

ARTEMISIA: Every time I looked up he was looking at me.

TUZIA: Are you working or talking? I could be upstairs.

ARTEMISIA: I am working. I can talk and paint at the same time. Did you see him? Did you see the way he was looking at me?

TUZIA: No. How much longer? Have you been counting?

ARTEMISIA: No?

TUZIA: He was looking at you, yes. Of course he is interested in you. You are Orazio's daughter.

ARTEMISIA: I don't think that's the reason. I was thinking he's the kind of person I should marry.

TUZIA: That's what you were thinking? He probably guessed that. Not marry. Not husband. That's not what he was thinking.

ARTEMISIA: He could paint the landscapes, the architectural surrounds. I could paint the figures. I don't like doing the landscapes.

TUZIA: I don't think so.

ARTEMISIA: Why? Someone will marry me, don't you think?

TUZIA: Yes.

ARTEMISIA: Who?

TUZIA: I don't know. Someone. Now don't bore me with this. How many more minutes?

ARTEMISIA: Five.

TUZIA: It's true, you do not have rosebud lips.

ARTEMISIA: My chin. I have a double chin. That's what you mean, isn't it?

TUZIA: *(Puts on her robe and walks over to Artemisia.)* I could make you look better. Stay there.

ARTEMISIA: What are you doing?

TUZIA: *(Adjusting Artemisia's clothes.)* Let me see. Your blouse. If you don't tie it so tightly around your neck . . .

ARTEMISIA: My blouse lower than this?

TUZIA: Lower. And dot a little red on your own cheeks.

ARTEMISIA: Is this right?

TUZIA: You could make it lower.

(Agostino enters knocking, Artemisia and Tuzia both jump.)

ARTEMISIA: I don't know why I jumped. I knew you were there. I don't know why I jumped.

AGOSTINO: I thought you would be painting. Painting. Always painting.

ARTEMISIA: I don't know why I jumped, I heard you come in . . .

AGOSTINO: *(Looking at painting.)* The modesty of Susanna. Her hands in the air.

TUZIA: Doesn't she look beautiful? I think she looks beautiful in that blouse. A little color in her cheeks.

ARTEMISIA: I haven't finished her wrist.

TUZIA: You do look beautiful. Fresh.

AGOSTINO: How much of this did Orazio paint? Here? Around the shoulders?

ARTEMISIA: Yes. That part. How could you tell?

AGOSTINO: It's not very well done. Did Cosimo pose for you?

ARTEMISIA: Tuzia posed.

AGOSTINO: How about Cosimo?

ARTEMISIA: No.

AGOSTINO: You're getting too much of an outline between the shoulders and the sky. The red cloak is very good. Did your father paint that too?

ARTEMISIA: I painted that part myself.

AGOSTINO: Tuzia, you can go upstairs. Give me your rag. I have to fix this.

ARTEMISIA: We're not stopping. I didn't say we're stopping.

AGOSTINO: *(To Tuzia.)* You can go upstairs. We don't need you.

ARTEMISIA: Stay downstairs. We need you, for posing, for . . . I don't want to stop painting.

AGOSTINO: We are not stopping. I want to work with you on some of these problems.

TUZIA: You can call me if you need me. Your brother is waking up anyway.

ARTEMISIA: I don't hear him. Stay. I said don't leave. I don't want you to leave.

TUZIA: Your father engaged this man to teach you. Let him teach you.

AGOSTINO: Let her go.

ARTEMISIA: Then bring Francesco down here. He can play down here.

TUZIA: If you need me, I will be in my palatial quarters.

(Tuzia exits.)

AGOSTINO: Get up on the platform. Let me see if I can fix this outline problem. *(Holding her paintbrush.)* Along these edges, something is not right, between the sky and the clothing . . .

ARTEMISIA: *(Trying to grab the paintbrush from him.)* Let me have the paintbrush. I'll do it.

AGOSTINO: *(Easily keeping brush out of her reach.)* Where is your rag? Give me your rag. *(Artemisia hands him an oily rag.)* Wrong size. Too small. You need to use a bigger one. I am going to paint over this. You get on the platform.

ARTEMISIA: *(Calling.)* Tuzia. I'm calling her. I am not posing for you.

AGOSTINO: I'll tell you when to call Tuzia. Get on the platform.

ARTEMISIA: Tuzia. I'm calling her. I will.

AGOSTINO: Get up there.

ARTEMISIA: No.

AGOSTINO: On the platform.

ARTEMISIA: Only for one minute.

AGOSTINO: Push up your sleeves. *(Pause, while she follows his directions.)* Further.

ARTEMISIA: No more. I'm not pushing them any higher.

AGOSTINO: I've asked you to push up your sleeves, not to undress. That's right. Past the elbows. Twist your body. That's right. And now your arms up, by your ears, very good, stay that way, don't move.

ARTEMISIA: Like this?

AGOSTINO: You are shaking. Stop shaking. Look at the floor.

ARTEMISIA: I am.

AGOSTINO: No. You are looking at me. Don't look at me. Look at the floor. Look at your knee. Neck bent down further to your shoulder.

ARTEMISIA: I'm only doing it for one minute.

AGOSTINO: You stay there. And I will correct this problem . . . haa!

ARTEMISIA: What?

AGOSTINO: Sometimes it hits me, when I fix something that fast — what a brilliant painter I am. Don't do it — stop jinxing yourself — yes. That is better.

ARTEMISIA: I want to see.

AGOSTINO: Don't move. I did not say you could . . .

ARTEMISIA: *(Interrupting, walking over to the painting.)* No more. Give me my brush.

AGOSTINO: I did not tell you to break your pose. I need you in that position.

ARTEMISIA: My brush. I want it back. Give it back to me.

AGOSTINO: You want your brush. Here it is. *(Holding it out in front of him.)* Here it is. Come and get it. *(She reaches out for it and he pulls it behind his back.)* Try again.

ARTEMISIA: Give it to me.

AGOSTINO: Here it is. Take it.

(She grabs it before he can move it away. Agostino holds tightly on to her hand.)

AGOSTINO: Now I have what I want.

ARTEMISIA: Can you give it to me?

AGOSTINO: *(Agostino starts to kiss her neck.)* That's what I wanted. A closer view. The neck bones diving into the shoulder blades. Sutura dentata. The teeth into the gums. The hair. Push it off the neck more. These hands. Hours of holding the brush in these fingers . . .

ARTEMISIA: Let go. Let go of me. No one touches me. No one, when I get married, then, not until then, get off me . . .

AGOSTINO: Yes. You want to say yes. Now quiet, no need to make so much noise.

ARTEMISIA: Let go. My head is hurting. My hands are hurting. Let go. I feel hot. Do you want me to call Tuzia or not? *(Calling, not loudly.)* Tuzia! *(To Agostino.)* I said stop. Did you hear me? I feel dizzy. Let go.

AGOSTINO: The air. The turpentine. Your skin is warm. Very hot. Take a walk with me, around the room. Make us both feel better. *(Leading her over to bed at back of studio.)* Over here. Away from all the paint fumes.

ARTEMISIA: Your hands, your arms off me. I'm going to be sick. Let go.

AGOSTINO: Don't fight me.

ARTEMISIA: I'll kick you. Do you want me to kick you?

AGOSTINO: *(Putting his handkerchief over her mouth.)* It's too hot in here. Not easy, holding you down. Don't fight so hard.
(Blackout. Struggle of the rape in darkness.)

Scene Eight: Naples 1638, 1 PM

Artemisia working alone on Judith Slaying Holofernes.

ARTEMISIA: *(Talking to herself, describing painting.)* And approached to his bed, and took hold of the hair of his head, and said, Strengthen me, O Lord God of Israel, this day.
(Prudenza enters, stands very still watching Artemisia.)

ARTEMISIA: Pushed to the edge of the bed, left hand holding head down by roots of hair. Right hand holding sword. *(Artemisia sees Prudenza and jumps in fright.)* Is that paint? Is that blood? *(Looking carefully at her face.)* No. It's mud. Move. Can you move? Can you only stand in one place? Move. Do you know how to move? Say something.

PRUDENZA: Drums banging. Outside your door.

ARTEMISIA: A charivari?

PRUDENZA: Yes. Because of you.

ARTEMISIA: *(Holding Prudenza's hands.)* Moving how many times. How many houses? How many cities? Stop. Stop following me.

PRUDENZA: Boys surrounding me. Throwing chicken heads, chicken blood. Banging. Didn't you hear the banging?

ARTEMISIA: Twenty-five years. That's not too long to forget. No. They can re-member forever. Twenty-five years. One hundred years. How about four hundred years?

PRUDENZA: Codazzi tried to protect me.

ARTEMISIA: Codazzi?

PRUDENZA: I told you before I left I had something to tell you.

ARTEMISIA: What? What does Codazzi have to do with this? Tried to protect. Yes. I know. Tried to protect. Why are they attacking you now? You?

PRUDENZA: I'm marrying Codazzi. *(Pause.)* They think Codazzi is too old to have a young wife. And a widower. They don't like that either.

ARTEMISIA: They're right. You can do better than Codazzi.

PRUDENZA: No. I can't. I can't do better than Codazzi.

ARTEMISIA: A second-rate Neapolitan painter.

PRUDENZA: He gets as many commissions as you do.

ARTEMISIA: You know why he wants to marry you, don't you?

PRUDENZA: I do know. Yes. Do you? I wonder.

ARTEMISIA: Not for your charms.

PRUDENZA: I'm sure you think you understand.

ARTEMISIA: Because you know to fill a vial of turpentine all the way to the top, or it will spoil. Because you know if you leave black pigment in the sun it will crack . . . because you know the difference between gesso and ca-sein . . . because you know . . .

PRUDENZA: *(Moving toward stairs.)* You don't know, do you? I'm going upstairs.

ARTEMISIA: I don't give my permission.

PRUDENZA: It's too late for permission. I am marrying him.

(Prudenza stops at base of stairs.)

ARTEMISIA: You're going off to work for another painter.

PRUDENZA: Not work for him. Marry him.

ARTEMISIA: He'll be getting a trained model, an assistant, and a good cook. He should be paying me.

(Prudenza starts walking upstairs.)

ARTEMISIA: Where are you going?

FRANCESCO: *(Entering.)* I'm back. Where are you going?

PRUDENZA: Upstairs. I'm taking off your blouse and tearing it up for rags.

ARTEMISIA: Yes. Go upstairs. Change out of those clothes. *(To Francesco.)* What did he say?

FRANCESCO: Who? Oh Ruffo. He served me a five-course lunch.

Scene Nine: Rome 1612. Painting Studio

Artemisia is a disheveled heap of torn clothes. She is threatening Agostino with a palette knife. Agostino, injured in the struggle, is trying to hide his pain from her.

ARTEMISIA: You have stolen something —

AGOSTINO: *(Opening his doublet.)* Throw the knife. If you need to throw the knife at me, aim at my chest.

ARTEMISIA: — that can never be replaced.

> *(Artemisia throws the knife. Her aim is not good, her throwing is not good, but the gesture has sincere fury. Agostino dodges easily.)*

AGOSTINO: You missed me.

ARTEMISIA: Torn clothes.

AGOSTINO: I have to find my scarf.

ARTEMISIA: Red stains. On my blouse.

AGOSTINO: My blood. *(Silence.)* Don't tell your father.

ARTEMISIA: Tell my father. Don't tell my father. I was a virgin. I'm not a virgin.

AGOSTINO: I didn't know that.

ARTEMISIA: He'll have you poisoned. He'll have you stabbed. He'll have you killed.

AGOSTINO: You can find a way to stop yourself from discussing this with Orazio. I promise. I'll marry you.

ARTEMISIA: My dress, my smock that I paint in, torn. Is this paint? Is this blood?

AGOSTINO: I need time to extract myself from the labyrinth I am in.

ARTEMISIA: Where is Tuzia? *(Weakly calling.)* Tuzia. Tuzia.

AGOSTINO: No. Don't call her. Think of my promise. Where is my scarf?

ARTEMISIA: Are you leaving?

AGOSTINO: I have to go. I was wearing a scarf around my neck.

ARTEMISIA: On the floor by the bed.

AGOSTINO: *(Picking up the scarf.)* We're bound together forever now, aren't we?

> *(Agostino exits. Artemisia picks up a mirror and looks at herself in the mirror, then at the Susanna painting then at the mirror.)*

END OF ACT I

Act II

Scene Ten: Rome 1612. Painting Studio

Six months later. Artemisia is taking a bath. Tuzia and Artemisia are singing together.

TUZIA: *(Singing.)* Lazy John, Lazy John
Will you marry me?
Will you marry me?
ARTEMISIA: *(Singing.)* How can I marry you
No shirt to wear?
TUZIA: *(Singing.)* Up she jumped and away she ran
Down to the market square
There she found a shirt for
Lazy John to wear.
Lazy John, Lazy John
Will you marry me?
Will you marry me?
ARTEMISIA: *(Singing.)* How can I marry you
No pants to wear?
TUZIA: *(Singing.)* Up she jumped and away she ran
down to the market square
There she found some pants for
Lazy John to wear.
Lazy John, Lazy John
Will you marry me?
Will you marry me?
ARTEMISIA: *(Singing.)* How can I marry you?
With a wife and ten children at home.
(Dunking her head under water.) Why isn't he here? Now. He didn't come over yesterday. Or the day before yesterday. What is he waiting for?
TUZIA: Must you see him every day? I'm not sure I like the effect he is having on you. I am not sure it is healthy for a young girl to be thinking only about painting and painting teachers.
ARTEMISIA: He will come. He won't come. Did he say he was coming or not? Did he promise or not? Should I ask him, why weren't you here yesterday? Or the day before yesterday? I hate this. I hate this. *(Dunks her head in water.)* What does he mean? Labyrinth.

TUZIA: A maze. A hard maze. A place you'd get lost.

ARTEMISIA: What if he changes his mind? Then what? Then what will I do? Have patience. What does that mean? Have patience. Stop waiting. I'll tell him stop waiting. What are you waiting for? I can't wait all year. *(Head dunked under water.)* Towel!

ORAZIO: *(Offstage.)* Are you out of the bath yet?

ARTEMISIA: No.

ORAZIO: Get out of the bath.

ARTEMISIA: I won't.

    (Orazio enters.)

ORAZIO: Do you know where the Judith is? The large Judith you copied?

ARTEMISIA: Why?

ORAZIO: *(From behind screen.)* I was in the shop down the street. I went up to see what he had today. A lot of paintings in there, hanging on the walls, on easels, and there on the floor looking — leaning on the wall, on the floor, there it is staring at me . . .

ARTEMISIA: What?

ORAZIO: Holofernes. Staring at me. The dead head of Holofernes and I pick it up. Pick it up. Hold it. And it's staring at me.

ARTEMISIA: Judith and Holofernes?

ORAZIO: My Judith and Holofernes. The one you copied.

ARTEMISIA: I know which one. The one you sold to Borghese.

ORAZIO: Yes. That one. And I'm thinking he got me by pure flattery. I gave him the painting for half what it was worth.

    (Artemisia gets out of the bath and gets dressed.)

ARTEMISIA: Why did you?

ORAZIO: He said he wanted it for his collection — he said he was putting it in his collection — of greatest, most famous Italian painters. I'm thinking it didn't take him long to sell that painting off. Greatest most famous Italian painters, and he got it for a hundred . . . and there it is sitting in a little shop, three houses down from us, selling for three times what I got. Now anyone wants that painting, comes in off the street, buys it.

TUZIA: *(To Artemisia.)* Now I really must have you over here. Can I trust you with chopping the basil? Ummm. I love the smell of basil. Uhmmm. *(Holding basil out to Orazio.)* Isn't it delicious?

ORAZIO: I have smelled basil before.

ARTEMISIA: You hold that end of the table. I'll hold this end. Why were you at the shop down the street?

ORAZIO: *(To Artemisia.)* Not why I was at the shop, when I was at the shop.

I was staring at the painting. The man thinks I want to buy it. He says I'll give it to you for three hundred. Three hundred. Pretty good, more than I got paid for it. One hundred. Remember? And I'm staring at it, and I'm looking at the head, lying there, the sleeves pushed back, and the hair. And I'm looking at the hair and suddenly I couldn't remember. Did she add the earrings? Or did she take them away? I couldn't remember. There they were. Earrings. Bright gold in the middle of dark hair. Yes. There they were. There they are.

ARTEMISIA: Your painting? With earrings? Down the street?

ORAZIO: No. Your painting with earrings, down the street. It's your painting. Once I saw the earrings I knew. The hair entwined in fancy braids, the same Artemisia hands. I know your painting.

ARTEMISIA: I didn't sign it.

ORAZIO: No. No signature. I looked. Further proof that it is your painting. We were going to sell it as an Orazio. Did you sell it as an Orazio?

ARTEMISIA: No. I didn't sell it. No.

ORAZIO: Then someone stole it. Someone stole it out of the studio.

(Orazio starts scrambling around, looking for the painting.)

ARTEMISIA: Stop. No one stole it. I lent it to Agostino.

ORAZIO: You lent it to Agostino. It's for sale. Now we know what happened. You lent it to Agostino. Agostino sold your painting.

ARTEMISIA: You think Agostino would steal my painting? When I lent it to him?

ORAZIO: Do I think he would steal? Yes.

ARTEMISIA: You trusted him. To teach me.

ORAZIO: I trust him to act in his own best interest. You've got to know the wolf you sleep with.

ARTEMISIA: And if he tells you something or makes a promise to you, do you believe him?

ORAZIO: What did he promise you? *(To Tuzia.)* Did you know about this?

TUZIA: I was here. I saw her give it to him.

ORAZIO: Why didn't you stop her from doing it? What is your job around here?

TUZIA: You hired him. How are you chopping those leaves?

ARTEMISIA: However you like, however you want me to.

ORAZIO: But you can't let her . . . she doesn't know . . . what does she know?

TUZIA: One by one, each leaf separately, not bunched up like bananas.

ARTEMISIA: And if he tells you something, or makes a promise to you, do you believe him?

ORAZIO: Depends what the promise is. About money, no. What did he promise you?

TUZIA: *(To Orazio.)* Taste this sauce I am making. Is it the most delicious you've ever tasted?

ORAZIO: Good. What did he promise you?

TUZIA: *(To Orazio.)* And a sip, take a sip of wine from my glass.

ORAZIO: You never give away your work.

TUZIA: It goes perfectly with the sauce.

ARTEMISIA: I don't like it. I like it with one spice. Not eight spices. I like it with one spice.

TUZIA: Orazio likes it.

ORAZIO: Yes. I like it that way. Me. Why did you lend him the painting?

ARTEMISIA: Too many spices. I am not eating dinner.

(Artemisia moves toward door.)

ORAZIO: Wait. Wait. Wait. No. No. No. You're not. You're not going anywhere.

AGOSTINO: *(Agostino enters, throws arm around Orazio, giving him a hug. To Tuzia.)* Smells delicious. Basil and sage?

ORAZIO: Wait. Wait. Wait. We're not talking about food here.

ARTEMISIA: I didn't give you the Judith.

ORAZIO: We're talking about paintings.

ARTEMISIA: I lent it to you. For you to borrow.

ORAZIO: Why did you steal the painting?

ARTEMISIA: Did you think I gave it to you?

AGOSTINO: No.

ORAZIO: She didn't give you the Judith.

ARTEMISIA: *(Simultaneously with Orazio.)* I didn't give you the Judith . . .

AGOSTINO: You didn't give me the Judith. I know you didn't give me the Judith.

ARTEMISIA: I lent it to you, and my father said he saw it down the street for sale . . .

ORAZIO: Selling for three hundred. Three times what I got for my Judith.

ARTEMISIA: . . . and I lent it to you. I didn't give it to you.

AGOSTINO: You gave Cosimo the note. You wrote I should give the painting to him. I am sorry you didn't have a chance to enjoy it, but I like to spread my generosity around.

ARTEMISIA: Who wrote? What note?

AGOSTINO: *(To Artemisia.)* The note was signed Artemisia.

ARTEMISIA: *(To Agostino.)* I never gave you a note. I don't even know how to write.

(Cosimo enters.)

COSIMO: I am here. I have done it. You can kiss me, congratulate me. I don't mind. *(Silence. Cosimo places money on the table.)* Here it is. Five hundred ducats advance.

ARTEMISIA: I don't know how to write.

COSIMO: I'm not surprised.

AGOSTINO: *(To Cosimo.)* You tell them. How you came to my room in the middle of the night with a letter, with Artemisia's name on the bottom. Telling me to give the painting to you.

ARTEMISIA: *(To Cosimo.)* I would never give you anything of mine. Nothing.

COSIMO: Right now we have more important things to discuss. Your father and your friend Agostino have been awarded one of the biggest commissions available in Rome at the present moment.

ARTEMISIA: That was my painting. My painting . . .

COSIMO: Don't interrupt me. One of the biggest commissions. Let me take the congratulations. The Casino of the Muses, granted to Orazio Gentileschi and Agostino Tassi, one thousand ducats . . .

ORAZIO: *(Interrupting.)* No one, no one steals a painting from me, and no one steals a painting from this young innocent girl. The rule here is: you steal that painting, you return that painting. Very simple. Either you bring back the painting or you pay for it.

COSIMO: Stole. Stole. You are wounding me with such harsh words. And innocent? I don't know if I would describe her as innocent. Today you should be congratulating me. Thanking me. Instead, you are insulting me.

ORAZIO: I haven't been insulting. I haven't even started. I've been kind. Kind. A dog would steal a painting from a sixteen-year-old girl.

COSIMO: *(Looking at Agostino.)* You are accusing the wrong person.

AGOSTINO: You stole the painting.

COSIMO: I don't like it. I'm not the thief around here. Tuzia, I smell what you are cooking and it smells delicious. I've been dreaming of the odiferous and the strong. The pungent. Onions, garlic, red wine, foods that are forbidden to me. There is someone who stole from you. Something more precious than the painting.

AGOSTINO: *(Interrupting, to Cosimo.)* Discretion, not food should fill your mouth now.

ORAZIO: Discretion. Garlic. Onions. Listen Cosimo, the painting was stolen by you.

COSIMO: I needed a doctor to cure me of this affliction I suffer from. But I wouldn't call it theft. I'd call it charity to a close and faithful friend. The doctor accepted the painting as payment. Rest assured, as to my crime, you were able to assist in my cure. You've done a good deed in your life. All your sins are now absolved.

ARTEMISIA: I don't care if you're cured. I don't care. That was my painting. You pay the doctor. Not me. I'll pay for my own doctor.

ORAZIO: *(To Cosimo.)* You're going back to the shop, up three flights of stairs, break down the door. You stole it once . . .

COSIMO: *(Interrupting.)* What Agostino did, that is theft. I didn't pretend to teach . . . while really doing something quite different. I didn't steal your daughter.

AGOSTINO: You've already done enough damage. I would stop right now. You say another word, I'll kill you.

ORAZIO: What are the two of you fighting about?

COSIMO: You were on the scaffolding. He was in her bed.

ORAZIO: I was what? He was where?

(Agostino jumps up and starts to strangle Cosimo.)

AGOSTINO: You'll die for this.

(Orazio breaks up the fight.)

ORAZIO: Doing what? What were you doing with her?

COSIMO: And I was just beginning to recover.

ORAZIO: *(To Artemisia.)* What were you doing with him?

COSIMO: Isn't it obvious? Agostino told me himself.

TUZIA: *(To Agostino.)* And I thought it was the chance to see my beautiful legs that brought him back so many times.

ARTEMISIA: Not enough times.

AGOSTINO: *(To Artemisia.)* I told you, have patience.

ARTEMISIA: I did. I do.

(Cosimo slinks out.)

ORAZIO: Open my eyes. Illuminate me. Open the eyes of this blind old man.

AGOSTINO: *(To Artemisia.)* I promised you. I intend to keep my promise.

ARTEMISIA: When?

AGOSTINO: Soon.

ORAZIO: *(Softly, to Tuzia.)* You, whose only job as far as I could see, was to watch my daughter while I was at work . . . so I could go and get a little work done.

TUZIA: Do not shout at me. I do not like to be shouted at.

ARTEMISIA: *(To Orazio.)* He is marrying me.

AGOSTINO: As soon as I get myself out of the labyrinth I am in.

ORAZIO: Marry you? Oh, good. Marry you. Marry you when he's married already.

AGOSTINO: I said . . . have patience.

ORAZIO: Or maybe you didn't know that?

ARTEMISIA: No.

ORAZIO: No. Of course not. He didn't tell you that part, did he? He omitted that part.

AGOSTINO: I mean to keep my promise.

ARTEMISIA: When I was crying, when I said I wanted to kill you, you said "Wait. Have patience — I will marry you." You said it, not me. You.

AGOSTINO: What I told you, I meant. Don't listen to him.

ORAZIO: *(To Artemisia.)* Don't listen to me. How about when I tell the truth?

AGOSTINO: He is trying to turn you against me. I made you a promise. I intend to keep that promise.

ARTEMISIA: You tell me. Do you have a wife? Yes or no?

AGOSTINO: I have been arranging things.

(Orazio throws a fork.)

ORAZIO: Arranging things?

TUZIA: Why doesn't everyone sit down? It will be absolutely inedible if we don't eat now.

(Orazio throws a glass.)

ORAZIO: No, we won't eat. *(In Tuzia's voice.)* Why doesn't everyone sit down? *(In his own voice.)* Or why doesn't everyone line up against the wall. And I can hit you one after the other. No. I'm not going to eat your food. I'm going to eat you. How do you like that? I am running three miles each way back and forth twelve times a day between this house and up that mountain — hill — chaos — making sure you have fresh pigment, making sure you have work, making sure you have some one to model for you, making sure the twelve idiots who work for me keep painting even when I am out of the room for one second. Everyone says your problem Orazio is you're taking on too many jobs, taking care of too many people, too much meat on the fire. But I say, oh I have my safety net. If I fall off the scaffolding, that's bad. But, if I fall off a scaffold and I've got someone to catch me, or a rope to catch on to, I'm doing all right. If I have an upstairs tenant who happens to be a pretty close friend of mine, who happens to not pay a ducat in rent, who assures me, that while I am at work, I can leave the worries of my household behind me, that she will watch my daughter like a hawk, take care of my baby boy like a mother, that is my rope. That is my safety net. I'll worry about your daughter. I am forty-five years old. You are thirty-three years old and you are fucking my daughter who is sixteen years old. Under my roof, in my studio. And what chance do I have of marrying her off now. That makes me mad. Very mad. I'll destroy you. You will never get near this house again. You will never get into the academy. You will never work in Rome. You will never touch her again. I promise you that. Let me build a cross and I'll nail all three of you to it. And when you're finished you can hang me on it too. And then you can come to my funeral ten minutes later. And you will not get one more shred of her and not one more shred of this either. *(Orazio picks up the money.)* Not one more shred of her.

Scene Eleven: Naples 1638

Artemisia is putting glue on panels and covering with canvas and preparing canvases by painting layers of white over green over white.

FRANCESCO: Five courses for lunch. Squab with raisins and nuts. Fresh green salad. I can't eat the food in England. That is why I am so thin. And Orazio will spend nothing on food. Ruffo and I had an interesting discussion. He listened carefully to what I was saying about the painters in the English court. Van Dyck, Orazio . . .

ARTEMISIA: Did he give you the money?

FRANCESCO: Yes. I have to say I was sounding very intelligent on the subject.

ARTEMISIA: Do you have it?

FRANCESCO: Yes. He loved having lunch with an artist.

ARTEMISIA: Put the money on the table before you forget.

FRANCESCO: I have a sore hip. Carrying your painting down to the harbor may have made it worse.

ARTEMISIA: Put the money on the table. *(Francesco puts the money on the table, Artemisia counts it.)* Did he like the Bathsheba? Did he say anything about it? One hundred. The full amount. *(Pause.)* Did he say he recognized the skill of the artist in its beauty? That it is the finest painting in his collection?

FRANCESCO: Ruffo liked your painting. He gave you what you asked. When I delivered the letter to the viceroy, he said he would not give you more money until he had the painting in his hand. He said if it's lapis she needs, I'll give her lapis. *(Francesco produces a vial of blue lapis.)* One hundred grams. Pure lapis lazuli. He told me to tell you he won't pay for the painting unless it is an exact copy of your earlier Judith. The one you painted after the . . .

(Prudenza enters wearing a V-necked smock.)

ARTEMISIA: *(Interrupting.)* I know which one he wants. *(To Prudenza.)* Are you feeling better?

PRUDENZA: I started packing.

FRANCESCO: Where are you going?

(Prudenza picks up the money.)

PRUDENZA: I should take this.

FRANCESCO: One hundred ducats. It's all there.

ARTEMISIA: Put it down.

PRUDENZA: *(Holding money.)* Threatening to not give me a dowry.

FRANCESCO: Are you getting married? Finally.

PRUDENZA: After all the hours I've given you.

ARTEMISIA: Put it down.

PRUDENZA: Twenty years of enslaved labor.

FRANCESCO: Who did you get to marry you?

PRUDENZA: *(Still holding money.)* Codazzi. What would you do if I didn't give it back to you?

FRANCESCO: *(To Artemisia.)* The painter Codazzi? How did you arrange that?

ARTEMISIA: I didn't. *(To Prudenza.)* Put it down.

PRUDENZA: It's only one hundred, anyway. You promised me three. I want my three hundred.

(Prudenza puts the money down.)

ARTEMISIA: Francesco brought back the lapis. Go and change.

PRUDENZA: Not until you give me the three hundred.

ARTEMISIA: The blue dress.

PRUDENZA: The blue silk dress? *(Retreating behind screen.)* I'll wear it to my wedding.

ARTEMISIA: That dress doesn't leave our studio.

PRUDENZA: That's what I'll wear to my wedding.

ARTEMISIA: The answer is no. I am thinking of what is best for you.

FRANCESCO: Codazzi is a very prestigious artist. He's a good choice for Prudenza. Why don't you want her to marry him?

ARTEMISIA: Because he is an artist. He'll have her working for him all the time.

(Prudenza emerges from behind screen in blue dress, admires herself in mirror.)

PRUDENZA: I'm not changing my mind.

ARTEMISIA: *(Walking over to mirror.)* You will. Let me cinch it up. *(Remem-*

bering the pose while she fusses with the dress.) . . . and then hands clenched tight, holding the sword tight, pulling the hair . . . Pull in your stomach.

FRANCESCO: I think there are a few Codazzi's in England. Orazio thinks you can't run a household. I can't wait to see his reaction when I tell him you've managed to marry his granddaughter off to Codazzi.

ARTEMISIA: I've decided. You can go back without me. *(To Prudenza.)* Pull in your stomach.

PRUDENZA: I am.

(Francesco crawls into bed and falls asleep.)

ARTEMISIA: Pull it in.

PRUDENZA: I am. The dress is too small for me.

ARTEMISIA: Is your smock rolled up inside?

PRUDENZA: No.

ARTEMISIA: Stand. Still. Don't look in the mirror.

PRUDENZA: I'm not.

ARTEMISIA: I can't pull the cord tight enough if you are looking in the mirror. What happened to you? Take it off. If you're going to wear this dress I need to find a longer cord.

PRUDENZA: Can you notice anything, is it possible, something outside of the canvas frame? *(Pause.)* Why do you think I can barely squeeze into one of your dresses, when they are always too big for me?

ARTEMISIA: Why? *(Silence.)* Are you pregnant? *(Silence.)*

PRUDENZA: The whole town knows. Why do you think they were harrassing me this morning? Throwing chicken feathers, throwing chicken blood. The whole town knows. You're the only one who doesn't.

ARTEMISIA: Behind my back, deceiving me.

PRUDENZA: You should have noticed how fat I was getting.

ARTEMISIA: How many months? How long have you known? How long?

PRUDENZA: Three months.

ARTEMISIA: *(Shrieking.)* Three months. *(Francesco wakes up.)* Hiding it from me. Working here with me, sleeping there with him. Saying how long can I stay here locked up with her. Running off to see him. Asking me to buy rose water. When you were pregnant already. You weren't thinking about rose water, oil of clove. You were thinking about your dowry. First I'll get permission. Then I'll get a dowry. Then I'll get married. Unless you're married already. Are you?

PRUDENZA: No.

ARTEMISIA: No. Not married already. That's good. Not married already.

PRUDENZA: I was waiting to get your permission.

ARTEMISIA: You didn't ask my permission to get pregnant, did you ? You're not getting my permission now. Money for your dowry. You're not going to get that either. Not one shred of it. *(Artemisia picks up money from table.)* Not one little shred of it and he's not going to get one more shred of you either. *(Remembering her father's words to her, Artemisia freezes and then imitates her father.)* Let me build a cross and I'll nail all three of you to it. Then you can come to my funeral ten minutes later. And you will not get one more shred of her. And not one more shred of this either. Not one more shred of her. *(Artemisia looks into the mirror.)* I say that when you are painting you should take a flat mirror and often look at your work in it. And it will appear in reverse, and you will be better able to judge its errors than in any other way. *(Quiet, sits.)* Under the mattress, by my pillow is a leather pocket, bring it to me.

(Prudenza brings a leather pouch; Artemisia opens the pouch and starts taking out a pile of coins.)

ARTEMISIA: Ten, twenty, thirty, forty . . .

PRUDENZA: What are you doing?

ARTEMISIA: . . . fifty, sixty, seventy, eighty, ninety, one hundred, fifty, two hundred, two fifty.

PRUDENZA: Under your mattress? That's where you hid it.

ARTEMISIA: Two hundred fifty. Yes. Three hundred. Don't talk to me when I'm counting, fifty, four hundred, four fifty . . .

PRUDENZA: The whole time in this room?

ARTEMISIA: . . . four fifty. My savings. Five hundred . . . five fifty . . . six hundred . . . six fifty . . . seven hundred . . .

FRANCESCO: I didn't bring any money with me.

PRUDENZA: You've had it there the whole time.

ARTEMISIA: My savings. I said seven hundred, didn't I? Seven hundred . . . seven fifty . . . eight hundred . . . eight fifty . . . nine hundred . . . nine fifty . . . one thousand. One thousand. For you. Go ahead. Take it. It's all for you. I want you to have it. Francesco! Take a message to Codazzi. Prudenza will be ready to marry him this evening.

Scene Twelve: Rome 1612. Prison

Agostino is pacing behind bars in a prison cell. Artemisia is outside the cell, standing in the shadows, not immediately visible.

AGOSTINO: If you want to marry me, I'll give you three choices. Come out of the shadows. You don't have to be afraid of me. I'm behind bars. I'll give you three choices. You press charges, I destroy you. Your father is not the only one with friends in high places, I have them too. And they do not like me being in here, not at all. Second choice: your father presses charges against me, you deny them. Deny everything.

ARTEMISIA: I don't like those choices.

AGOSTINO: That's the way it is. Those are your choices.

ARTEMISIA: And third. What is my third choice?

AGOSTINO: Third choice: you and your father drop charges, I walk out of here and marry you.

ARTEMISIA: Third choice. That's the only choice. The other two are not choices.

AGOSTINO: No, I gave you three choices.

ARTEMISIA: Third choice. How can you marry me if you are married already?

AGOSTINO: Because I am not. They brought a letter to me here, in prison. *(Pause.)* She's dead.

ARTEMISIA: She's dead? For how long? How did she die?

AGOSTINO: That's not your problem. She was a wicked woman.

ARTEMISIA: You should have told me. You should never have promised me.

AGOSTINO: Get your father to drop charges.

ARTEMISIA: Then what?

AGOSTINO: Then I will keep my promise.

ARTEMISIA: No, I mean then what, about the court?

AGOSTINO: If you drop charges, you don't testify. There is no court.

ARTEMISIA: Too late. I gave my testimony already. The notary came to the studio.

AGOSTINO: What did you tell him?

ARTEMISIA: I told him about that day. I told him what happened. So now, what are my three choices? No choices, right? No choices. *(Silence.)* And the midwives came. I forgot. Two midwives came.

AGOSTINO: And what did they find?

ARTEMISIA: I don't know. Put their fingers in. I don't know. They don't tell me, they tell the court.
(Silence.)

AGOSTINO: Your father cannot do this to me. I don't know who he thinks he is. I care more about you than he ever did. I'd give you the bread out of my mouth. But him, if he cared about you a fraction of the amount he cares about the copy of his Judith, he would drop charges immediately. *(Pause.)* Contradict your father's charges. Deny everything. Say you don't know me. You never met me. If the midwives swear you are not a virgin, tell them it was someone else. Tell them it was Cosimo. He's dying anyway.

ARTEMISIA: He has the French pox.

AGOSTINO: Say it was the pigment grinder, or the plasterer, one of your father's employees . . .

ARTEMISIA: No, I can't say that. I told them already.

AGOSTINO: Remember: you choose. You can get your father to drop charges.

ARTEMISIA: And if I try, and I convince him, what will you do?

AGOSTINO: Give me your hands. *(Agostino kisses her hands.)* Soon we'll be together.

ARTEMISIA: And you promise?

Scene Thirteen: Naples 1638. Painting Studio

Prudenza looking at herself in the mirror in the ill-fitting blue dress. Judith and Holofernes *on the easel.*

ARTEMISIA: And he promised you?

PRUDENZA: Yes.

ARTEMISIA: And you trust him?

PRUDENZA: Yes. *(Pause.)* I kept delaying. Not him. *(Prudenza retreats behind screen.)* Shall I take this bolt of cotton? I can use it to make the clothes I need.

ARTEMISIA: The Egyptian cotton? You're right. Take it. Make undergarments. *(Pause.)* But before you take that, look under my bed. In my chests. You'll find everything you need: smocks, dresses, nightshirts.

PRUDENZA: In the Susanna chest?

ARTEMISIA: Yes. Take the whole chest.

PRUDENZA: *(From behind screen.)* Can I take these ribbons? You never wear them.

ARTEMISIA: Take them.

PRUDENZA: I'll take the whole Susanna chest. There are a lot of things I can use in here.

ARTEMISIA: I already told you to take it. If you could get in position for one minute, I could probably paint the rest from memory.

(Prudenza emerges from behind screen with a bundle of worn pages.)

PRUDENZA: Roman court. 1612. Rapes and procurements. For the curia and the . . .

ARTEMISIA: *(Interrupting.)* Stop. Put that back. Where did you find it?

PRUDENZA: In the bottom of the chest. "For the curia and the state versus Agostino Tassi, painter." A rape trial? "The state versus Agostino Tassi painter, Before the Illustrious and Excellent Lord Heironimo Felicio.

ARTEMISIA: *(Trying to grab the papers away.)* Stop reading. Put it back. I didn't say you could read it.

PRUDENZA: *(Keeping it away from Artemisia.)* You said I could take the whole chest. *(Reading.)* "Lord Decio Cambio, Notary. Pro charitate. Ostilio Toccio, Substitute Notary." *(Turns a page.)* "Index of the witnesses: Petition of Orazio Gentileschi to His Holiness, Donna Artemisia Gentileschi, examination by the midwives, Donna Tuzia, Agostino Tassi of Rome . . ." *(Turns the page.)* "Petition of Orazio Gentileschi to His holiness: Most Holy Father. Orazio Gentileschi, painter, most humble servant of your holiness respectfully reports to you how a daughter of the plaintiff, Artemisia Gentileschi, has been deflowered by force and carnally known many many times by Agostino Tassi."

Scene Fourteen: Rome 1612. Courtroom

The painting studio is transformed into a courtroom. Artemisia's copy of Judith and Holofernes *is brought out into center stage and placed on an easel. A witness stand is brought in.*

ORAZIO: Orazio Gentileschi, painter, most humble servant of your holiness, respectfully reports to you how, as a result of the complicity of Madame Tuzia . . .

TUZIA: Why Orazio is bringing charges against me, I don't know. Her father had great hopes about Artemisia becoming a painter. I am sure now that he is very disappointed. When I first moved into the Gentileschi house, Orazio hugged me, warmly, saying that he was happy his daughter and I were friends and she could enjoy herself a little, as she was always alone and didn't have anyone. I have seen Agostino alone in the room many times with Artemisia. And many times I have reproved her. She would say "What is it you want? Mind your own business and don't meddle in matters that don't concern you."

ORAZIO: As a result of the complicity of Madame Tuzia, my tenant, my daughter, Artemisia Gentileschi, has been deflowered by force and carnally known many, many times by Agostino Tassi.

COSIMO: Agostino told me many times that he was in love with Artemisia and had promised to marry her. However, he was unable to do so as he was married already. Agostino's wife, Maria, angered him greatly when she betrayed him and ran away with a lover. Agostino was disgraced by her flight and came to Rome in desperation. Recently, Agostino showed me letters that his wife had been killed. He bragged to me that he was responsible for her death, showing me records of payments received from merchants in Lucca. Whether or not Agostino was responsible for his wife's death, I don't know. I do know that Agostino came to know the said Artemisia carnally and he deflowered her, as Agostino himself told me many times in confidence.

ORAZIO: Agostino through his intrigues, took from the hands of the same young woman a painting of Judith large in size. And because, Holy Father, this is such a nasty deed, giving such serious and great injury and damage to the poor plaintiff, especially since it was done under the trust of friendship, it is like a murder. Thus kneeling at your Holy feet, I implore you in the name of Christ to take action against this ugly intemperance by bringing to justice those who deserve it.

NOTARY: I am reading the transcript of the examination that the aforenamed woman had undergone at another time on March twenty-eighth, 1612. *(Reads Artemisia's testimony.)* He threw me onto the edge of the bed, pushing me with a hand on my breast . . . he put a knee between my thighs to keep me from closing them. Lifting my clothes, with so much trouble, he placed a hand with a handkerchief at my throat and on my mouth to keep me from screaming, he let go of my hands, which he had been holding with his other hand. He put both knees between my legs with his member pointed at me he began to push it inside. I felt a strong burning. It hurt very much, but because he held my mouth with a handkerchief, I couldn't cry out. I tried to scream, calling Tuzia, I scratched his face and pulled his hair before he penetrated me again. I grasped him so hard, I even removed a piece of flesh. All this didn't bother him at all — he kept doing his business, which kept him on top of me for a while holding his member inside me. I was crying saying, "I'd like to kill you because you have dishonored me." And to stop my crying, he said, "Give me your hand. I promise to marry you as soon as I get out of the labyrinth I am in." Later he induced me to yield lovingly, many times, to his desires, since many times he reconfirmed this promise to me. Asking me to have patience.

Scene Fifteen: Naples 1638. Painting Studio

Prudenza still dressed in blue dress is reading the trial text.

PRUDENZA: *(Reads Prudentia's testimony.)* He threw me onto the edge of the bed, pushing me with a hand on my breast . . . he put a knee between my thighs to keep me from closing them. Lifting my clothes, with so much trouble, he placed a hand with a handkerchief at my throat and on my mouth to keep me from screaming , he let go of my hands which he had been holding with his other hand. He put both knees between my legs . . . This happened?

ARTEMISIA: I know. I know. I know.

PRUDENZA: . . . he began to push it inside. I felt a strong burning. It hurt very much but, because he held my mouth with a handkerchief I couldn't cry out. I tried to scream, calling Tuzia, I scratched his face and pulled his hair before he penetrated me again.

ARTEMISIA: I know. I know. I know.

PRUDENZA: You never told me.

ARTEMISIA: What was I thinking? Why did I say anything? Why did I say those words? He threw me onto the edge of the bed . . . Why did I say that? He put both knees between my legs with his . . . What was I thinking? A strong burning. What was I doing? What was I telling the notary? I should never have told him.

(Prudenza lays down text and begins to braid Artemisia's hair.)

PRUDENZA: My father?

ARTEMISIA: No. Not your father. Quiet courtroom. Everyone listening.

PRUDENZA: Agostino was my father, wasn't he?

ARTEMISIA: No. Not your father. 1612. Three years before you were born. Orazio refused to drop the charges. I begged him. I asked him. "Please drop the charges. Agostino promised he will marry me." My father refused to drop the charges. The notary's voice shouting in my ear. Is this the testimony you gave to the court three months ago? Are these your words? Is this your testimony? Orazio was watching me. Agostino was watching me. Father on the right side. Lover on the left. Each were waiting for me to betray the other. Are these your words? Is this your testimony?

Scene Sixteen: Rome 1612. Courtroom

NOTARY: *(To Artemisia.)* Are these your words? Is this your testimony?

ARTEMISIA: *(To Agostino.)* I tried to get my father to drop charges.

NOTARY: Are these your words? Is this your testimony?

ARTEMISIA: *(To Agostino.)* He wouldn't. He refused.

NOTARY: Are these your words? Is this your testimony?

(Artemisia is silent.)

AGOSTINO: *(To Artemisia.)* Answer him. Do it. Deny the charges.

NOTARY: Will you confirm your testimony? Your father pressed charges against the said Agostino Tassi. A notary came to your painting studio to interview you. What the court requires is confirmation of your testimony. Are these your words? Is this your testimony?

(Artemisia is silent for a very long time.)

AGOSTINO: She's not speaking because she knows the words she said are lies. Never have I had carnal intercourse, nor desired to, with the said Artemisia. I visited her house with the honor and respect which one shows in a friend's house. I have never deceived my friend, Orazio, nor her. Everything that Artemisia said and everything written on that paper is a lie.

NOTARY: *(To Artemisia.)* Are these your words? Is this your testimony?

(Artemisia is silent for an even longer time.)

AGOSTINO: Not only have I not raped the said Artemisia, but I have never had sexual relations with her. If Artemisia confirms that I have had relations with her and deflowered her I will tell her to her face she is not telling the truth. Whenever I visited her house there was always some man around. A stone cutter named Marco with whom you couldn't trust a female cat. Pasquino from Florence who boasted publicly that he had had Artemisia.

ARTEMISIA: Everything in the document is the truth.

AGOSTINO: It is not. You are lying through your throat. I didn't rape you. She is lying. If Artemisia says that I've taken away her virginity, she is telling lies . . .

ARTEMISIA: *(Interrupting.)* Everything I said is the truth. You know it's the truth.

AGOSTINO: In that case, why didn't you bring suit earlier? Why wait until now?

ARTEMISIA: He knows why I waited. I hoped something else could be arranged. Not this.

AGOSTINO: You wanted me as your husband. Say it. You were hoping that if you testified against me, you could have me as your husband.

ARTEMISIA: I hoped to have you as a husband, but now I don't. Everything I have said in my testimony is the truth.

AGOSTINO: If everything she says is the truth, let her give her testimony wearing torture rings.

ARTEMISIA: If it was not the truth, I wouldn't have said it.

NOTARY: *(Producing torture rings.)* In order to remove any mark of infamy, to remove any doubt about the things you said, so it does not appear that you are a partner in the crime, mostly to corroborate and strengthen your testimony, are you willing to confirm your testimony under the torture of thumbscrews?

ARTEMISIA: Yes.

(Notary attaches torture rings.)

ARTEMISIA: I told the truth. I wish it were a lie.

(The notary tightens the rings.)

ARTEMISIA: But everything in my testimony is true. True. True. True. He knows it's true. Ask me again. I'll tell you again. True. True. True. True. True. True.

AGOSTINO: Stop it. What's wrong with you?

ARTEMISIA: I didn't mean yes, I meant no. I said no. You kept saying yes. Yes.

AGOSTINO: You will pay for these lies.

ARTEMISIA: You know it's true. Everything I've said. Everything I said in my testimony. True. He knows it is true.

AGOSTINO: Why are you telling this? Why? It's your father, isn't it? Because he owes me money, isn't it?

ARTEMISIA: *(Holding up torture rings.)* These are the rings you gave me. These are the promises you made.

AGOSTINO: A lie. Everything she says is a lie.

ARTEMISIA: I trusted him.

AGOSTINO: I trusted her.

ORAZIO: I trusted both of you. In my house. Under my roof. Both of you.

ARTEMISIA: I said no.

Scene Seventeen: Naples 1638. Painting Studio

Prudenza in blue dress; Judith Slaying Holofernes *on the easel. Artemisia holds a ring in torture ring position.*

ARTEMISIA: These are the rings you gave me. These are the promises you made.

PRUDENZA: Whose ring is it?

ARTEMISIA: *(Giving ring to Prudenza.)* It was my mother's. Your namesake. You take it. Orazio tried to give it to me as I was sent off to Florence to marry your father. I threw it back at him. Marrying me off to an out-of-work painter. Old. Toes gnarled up.
(Prudenza takes the ring and puts it on her finger.)

PRUDENZA: Gold. Beautifully carved.

ARTEMISIA: And the stolen painting. My Judith. The pope decided the evidence was inconclusive and claimed the Judith for his private painting collection in the Vatican.

PRUDENZA: What happened to Agostino after the trial?
(Francesco enters unseen.)

ARTEMISIA: They released him. Eight months later. And Orazio and Agostino worked on the casino of the muses together. After the trial, after the scandal. The two of them worked together on the ceiling. Me in Florence. With your father. Agostino and Orazio working together on the Casino ceiling. I was far away in Florence under the wing of the Medicis. Friend of Galileo's. First woman admitted to the Academia del Disegno. Cosimo got me one Judith commission after another. He pitched them as revenge paintings. Me as Judith. Agostino as Holofernes.

FRANCESCO: Codazzi will meet you at St. Catherine's church at six o'clock.

PRUDENZA: Where do you want me? I am ready to pose for you.

ARTEMISIA: On the platform. Francesco, you too. Lie down. Head back. That's right. That's it. Perfect. *(To Prudenza.)* Hands extended. Holding the sword tightly. *(Pause.)* Sword pointed down. Weight on your left arm. *(Pause.)* Left hand holding head down by roots of hair. *(Long pause, Artemisia stares at her a long time.)* No. I can't do it. Climb down. *(To herself.)* two rectangles twenty feet by fifteen feet, two rectangles twenty feet by ten feet, four corner roundels each twelve and a half feet in diameter, one central roundel twenty feet in diameter . . .

PRUDENZA: Are you thinking of helping him?

ARTEMISIA: Wrap the canvases. I'll go to London. Where it is cold and damp and the paint never dries.

PRUDENZA: They worked together after the trial.

ARTEMISIA: Orazio Gentileschi and Agostino Tassi. Those were the names on the contract for the casino ceiling. *(Pause.)* And now he wants me to help paint the ceiling at Greenwich House. He'll be down on the floor bragging to his friends about what a great painter I am. I'll be up on the scaffolding doing all the work.

PRUDENZA: Let him paint it himself.

ARTEMISIA: I'll shout down at him, "Stop talking. Do you want to talk or do you want to paint?" I wonder if he has already laid out the design. One last letter.

(Prudenza looks for paper.)

ARTEMISIA: To the viceroy . . . Please do not ask me to paint a copy of a former work, without invention. I will not paint another Judith and Holofernes. Did you get that?

PRUDENZA: Yes.

ARTEMISIA: *(Dictating.)* I will not paint another Judith and Holofernes. For when the composition has been realized, when the light and dark areas have been defined, when the planes of the space have been established, the rest is a trifle. With this I end, kissing your hands and wishing you every happiness. Today the tenth day of June, 1638. Your most devoted and grateful servant, Artemisia Gentileschi.

(Prudenza brings over letter for Artemisia to sign.)

ARTEMISIA: Whatever you want, take. Whatever you don't want, throw it away. *(In Orazio's voice.)* Piles of old clothes. Who will wear them? Throw them out. Old rags, broken things, things that are worn out, useless. *(Repeating the words of Orazio's letter.)* When I assessed the ceiling, it came into my head that this is the ceiling I will paint with Artemisia. Gentileschi and Gentileschi. Father and daughter. Figures, lighting, perspective.

(Lights fade out on Artemisia, Prudenza, and Francesco. Tuzia enters and sings the following song, accompanying herself on the lute.)

TUZIA: One you'll have sorrow, two you'll have joy,
Three get a present, four get a boy,
Five receive silver, six receive gold,
Seven's a secret that's never been told,
Eight a love letter with promises three,
Nine means your true love's as true as can be.

END OF PLAY

Self Defense

or Death of Some Salesmen

By Carson Kreitzer

This play is dedicated to Aileen Wuornos,
and all those whose names we don't know.

PLAYWRIGHT'S BIOGRAPHY

Self Defense finishes out Ms. Kreitzer's *Women Who Kill* triptych, begun in 1993 with *Valerie Shoots Andy,* an investigation of Valerie Solanas's 1968 assassination attempt on Andy Warhol, followed by *Heroin/e (Keep Us Quiet.),* featuring Ellie Nesler, who entered a California courtroom and put five bullets in the man who molested her son. *The Slow Drag,* a jazz cabaret about a woman who passed as a man to play the music she loved, transferred from London's Fringe to the Whitehall Theatre in the West End, following an original Off Broadway production at The American Place Theatre. Other work includes *Freakshow, Take My Breath Away,* featured in the Brooklyn Academy of Music's 1997 Next Wave Festival, *Dead Wait,* and *The Love Song of J. Robert Oppenheimer,* current winner of the Lois and Richard Rosenthal New Play Prize. Ms. Kreitzer holds a degree in theater and literature from Yale University and has received grants from NYFA, New York State Council on the Arts, the National Endowment for the Arts, and TCG, two Jerome Fellowships, and a McKnight Advancement Grant. She is currently in residence at the Playwrights' Center in Minneapolis.

ORIGINAL PRODUCTION

Self Defense, or Death of Some Salesmen was first produced by Perishable Theatre in Providence, Rhode Island, on November 3, 2001, directed by Vanessa Gilbert, with the following cast:

Jo	Lynne McCollough
Lu	Casey Seymour Kim
Chastity, Jean, etc.	Anushka Carter
Daytona, Cassandra Chase, etc.	Marilyn Dubois
Coroner, LeeAnn, Pandora, etc.	Wendy Overly
Captain, Marty, Judge, etc.	Paul Buxton
Bucket	Kerry Callery
Drums, Prosecutor, Flaky Lawyer, etc.	Richard Noble

It was subsequently produced by Frank Theatre at the Playwrights' Center in Minneapolis on February 7, 2002, directed by Wendy Knox, with the following cast:

Jo	Phyllis Wright
Lu	Kim Shultz
Chastity, Jean, etc.	Sandra Struthers
Daytona, Cassandra Chase, etc.	Bianca Pettis

CORONER, LEEANN, PANDORA, ETC. . . . . Maria Asp
CAPTAIN, MARTY, JUDGE, ETC. . . . . Tom Sherohman
BUCKET . . . . Ron Menzel
DRUMS, PROSECUTOR, FLAKY LAWYER, ETC. . . . . . John Riedlinger

The New York premiere was produced by New Georges and Reverie Productions at HERE Arts Center on May 25, 2002, directed by Randy White, with the following cast:

JO . . . . Lynne McCollough
LU . . . . Carolyn Baeumler
CHASTITY, JEAN, ETC. . . . . Carolyn DeMerice
DAYTONA, CASSANDRA CHASE, ETC. . . . . Melle Powers
CORONER, LEEANN, PANDORA, ETC. . . . . Dee Pelletier
CAPTAIN, MARTY, JUDGE, ETC. . . . . Stephen Bradbury
BUCKET . . . . Mark Zeisler
DRUMS, PROSECUTOR, FLAKY LAWYER, ETC. . . . . Dan Illian

NOTES FOR *SELF DEFENSE*

Although this play is a work of fiction, it is inspired by events in the life of Aileen Wuornos, who was executed by the State of Florida on October 8, 2002. It takes texts or inspiration from courtroom transcripts, newspaper accounts, televised interviews, and the book *Dead Ends* by Michael Reynolds. Many thanks to Phyllis Chesler for her comprehensive and passionate essay "A Woman's Right to Self-Defense" in her book *Patriarchy* and to Nick Broomfield for creating the stunning documentary film *Aileen Wuornos: The Selling of a Serial Killer.*

ACKNOWLEDGMENTS

Self Defense was commissioned with public funds from the New York State Council on the Arts and developed in residencies with Mabou Mines, the Playwrights' Center, and A.S.K. Theater Projects, and with the assistance of a Theater Communication Group extended collaboration grant.

Thanks to everyone who helped make this play a reality — over the years, too many to list here. Special thanks to Dick Beebe, Susan Bernfield, Lisa McNulty, Mead Hunter, John Walch, Rachel Lloyd, and Dawn Botkins, who gives me hope in this world.

In future productions of this play, I would like the program to contain contact information for local antideath penalty groups and, if possible, local groups that help women break away from prostitution. The U.S. Campaign to Stop Commercial Sexual Exploitation of Children & Youth can be of assistance in finding a local group. Contact: Aiko Yoshi at (202) 244-1986 or via their Web site: www.stopcsec.us.

CHARACTERS

WOMEN:

JOLENE PALMER (JO): Prostitute on death row for the killing of seven johns.

LU: The lover who turns her in.

CHASTITY AND DAYTONA: Two strippers: the first suspects.

PANDORA: Their cohort.

LEEANN: Born again woman who adopts Jo in jail.

JEAN: Jo's overworked public defender.

CASSANDRA CHASE: Famous feminist.

ANNIE AMES: Hollywood producer.

Coroners 1, 2, and 3, Reporter, Waldren's Girl.

MEN:

CAPTAIN: The man in charge.

BUCKET AND DRUMS: Two undercover cops.

MARTY: A decent john. She doesn't kill him.

Judge, Shrink 1 and 2, Prosecutor, Flaky Lawyer, Cameraman.

DOUBLING

These roles can be played by eight actors, with Chastity, Daytona, and Pandora forming a thanatos/eros Greek chorus of sorts, doubling as strippers, coroners, and all other female roles as follows:

Chastity/Reporter/Jean/Coroner 3/Woman 1

Daytona/Coroner 2/Cassandra Chase

Pandora/Waldren's Girl/LeeAnn/Coroner 1/Woman 2

Lu doubles as Annie Ames.

The men double as follows:

Captain/Bystander/Marty/Judge/Guard

Bucket/Shrink

Drums/Shrink 2/Prosecutor/Flaky Lawyer/Cameraman

SETTING

This play is envisioned with a two-level set, with three playing areas below: center Jo's jail cell, with a pay phone nearby, stage left the suggestion of a police station, and stage right the hotel/apartment spaces. All this should be accomplished with as little furniture as possible. The courtroom scenes are down center. The upper area serves for the phone surveillance scenes as well as any characters who have to appear and disappear suddenly, like the coroners. Two poles, of the sort seen in strip clubs, essentially separate the three downstage areas, and at either side of the stage a television set is suspended, where the act titles, newscasts, etc. appear. The specifics of this design are not important (I have now seen the play performed with the audience on one, two, and three sides, always with a single-level set.); what is important is a multiplicity of playing areas and the ability to switch scenes instantaneously.

Self Defense

Prologue

Dim spot rises on a lone woman in a jail cell.

JO: I try to remember a time when I was not ashamed.
   I gotta go pretty far back.
   I don't even know . . . if I just can't remember back that far or if there
   never was one.

   They take your baby away at fourteen, that's a . . . Even before that, when
   I was a kid, I was ashamed. An gettin' beat.

   Alls I know is, when I was takin' care a you, I was not ashamed.
   Of anything I had to do.
   'Cos I had a reason. I had you to take care of.

   Like an angel on this earth, breathin' next to me.
   And nothin I did could leave a stain on me.

   'S the only time in my life I have not been ashamed just a livin'. What I
   had to do to keep my own miserable self breathing.

   But if I was alive so you could live, well that made sense.
   An' if I gotta die so you can live, that makes the most sense a anything
   I've heard yet.
   (She lights a cigarette. Lights up on Bucket, testifying in court.)
BUCKET: Well sir, bodies in the swamp off I-95 are not too unusual. So it
   took us quite a while to make the connection, between the five counties
   involved, that there could be a serial killer at work.
   *(Seven shots. BANG. BANG. BANG. BANG. BANG. BANG. BANG. Si-
   multaneous with the last three shots, lights up on three coroners, all female.
   Lab coats, glasses, hair up. High heels.)*
JO: You know, tonight is the beginning of a war?
CORONER 1: The remains are those of a nude Caucasian male.
JO: And it'll be eight o'clock in the morning in Iraq. And there's gonna be the
   bombing and they're checking out for terrorists in the United States 'cos
   they're probably planted.

CORONER 1: The skin and soft tissue is absent from around the mouth and eyes.

JO: They're infiltrated all over the United States and they're just gonna start some shit.

CORONER 1: There is no external ear tissue present.

JO: They been waitin' for this, you know. Just waiting for us to make that aggressive move.

BUCKET: In the first case, we determined the course of our investigation based on certain behaviors.

CORONER 2: *(Stepping up to examine the body.)* The genitalia are missing. Though whether removed or simply decomposed or chewed off by animals is impossible to determine.

JO: And they can start all their terrorist missions. Blowing shit up. And quiet stuff, too. Puttin' chemical warfare in the air conditioning systems. Poisoning people's brains. They know how to do all that shit.

BUCKET: Victim was found to frequent topless bars in the area, as well as frequenting prostitutes.

CORONER 3: X-rays reveal six metallic projectiles. Small-caliber bullets. One in the clavicle.

JO: 'Cos we taught 'em, right?

CORONER 3: Three in the back, one of them imbedded in the spinal column.

JO: Thought we could just give 'em this knowledge, our special CIA tactics, help 'em win their little war. Didn't think they'd be gettin' all cocky and turn around and put fuckin' legionary's disease in the air conditioning.

CORONER 3: One on the left side. Two in the chest.

JO: Biting the hand . . . that was feeding them all those years.

LU: *(Voice on phone.)* Why don't you just get it over with and tell them what you done?

JO: Louise. I didn't do anything.

BUCKET: He was last spotted at the 2001 Odyssey, a, uh, gentlemen's club.
(Lights and music up Sleazy, INXS's "Suicide Blonde.")
(The coroners step forward, shedding glasses and lab coats as in a porn film, revealing strippers outfits below. Two attach themselves to the strip-bar poles stage left and right [Chastity and Daytona], the third [Pandora] wanders off to sit with someone. The TV monitors proclaim:)

Act I: Paranoid and Pussy-Crazy

Lights up on police station.

CAPTAIN: Not much to go on with this Waldren guy. I think the drug angle is a bust, then we've got him changing his locks every six months or so, then we've got the topless joints.

BUCKET: And the dating service.

CAPTAIN: So he's paranoid and pussy-crazy, with bad business habits.

BUCKET: Yeah. And dead.

(Spots pick out the two strippers at either side of the stage.)

CHASTITY: So you know about the locks? Changing the locks? He was just weird about things.

DAYTONA: He gave me a TV an a VCR.

(Spot picks out Waldren's Girl [Pandora in a pink waitress uniform].)

WALDREN'S GIRL: Well, he was obsessed with pornography, extremely paranoid, drank heavily, smoked a lotta weed. He could be so sweet, and then the next minute he'd turn around and . . . scare the hell outta you. *(Beat.)* What else can I tell you? You know about the locks?

BUCKET: Yes, Ma'am. Was he the type who would pick up hitchhikers?

WALDREN'S GIRL: Well, if they were female, yeah. You know?

(Blackout. Spot on Jo: Jail cell.)

JO: I am not a difficult person. I'm not a fighter.

Often, with my clients, I'd talk about Jesus or I'd talk political. Or both at once. And we never got into arguments.

So you see, there was no need for them to go — looking for the nearest weapon, to try to use it on me, to — *(Beat.)* If it was in Western days they'd put me in a noose and watch . . . let the town watch me die.

(Police station. Chastity in slinky lycra dress, Captain and Drums.)

CHASTITY: He wanted to date me, but I told him I'm gay.

CAPTAIN: By date, you don't mean go to the movies, have dinner . . .

CHASTITY: No. Sex. You know. Have sex.

CAPTAIN: For money.

CHASTITY: Yeah.

CAPTAIN: All right, Chastity, just trying to establish a few things here. You don't have to worry. We're Homicide, not Vice.

CHASTITY: Right.

CAPTAIN: OK. So, he propositioned you, you refused.

CHASTITY: Yeah, I didn't want to. I don't do that. I mean, I'm gay. I live with someone, you know? I've got a girlfriend.

CAPTAIN: Do you mean to tell me that you don't have sex with customers at the club?

CHASTITY: Sure. I've done that.

I'm saying I didn't want to. I'm saying I told him no. He kept at me. He said we'd go over to his repair shop in Clearwater. I said I'd do some lap dances.

CAPTAIN: Lap dances?

CHASTITY: What it sounds like.

CAPTAIN: This is the last day in November?

CHASTITY: Yes. He said he'd give me a TV and a VCR for some dances at his shop. Me and Daytona, we talked it over, I told him, OK, if you bring some cash. So he gave me fifty bucks and a nineteen-inch Magnavox and a Fisher VCR . . . took us out there and back home. I don't have a car. We went in his van. Kind of red or maroon. Then when we were done, brought me back home, hooked up the Magnavox and the VCR, and left with her. Wasn't there more than twenty, twenty-five minutes.

CAPTAIN: *(Kindly.)* How about you suck me off or I turn you in on the prostitution?

CHASTITY: I'm sorry?

DRUMS: That's right. You're a sorry sack of shit, that's what you are.

CAPTAIN: *(Still kindly.)* It won't take long. I'm not getting any at home.

CHASTITY: *(Rubs her nose, looks around.)* Well, all right. Will you be needing me for further questioning?

CAPTAIN: That depends.

(Blackout. Spot on Jo.)

JO: Now they're saying that I'm a man hater. That's not true. I don't hate men. Why, some of my best friends are Johns.

But the problem is, the problem was the Gulf War, see? All my regulars were getting called away to the Gulf, to go defend Uncle Sam in the desert, make sure we got enough oil to keep the semis running.

I mean, oil's a very important thing for this country's economy. Shit, I know that. Make my money long the side of the highway. I know all about the importance a oil to the American economy. But that Gulf War shit, that was taking alla my regular customers away. Hadda move on. Hadda get in cars with strangers that I didn't know very well. And subsequently, on several occasions, I was called upon to defend myself. *(Phone rings. She looks at it, doesn't answer. Phone rings again. Sound of a car crash. She jumps, panics.)* GET AWAY FROM THERE, YOU STUPID BITCH. THAT'S A DEAD MAN'S CAR YOU JUST WRECKED.

Can . . . Can I get something to drink in here, please? I . . . I suppose you would call me an alcoholic, because I do suffer when it leaves my system. I'm never . . . without a drink for too long.
If I'm without a drink for too long I really start to feel it. Bad. And I been without a drink too long already. It's only . . . It's only gonna get worse.
(Police station.)

DRUMS: We got a picture of the other one, Daytona. Note the —
(A spot rises slowly on Daytona. Acid-wash jeans, tank top. Tattoos.)

BUCKET: Christ, that's a lotta tattoos.

DRUMS: Precisely.

BUCKET: *(Reading.)* "Property of Bruiser." *(Whistles.)* Nice.

DAYTONA: Sure. He gave me a TV and a VCR.

DRUMS: That's a lotta ink on a young girl's flesh.

BUCKET: Are you thinking what I'm thinking?

BUCKET AND DRUMS: Outlaw Bikers.

DAYTONA: I met Waldren around early November at the 2001 Odyssey. I met him through a girl. Pandora.
(Lights up on Pandora, pouring a drink behind a bar.)

DAYTONA: So named for her box. Which had the power to destroy the world, she said.
(Pandora smiles. Lights out.)

DAYTONA: The next time I see him was late November, and Chastity and I started talking to him about having a good time. We told him we'd each charge three hundred dollars for three dances. He asked us if we'd like a TV and a VCR instead of the three hundred. And we accepted and left with him in a van — I think it was blue or maybe green — and headed for Clearwater. We smoked a joint on the way over and drank some beer. Stopped at a Jiffy store, got some food, and went over to his shop. Went through and we picked out a TV and VCR. A Zenith. He loaded them up in the van and then we all got undressed in his office. Chastity had sex with him and then I went on with her. He took us back about four or it was five. He took me home first, brought in the TV and VCR. Hooked them up for me. Fifteen, twenty minutes and he was gone.
(She walks into scene with cops.)

DAYTONA: My boyfriend is really gonna kill me.

DRUMS: Your cooperation is imperative —

DAYTONA: He's just gonna kill me if he finds out what I've been telling you.

DRUMS: Well, there's no way he's gonna find out. We wouldn't want you getting hurt.

DAYTONA: I didn't fuck him.

DRUMS: OK.

DAYTONA: *(Rubs her nose.)* It was Chastity. I didn't fuck him.

DRUMS: OK. And he —

DAYTONA: Gave me a TV and a VCR, yeah.

BUCKET: Could we see those, please?

DAYTONA: *(Hangdog.)* Hadda sell 'em.

DRUMS: What?

DAYTONA: *(Precise.)* I had to sell them.

DRUMS: Why?

DAYTONA: Needed the money.

(Blackout. Spot on Jo.)

JO: I told her she should quit her job, 'cos she was making like $150 bucks a week and I was making like $150 bucks a day. When I went out. And it was no problem you know, I . . . I wanted to take care a her.

I liked it that I was able to . . . that there was somebody I could take care of.

An' you could get all . . . . psychological about it if you want, say it's on account of that baby I had when I was fourteen, that they took away. *(Laughs.)* You'd think I'd learn my lesson. That was the first time I got raped in a car. Cuttin' school, trippin' on acid and a quaalude. Didn't want to go to the cops 'cos I thought they'd know. Give me a blood test or some shit, throw me in jail. Saw that motherfucker around town all the time. He saw me, gettin big. Musta known. I didn't tell nobody who it was. You'd think you could get in a car with a friend of your dad, right? Somebody you've seen around the house? But you can't . . . you can't let 'em kill you. You know? You gotta beat it.

Anyway, you could say it was because of that, but I don't think that's it. I think it's simpler than that.

An' she's just the most . . . good . . . person I've ever met in my whole life. She's one person out of this whole goddamned life that's actually a good person. And I was just glad I could take care of her.

CHASTITY: *(Appears in spot.)* I know nobody's asking me, but I think it's about time we had a female serial killer.

(Police station.)

CAPTAIN: Done with the interviews?

BUCKET: Yes, sir.

Neither one slept with him, and they both got dropped off first.

CAPTAIN: We have anything solid on them?

BUCKET: No, sir.

CAPTAIN: Let 'em go, keep an eye on 'em. All we can do. You like 'em for it?

BUCKET: Not really, sir.

DRUMS: They lied. They've got no alibi's except each other, and can't even agree on a story . . .

CAPTAIN: Let 'em go. Keep an eye on 'em. No other suspects?

BUCKET: Not unless someone killed him 'cos he gave a stripper their VCR.

CAPTAIN: Keep on it. Something's gotta break.

(Soft lights up on Jo and Lu, bedroom. Lu lying in bed. Jo sitting on the edge.)

JO: *(A low, insistent whisper.)* Honey, I

I killed a man today. I just gotta . . . I gotta talk through this a little bit. I know it upsets you an' I understand that. Christ, don't I spend my whole life tryin' to keep you clean from all this shit. Keep it away from you. Keep it from touching you. But this is . . . this is too much.

Today . . . Out in the woods. I had to make the choice. Him or me. I mean, part of it was instinct, a big part a how I managed it. You just . . . when you have to. When you know you're gonna die if you don't get this right. But for the instinct to kick in, I had to . . . I don't know how to explain it. Empty myself out. Of the fear, the attitude of, I'm a worthless piece a shit an' this was gonna happen sooner or later. I had to turn my brain to thinkin' No, fuck this. I am not gonna die out here. I had to decide that.

Shit, I'm so stupid sometimes. Thinkin' you can trust people. If they seem nice an' all. 'Cos he, you know, he seemed . . . but that was Bullshit. All parta this plan, get me into the woods get me away from where anybody might hear, might happen by. An he, shit, I'm tellin' you he had this thing planned out. It was . . . I never been so fuckin' scared. Not in a while. I thought those days were over, me gettin' inta cars like a fuckin' teenager, thinks they're invincible. That's why I just been stickin' to my regulars, years now. I told you that.

But I know. You gotta have your things. An' the cable TV. I know, sweetie, you get bored when I'm not here during the day. I know. I know I gotta take care a you. An don't you worry, I'm gonna do it. I'll just . . . keep my eye out. Watch myself.

'Cos I swear, honey, I thought I wasn't gonna make it back to you today. That's what I thought.

(A light snore from Lu.)

JO: Look like an angel when you're asleep, I swear it. An angel.

I'll take care a you. Always.

Don't know what I'd ever do without you. Baby.

(Blackout. Pin spot up on the Coroner, Reporter on Video.)

CORONER (PANDORA): Nude white male, between the ages of twenty-seven and fifty. Five feet ten inches tall. Can only approximate a time of death: Five days to two weeks.

REPORTER (CHASTITY): An eight-month string of unsolved murders has left investigators in north-central Florida facing the possibility of a serial killer — or killers — preying upon highway travelers throughout the region.

CORONER (PANDORA): The skin is absent from the anterior chest and abdomen,

REPORTER (CHASTITY): Since early this year, five middle-aged white males have been discovered alongside roads and in woods dead from gunshot wounds.

CORONER (PANDORA): *(Continues.)* as is the vast majority of skeletal muscle and other soft tissues. The inside of each arm from the axilla down to the hands has exposed bone.

REPORTER (CHASTITY): A sixty-six-year-old evangelist, missing since January, is also feared murdered. The latest victim, a former Alabama police chief, was found in September, nude except for a pair of tube socks.

(Police station.)

DRUMS: We know they liked Busch.

BUCKET: Pardon?

DRUMS: Beer. Cans found in the car.

CORONER: Nude white male, between the ages of thirty and sixty. Five feet nine inches tall. Time of death: between two and three weeks. Cause of death nine .22 caliber bullets. Decomposition so severe that even the .22 caliber projectiles have deteriorated.

(Bucket gives a press conference. Daytona leans on a pole.)

DAYTONA: I danced a lotta the bars around Orlando.

BUCKET: White middle-aged men driving around Florida are are targets right now.

The Circus.

The Booby Trap.

The Candy Bar.
Scores.
The Naked and the Dead.

Make Your Money, Girl.

All our victims are white
males traveling alone.

Motorists are strongly
advised not to pick up
hitchhikers.

DAYTONA: That's a lotta laps. Know what I mean?

(Spots out on Bucket and Daytona. Video up: Reporter. [Captain is unaware of the video.])

REPORTER: On the morning of July 30, Lane Michaelson left the Gilchrist Sausage Company in Ocala on his delivery route, which would take him through the Ocala National Forest. He failed to return. At approximately four AM, the dark brown Ford truck carrying a silver refrigerator box with "Gilchrist Sausage Company" painted on both sides was spotted on the shoulder of State Road 19 —

REPORTER AND CAPTAIN: just south of its intersection with Highway 40 —

CAPTAIN: twenty miles east of Ocala. The doors to the cab were unlocked, but the refrigerator box was secured.

DRUMS: This guy got killed making a sausage delivery?

CAPTAIN: Apparently.

DRUMS: And if we *are* dealing with a hooker here. So I mean, this guy *got* it . . . making a sausage delivery. If you know what I mean.

CAPTAIN: I get it. I just fail to see the humor in it.

DRUMS: Sausage delivery. Sorry. It's just funny. Forget it.

CAPTAIN: I'll try.

DRUMS: Wycowski'll think it's funny.

CORONER: It is in fact a misnomer to label Jolene Palmer the first female serial killer.

There have been others. Some place the number at thirty-five or so. But Jolene Palmer differed from these cases because she was closer to male patterns of serial killing. She used a gun. She killed strangers.

Most women killed members of their families, with poison.

(She smiles. Blackout. Lights up on Jo and Lu. The apartment is a filthy mess. Lu looks out the window.)

LU: Where'd ya get the car?

JO: Borrowed it.

LU: He didn't have no money?

JO: Borrowed it from a *friend.*

(Lu nods. Beat.)

LU: He didn't have no money?

JO: Ah, that's right. You're a laugh riot, that's what you are.

LU: Just kidding. Jeez. 'S a nice car. I always wanted a red Camaro.

JO: 'S a Firebird.

LU: Lemme drive it.

JO: No. I said I borrowed it.

LU: So what's that mean?

JO: That means I gotta keep it in one piece.

LU: Ha ha very funny.

JO: What is this? *(Kicks a bag of chips on the floor.)* You know, I leave you in charge of this place, and look at it! You can't clean worth a shit. It's no wonder they fired you at that motel. Prob'ly the shittiest maid they ever seen.

LU: Whyn't you clean up, if you don't like it?

JO: ME? *(Comes right up against her.)* WHAT AM I DOIN' ALL DAY? HUH? TO PAY FOR A ROOF OVER YOUR HEAD AN' FOOD ON THE TABLE? YOU CAN'T EVEN IMAGINE WHAT I'M DOIN' ALL FUCKING DAY. TO COME HOME TO A FILTHY HOUSE AN' YOU SASSIN' OFF TA ME?

LU: *(Very small.)* I'm sorry.

JO: Shit, honey. How come you make me get so mad at you like that? You know I love you.

LU: Yeah.

JO: Look, let's get atta here. How 'bout I take you to Red Lobster.
(Lu doesn't respond.)

JO: I'll help you clean up when we get back. Can't get no more roaches than we already got, right?
(Lu shrugs.)

JO: Come on, get dressed.

LU: I am dressed.

JO: You don't wear fuckin' sweatpants to Red Lobster. For Chrissakes. Now you're just tryin' to make me aggravated.
(Lu stomps out. Jo shouts after her.)

JO: I *buy* you *clothes.* Put on somethin' nice! *(Alone.)* Get a nice dinner. Few drinks on the way home. Stop at the Kwik-e-Mart, pick up a buncha roach motels. Have this place cleaned up in no time. 'S gonna be alright.
(Lu comes back in wearing jeans.)

JO: That's better.

LU: I wanna drive.

(Beat.)

JO: Sure, baby. Anything you want.

(Blackout. Strip club back up full: "Suicide Blonde," Chastity and Daytona at their poles dance casually, not putting much effort into it.)

DAYTONA: You know, I think it's kinda funny we finally got a female serial killer.

CHASTITY: *(Laughs until she snorts.)* Yeah!

I mean, it wouldn't be funny if it happened to my brother.

But if it happened to my stepfather?

That'd be funny.

(Music up loud. Chastity and Daytona become more suggestive. Money begins to rain down from the sky. Music crescendoes into the sound of a car crash. Chastity and Daytona stop, bend down to collect the money. Jo and Lu run onstage, disheveled and bloody. Jo holds license plates in her ripped-up hands.)

LU: I think I got a c'cussion. I gotta . . . I gotta sit down for a minute.

JO: YOU STUPID BITCH. THAT'S A DEAD MAN'S CAR YOU JUST WRECKED. COME ON.

(They run offstage. In separate pin spots: Drums testifies in court, Bucket is taking a statement from a witness.)

DRUMS: The whole case was finally about to bust wide open —

BYSTANDER: She just ripped them plates off with her bare hands. She's gotta be real strong. It was her and another girl. I said I had called for help, and they just took off inta the woods.

(Blackout. Lights up on the apartment, only slightly cleaner. Lu lying on the floor, watching TV.)

TELEVISION REPORTER: Christian Missionary Walter Thorpe left his home to visit relatives in Arkansas. He never arrived. The victim's vehicle was found abandoned in Marion County, Florida, after a crash. Two white females were seen exiting the vehicle and leaving southbound on foot. Here are the police sketches, drawn from eyewitness accounts of the two. *(Lu stares at the TV in transfixed horror.)* The first is blonde, twenty-five to thirty, five eight to five ten, last seen wearing jeans and a camouflage T-shirt. Her companion is heavyset, twenty-five to thirty, five three to five five, wearing a plaid shirt and baseball cap. *(Lu rocks back and forth, emitting a high, keening whine.)* Anyone with any information on the whereabouts of these two should contact local police immediately. They are presumed armed and may be dangerous. Repeat: these two women are suspects in the recent string of highway murders. They may be the nation's first female serial killers.

LU: *(Small, scared voice.)* Shit.
　　(Blackout. Apartment. Jo enters, drunk.)
JO: Lu? *(Looks in the bedroom.)* Lu? *(Beat.)* Aw, shit.
　　(Blackout. Music: "Runaway" by Del Shannon.)

Act II: The Last Resort

Music continues as lights come up on a masculine apartment. Plaid sofa, per-
haps. Jo stands just out of the shower, dressed but with her hair wrapped in
a towel. A nondescript middle-aged man, Marty, is with her. It's his apart-
ment.

JO: I can't believe you got this record. I been wanting to listen to this song
　　ever since . . . .
　　How come you think he blew his head off?
MARTY: I dunno.
JO: 'Cos he only had that one hit?
MARTY: I guess.
JO: Shit, it's a good song, though. A lotta people don't even have that. A song
　　they wrote, that can make people feel things, or remember shit, you know?
　　Been wantin' to hear this ever since I walked into that empty house. That
　　song's the first thing went through my head. I swear, I never been so heart-
　　broken in all my life. I been through some shit, but this is the worst. I
　　don't know if I can even go back in there. It's so empty. Everything in
　　there remindin' me a her every second. It's too much to bear, it is. *(Beat.)*
　　How about if I stay here for a few days. With you. That be OK?
MARTY: Uh . . . you gonna charge me?
JO: You gonna charge me *rent?*
MARTY: *(Looking down and smiling.)* Naw.
JO: Well then let's call it even. How about we try that again. Hey, Marty. How
　　about if I stay here a couple days.
MARTY: I'd like that.
JO: Well all right then. Get me outta that house. And we can commiserate
　　about our wives that left us.
MARTY: OK. *(Pause. He looks at her.)* You wanna Jack and Coke?
JO: That sounds great. I'd love one, Marty. *(As soon as he leaves the room, her*
　　smile fades.) Where'd you go, little girl? Can't take care a herself.
　　(Blackout. "Runaway" swells, then fades. In darkness:)

COP VOICE: Ma'am. You'd better come with us.
  (*Lights up on Lu and the Captain, upper level.*)
LU: I don't want no —
CAPTAIN: Now, you've got some rights here we need to read you.
LU: I don't want no rights, I just —
CAPTAIN: Right to remain silent, right to an attorney, all that. Like you hear
  on TV.
LU: I don't want no right to remain silent, I just wanna get all this straight.
CAPTAIN: You waive, then?
LU: Yeah, I waive. I just —
CAPTAIN: You waive your right to an attorney —
LU: I just wanna get all this straight.
CAPTAIN: You waive your right to remain silent on the grounds that it might
  incriminate you —
LU: That's what I wanna get straight. I didn't have nothing to do with this. I
  didn't do nothing wrong.
  (*Blackout. Spot on Chastity.*)
CHASTITY: The cops around here have been pretty jumpy since Gainesville.
CAPTAIN: (*Addressing his posse.*) All right, men. We've been trailing this bitch
  for a year.
CHASTITY: You remember Gainesville, don't you?
CAPTAIN: Makin' fools of us. Six bodies, one missing Missionary probably gonna
  turn up any minute chewed up by swamp rats.
CHASTITY: Got a lotta press. The college students. Five, I think. Creepy shit.
  This guy taunting the cops with his knowledge of police procedure. Wash-
  ing the bodies down with cleansers. One girl got her head cut off, put
  on a turntable next to her. Just goin' round and round when the police
  came in. Round and round.

  Her body posed in a sexually provocative position, whatever that means.
  Read that somewhere.
  'Course maybe that's just what the Crime Reporter thought, when he saw
  her naked and tossed away like . . . a dead thing.

  I'm serious. People take jobs they like.
  You think about that next time that nice man is helping you try on shoes.

  Course, then that means I picked that job at Platinum's 'cos I liked it.
  An' I guess that's true in some ways, not so true in others. I like the money.
  The hours suit me fine. Guess I like . . . feelin' like a star, a little tiny bit.
  But I wasn't talkin' about me. I was talkin' about those College Girls.

CAPTAIN: Not the kind of thing we want the state of Florida remembered for.

CHASTITY: Daddies burning rubber all over the state, whisking their little girls home from the dorms. They got him, finally. Turned out it was 'cos his Daddy used to beat him all the time. *(Beat, serious.)* Why would anybody do that to a child?

CAPTAIN: So get out there and bring her back to me. Hog-tied if at all possible. That's all.

(Spot on Annie Ames, a Hollywood producer. She talks excitedly on the phone.)

ANNIE: Now open to page four. What am I — ? Just do it. Something very intriguing is happening in Florida. I know, of all places. *(Whoever she's talking to locates the page.)* Uh-huh. Uh-huh. It's *Silence of the Lambs* meets *Thelma and Louise!* We're gonna have to recast Louise, though, my God. The minute these two are in custody, I'm hopping on a plane. I'm gonna get this for us.

(Spot out. Drums testifies in court.)

DRUMS: My partner had some rather . . . unorthodox undercover methods. However, he was outstanding at gaining a subject's trust.

(Lights up on the Last Resort, a biker bar. Behind the bar, Pandora pours a drink: the exact image we saw earlier. Music: The Derailers, "Painful Days and Sleepless Nights." Bucket and Jo are dancing.)

DRUMS: I tended to hang back and let him operate, taking on more of a liasing role.

(Drums walks into scene.)

BUCKET: *(Leads her off the dance floor, back to the bar.)* What's a nice girl like you doin' at the Last Resort?

JO: Well I suppose it's my last resort, innit?

DRUMS: *(On a walkie-talkie.)* Jerry, we're with her. Sitting over here in a dump called the Last Resort, knocking back a few brews. Jenkins's dancing with her. I'm going back in.

BUCKET: Buy you a beer?

JO: You don' have to ask twice.

BUCKET: Buy you a beer?

JO: Comedian, huh? *(Calls to Pandora.)* Corona. And don't forget the lime. *(To Bucket.)* It's the little details, you know? Place like this, got no class. Don't get the little things right.

BUCKET: Ain't that the truth.

JO: Name's Jo, by the way.

BUCKET: Mine's Bucket. This here's Drums.

JO: Thanks for the beer, Bucket.

BUCKET: Oh, anytime, anytime.

JO: What's that sound like . . . ? Bucket and Drums. Bucket and Drums. Oh,
I know. Don Johnson. Right? Miami Vice.

Crocket and . . . that other one —

(Drums blanches, looks panicky. Bucket doesn't miss a beat.)

BUCKET: Tubbs. Yeah, it's a bit of a personal joke . . . on the law, you know?
We're down here to move some product, if you catch my drift.

JO: Uh-huh. Certainly. Certainly do catch your drift. 'Fraid I can't help you
out in that department.

BUCKET: Aw, that's all right, Darlin', we don't need no help. We know who
we're dealin' with.

JO: Better that way.

BUCKET: Only way to do business. But's mighty sweet a you ta even think about
helpin' out. Ya see that, Drums? That's what I like about Florida. Everybody's so friendly and helpful.

(Drums stands, wooden.)

JO: Well, no reason not to be. I heard that about the North, that everybody's
real rude. I wouldn't like that. I'll stick with Florida. Hot, though. Fuckin'
huge palmetto bugs. You guys seem all right, though.

BUCKET: Yeah, we're all right.

JO: I think I'm a pretty good judge of character. An' you guys are all right.

BUCKET: Yeah, we're all right.

JO: *(Lifts up her shirt.)* Wanna see where I got shot with a .22?

(Bucket whistles.)

JO: Yeah, I done some shit. *(She stands.)* I'monna go play the jukebox. *(Fishes
in her pockets.)* Aw, shit. Don't think I have any change left.

(Bucket hands her a few bills.)

BUCKET: Wouldn't mind some Hank, Senior if they got any.

JO: *(Impressed.)* All right, you are now officially in my good books.

(She staggers off. Drums hisses under his breath:)

DRUMS: I told you those were stupid names.

BUCKET: Shut up.

(Lights up on Lu and the Captain, upper level.)

LU: And she ain't no five eight, neither.

CAPTAIN: Pardon?

LU: On the news. With them sketches. Everybody said she was five eight or
ten. That's just how she acts. She's five five.

CAPTAIN: All right.

LU: She just acts bigger.

(Jo returns. Hank Williams "Long Gone Lonesome Blues" begins to play.)

BUCKET: Well, howdy lady.

JO: Fancy meetin' you here.

(Bucket pulls a pack of cigarettes out of his shirt pocket, offers her one first, which she takes. As she leans in for him to light it, she notices something in his shirt pocket.)

JO: Juicy Fruit?

(Bucket nods, lighting his own cigarette.)

JO: Well ain't you a boy scout.

BUCKET: Oh, not in a long time. You 'bout ready for another?

JO: Wouldn't say no.

BUCKET: *(Waving the bartender over.)* "The Last Resort." A colorful appellation.

JO: Nothin' but the truth. Look around you.

(Music down to a faint underscore. Light on Lu and the Captain.)

LU: I'm just scared is all, I'm just scared. I didn't have nothing — Didn't have nothing to do with all this shit. I'm just scared. Are you gonna charge me, or — *(No response.)* I dunno, maybe I oughta have a lawyer here. Whadda ya think?

(Music back up. The Last Resort.)

JO: Y'all gonna stick around for the pig roast? I hear it's really somethin'.

DRUMS: I'll be right back. *(Ducks outside to use his walkie-talkie. Static, motorcycle engines.)* The bonfire pig-roast number is going down when it gets dark. You just heard a couple more come in. This place is gonna be crawling with bikers when the sun goes down. I would advise making a call real soon.

COP VOICE: Copy.

DRUMS: *(Static.)* She disappears into a passel a bikers, we're fucked.

COP VOICE: Understood.

DRUMS: WHITE MIDDLE-AGED GUYS ARE AT RISK HERE. I don't wanna hear about another body in the swamp after we let her hop on somebody's bike and bust the state.

(Phone rings next to Captain. He picks it up.)

COP VOICE: The undercover wants to know what to do about the pig roast. The bikers are coming in.

CAPTAIN: *(Beat.)* Take her.

(Instantaneously, two Cops appear and muscle Jo out of the bar. "Long Gone Lonesome Blues" fades as they drag her out.)

JO: Hey, what the — Fuckin' Cops. I pay my taxes. Pay your fuckin' salary.

What is this bullshit anyway, never get tired a hassling citizens. That old concealed weapon thing? That's not even in this state, whadda you care? Arright, arright, I'll come with you. I'll come along peaceably. But this is bullshit. You hear me? Bullshit.

(They leave her center stage.)

JO: I've a good mind to sue for harassment an my constitutional rights or some such. *(Phone rings.)* I don't need no lawyer. How'm I gonna afford a fuckin' lawyer? This is bullshit anyway. Outstanding warrants charge. Bullshit. Fuckin' concealed weapon. *(Under her breath.)* They ain't got nothin' on me. No prints. No witnesses. No gun. No nothin'. They don't even know about that shit. They don't know nothin' about that shit.

(Blackout. Sound of four shots.)

Act III: Bullshit Weapons Charge

BUCKET: Sir, we've got nothing.

No prints. No witnesses. No gun. No nothing.

CAPTAIN: We've got her.

(They look over at Lu, eating Cheetos and drinking a Sunkist.)

BUCKET: You think it'll work?

CAPTAIN: It'll have to.

(They approach her. Stand over her. She stops eating Cheetos and looks up, apprehensive.)

LU: What?

(Blackout. Lights up on Jo, staring at pay phone. Phone rings once, twice. She picks up. Lights up on Lu, in upper area, surrounded by cops on headphones: Bucket and Drums plus Chastity, Daytona, and Pandora dressed as cops. With each blackout, they assume different "surveillance" positions. Empty coffee cups and cigarettes proliferate.)

LU: Jo?

JO: Yeah.

LU: Hey.

JO: I got your message. What are you doin'?

LU: Nothin'. What the hell are you doin'?

JO: Nothing. I'm sitting here in jail.

LU: I came down here to see what the hell's happenin'.

JO: Everything's copacetic. I'm here for a . . . a . . . carryin' a concealed weapon back in '86 . . . and a traffic ticket.

LU: Really?

JO: Yeah. It's bullshit.

LU: 'Cos there's been officials up at my parents' house askin' some questions.

JO: Oh-oh.

LU: And I'm gettin' scared.

JO: Hmmmm. Well, you know, I don't think there should be anything to worry about.

LU: Well, I'm pretty worried.

JO: Well, all I can say is just, uh, you know . . . don't. OK?

LU: Don't what?

JO: Don't worry. About anything, all right?

LU: Well, it's pretty hard not to worry when —

JO: This . . . you know, this phone . . . they listen to everything you say on the phone.
(Beat.)

LU: They do?
(Blackout. Lights up.)

JO: I'm sure this is just all a case of mistaken identity. Somebody musta said at work, Oh, wait this looks like, you know, maybe Lu or . . . Jo. Probably that . . . boss of yours, just wants to get us in some shit, 'cos you beat him up that time. You know? I mean, I gotta say, it is something, the way those pictures do look like us, so I guess it could be a natural mistake. But I'm sure this is all just a case of mistaken identity. That's what it is.

LU: I just don't want my life messed up for something you did.

JO: *(Slowly.)* Louise, I didn't do anything.
(Blackout. Lights up.)

JO: You know we're not the people. This is a bunch of fuckin' bull.

LU: Why do you want to lie about it?

JO: I don't need to lie about it, Lu, I don't . . . I didn't do anything.

LU: Now you know you told me before —

JO: Lu, I didn't tell you nothin'.

LU: Don't lie.

JO: What is this shit? You got somebody there listenin?

LU: No.

JO: I'm telling you. Any . . . any kind of car that I ever borrowed from somebody was a car because I borrowed it. I do not know anything about this *shit*.

LU: OK.

JO: And neither do you.

> (*Blackout. Spot on Jo. We hear her voice on tape.*)

JO: (*On tape.*) You know, tonight is the beginning of a war?

And it'll be eight o'clock in the morning in Iraq.

And there's gonna be the bombing and they're checking out for terrorists in the United States.

'Cos they're just gonna . . . start some shit.

DRUMS: (*Listening to playback.*) What the fuck is this ? Nineteen hours of tape and we got nothin' but her fuckin' *theories* on the fuckin' *universe*.

> (*Lu and Bucket in the phone/surveillance area.*)

BUCKET: Louise, listen to me. You know all this shit you're sayin? Whinin' to her about how the cops are gonna be up your ass?

All that shit you're sayin'? It's for real.

YOU DON'T HAVE IMMUNITY, HERE. You didn't make no immunity deal. If we don't get her, we got you. Accessory to murder, shit, if she gets outta this, maybe just plain ol' murder. I mean, all we got is your word *she* did it, not *you*. We got your fingerprints at the scene, you takin' joyrides, wrecking a dead man's car. Doesn't look too good. Does it? DOES IT?

> (*Miserable, Lu shakes her head.*)

BUCKET: So I want TEARS. You got one last shot, here. If she loves you, she's gotta confess. Or I'm not shittin' you here, we'll take you in her place. Don't think we won't do that.

> (*Lu nods. Stares at phone. Bucket moves a bit away, talks to the Captain on another phone.*)

BUCKET: Chief? Yeah, this is gonna be the day. Yeah. I just gave her a lil' acting lesson.

> (*Phone rings. Twice. Shaking, Lu picks it up.*)

LU: Hello?

JO: Hey, I called early this mornin' 'cos I didn't know if you were leavin' or —

LU: (*Starting to cry.*) They're comin' after me. I know they are.

JO: No, they're not. How do you know that?

LU: My whole family . . . they been talkin' to my sister. I just know —

JO: Honey —

LU: I'm not goin' to jail for something you did! It's not fair! My family is a nervous wreck up there, my mom keeps calling me, she doesn't know what the hell is going on —

JO: Lu? I'm not gonna let you go to jail. You hear me? Lu, listen.

LU: You evidently don't love me anymore.

JO: Lu, why would you say something like —

LU: *(Crying.)* I mean, You're gonna let me get in trouble for somethin' I didn't do . . .

JO: Louise, I said, I'm *not!* Quit cryin' and listen. Go ahead and tell 'em what you need to tell 'em, OK? Do what you gotta do. I love you.

LU: I'm not so sure anymore.

JO: I do.

LU: I don't know if I should keep on livin' or . . .

JO: No, Lu, Lu, listen. Lu, listen. I'm not gonna let you go to jail. Listen, if I have to confess, I will.

(Silent jubilation and high five-ing from the officers.)

LU: Jo, why in hell did you do this?

JO: I don't know, baby. I don't know. Just hold onto the phone for a little while, please, can you please? I'll probably never see you again, you know that?

LU: Yes.

JO: I love you. Honey, I'm not gonna let you get in trouble. Awww. It's the end of the world, I'll have you know. The end of the world.

CORONER: *(Appears on spotlight.)* I've seen a lot of dead hookers. In my line of work.

(Spot out.)

JO: Hey, you know what? I'm gonna be famous. Like Bundy.

LU: What a way to be famous.

JO: Yep. Like Bundy. And If I write a book or anything, I'm gonna give you the money. You definitely deserve it. You know, I'll never love anyone like I love you. I'll probably die of a broken heart pretty soon anyway. I'll never have another relationship.

LU: I prob'ly won't either.

JO: Well, Lu, I gotta admit I'm glad to hear that.

LU: You turned me against everybody. I won't trust a person for the rest of my life.

JO: That's good! Because you know what? *People aren't right.* Pollution's fucking up their heads . . .

LU: Why don't you tell 'em now.

JO: You want me to tell 'em now?

LU: Tell 'em now. Get it over with.

JO: All right. *(They hang up the phones.)* All right.

(She stares at the phone. As lights fade:)

BUCKET: Guess she really loves you.

LU: *(Beat.)* Yeah.
  (Blackout. sound of three shots.)

Act IV: Confession

Lights up. Police station.

JO: Well, I came here to confess to murder.
  (Blackout.)
CAPTAIN: I'm Captain Roswell. And you remember Sergeant Jenkins.
BUCKET: *(Bringing her a coffee.)* They didn't have any cream and sugar, so I
  put in —
JO: Truth serum?
BUCKET: Sweet-n-Low. I put in some of that Sweet-n-Low.
  (Blackout.)
DAYTONA: Although Self Defense was mentioned a total of forty-three times
  in the videotaped confession, those words were never heard in the sec-
  tions of the tape shown to the jury.
JO: That other girl. She . . . she didn't have nothing to do with this. She's
  just . . . a friend. She didn't know nothing about any of this. *(Lights a
  cigarette.)* And that's why I'm doing this. Because I don't need her gettin'
  messed up for somethin' that I did. I know I'm gonna miss her for the
  rest of my life. She's a real good person. *(Cries, smokes.)* So sweet and kind.
  (Spot on Coroner. Confession scene continues, silent.)
CORONER (PANDORA): I've seen a lot of dead prostitutes, in my line of work.
  A lot. And it's not supposed to be something you get upset about. I am
  a doctor, after all. A doctor of the dead. And it's like cancer or something,
  as a doctor, you're not supposed to get upset about it. Curse God or —
  You're supposed to speak in calm, rational terms. Not alarm the patient.
  Comfort the family.

  A coroner's main job is to listen.
  Find out how this thing happened. Make the call.
  Natural causes. Suicide. Homicide.

  And these girls who come in, ripped up some of 'em in ways that speak
  of a hatred I can barely begin to comprehend.

  I've been listening to their bodies. For years. Listening to stories of des-
  ecrations of the human body not to mention the spirit that I can only
  call evil. Although I never had much of a dialogue with God or any sort

of metaphysical thing. Suddenly I am forced to have this conception of evil. This knowledge.

The listening — adds up. Sometimes I feel it is eroding me, like a high whistling wind over sandstone. I am becoming . . . mute and rough and rounded.

I didn't come to this job with any fancy ideas about justice. The . . . orderliness appealed to me. The ability to find truths. Add detail upon detail, layering to conclusion.

Without too many people cluttering things up, if you want to know the truth. I . . . have a little trouble dealing with people. Figured I could do my job, do it well, have a large degree of privacy in my life. These things are important to me.

The ideas about justice — started springing up at me. After the bodies had been piling up. For a while. Girls, women, who should not have been on my table. Sure, I get some ODs, suicides, but it's the others. The ones who shouldn't have been on my table for another forty years. Who should never have gone through what they went through to get to my table. And they're whispering to me —

Unsolved. unsolved. unsolved. unsolved.
(Spot out. We return to confession.)

JO: I just wish I never would've done this shit. I wish I never woulda got that gun. I wish to God, I never was a hooker. And I just wish I never woulda done what I did. I still have to say to myself, I still say that it was in self defense.

And I do. I feel bad for the pain I have caused some families. But I do have to say one thing, though, their families must realize that no matter how much they loved the people that died, no matter how much they love 'em, they were bad. They were gonna hurt me. So, they have to realize that fact, that this person, no matter how much they loved 'em or how good they felt they were, this person was either gonna physically beat me up, rape me, or kill me. And I don't know which one.

I just turned around and did it before they did. Is all.
(Spot on Lu, upper area, on the phone.)

LU: Hello? Mr. Broadstreet? I, uh, I wanted to talk to a lawyer about all this . . . I was given this number by the detectives who are involved in the case, they said you could help me. I'm Louise Raines. Yeah. I'm her . . .

Yeah. I just figured I really need to be talkin' to a lawyer. I never been involved with nothing like this before . . . Anyway, that cop said you could help me. That you'd be the best person to talk to. *(Squeezes her hand over her eyes for a moment.)* 'Cos you're representing them already. He said — he said you could get us a better deal, like a package deal with Republic Pictures. That we'd get more money than if we all signed separate deals. I just — I'd feel better knowing you were there to field the . . . various offers, right? Like, somebody on my side. To make sure I get the best deal out of this. Right? OK then.

(Blackout. Sound of two shots.)

Act V: Jesus Told Me to Write to You

On TV's, footage of Jo being taken from the courthouse and stuffed into a squad car, handcuffed, orange jumpsuit. She smiles and nods to the camera, as though it is held by loyal supporters. A spot comes up on a woman watching this on TV. She takes pen to paper, composes aloud.

LEEANN: Dear Jolene: You're gonna think I'm crazy, but Jesus told me to write to you.

(Spots up on Cassie watching the footage and Annie on the phone.)

CASSIE: Cancel my seminars and get me to La Guardia!

ANNIE: Can you tell me if you have a prisoner there by that name? I'm calling from Los Angeles . . . Look, do you have a superior I could talk to?

(Blackout. Spot warms on Jo pacing her jail cell.)

JO: 'cuz you just hit the one piece a Roadkill wouldn't *fucking* lie down, didn't-cha. Didn'tcha.

Thought you could just let cher foot press heavy on the accelerator. Do what you want. Listen to a woman scream in the woods off Highway 101.

Thought you'd be left with nothing but a splash of guts and hair. Instead your truck comes dead-lock stop, you're heading for your own windshield sixty-five *fucking* miles per hour. *(Low.)* I lay down and I lay down and I lay down but no more.

I stood *up*.

And your world comes crashing to the ground.

(Blackout. Lights up on Jo and her lawyer. Jo is handcuffed.)

JEAN: I'm not gonna lie to you, this is gonna be pretty tough. They've got your confession . . .

JO: Yeah, I had to do that.

JEAN: I'm going to try to get it thrown out on the grounds that you were intoxicated at the time, but —

JO: Hey, if that works you can ask them to throw out the last twenty years of my life.

JEAN: I don't think it's going to work.

JO: Look, I'm sorry if that confession thing makes your job harder. But, you know, I just told them what happened. I told them I acted in self defense. Can't hurt to tell the truth, right?

(Jean stares at her for a moment.)

JO: Right?

JEAN: We'd be in a much better position if you hadn't told them anything.

JO: Sorry about that. I said, I had to do it. They had my wife, you know? So I had to tell them she had nothing to do with all this. I had to protect her. Nothin' on earth I wouldn't do for that woman.

JEAN: Jo, there's something I have to tell you. It's about Louise.

(Blackout. Spot on Jo.)

JO: You feel something and you think that makes it real.

I mean, I . . . I loved that woman like in all the fairy tales, you know? I usedta lay awake an' just listen to her breathe. An she'd . . . turn over in her sleep, maybe, an' the feeling would just well up inside me.

Even if she's looking stupid and drooling on the pillow, still I'd just be all fulla this feeling of being in love. That this is it, you know, she's the one.

What was *she* thinking, lying there in our bed, next to me in the dark? She's just thinkin', well, this'll do for now. Got a roof over my head. An' this crazy bitch willin' to go out and suck cock six, seven hours a day to take care a me.

What kind of a person . . . is that? That I was in love with. That I'm goin' to the chair because a her.

(Courtroom. A boom box sits atop a table, playing the following into the court record:)

LU: *Now you know you told me before —*

JO: *Lu, I didn't tell you nothin'.*

LU: *Don't lie.*

JO: *What is this shit? You got somebody there listenin?*

LU: *No.*

JO: *I'm telling you. Any . . . any kind of car that I ever borrowed from somebody was a car because I borrowed it. I do not know anything about this shit.*

LU: *OK.*

JO: *And neither do you.*

(Blackout. Lights up on Jo in her cell. Prosecutor and Lu in court.)

PROSECUTOR: The prosecution would like to call to the witness stand — Louise Raines.

JO: There are, y'know, there are certain . . . activities that are just known to carry a Death Sentence. I'm not talking about Law here, I'm not talking about being illegal. I'm talking about the list a activities that, if you pursue them, these could very easily lead to death.

Prostitution, for example. Everybody knows, you sink that low, you got a real good chance a endin' up dead. That's a line a work with a real high mortality rate.

Everybody knows that. Except maybe for kids, think they're invincible. Think that doesn't apply to them. That's why I was always so careful, kept to my regulars. 'Cos I knew.

Alls I'm saying is *I want killing women to be added to that list.* And I'm not talking about a court of law, getting Caught. I'm talking about right there, at the time. Knowing, this is an activity that, if you engage in this activity, you could easily wind up dead.

'Cos killing women is not on that list right now.

LU: She told me she shot him and covered him with a piece a carpet, and so when I saw that on the news I put two and two together.

PROSECUTOR: What did you say when she first told you she'd killed a man?

LU: I said . . . I didn't want to hear about it.

JO: An' you know what?

Dyin' to protect someone you love, now that's one thing.

That's a choice I can make. As opposed to dyin' 'cos a trick decides he wants a special thrill, wants to get him some a that hooker murder he's heard so much about. Now that's not a death I can live with. Dying to protect somebody you love.

Even if you turn out to be wrong. Still.

That's a helluva lot better reason. That's something I can live with.

Not gonna be too long, anyway.

(Jo sits, catatonic. Everything about her has given up. Jean appears in the doorway.)

JEAN: Jo? There's somebody I want you to meet. *(Motions behind her.)* Her name's Cassandra Chase. She's a noted feminist scholar —
    (Cassandra Chase [Cassie] enters, New York bohemian.)

JO: Feminist?

CASSIE: *(Somewhat overexcited.)* It is an *honor* to meet you. Jo, may I call you Jo? I've been following your case with quite a bit of interest since, well, since before we knew who you were. A string of white middle-aged men left rotting in the swamp! How outrageous, yet fitting. The ultimate retribution for their crimes —

JO: They all tried to kill me, yeah.

CASSIE: *(Suddenly dead serious.)* I understand. And I'm here to tell you that you are not alone. There are a lot of other women out there who feel the way I do, and we're behind you 100 percent.

JO: The women are behind me? Far Out.

CASSIE: I flew down here at my own expense to help.

JO: Yeah, how're *you* gonna help?

CASSIE: Jo, *I know why you did what you did.*

JO: *(Muttering.)* 'Bout time somebody's talking sense. Seems like the whole world's gone crazy, can't understand a simple thing like I had to defend myself.

CASSIE: We are at war, here, Jo. Women like you are the front-line casualties.

JO: Shit, yeah. It's a war zone out there. It's crazy, man.

CASSIE: I'll be called as an Expert Witness —

JO: What makes you an Expert?

CASSIE: Well —

JO: You'd think by now I'd be the Expert.

CASSIE: Of course. My testimony will serve to contextualize — *(She hesitates, switches tactics.)* — back you up. Explain how something like this could have happened.

JO: *(Shakes her head.)* You gotta pardon me, but I never thought anybody like you would ever give a shit about me, or what-all goes on at the bottom of the food chain down here.

CASSIE: I care very much. And I'm here to help.

GUARD: *(Appearing at the door.)* Playtime's over, ladies.

CASSIE: I'll be back.

JEAN: And I'll see you in three days. Just don't . . . don't talk to anybody, OK?
    (Lighting shift: courtroom. Judge and two psychiatrists.)

SHRINK: You can definitely see that she suffers from mild cortical dysfunction, though to the layperson that might not be immediately obvious.

(In a sudden burst of glorious light, LeeAnn Bennett appears, suspended, holding a gilded harp. She is lowered impossibly slowly from the flies.)

LEEANN: Dear Jolene: You're gonna think I'm crazy but Jesus told me to write to you.

SHRINK: What with her childhood, home life, as mentioned earlier, the organic factors, genetics, a traumatic blow to the head at fifteen, the cortical dysfunction is not only to be expected, it is to be expected both from organic and inorganic factors — a cortical dysfunction doubly determined.

LEEANN: I was just sittin' there in my daddy's hospital room, prayin' and prayin' for his bypass operation to be successful, and thank the lord he did come through it, Jesus is a fair man he does answer prayers. But when I was there in that hospital room with the stench of death comin' for my daddy, I saw your picture in the paper. An' I thought, she can't have done all those horrible things they're sayin' she did. Look at her. I could see right through to your soul, Jolene, and I could see that you were a good person, a kind person, a person to whom bad things had happened in her lifetime. Not a bad person. An I just knew — Jesus himself meant for me to see that picture. An it was Him put those clear, clear thoughts into my head. So I am writin' to you now, to offer the hand of friendship and the support and love of Jesus Christ Himself, through his messenger here on earth, and that is me.

SHRINK 2: I would have to agree with my esteemed colleague on the cortical dysfunction, I might even go so far as to call it a mild cortical impairment.

JO: Mother fuckers. Talkin' like I'm crazy, 'r stupid, 'r both all the time. I'll fuckin' cortical impair you.

SHRINK 2: Her repeated courtroom outbursts illustrate my point quite succinctly. She has no concept, not only of what would constitute appropriate behavior, but also that these repeated outbursts are not in her best interest as a defendant —

JO: I don't know what I'm supposed to be doing here anyway, if you're all just gonna go around talking in your fucking made-up language, your fuckin' lawyer talk, shrink talk, what am I doing here? Exhibit Fucking A?

SHRINK 2: Her inability to temper her own desire for what she perceives as power, the voicing of her displeasure with these proceedings, is roughly on the emotional level of a high-school student —

JO: You Mother Fucker —

SHRINK 2: "sassing off" to a teacher or other authority figure —

JUDGE: If you do not restrain yourself, Ms. Palmer, you will be bound and gagged for the remainder of these proceedings.

JO: Is that even legal?

JUDGE: It most certainly is.

SHRINK 1: Though in this metaphorical analysis, the age of a high school student is deceptively high. I would more often put her behavior in the three-to-five-year-old range,* with an analogous understanding of right and wrong, ego gratification versus conception of a future, etc.

(Lighting shift: courtroom fades, leaving Jo and LeeAnn by the end of her speech. LeeAnn finally alights but continues her address straight out to the audience.)

*LEEANN: *(Overlapping.)* Jesus gave me the clear sight into your eyes. To see that maybe you are a sinner, but we are all sinners. Every last one of us. Anyone who doesn't think so is lying to himself. And you can lie to yourself, but you can't lie to Jesus. With His help, I can see that you and I are not so very different. I've had my hard times myself. I didn't kill anybody, of course, but when I was having my trouble with alcohol, before I got sober, I did some things I'd rather forget. An' I had some BAD THOUGHTS. I did.

JO: *(Looking at her for the first time.)* Lady, you don't know what bad thoughts are.

LEEANN: *(Turning to Jo with delight.)* I do. And if I don't, Jesus does. And do you know what? His heart is so big he can forgive everything you got weighing down on you. He could even forgive you if it was worse than it is.

JO: It's pretty bad.

LEEANN: I know. I know it's bad. But we can get through this together. Take my hand and I will lead you into the clear light of the Lord Jesus Christ's sweet forgiveness.

JO: *(Amazed.)* You know, I musta . . . . I musta prayed for this. 'Cos I remember. When I knew all this shit was goin' down. I remember saying, inside my head, Please, God. Send me somebody to help me through this.

LEEANN: That must be it! You asked Him. He asked me!

JO: Please, God, send somebody who can help me get through this thing. Somebody who could — just once. Just once before I check outta here. Somebody who could actually love me.

LEEANN: Praise God.

(LeeAnn immediately gives a press conference.)

LEEANN: If everybody could know Jolene the way I do, there's not a jury in this land that would convict her. She is truly a good and kind person. I love her more than I've loved anyone in my life, including my husband.

It's not a homosexual perversion. It's a soul binding. We're like Jonathan and David in the Bible.

If I was Houdini and could bust her out of that place I'd do it. And we'd roam the country and live like vagabonds and have adventures.
(Jo in handcuffs, being transported from one point to another. Runs into Bucket in the hallway.)

JO: Hey.

LEEANN: But of course I can't.
(Spot out on LeeAnn.)

JO: Hey BUCKET.

BUCKET: Uh, actually it's David.

JO: Yeah, well I'm just gonna stick with BUCKET. OK with you, BUCKET? So this all part of your master plan? Buy her a beer, get her a cup a coffee, EXECUTE THE BITCH?
(He looks away.)

JO: Just let me ask you one thing.
BUCKET.
You got files marked NHI down at the sheriff's?

BUCKET: *(After a moment's hesitation.)* No.

JO: I bet you don't have no string a unsolved prostitute murders this year, huh? In Citrus. In Pascoe. In Dixie.
Since I started doin' your job for you.
How many unsolved prostitute murders you got in the last, say, ten years.

BUCKET: Look, I really don't have the data on that —

JO: I BET you don't. I just bet you don't. *(As she is dragged away.)* Well, you just go through those files, there. Look for yourself. How many unsolved prostitute murders you got on the books this year?

LEEANN: It's clear to me that Jesus is calling her to come home to Him. And this state has the Death Penalty, thank the Lord, so why not take advantage of it?

I tell you, I'd go in a flash, if the Lord was calling to me. But I have not been given the opportunity. So I just have to wait. And do His work on earth as best I can.

DAYTONA: NHI. Is a police term.
Prostitutes. Biker girls. If no family comes forward to put the heat on. Or if the family is powerless. Poor. Non-English speaking.
Goes in a file marked NHI.
No Humans Involved.

(Blackout. Spot on Jo, jail cell, alone.)

JO: I'm an American Citizen. I go out. Make my money. Support my wife. I pay her rent. Buy her things. Make sure she's got clothes to wear and a nice place to live and plenty of beer in the fridge. And cable. Right? And there's people tryin' to kill me. Now I got a right to defend myself. That feminist chick said there's a store owner out in LA who killed five times in one year, because his *store* was gettin' robbed. Shit, maybe they were gonna kill him. Maybe they were just gonna take a couple a TVs. You don't hear nobody tell him, well maybe you should stop *selling* your TVs in this bad area. Maybe you should just give up the only way you know how to make a living. Everybody says, Oh yeah, well, he was defending his *property*. His TVs. And he's not even *from* here. Pakistani'r some shit. Never charged him with murder.

(Jo with Cassie and Jean.)

JEAN: I think it's going pretty well.

JO: What are you talking about? They're making me look like an idiot in there.

JEAN: That's not true. It's a matter of the legal language —

JO: I may not know the fuckin' language, but I know when people are making me look like an idiot. Or fuckin' crazy. Why don't *you* call some shrinks, on *my* side?

JEAN: They *were* on your side.

JO: What are you —

JEAN: Jo, you've got to look at what's going to be the most advantageous light to put you in, for the case. You understand —

JO: Understand? Understand fucking what? Look, you get Cassie in there. Tell 'em the Women are behind me. 'Cos they fuckin' *understand*. What's goin' on here.

JEAN: Ms. Chase is set to testify tomorrow. Battered woman syndrome, leading to diminished capacity — it's very compelling stuff.

(Beat. Jo turns to Cassie, stunned.)

JO: *(Soft.)* You fuckin' bitch.

JEAN: Jo —

JO: She's gonna tell them I'm crazy?

JEAN: Diminished Capacity. It's a legal term.

JO: Comin' in here all nice like you're my friend, sayin' you understand —

CASSIE: Jo, I do understand. This is my area of expertise. My testimony on Battered Woman Syndrome will help the jury understand why your history of abuse might lead you to both underperceive and overreact to later instances of abuse . . .

JO: I ain't no fuckin' syndrome. This is just shit that happened. To me. And now all I wanna do is tell the people what happened, get right with Jesus, and get outta here.

CASSIE: Is that really what *you* want?

JO: What'd I just say?

CASSIE: I'm afraid your association with LeeAnn Bennett may not be in your best interest.

JO: *(With quiet fury.)* You know what's in my best fucking interests? That LeeAnn — the one truly good person I have ever met in this life — That she's been sent here as a blessing by God, that's what's in my best fucking interests. You know what's not? City bitches like you goin' in that room tomorrow and telling them I'm crazy.

JEAN: Jo, it could mean your life. I'm very serious.

JO: WELL SO AM I. You are not gonna go in there and tell them I'm crazy. It's not true. If I gotta get myself another lawyer, I'll do it. Don't you worry, I'll do it.

JEAN: *(Takes a deep breath.)* Do you want another lawyer?

JO: No, I want you. *(Beat.)* And I want you to take that bitch off the schedule tomorrow.

CASSIE: Jo —

JO: Are we totally clear here? I have just unemployed you. Now get atta here. *(Cassie leaves, flustered. Jean stares at Jo, then follows Cassie out. Lights dim to spot on Jo.)*

JO: If I say I'm crazy, that means they didn't do it. Them bastards with the "suck my dick, I'm a cop" routine. Neither one of 'em was a cop. Well, that one was a retired cop. Other one was a fuckin' security guard or something.

If I say I'm crazy, then none a them bastards tried to kill me. I'm just a hooker got her head knocked around one too many times, went nutso. Up and started shooting men.

Then how come it's only seven, motherfuckers?

How come I'm not standing on a pile a 200 corpses? Huh?

Maybe 'cos most of the men I interact with in my daily business do *not* try and kill me.

Only some of 'em, do.

Maybe seven of 'em.

Do.

(Jo stares forward. Lights fade on her. In twin spotlights, LeeAnn and Annie.)

LEEANN: Jo —

ANNIE: Jo. I'm so glad I finally got you on the phone . . .

LEEANN: Of course I don't mind another collect call. They're runnin' up into the thousands, but the Good Lord will provide.

ANNIE: Listen, I want to make the movie of your life.

LEEANN: Oh, Jo, you know He will!

ANNIE: Don't you understand —

LEEANN: Can't you feel His love, shining down on you.

ANNIE: It's gonna happen. It's already happening. Those cops who arrested you are making their own movie —

LEEANN: The smiling light of Jesus Christ.

ANNIE: well they sold their story, is what I'm saying.

LEEANN: Don't cling to what's meaningless.

ANNIE: So now it's your turn.

LEEANN: I have the truth.

ANNIE: Your side of the story needs to be told.

LEEANN AND ANNIE: *I am offering you life everlasting —*

LEEANN: wrapped in the embrase of God.

> *(Jo kneels in her cell, praying. Spots out. [Note: Here, with the addition of a lab coat, LeeAnn once again becomes the Coroner. This can be done on or offstage.] Light up on the Coroner, examining a body and speaking into a microcassette recorder.)*

CORONER: I would estimate her age to be between fifteen and eighteen. Multiple contusions on the face and neck. Lacerations from a very thin blade, most likely razor or boxcutter. Seven lateral cuts across the face, one across the neck, severing the jugular and the larynx, most likely cause of death, though several of the torso cuts are severe enough to have —

> *(Bucket appears in the doorway. She starts.)*

CORONER: Jesus Christ.

BUCKET: Sorry.

CORONER: Didn't anyone* teach you to knock —

BUCKET: *(Overlapping.)* *The door was open —

CORONER: detective?

> *(Beat.)*

BUCKET: I'm sorry.

CORONER: What do you want? I sent it all upstairs.

BUCKET: Yeah, I got it. Thanks. There's just —

CORONER: It's all in the paperwork. Anything you might need. All there.

BUCKET: No, it's . . . . Yeah, thank you, it's very thorough. I'm not . . . uh . . .

my partner is going to be handling the testimony from here on out. I just . . . *(He reaches in his pocket and takes out a pack of Juicy Fruit. Offers it to her before taking a stick.)* Juicy Fruit?

CORONER: No. Thank you.

BUCKET: I'm trying to quit. Smoking. They keep . . . sending me in. I was quit for three weeks this time, then they sent me in and I had to . . . you know, you can't be infiltrating the bad guys chewing Juicy Fruit.

(She stares at him. He puts the gum away. Clears his throat.)

BUCKET: I wanted to ask you a question.

CORONER: Uh-huh.

BUCKET: Is she or isn't she?

CORONER: What?

BUCKET: A serial killer.

CORONER: Don't be ridiculous.

BUCKET: Is she or isn't she?

CORONER: She did not stalk. She did not plan.

BUCKET: Seven.

CORONER: She did not keep trophies.

BUCKET: Yeah, she did.

CORONER: You don't pawn trophies. You keep them.

BUCKET: Number of bullets?

(Coroner does not answer.)

BUCKET: First one was four. By the end, she's using nine. She had to reload.

CORONER: She's not here. *(Gestures at the dead girl on the table.)* And she coulda been.

BUCKET: *(Looks at the girl.)* Young.

CORONER: Yes.

BUCKET: So how come Jolene didn't —

CORONER: What?

BUCKET: How come she made it to twenty, let alone thirty-five.

CORONER: *(Shrugs.)* Good instincts.

BUCKET: And then seven. In one year.

(They look at each other.)

CORONER: Good instincts.

(Blackout. LeeAnn's voice.)

LEEANN: *(On the phone with Jo.)* You can help out with the horses and live here on the ranch. *(Beat, brightly.)* Or, if they convict you, go home to Jesus.

(Spot on Jo, jail cell.)

JO: Now they got their fucking movie coming out, and I haven't even been convicted yet. That's gotta be illegal. I swear. "First Female Serial Killer." And I haven't even been convicted yet. I'm right in the middle of this shit.

An they got me bein' played by SOMEBODY I NEVER EVEN HEARD OF. They coulda at least got Jodie Foster or something.

I know I . . . ain't that Pretty, but they could rough her up some. We know she can play a hooker. She was real good in that Taxi Driver. Actually, I looked . . . well, I looked a lot like her when that movie came out. Don't look nothing like her now. Maybe I would, if I got to go home after shooting, instead a . . . Course, at that time home was a car out in the woods. Fuckin' . . . freezing. I was cold all my life, Florida always sounded like a good deal.

Anyway, we know she can play a hooker, we know she can get raped. How about coming full circle and we see her packin' a little Justice? Huh? Now there's a movie I'd pay money to see.

Not some fuckin' bullshit lying-ass TV crap fuckin' Marg Helgenberger fuckin' Alyssa Milano. Who the fuck are these people?
(Blackout. Lights up on the courtroom. The Prosecutor speaks.)
PROSECUTOR: The evidence is clear. This man-hating lesbian became a prostitute for the control over men. And when that thrill was no longer enough, she moved on to the ultimate control — murder.
She lured Tom Waldren into the woods in order to kill him and steal everything he had — his car, his personal possessions, even up to and including his life.
JO: What in hell is he talking about?
PROSECUTOR: Possessions belonging to Mr. Waldren were recovered from the OK Pawn shop and Lucky Pawn, both in Tampa, including a Polaroid Impulse Camera, a Remington Micro-screen Razor, and a Toshiba Video-cassette Recorder.
JO: What the fuck? Is this guy insane?
JEAN: Shhh.
PROSECUTOR: In addition, in a mini-storage unit owned by the defendant, police recovered a plaid hunting jacket identified as belonging to the victim, as well as a set of tools belonging to —
Oh, I'm sorry, the tools did not belong to Mr. Waldren . . .
JEAN: OBJECTION!
JUDGE: Sustained. Watch yourself, counselor. Stick to the issue at hand.
PROSECUTOR: Yes, sir.

(Blackout. Jo and Jean.)

JEAN: You *did* steal their possessions —

JO: What was I supposed to do, leave it laying there? These, of course, were instances where I was not getting paid for my time. What, I had some big moral imperative after these guys tried to kill me, not to fuckin' take their *stuff?*

JEAN: It just doesn't look good.

(Beat.)

JO: You gotta let me take the stand.

JEAN: I'm not at all sure that's in your best interest.

JO: How else are they gonna understand what happened? I'm the only person that can tell them exactly what happened that night.

JEAN: If you take the stand that's going to leave you open to a cross-examination. It's gonna be pretty brutal.

JO: I can take it. *(Beat.)* It's what I want to do. You just go set it up.

(Blackout. Spot on LeeAnn, press conference.)

LEEANN: At ten-fifteen this morning, all the paperwork was completed and we got the final stamp makin' it legal — I have adopted Jolene Palmer as my own daughter. And she has taken me as her adopted mother. My good friend in Christ Terry McNeil handled the adoption for us.

(Flaky Lawyer smiles and waves.)

LEEANN: He may be a lawyer, but he's going to heaven! Isn't that right, Terry? Now in addition to our great spiritual bond, I am also her next of kin. Should the occasion arise, it is to me to give her a beautiful Christian burial.

(Spot on Jo, jail cell.)

JO: They say If a tree falls in the forest an' nobody hears it, does it make a sound? Well that's a stupid fuckin' question. But I'll tell you the answer, 'cos that was nearly me. An' yeah, you make a lotta sound. Even if it's just your own breathing. And blood pounding an' little twigs under your feet. Even if you don't scream, 'cos you know there's nobody gonna hear you. Yeah, you make a lotta sound. The sound a being alive.

Right up until you're not.

An' if you fire a .22 in the forest, he feels it first. Then he hears it. I think.

(Light up on the Captain and Bucket in the station house. Bucket is surrounded by files.)

BUCKET: I've been going through the unsolved prostitute murders —

CAPTAIN: The NHI files?

BUCKET: *(Beat.)* Yes. Sir, she's right. There are significantly fewer prostitute murders this year.

CAPTAIN: You're not saying you believe her?

BUCKET: Well —

CAPTAIN: That she happened to be picked up by seven men who are killing prostitutes in the area? What are the odds?

BUCKET: well —

CAPTAIN: Or that she got the *only* seven?

BUCKET: I admit, it's —

CAPTAIN: They're just plain scared, is all.

BUCKET: Exactly. That's what I was saying. That maybe that is not a bad thing. *(Beat.)*

CAPTAIN: Are you worried about Prostitute Quality of Life, here? Are you concerned that not enough fucking Hookers will choose the Sunshine State to ply their trade?

BUCKET: No, sir.

CAPTAIN: We're never gonna run outta hookers.

BUCKET: No, sir.

CAPTAIN: Now, if white middle-aged businessmen pick someplace else to live and work and spend their hard-earned vacation dollars, THEN we're in TROUBLE.

BUCKET: Yes, sir.

(Blackout. Sound of a shot.)

Act VI: Self-Defense

Lights up. Courtroom.

JEAN: In your own words, tell us what happened next.

JO: We both started to get undressed. I said Tom, I can't do this without rubbers . . . he went back to the trunk of the car to get some . . . I started to take off my clothes first, I always do this to let them know I was all right, I'm honest . . . He came back . . . and he's unzipping his pants . . . then he says he doesn't have the money. He said I only got a little for breakfast and gas. And I said Tom no way, we've got to call this off and started to get my clothes out of the back . . . and out of the corner of my eye I saw him coming toward me . . . he put a cord around my neck . . . he said Yes you are, bitch, you're going to do everything I tell you or I'll kill you like the other sluts I done before. I don't care. Your body will still be warm for my huge cock. You want to die, slut? Are you gonna do what I tell you to do and I just nodded yes. He tied my hands and tied them to the steering wheel . . . he got out of the car and told me to slide up . . . said he was going to see how much meat he was going to pound in my ass.

I'm sorry. This is very difficult for me. I don't — this is very embarrassing. I'm sorry.

He got undressed and threw his clothes on the floor . . . he lifted my legs all the way up to where my feet were near the window. Then he started having anal sex. He's doing this in a very violent manner . . . And then I don't know if he came . . . or climaxed or whatever . . . I don't know what the proper word is, I'm sorry, I talk street talk . . . But he took himself very violently out and put himself very violently in my vagina. I was crying my brains out . . . he said he loved to hear my pain. That my crying turned him on.

He got out and went to get something from the trunk. He got a red cooler and a blue tote bag . . . there were two liter bottles of water, a maroon towel, a bar of soap, a toothbrush, and a bottle of Visine. I said to myself, this guy is going to kill me or dissect me, I don't know.

He said the Visine bottle was one of my surprises. It turned out to be filled with rubbing alcohol. He emptied it into my rectum. It really hurt bad because he tore me up a lot. And he squirted it in my vagina. Which really hurt bad. And in my mouth. He pulled back my head and squirted it in my nose. He said I'm saving your eyes for the grand finale.

He put the Visine down on the dash. And I was . . . really pissed.

I was yelling at him, and struggling to get my hands free. Eventually he came back and untied me, put a stereo wire around my neck, and tried to rape me again. He's chokin' me and I grabbed his hand and he slapped me real hard in the face, and I got both feet against him and pushed him away.

And he got up on his knees and said, "You're gonna be a lot of fun."

An' I jumped up real quick and spit in his eyes. And he's wipin' his eyes, he says, "You're dead, Bitch." And I lay down real quick and grabbed my bag, pulled out my .22 and started shooting and I shot as fast as I could. I shot two times, I think.

And he lurched toward me
and I shot him some more.
And he stopped moving.
(Silence.)

JEAN: No further questions.

LEEANN: *(Tears in her eyes, absolutely honest and true.)* Jesus is calling you, Jo-lene. He wants you to come home to him.

JUDGE: Do you need to take a break?

LEEANN: He's waiting for you. Waiting with his loving, open arms.

JO: No . . . I'm . . . I'm all right.

JUDGE: Cross?

(The Prosecutor stands. Bucket appears downstage in spot.)

BUCKET: When I saw what happened to her in that courtroom, I almost wished . . . we'd a missed her. Woulda been hell on my record, but I never woulda had to see that.

PROSECUTOR: That was a very moving . . . story.

But isn't it true you have six other cases, just like this one, pending against you.

JEAN: Objection!

JUDGE: Overruled.

JEAN: Your Honor —

JUDGE: You put your client on the stand. You know Prior Bad Acts are —

JEAN: Alleged prior bad acts. My client has not been convicted of anything —

JUDGE: Overruled.

(Blackout. Spot on LeeAnn.)

LEEANN: He's waiting, Jolene. Waiting to take you into his bosom and forgive.

(Lights up on courtroom.)

JUDGE: Do you have anything else to say before sentence is passed?

JO: Just that I am sorry for the pain I have caused, and if you feel that I need to die for my acts of self defense, so be it. I have made my peace with the lord Jesus Christ.

JUDGE: Jolene Palmer, you are sentenced to die for the murder of Tom Waldren.

(Beat.)

JO: Mother fuckers.

JUDGE: Ms. Palmer —

JO: I was raped. I was raped and you say I gotta die?

JUDGE: Sit down.

JO: You know, I just hope someday you know . . .

JUDGE: Ms. Palmer —

JO: I hope your wife and daughters get raped in the ass.

JUDGE: Bailiff —

JO: *(To the jury.)* SCUMBAGS OF AMERICA!

(Blackout. Spot on Daytona.)

DAYTONA: Yeah, he gave me that TV and the VCR. Didn't have the three hundred in cash. Hooked 'em up for me and everything.

You ask me how I feel, how do I feel about him bein' dead. Well, it's weird anybody you knew even a little bit winds up dead. So I feel bad. But you know what? I'm not surprised.

How about that. The kinda stuff he was into, the kinda impulses he was useta gettin' satisfied, I'm not surprised the man is dead.

So now it's my turn to be not surprised. Just like people are not surprised when one a my kind turns up dead. Cops, people. Not unless it's College Students, oh a Nice Girl got her fuckin' head cut off, then everybody's surprised. Everybody's up in arms, doing shit. Mobilizing special police task forces. Yeah, maybe if I was a college co-ed somebody'd give a shit if I wound up dead. Somebody'd try and figure out how it happened.

But I aint no fuckin' college girl. My body winds up in a ditch, they're not gonna waste too much of a day on it. And whoever it was that decided I didn't count and no one would give a shit if he dumped me out by the side of I-95, whoever it was driving the last car I got into, he's hangin' around going to the grocery store, playing with his fuckin' kids maybe, watching the five-second blip about it on the evening news and probably none the worse for wear.

He had, that Waldren guy I'm talking about now, had what you call bad impulse control. So usedta throwin' around money, acting like the big man. I mean, this is the kind of guy wants what he wants. If he doesn't have the three hundred in cash, he'll go open up his repair shop and give you somebody's TV and VCR they're probably waiting to have fixed. Tell them there's been a break-in or some shit, I don't know. I mean, he never hurt me, but those things are tricky. You never know what's gonna set somebody off.

So yeah, I'm not surprised Mr. Waldren met with an untimely death. I feel bad for the guy, but I'm not surprised.

LEEANN: You shouldn't have said that. I'm very disappointed in you, Jolene. the way you behaved in court. Calling those people . . . the you-know-whats of America. That was not very Christian of you. I'm just . . . I'm just very disappointed. That's all. I would almost think you don't *want* to go home to Jesus.

JO: Yeah. You might think that, huh?

DAYTONA: An' I'll tell you why they're not buying that Self Defense. What Self?

Plain an' simple. Ask any one of 'em. They don't see a self there to defend. They even say — she sold herself for money. Sold her Self. No right to fuckin' defend it now.

(Blackout. Sound of six shots.)

Act VII: Deathwatch

Spot up on Flaky Lawyer.

FLAKY LAWYER: Having performed Ms. Palmer's adoption by my dear friend in Christ, LeeAnn Bennett, I have been asked to take over her criminal defense as well. And yes, we do have a strategy.

My client has accepted Jesus Christ as her personal savior, and therefore would like to confess to her sins and ask pardon for them.

Not from this court, of course, but from the only one who has the power to judge, Our Lord Jesus Christ. *(Angelic music.)* For this reason, she will be entering a plea of "No Contest" in the remaining six trials.

MARTY: *(Appears on TV.)* I don't know why she didn't kill me, too. I suppose I was in danger for my life the whole time.

FLAKY LAWYER: I am the Dr. Jack Kevorkian of the legal world. I am helping my client to commit suicide, which is what she wants.

MARTY: *(On TV.)* She had Death Row eyes. I don't know what that means, exactly, but that's what I thought. Death Row eyes.

I always liked her, though.

(Pin spots on the Judge and Jolene.)

JO: People think a prostitute can't be raped. That that just means somebody didn't pay. It's not about the fuckin' money. If that was it, you know, I'd say I got *robbed.* It ain't about money.

JO: It's about using me to take out all your hate at somebody else, at the world, No Contest
at whoever made you feel powerless an' weak an' limp-dick an' stupid, takin' whatever shit you got inside you out on me.

JUDGE: For the murder of Dick Relaford, how do you plead?

It's about not knowing if this is the time you're gonna die. No Contest.

JUDGE: For the murder of Harry McAdams, how do you plead?

JO: It's about havin' whispered close in your ear You're gonna die, you worthless piece a shit, an' *knowing* it's true.

Knowing you're gonna die. Knowing you're a worthless piece a shit.
NO CONTEST

JUDGE: For the murder of Walter Thorpe, how do you plead?

It's about having a knife shoved up inside you, having a person deliberately cut down, slicing your cunt open through to

your asshole and going to the hospital bleeding through a hotel towel,
NO CONTEST

JUDGE: For the murder of Lane Michaelson, how do you plead?

bleeding on the floor, having them call you a whore while they're lookin' at what that man did to you. An' you can't go to the cops 'cos he *was* a fuckin' *cop*. An they don't treat you like you're *anything*.
NO CONTEST.

JUDGE: For the murder of Anthony diBlasi, how do you plead?

But I am something. An' if it takes six shots from a .22 to show you that, I'm gonna *do* what it takes.

(Blackout. On TV.)

WOMAN ONE: I hope she goes to Old Sparky. You know who Old Sparky is, don't you? Uh-huh. Old Sparky's just a-waitin' for her.

(Lights fade up on Bucket, obsessively watching videotape. Open file folders surround him. Drums walks by, does a double take.)

DRUMS: What are you doing?

(Bucket doesn't answer.)

DRUMS: Case is closed. We got the bad guys.

(Bucket snorts.)

DRUMS: Seriously, man. What are you looking for in there?

BUCKET: *(Looks up at him. Beat.)* The one who didn't deserve it.

(Drums just stares. Bucket continues, placidly.)

BUCKET: You know. So I can sleep at night.

DRUMS: Jesus Christ —

BUCKET: those of us not Technically Advising any movies have more free time on our hands . . .

(Takes TV off "pause.")

WOMAN TWO: My brother never would have picked up a prostitute.

DRUMS: Yeh, right.

(Bucket hits "pause.")

BUCKET: Yeah, she sounds funny, doesn't she? Naïve. But she could be right. You know who her brother is?

(Drums shakes his head.)

BUCKET: Sausage Delivery Guy.

DRUMS: *(Cracks up.)* No way.

BUCKET: He's my great hope. No priors, no beat-up ex-wives. A sister who loves him. Speaks pretty well for the guy. I'm thinkin' it's him. The one who just triggered off her radar somehow, maybe he was just reaching for something in the glove compartment. She took it as a threat.

(Takes it off "pause.")

WOMAN TWO: She must have been posing as a stranded motorist, because my brother would never have stopped to pick up a prostitute, but a woman in trouble? He would definitely have picked up a woman having car trouble, dropped her off at the nearest garage.

DRUMS: Oh, come *on* —

BUCKET: Sounds funny, huh?

As implausible as killing seven men in the course of one year in self defense.

But she could be right.

DRUMS: *(Incredulous.)* You got the hots for her. What are you doing, going down to that cell for a little ten dollar blow job, lighten up the day?

(Bucket stands. The gesture is filled with menace. Drums edges for the door.)

DRUMS: You're the one should be talking to those shrinks.

Been undercover too long. Don't know you're Cop anymore. Think you're some kinda cowboy for Justice. It's bullshit, Dave.

You're Cop. Just like me. *(On his way out.)* Go home, man.

(Bucket returns to his research. Pushes a button on the remote. TV unfreezes to:)

WOMAN TWO: I miss him so.

She's gonna burn in hell for what she did. That is the only comfort I have. She's gonna burn in hell.

(Jo. Jail cell. Alone.)

JO: First time. I made it outta that one alive.

An' I made a vow to myself.

Not in words or anything, just in the chemicals in my brain, in the nerves, in the muscles, in my blood. I made the vow that nobody was ever gonna do that to me again.

I was never gonna feel that fear. Again.

Anybody who fucked with me. Was gonna feel that fear.

The only way I could go back out there again. Was knowing. In my body. I'm not gonna die out here.

Maybe you will. I won't.

Took me seventeen years, but

I stood up.

That moment. I became a threat to them. Couldn't just be kicked around anymore.

Had blood on my muzzle. Blood on my fur.

And it tasted . . . good.

I knew.

They had to take me out.

(Blackout. Lights up on Drums and Lu.)

DRUMS: We been getting some heat on that movie deal. Just "no comment" if anybody asks.

LU: I did the right thing, right?

DRUMS: Yeah.

LU: She was killin' people.

DRUMS: Don't see what the big fuss is about. Biggest case a my career. And a subject people naturally want to hear about . . .

LU: She had to be stopped . . . she wasn't gonna stop.

DRUMS: I told them all the money goes to a victim's charity fund —

LU: It does?

DRUMS: It does now.

(Blackout. Jo. Jail cell, alone.)

JO: All this shit never woulda happened. That damn Gulf War. Now boys come back with th' syndrome. 'Cos they been doin' medical experiments on 'em. Our own boys! This is the greatest country in the world, always has been, but them boys in charge been fucking up pretty bad lately.

(Bucket approaches.)

BUCKET: Howdy, lady.

(She snorts at him.)

BUCKET: Buy you a beer?

JO: Fuckin' comedian.

(He pulls a Corona from behind his back, passes it to her through the cell bars.)

JO: No lime?

BUCKET: It's a felony to bring citrus fruits into a maximum security environment.

(She eyes him. Takes a swig.)

BUCKET: Mind if I join you?

JO: Suit yourself.

(He reveals a six-pack in a bag. Takes one.)

JO: So you just come to stare at the animals or what?

(Beat. He takes a drink.)

BUCKET: Or what. *(Drinks again.)* You were right.

JO: What?

BUCKET: Unsolved prostitute murders are down significantly this year.

JO: *(Whistles.)* How much?

BUCKET: Significantly.

JO: Come on, man, give me the number —

BUCKET: Well, you know we don't have statistics or anything, but just simple numbers is, last year was eleven, this year is four.

JO: Holy Shit!

BUCKET: Now, that doesn't mean anything — that's just last year to this year, simple comparison —

JO: So I coulda saved as many people as I killed. *(Shakes her head.)* I was just talkin' out my ass, you know.

BUCKET: I know.

JO: But I was right.

BUCKET: Yeah. You were right. *(They drink in silence for a moment.)* I'm leaving the department.

JO: 'Cos a me?

BUCKET: Yeah. My opinions have become rather unpopular around here.

JO: Well, shit, yeah, you'd better find yourself a new place to hang your hat. Before you find yourself goin' in first someplace and your backup never shows. Right?

BUCKET: That's, yeah, that's one a the things on my mind. These boys aren't like that, but still. You want to get along with your department.

JO: *(Takes a swig.)* Well, I'm flattered that you'd get yourself in trouble over me. That's kinda sweet.

BUCKET: Just what I see.

JO: More'n my girlfriend ever did.

BUCKET: Yeah, she's a piece a work.

JO: Must be the economy, man. All these people got nothin' on their minds but takin' advantage of me. 'Cos LeeAnn is really a horse a the same color.

Tellin' me she loves me, an Jesus loves me. I think she was lyin' for both of them. Love somebody who's not me. Love some perfect good Reformed Sinner. Now I been a sinner, all right. But not in the ways they think. An' not in being still alive, after all that shit I been through. I should get a fuckin' medal just for being still alive.

I tried to kill myself once. Shot myself in the stomach with a .22. But I didn't really want to die, I guess. If I did I coulda just taken the

Cops' way out, swallowed it. That's what you cops do, right, just blow the back of your brain out?

BUCKET: Uh, yep. That's what we do.

JO: Maybe I just didn't wanna put nothin' else in my mouth. *(Both smile at her joke.)* An' if *I* don't get to do it, nobody *else* is damn well gonna kill me. *(An uncomfortable silence.)* Sure woulda been easier, take it lying down out in them woods. Coulda got this whole thing over with a long time ago.

(Jo stares forward for a moment. Blackout. Spot on Lu.)

LU: She said she did it for me.

She didn't do this for me.

She was doin' this before she met me. Since she was sixteen, she said. But you know, she . . . she lies all the time.

She said that she loved me. But you know, she loved . . . that I wasn't good at things. I made her feel important. That's not so great, right?

An now she's gonna die.

An' nobody is ever gonna love me like that. Again.

(Blackout. Jo in her cell. Asleep on the narrow cot. Two angels float above her. They clearly have Chastity and Daytona's stripper outfits beneath flowing diaphanous layers of white. And, of course, wings.)

GOODNESS: Look at her. Sweet thing.

MERCY: Tired eyes.

GOODNESS: Even when she's sleeping. She's tired.

MERCY: I can't do this.

GOODNESS: Yes you can.

MERCY: No, I can't.

GOODNESS: It's our job.

MERCY: Then in His infinite wisdom he should have picked someone who was capable —

GOODNESS: He has.

MERCY: Without falling apart entirely —

GOODNESS: You won't.

MERCY: I'm going to dissolve . . .

(Jo tosses on the bed.)

GOODNESS: Look what you've done!

MERCY: I'm sorry —

GOODNESS: You're waking her up!

MERCY: I told you! I'm not cut out for this —

(Jo sits up in bed, startled.)

JO: Fuck's that?

Get the fuck outta here.

GOODNESS: Hello, Jolene.

MERCY: Hello.

JO: And who are you two supposed to be?

GOODNESS: *(Gesturing to herself and her companion.)* We're Goodness and Mercy.

MERCY: We're here to follow you the rest of your days.

JO: And keep me up nights?

MERCY: I'm sorry. That was me. I just can't —

GOODNESS: She has trouble being objective.

MERCY: It's just so awful. Look at you. Such a sweet face. And you — *(She touches Jo.)* So full of love. And Fear! Ah! And . . . and . . . ANGER. *(Pulls her hand away.)* Oh, I feel . . . ill. I have to sit down.

(She lies on the floor.)

GOODNESS: We know . . . your path. We are here to guide you at the end.

JO: You friends a LeeAnn?

GOODNESS: Who?

JO: Never mind.

MERCY: *(Sitting up.)* Whew! I don't know how you —

how you — HOLD all that without —

GOODNESS: They're all like that.

MERCY: They ARE?

GOODNESS: That's why you have to be careful about touching. Will you remember?

MERCY: I'll remember.

JO: Surely goodness and mercy shall follow me all the days of my life —

GOODNESS: Yes!

MERCY: Yes! That's us!

JO: And I will dwell in the house of the Lord for ever?

MERCY: *(Looking at Goodness.)* Uh, I guess. Yeah.

GOODNESS: That . . . that sounds right.

JO: You don't know?

GOODNESS: Well . . .

MERCY: *(To Goodness.)* That must be right! Right? Because the part about us was right. I know that was right.

GOODNESS: It's complicated.

JO: It's complicated? That's all you got to tell me?

GOODNESS: I'm sorry.

JO: I can't even hallucinate no shit that makes sense?

MERCY: Please. We're here for you. To help you sleep. To bring you . . . comfort.

JO: Where were you when I was prayin' my Goddamn head off?

MERCY: *(Honestly.)* I don't know.

JO: Or during my trial? Huh? How come a whole mess a you didn't blow the roof off that place. Tell them I was tellin' the truth. Tell them to get their freakin' hands off me 'cos I'm a child of God. *(Looks between them.)* Yeah, I know the rap. Mysterious ways. Him and them fuckin' mysterious ways.

GOODNESS: I'm sorry we woke you.

MERCY: Yes, come, lie down. I could sing to you. Did your mother sing to you when you were a little girl?

JO: No.

MERCY: *(Appalled.)* She didn't?

JO: My Grandmother did sometimes. But that was only if we'd got beat. so I don't like it very much.

MERCY: Come, lay your head in my lap.

(She does. The instant Jo touches her, Mercy is shaking. Controls her voice with difficulty.)

MERCY: There, now. *(She strokes Jo's hair.)* Sleep. Sleep my child. Yes.

(There are tears streaming down her face. Jo is asleep. She disengages herself carefully, placing Jo's head gently on the cot, then grabs the cell bars for support and hangs there, gasping.)

MERCY: I can't.

GOODNESS: No. That was good.

(Blackout. Spot on LeeAnn. Press conference.)

LEEANN: Jolene is not available for comment right now — *(Listens to a question.)* Refused my phone calls? Why that is not true! Not true at all! I don't know who's been telling you such things, but — Just last week. I told her about every one of the horses. She always wants to know how the horses are doing. But what she most wants is to be in the arms of Jesus. When all this . . . Strife. Is over. She just wants to go home.

(Spot out. Video up. Chastity, being interviewed.)

CHASTITY: I been thinking. I should probably get a new job. I mean, it's one thing if you're twenty-two. But I'm gonna be twenty-three next month. This girlfriend of mine, she went to school to be an optometrist, and she makes pretty good money. Not like I was making, but pretty good. Maybe I could do that.

(Spot comes up on Reporter, with microphone, and Daytona, who takes out a small black case, her "works.")

REPORTER: The term "media circus" has been much bandied about by law enforcement in this case, giving people the impression that the media are a voracious pack of vultures —

DAYTONA: My Man —

REPORTER: interfering with Justice.

DAYTONA: has never laid a hand on me.

REPORTER: But perhaps the real reason for all this talk of Media Circus is fear that we can do their job better than they can.

DAYTONA: He gets me what I need.

REPORTER: Or choose to.

DAYTONA: He understands about the bad shit in my head.

REPORTER: For while law enforcement and Jolene Palmer's public defender could not find any evidence to back up her claim that Tom Waldren sexually assaulted her —

DAYTONA: That I just gotta drown it out sometimes. He doesn't mind.

REPORTER: we had no trouble locating his prison record from Maryland, where he served ten years for attempted rape and aggravated assault.

DAYTONA: An' sometimes we just take off. Don't tell nobody. Get fired from both our jobs. *(Daytona cooks up.)* Wind in my face, my arms around his body, strong and warm. The bike between our legs.

REPORTER: This is Brenda Case, Eyewitness News.

CAMERAMAN: OK, got it.

REPORTER: Jeez, whaddaya gotta do to get ten years for *attempted* rape?

CAMERAMAN: Easy — pick the wrong guy's daughter.

(Daytona shoots up.)

DAYTONA: Rode clean up to New York City once.

JO: *(Quiet.)* Ever since I can remember. I hated cops. Anybody. Tryin' to tell me what to do. But the funny thing is, I was always proud to be an American. Greatest country in the world.

DAYTONA: *(Untying rubber tube from around her arm.)* You ever see those kids play bucket drums in New York City?
Fuckin' incredible.
Outta . . . nothin', you know?
Empty industrial-size buckets a —
well, it doesn't matter what. Just the buckets.

JO: *(Addressing a crowd of reporters.)* How many times you gotta fuckin' kill me? Citrus, Pascoe, Dixie. Everybody fightin' over who gets to pull the switch. I'm trying to save the taxpayers money, here.

DAYTONA: Tahini or some shit, I think.

(Light on Bucket, coming home with a bag of groceries.)

BUCKET: Suzette?

JO: *(In court.)* I'm sick a all this re-electoral bullshit. Everybody tryin' to get reelected on who gets to fry me. I flatly don't want to be here. I want to go back to prison and wait for the chair so I can get the hell offa this planet which is full of evil and your corruption in these courtrooms!

DAYTONA: Whaddaya think they do with all that tahini, huh? that's a lotta tahini.

BUCKET: Suzette?

JO: Drag me all the way down here just so I can say it one more time.

No Contest. *(Beat.)* Now take me home.

BUCKET: *(Pulls out a box of cat food, shakes it.)* I got the kind you like.

JO: I got five death sentences already.

How many times you got to kill me?

Can't do it but once.

CORONER: She's going to the same chair as Bundy.

I personally find that ironic. Though I realize some don't.

You know, I'd heard about it, but I didn't really believe . . . Thought it was something of a local legend. But then I saw the clip on TV. When the judge sentenced Bundy, who had, by the way, all kinds of fancy lawyers representing him Pro Bono, not to mention the loving support of his mother and new girlfriend, when the judge sentenced him to two death sentences for the murder of over thirty women, he acted like — He —

He said, "You're a bright young man. I would have liked to see you practice law in my courtroom. But you went the other way, son."

Called him son.

Like it was some awkward misunderstanding that led them both to that position.

(Light of a TV set comes up. Lu lies on her stomach in front of it. Jo approaches her.)

JO: Lu. I killed a man today.

(Pause.)

LU: I don't think I like the color we painted in here.

(Blackout.)

END OF PLAY

U.S. Drag

By Gina Gionfriddo

But there is no drag like U.S. drag. You can't see it, you don't know where it comes from. Take one of those cocktail lounges at the end of a subdivision street — every block of houses has its own bar and drugstore and market and liquor-store. You walk in and it hits you. But where does it come from?

William Burroughs
Naked Lunch, 1959

PLAYWRIGHT'S BIOGRAPHY

Gina Gionfriddo has been the recipient of the 2001–2002 Susan Smith Blackburn Prize for *U.S. Drag*, the 2002 Helen Merrill Award for Emerging Playwrights, a Lucille Lortel Fellowship, and a Rhode Island State Council on the Arts Fellowship. Her work includes *After Ashley* (Eugene O'Neill Playwrighting Conference), *U.S. Drag* (Clubbed Thumb, New York), *Guinevere* (Eugene O'Neill Playwrighting Conference), and *Briar Rose* (Providence New Plays Festival). Her plays have received developmental support from ACT (A Contemporary Theater), Denver Center Theatre Company, Trinity Repertory Company, Atlantic Theater Company, Connecticut Repertory Company, Cherry Lane Alternative Company, The Barrow Group, Perseverance Theatre Company, Philadelphia Theatre Company and Chicago Films. She has held residencies at the MacDowell Colony, Yaddo, and Hedgebrook. She is a graduate of Barnard College and Brown University's MFA playwriting program and has taught at Brown University and Providence College.

ORIGINAL PRODUCTION

U.S. Drag was first presented by Clubbed Thumb at HERE Arts Center in New York City. It was directed by Pam MacKinnon. The designers were Craig Siebels (sets), Randy Glickman (lights), Alysia Raycraft (costumes), Robert Gould (sound), and Monica Bill Barnes (choreography). The stage manager was Morgan Robinson. The cast was as follows:

ALLISON	Meg MacCary
ANGELA	Maria Striar
JAMES	Erich Strom
NED	Ian Helfer
EVAN	Vin Knight
MARY	Effie Johnson
CHRISTOPHER	Mather Zickel
STORE MANAGER/JANICE/BARTENDER/CHRISTEN	Annie McNamara

U.S. Drag was developed in readings and workshops by Brown University, Connecticut Repertory Company, Denver Center Theatre Company, Chicago Films, and Basic Grammar.

PRODUCTION NOTES

Please make an effort to "twin" Allison and Angela, though not in such a way that it becomes cutesy or precious. Allison and Angela are usually in close physical proximity to one another and may share moves, gestures, tics, etc. There is a sense of mysterious connection or nonverbal communication of the sort biological twins sometimes report.

CHARACTERS

ALLISON: Twenty-five.
ANGELA: Twenty-five.
JAMES: Thirty to thirty-five.
NED: Twenty-five to thirty.
EVAN: Thirty to thirty-five.
MARY: Thirty to thirty-five.
CHRISTOPHER: Thirty to thirty-five.
STORE MANAGER/JANICE/BARTENDER/CHRISTEN: Thirty to thirty-five.

SETTING

Manhattan.

U.S. Drag

An apartment in Manhattan. Evening.

ALLISON: Cointreau.

JAMES: I don't know what that is.

ALLISON: It's an orange liqueur —

ANGELA: If he doesn't know what it is, he doesn't have it.

ALLISON: Duh. I'm just telling him. It's an orange liqueur.

JAMES: I don't have it.

ALLISON: Triple sec. I could do it with triple sec. Do you have that?

JAMES: No.

ALLISON: Well, I don't know what to do, then.

JAMES: I was hoping to speak with you.

ALLISON: Sure sure sure. We just need drinks.

ANGELA: Like we told you at the bar, we'll sign the petition. That's no problem.

ALLISON: Yeah, go get the petition. We'll drink, we'll sign. It'll be cool.

JAMES: But you don't know anything about the case. I don't want you to sign when you don't know anything about the case.

ANGELA: Tell us. We're listening.

ALLISON: Yeah, I can multitask. Just start talking.

(*A pause, James looks uncertain. This isn't as he planned. Awkwardly, he begins.*)

JAMES: It was July. In Texas. In a heat wave. It's important that you understand that. It was intolerable — this heat. She was uncomfortable. The children were uncomfortable. They slept on the couches downstairs because there was air conditioning —

ALLISON: Wait. They didn't have central air?

JAMES: No.

ALLISON: But you said they were rich. You don't have any citrus vodka, do you?

JAMES: They were comfortably — No, I don't.

ALLISON: That just seems weird, you know? To have a lot of money and a big house and no central air.

ANGELA: In fucking Texas.

ALLISON: Seriously, that's bizarre. How about citrus fruits?

(*Pause.*)

JAMES: No.

ANGELA: *(To Allison.)* We can do wine if it's good wine.

ALLISON: *(To Angela.)* Is this good?

ANGELA: I'm not the fucking *Wine Spectator*, Allison. Ask him.

ALLISON: Is this good?

JAMES: I . . . like it.

ALLISON: Fine, but wine makes me tired.

ANGELA: So drink vodka.

ALLISON: He doesn't have any citrus —

ANGELA: Drink it straight with ice. Just sit down and stop being a crybaby.

ALLISON: I'm not a crybaby 'cuz I don't like wine.

ANGELA: No, you're a crybaby because you'll drink six cosmopolitans no problem, but straight vodka is like too harsh for your petite constitution.

ALLISON: Are you getting mad at me?

ANGELA: No, but you need to make a drink and sit down and listen to this man's story.

ALLISON: James, I'm totally listening.

    (Pause.)

JAMES: They slept downstairs. Darlie and the boys. Damon and Devon. Her husband, Darren, slept upstairs with the baby. Drake.

ALLISON: Oh God — they all had "D" names? That's tacky.

ANGELA: I'm sorry — why didn't everyone sleep downstairs if the heat was so bad?

ALLISON: That makes no sense.

JAMES: *(Getting frustrated.)* They slept. They all slept. In the early morning hours, an intruder entered the house. With a knife. He stabbed the boys. He was in a frenzy. He butchered them. Their tiny bodies were covered with . . . wounds. Darlie awoke. The children were crumpled . . . at her feet. There was blood everywhere. The children were dead —

ALLISON: She slept through the frenzy?

JAMES: She rose from the couch to meet the intruder. He cut her throat. From ear to shoulder. The blade cut within inches of her carotid artery. She nearly died. Her arms were blackened with defensive bruising as she tried in vain to fend off his blows. I can show you the photographs . . .

ANGELA: But I thought he had a knife.

JAMES: He did.

ALLISON: He beat her with a knife?

JAMES: No.

ANGELA: So how did her arms get so bruised?

JAMES: She . . . I don't know, but there are photographs. I have photographs of her injuries. Her slashed throat, her blackened forearms. The photographs alone exonerate this woman. It is a physical impossibility to believe that Darlie Routier's catastrophic injuries were self-inflicted.

ALLISON: Then he went upstairs and killed the others?

ANGELA: He probably robbed them, too.

ALLISON: You think he robbed them before he finished them off?

JAMES: No. No. He didn't rob them. He didn't go upstairs. He left. He dropped the knife and fled into the night. Darren and baby Drake were . . . spared through what could only seem to us a divine . . . grace. Darlie called 911 —

ANGELA: OK, wait. She has a cut throat and black arms and her husband is totally fine?

JAMES: Yes.

ALLISON: Hello.

ANGELA: Yeah . . . .

ALLISON: James, there are problems with this story.

JAMES: No —

ALLISON: People are sleeping through frenzies . . . for starters.

ANGELA: Just a wild guess, but I'm gonna go out on a limb and guess the knife came from their kitchen.

JAMES: Yes —

ANGELA: Right . . . and the intruder — the . . . unarmed, nonrobbing, selectively slaughtering intruder — he did this because . . . ?

JAMES: He's a psychopath.

ANGELA: Mmm hmm.

JAMES: You can't attribute motives to a psychopath.

ALLISON: I dunno, James.

ANGELA: So, the deal is they think the wife did it?

JAMES: SHE IS ON DEATH ROW! She was convicted of murder. They are going to kill her if someone doesn't do something.
       (Pause.)

ALLISON: We don't like Darren. We think Darren did it.

ANGELA: The thing is, James . . . Nobody does something for nothing. You do things to get things. Rapists get a rape, thieves get stuff, murderous spouses get insurance money. I suppose there are thrill killers, but . . . generally if you're gonna thrill kill you bring your own fuckin' knife.

ALLISON: Did the children have insurance policies?

JAMES: I don't know . . .

ALLISON: You should probably look into that.

JAMES: She is innocent and they are going to kill her.

ALLISON: Right.

ANGELA: Jumping backwards, James . . . Is she, like, a friend or a friend of a friend or . . . What is your connection to all this?

JAMES: She is an innocent woman who is going to be executed and I cannot . . . Any compassionate person cannot sleep at night, cannot live with himself if he lets this happen. If he lets this happen, he by his inactivity acquiesces. He is in his own way guilty if he knows this injustice and he does nothing.

ANGELA: That's a tough one, James. I mean, there's kids starving to death with flies all over their faces, but we can't all join the Peace Corps, you know? Bad things happen and, um . . . you do what you can. You can't go to pieces over, like, this woman you don't even know.

ALLISON: It's sweet he cares, though. *(To James.)* Like those letters you wrote . . .

JAMES: Which ones?

ALLISON: Back at the bar, you said . . . The Green River Killer. I thought what you did was cool. How even though the police didn't catch him, you knew how hard they worked so you wrote them little thank-you notes. I remembered that 'cuz I thought it was so sweet.

JAMES: They tried. The fact of their failure did not negate their dedication, their extraordinary work on behalf of Seattle's shadow women. I know the pain one feels in impotence.

(Allison casts Angela a look.)

JAMES: You try. You do your part. And most often, you fail them. Women. They die. *(Snapping back.)* I do my part. And my part is insignificant, but I feel — I have to feel — that the sum total of insignificant parts amounts to impact. From the accumulation of microscopic particles, emerges an entity visible to the naked eye. Invisible alone, in numbers we can matter. We will. Matter. *(Pause.)* Will you sign the petition now?

ANGELA: Sure.

ALLISON: But we don't agree with him. Do we?

ANGELA: Intruder, husband. Whatever. We don't think she did it.

ALLISON: 'Cuz of the whole black arms thing?

ANGELA: I guess.

JAMES: I'm more than happy to show you the pictures. I'll do that. I'll show you the pictures from the hospital and then, in good conscience, you will sign the petition. I want your signatures in good conscience. I wouldn't have asked you here otherwise. I could get signatures in a bar, on the street.

People are thoughtless, they'll sign without thinking. I don't want that.
I want you to understand.

ANGELA: OK, great. Show us the pictures and then we'll sign the petition.

JAMES: I'm going to give you a list of key persons in the Texas government
and a sample letter. A couple of dollars postage could save a life.

ALLISON: We're writing letters now?

ANGELA: Definitely we can do letters. Give us everything.

JAMES: I will.

(James goes to his bedroom to get the petition.)

ALLISON: Fuck, he's gonna ask us for money next.

ANGELA: No, he won't. He's all about hearts and minds and fucking Zen in-
terconnectedness. And he's loaded. He's not thinking about money.

ALLISON: This is a lot of work for free drinks.

ANGELA: You're the one who had to keep drinking.

ALLISON: I thought we were just gonna hang out. Listen to music and stuff.
I don't want to look at pictures of bruises.

ANGELA: Fine. We can leave after this.

ALLISON: And go out some more?

ANGELA: We can go out. We still have no money for drinks, though.

ALLISON: Tell him we need money for stamps or something.

ANGELA: I'm handling it, OK?

ALLISON: How?

ANGELA: Cab fare. Duh. If he's so bent about women dying, I think we can
make a case for cab fare. Did you tell him we live together?

ALLISON: I don't remember.

ANGELA: Think.

ALLISON: I don't remember! What difference —

ANGELA: Two addresses, two cabs, genius. I swear to God, they're gonna yank
your summa.

ALLISON: Excuse me?

ANGELA: Yank your summa. You just don't think. How are you summa cum
laude and I'm only magna and I'm the only one who can think?

ALLISON: I can think; I'm just nervous.

ANGELA: He's harmless.

ALLISON: Right. Yeah, I feel especially good about the part where he went to
retrieve pictures of battered women from his BEDROOM.

ANGELA: He's a rich lonely bleeding heart. He's fine.

*(James enters with papers. He shows them the photographs of Darlie Routier's
bruised arms.)*

JAMES: You see . . .

ALLISON: Yuck.

JAMES: You see . . .

ALLISON: Yep, the arms are black. I can now comfortably sign the petition.

JAMES: It's a physical impossibility —

ALLISON: Definitely. You can put those away now.

ANGELA: *(Taking the photographs.)* Her arms are BLACK.

ALLISON: Give them back to him.

ANGELA: I didn't know bruises could be that color.

JAMES: The pictures aren't doctored!

ALLISON: James, we know that. Put the pictures away.

(Allison finishes signing the petition and gives it to Angela.)

ANGELA: *(Reading.)* " . . . drafted by the Justice for Darlie Foundation and I . . . " Me is the object, so it would be "me" rather than "I," but it's an awkward construction. Why not "The bla bla bla foundation and I drafted . . ." That sounds better, right?

ALLISON: His way sounds fine. Sign it.

JAMES: I value your suggestions —

ALLISON: What do you do for a job, James?

JAMES: This. I do a substantial amount of advocacy —

ALLISON: Do you get paid for it?

JAMES: No, I don't. *(Pause.)* I apologize. I've forgotten what you two do?

ALLISON: We didn't say. Actually.

JAMES: Oh.

(Pause.)

ALLISON: We're currently between things.

JAMES: It's a difficult time. What is your . . . vocation?

(Pause.)

ANGELA: Allison and I went to college together. We have degrees with distinction. We worked very hard. We're not going to make copies for minimum wage in the windowless basement of Condé Nast while women with inferior minds and shoddy grammar make six figures upstairs.

ALLISON: We write better than they do. We dress better than they do. Which should count for something at a fucking fashion magazine. But if you tell them that —

ANGELA: Our sense of self worth is predicated on being treated fairly and respectfully. We're not going to do mind numbing work for poverty wages when we're capable of more.

ALLISON: We also don't want to be poor.

ANGELA: That's not —

ALLISON: Speaking for myself . . . My sense of self worth is predicated on living comfortably. I don't have to be ashamed of that. I am entitled to comfort. As I define it.

ANGELA: You define it as buying $35 mascara and drinking two lattes a day.

ALLISON: And you want to bum around Europe contemplating art. Which is fine for you and I respect that. We're different.

ANGELA: We're between things.

JAMES: Were you fired . . . from Condé Nast?

ALLISON: Our situation became untenable.

ANGELA: There's working your way up and then there's spending fifty hours a week wedged between large cancer-causing machines.

ALLISON: That room was like an Erin Brokovich saga waiting to happen.

JAMES: You're unemployed. That's difficult.

ANGELA: It's perilous in all sorts of ways. I mean, here it is midnight and we have to take the subway. Alone. Individually. To opposite boroughs.

JAMES: No! You can scrimp on many things, but not on safety. Here.

(James hands them each $20.)

ALLISON: Twenty — wow. Thank you so much.

JAMES: You can't put a price on safety, on your future.

ALLISON: Totally not, I know. You are a sweetheart.

ANGELA: Thank you so much.

(Pause.)

ALLISON: Are we done here? I mean I'm insanely tired and we do need to JOB HUNT in the morning, so . . .

JAMES: Just one . . . other thing. *(He gives them each a flier.)* This is Ed.

ALLISON: OK, James —

ANGELA: Yeah — we're pretty fired up about the whole Darlie thing. I don't think it's such a good idea to go splitting our focus.

ALLISON: He also looks creepy and guilty.

JAMES: He is! Guilty. He is guilty of multiple assaults. Here. In New York. I'm only asking you to be careful. To take note of his face. And to take care.

ALLISON: Why is there a hundred thousand dollar reward?

JAMES: Victim ten is a nurse. Her name is Jessica. She lives on West 19th Street. She's in a coma. He put her in a coma. I went to her apartment. Her mother was packing her nightgowns for the hospital. I said, "I read the newspaper. I am sorry. This should not have happened to Jessica. How can I help you?" She was angry. That's normal. She asked me to leave. I understood. I left a bit of literature. Church services, a map of the city.

Her mother is from Orlando. Florida. I gave her my phone number and a loaf of banana bread.

ALLISON: That was . . . cool of you.

ANGELA: Why is there a hundred thousand dollar reward?

JAMES: He struck at a bank and a museum. These organizations have contributed, generously contributed, their resources —

ANGELA: *(To Allison.)* Starbucks put up more than that when those kids were killed in DC —

JAMES: That's a terrible case! They were young, they were —

ALLISON: OK, we have to go now.

JAMES: Just remember.

ALLISON: Definitely. Bad Ed. Bad.

ANGELA: One hundred thousand dollars.

(James and his apartment seem to melt away. Another apartment assembles in front of us as the girls remain in spotlight.)

ANGELA: One hundred thousand dollars.

ALLISON: It's a big city, Angela.

ANGELA: It's a hundred thousand dollars.

ALLISON: It's an enormous city.

ANGELA: For information. A hundred thousand dollars. And all you need is information.

(We are now in Allison and Angela's apartment. (Well . . . It's a share.) They collapse into bed in their clothing. They pass out. Lights indicate the arrival of morning. Ned, their roommate and the leaseholder, enters. He is dressed for work on Wall Street. He looks at the girls in bed . . . curled up together, still in their club clothes. He appears disgusted but unwilling to look away. Finally, he kicks the bed and wakes them.)

NED: I want to do it this weekend.

ALLISON: *(Waking, startled.)* Hey!

NED: I want to do it this weekend.

ALLISON: *(Poking Angela awake.)* Do what?

NED: The party. *(No answer.)* The party. This weekend I want to have the party.

ANGELA: You want to have a party? That's cool. We'll come. We like parties.

ALLISON: Yeah, we love parties. Parties are great. We'll dress up . . .

NED: *(He might lose it . . .)* We talked about a party. PARTIES. Many parties. We talked about PARTIES.

ALLISON: You want us to come to a party?

ANGELA: We can do that.

ALLISON: I feel like we've established that we'll come.

ANGELA: Yeah, all this excess verbiage . . .

NED: You guys . . . You guys . . . When you guys moved in, OK? One of the reasons . . . OK, because of my job I don't have like . . . time to meet people . . . OK? Remember? I told you that. I said . . . 'Cuz like, I can afford . . . I make a lot of money, but . . . my group said I need . . . I mean . . . . I don't NEED roommates. I told you that! I don't need roommates!

ANGELA: Ned, we need to take our showers.

ALLISON: Yeah, you're supposed to be gone by eight so we can be nude and stuff.

ANGELA: We wouldn't have moved in if we knew you were gonna like wake us up and scream at us.

NED: When you moved in you promised. You said you would have parties! The only reason I let you move in is to have parties!

ALLISON: So have a fucking party, Ned. We'll show up.

ANGELA: We'll dress up, we'll be beautiful.

NED: I DON'T HAVE ANY FRIENDS! You said we would have parties with all of your friends. THAT IS WHAT YOU SAID! You have lived here for three months and there have been no parties! There have been no friends! I want you out! You . . . mis-rep-re-sen-ted yourselves and I want you OUT!

(Pause.)

ANGELA: OK.

ALLISON: *(Following lead.)* OK.

ANGELA: OK, I remember . . .

ALLISON: Ned, you can't like ask us important things in the morning when we've been drinking all night.

ANGELA: See, this is why you have no friends. Your timing is really bad.

NED: You said there would be parties. You said that you had friends.

ANGELA: The thing is, you know, our friends are out of town.

NED: All of them?

ALLISON: About like eighty something percent.

ANGELA: This is what's called "pilot season," OK?

ALLISON: Right. Our friends are in California . . .

NED: You have friends on television?

ANGELA: Listen: We have friends who are *trying* to be on television. That's why they went to California.

ALLISON: Duh.

NED: OK, when will they be back?

ANGELA: In the spring. Unless they get contracts . . .

NED: What if they don't come back?

ALLISON: We're making new friends, Ned. We were out until five.

ANGELA: Yeah, we're doing the legwork here. We're drinking ourselves to death.

ALLISON: And smoking. We're out ruining ourselves. We're gonna die at like fifty just so you can have a party.

ANGELA: We need more time.

ALLISON: And money. We need money.

ANGELA: We're doing the work, see . . .

NED: OK, fine. But I can't wait until spring.

ANGELA: Christmas. Everyone will be back for Christmas.

ALLISON: Yeah, we'll have a Christmas party. We'll make eggnog.

ANGELA: We'll start planning it now. We might need money, though.

NED: No money. Your rent is late already. No more money.

ALLISON: We need money.

NED: You need jobs. You told me you had jobs. You lied. You don't have jobs.

ANGELA: Your problem with people is you expect too much. You can't expect us to go out at night and be fascinating after we've been working all day. You can't have everything.

ALLISON: Yeah, we're doing a sort of a job and we're not even getting paid for it.

ANGELA: Even like a hundred a week —

ALLISON: Each . . .

ANGELA: . . . would just really help.

NED: You have until Christmas. That's all.

(Ned leaves. A beat.)

ALLISON: We need money.

ANGELA: Publishing. We can get entry-level jobs in publishing. They cannot deny us publishing jobs when we have English prizes.

ALLISON: I don't want to be entry level! Entry level is boring! Entry level is poor!

ANGELA: We just have to get some money coming in. Plus I think we'll have more credibility at happy hour if we actually have jobs to . . . not . . . be happy about.

ALLISON: It's just hard. It's hard!

ANGELA: I know.

ALLISON: It's hard to work for a little when what you want is a lot. *(Pause.)* I want a lot. And I can't wait 'til I'm fifty. I want a lot while I'm still pretty enough to enjoy it. What the fuck do we have to do to get a lot??!!

(Angela retrieves the Ed flier and shows it to Allison. As they consider it . . . Evan enters. He addresses an audience in his apartment. Angela and Allison enter during his speech.)

EVAN: We are not the police, OK? What we are is a community advocacy and impact group. Our name, which is an acronym, is SAFE. That stands for "Stay Away From Ed."

Basically, we just feel like there's this guy out there like hurting people and the police are just really focused on trying to catch him. Which is great. That's really important. But in putting all their energies into the investigation they're really not attending to our needs and our feelings and our fears as citizens and potential victims.

SAFE is not about catching Ed. That's actually really sort of against our mission statement. Because what we're really about is, you know, staying away from Ed. Keeping SAFE.

We are, again, not a police force. We are a grassroots community impact movement. We are mounting a campaign to increase awareness and keep people safe.

The campaign . . . *(Evan unveils a poster. It has the word "help" in a circle with a line through it.)* The campaign, which I designed myself, is called — just really simply: Don't Help.

(Evan shows another poster. This one says explicitly "Don't Help.") As you all know, Ed's MO — or, mode of operation — is to ask his victims for help. He pretends to be sick or handicapped or injured in some way. Typically, he asks for help. His last victim, you recall, acted under the mistaken impression that Ed was blind and needed help punching in his ATM code. Now, I'm sure I don't need to tell you that there was no ATM and there was no bank and that woman — Mary Stone, who is with us tonight — is very lucky to be alive.

Our strategy here is really, really simple. We don't ask anybody to do anything. In fact the only thing we do ask you to do is do nothing.

(Gesturing at poster.) Don't help. "Just Say No" — if it hadn't been used as an antidrug slogan — would have worked really nicely, too. But I'm happy with this.

Our goal is to just paper the city with "Don't Help" literature so that people will know that just . . . now is not a good time to help. *(Gesturing at poster.)* Don't help. Decline to connect. We also have . . .

(Unveiling third poster that reads . . .) "A good Samaritan is a dead Samaritan." We've got to get the word out. We can make a difference.

Because while we may not be able to catch Ed, we can just . . . not help each other and sort of beat him at his own game.

Thanks, you guys. *(Evan makes a "halt" hand gesture and says . . .)* SAFE.

(Allison and Angela approach Evan.)

ANGELA: We want to join the Ed squad.

EVAN: Great!

ALLISON: We want to find him. We want the reward.

EVAN: OK, I don't know if you guys maybe came in late. We're really not a police entity. We have a defensive rather than an offensive philosophy, mostly because we're civilians and we're unarmed and have no training.

ALLISON: How much are you paying?

EVAN: We're an entirely volunteer organization. So we don't pay at all.

ANGELA: Who can we talk to about the reward?

EVAN: Probably the police, but you guys need to really be careful. If you could conceptualize a different kind of heroism, for a second. Dissemination of information can be a really powerful act . . .

ANGELA: Can you get a *reward* for it?

ALLISON: We're mostly interested in the *reward.*

(Mary Stone approaches.)

MARY: I'm sorry, I don't mean to eavesdrop, but I heard you girls . . . Ed is not a TV villain. He is very, very real and he almost took my life. Please do not attempt to lure or capture him. *(Pause, points to her eye, screams.)* I was tricked by a blind man who wasn't really blind and I MAY NEVER SEE AGAIN!

(A beat.)

ALLISON: Shit.

ANGELA: Sorry . . .

(Mary runs off.)

EVAN: So . . . Are you guys into postering or what?

• • •

A bookstore in Manhattan. Angela has caved in and taken a job she feels is beneath her.

MANAGER: We have to start you at minimum wage, you understand that. The wage goes up a dollar with an MA or MFA and then a Phd brings you up to eight.

So if you get, you know, an advanced degree while you're working here, you should let us know.

ANGELA: Right.

MANAGER: What would you consider your specialty?

ANGELA: Books. I love books.

MANAGER: That's important. Obviously. We're a bookstore. I mean when you did your English major, where did you concentrate?

ANGELA: My dorm.

MANAGER: That's funny. I mean in literature. Do you have a specialty?

ANGELA: Yeah . . . English.

MANAGER: *(Writing.)* English, great . . . What period?

ANGELA: Whatever you need.

MANAGER: Classic or contemporary?

ANGELA: Pretty much both.

MANAGER: All around Anglophile?

ANGELA: That too.

MANAGER: OK, well, that's gonna be sticky because Kurt is our Brit Lit person and he's really sort of a control freak. How would you feel about special events — temporarily, until we can fit you in?

ANGELA: OK.

MANAGER: Our fall reading series kicks off tonight. Christopher Collins is reading from *Breaking the Boy* so it's . . . well, I don't have to tell you — red carpet, whatever he wants, the whole nine yards. If you could just sort of be with him until he goes on . . .

ANGELA: Be with him?

MANAGER: Put him at ease. Tell him how great it is to have him here. They say he's a really nice guy.

• • •

Christopher Collins' hotel room. He looks like he hasn't slept in years and just crawled out of bed.

CHRISTOPHER: My parents sent me a telegram in Boston: Read book *(Stop.)* Wish you would die *(Stop.)* So we could live again *(Stop.)* You're dead to us now *(Stop.)* Good-bye *(Pause.)* I called my sponsor, he said: "If you ever doubted that you are a victim — of toxic parenting of the most virulent kind . . . " I mean you don't send a telegram like that to someone with as many problems as I have, right? You just don't.

ANGELA: That really sucks.

CHRISTOPHER: I'm lucky to be alive. I'm lucky to be sitting here right now. What I've been through — I should be DEAD. I'm sorry — What's your name again?

ANGELA: Angela.

CHRISTOPHER: Angela. I'm at the top of my career. I have a *New York Times* Notable Book. I was interviewed in *Time* and *Newsweek*. This should be the happiest time of my life and all I do is cry. The people who brought me into this world want me dead. How am I supposed to process that?

ANGELA: We could raid your mini-bar.

CHRISTOPHER: I don't drink. *(Pause.)* I probably shouldn't put this all on you but . . . you know. You're the only one here.

ANGELA: Right . . . How about if just I raid your mini-bar?

CHRISTOPHER: I'd rather you didn't. *(Pause.)* Do you have any cigarettes?

ANGELA: Yes.

CHRISTOPHER: You remind me of my sister. My sister smokes five packs of cigarettes a day and lives in a trailer. She cuts hair. She's almost as smart as I am and she's cutting fucking hair. My parents did that. They beat the spirit out of her. They spiritually murdered her. And now they want me.

ANGELA: They definitely sound like assholes.

CHRISTOPHER: I should give you something. For being so nice to me and letting me bum your cigarettes. I should give you something.

ANGELA: OK. You can give me something. Great.

CHRISTOPHER: Have you read my book?

ANGELA: No.

CHRISTOPHER: I'm gonna give you one. *(Pause.)* Is that really weird? Was that a bad thing to say? Now do you think I'm like really full of myself because I offered you my book?

ANGELA: What?

CHRISTOPHER: I'm going to give you one. I'll sign it for you.

ANGELA: Great. Is it valuable now?

CHRISTOPHER: Well . . . collectible. Because there's a finite number of copies in the first printing —

ANGELA: Collectible like worth money?

CHRISTOPHER: Well, only if I die.

ANGELA: Then how much?

CHRISTOPHER: I love your demeanor. Your black humor, your quiet irony. It's really sexy. *(Pause.)* Was that really inappropriate to say? Did I just really, really fuck things up?

ANGELA: How much is it worth if you just get hurt?

CHRISTOPHER: You're amazing. I'm gonna write that. To . . . shit I abused myself so bad. I lost brain cells. I can't believe this —

ANGELA: Angela.

CHRISTOPHER: Angela. Sorry. You have to understand I did *everything*. Before I got sober, I did everything. In big, huge disgusting quantities. I went to counseling, they were like "you should be dead." I was the worst they'd ever had.

ANGELA: *Breaking the Boy.* Is it a novel?

CHRISTOPHER: It's creative nonfiction.

ANGELA: What does that mean?

CHRISTOPHER: It's my history as I experienced it.

ANGELA: But is it true?

CHRISTOPHER: Truth is an individual construct. If you believe in only one truth, you can believe in only one storyteller. Postmodernism completely exploded that idea, revealed it for what it was — sexist, racist, classist . . . a way to marginalize and/or discount the experiences of certain groups.

ANGELA: So it's . . . not true?

CHRISTOPHER: It's my truth.

ANGELA: What's it about?

CHRISTOPHER: It's about child abuse. Two children, a boy and a girl, enduring unspeakable tortures at the hands of their parents. Somehow, miraculously, they survive. The girl becomes a hairdresser and the boy becomes a writer.

ANGELA: Wow. Your parents abused you?

CHRISTOPHER: Symbolically. What they did to my mind, my soul . . . burning me with cigarettes would have been a relief.

ANGELA: Why do they want you dead?

CHRISTOPHER: There's a scene in the book where my mom blindfolds me and hangs me upside down until I pass out. The spirit of the scene is true. When I didn't make the tennis team, my mom just turned her back and walked out of the room. Hanging upside down in the dark is exactly what that felt like.

ANGELA: So why do they want you dead?

(Pause.)

CHRISTOPHER: I was on the *Today Show* last week. Katie Couric wanted to know if my parents really did that — hung me. She said, "Is that true?" and I said, "Yes, it is." Because it is true. It's my truth. So now my folks are like shunned at the country club or something, I don't know. *(Pause.)* You're so beautiful. You remind me of my high school girlfriend. She had a life-threatening eating disorder and I didn't try to help her. The only thing I loved back then was pot. *(Pause.)* Did that make you uncomfortable?

ANGELA: Which part?

CHRISTOPHER: A movie studio bought my book. They sent me this check which is like more money than my dad made in his whole life. I didn't cash it for a week. I just lay in bed sort of clutching it and crying. Because of my folks. Because I couldn't call them and tell them about it. *(Pause.)* Could we like . . . just lie on the bed and have you hug me?

ANGELA: I guess so.

CHRISTOPHER: I know that's really weird and now you probably hate me and I've ruined everything, but . . . I swear to God I won't touch you. I find sex really frightening, but I haven't slept in three weeks 'cuz my parents want me dead —

ANGELA: Whatever. It's my job. For $6.50 an hour, you know . . . Whatever you want within reason.

CHRISTOPHER: $6.50 an hour? That's horrific. I'll give you some extra if that isn't really crass and offensive.

ANGELA: Not at all. I'm really poor. *(Pause.)* My . . . sister is even . . . poorer.

CHRISTOPHER: OK, get on the bed. Please don't be frightened.

(Angela lies down on the bed. Christopher gets behind her with two pillows. For a moment it looks as though he might be moving toward smothering her.)

CHRISTOPHER: *(Like a child.)* I like two pillows. *(He gets on the bed and wedges the pillows behind her head. He lies down and "spoons" her aggressively from behind, throwing much of his weight on her body.)* Now let's just sleep like this, OK? Are you OK?

ANGELA: It's pretty uncomfortable . . .

CHRISTOPHER: You smell like powder. You remind me of my babysitter. I was never breast-fed.

ANGELA: No?

CHRISTOPHER: That wasn't a come-on, I swear to God. I can't believe I said breast. I'm such an asshole. I fuck everything up.

ANGELA: My neck kinda hurts with you pressing on it like that . . . Wanna sleep on my stomach? I feel like I'm gonna fall off the bed.

(Christopher is snoring. Angela stares at the wall.)

• • •

Allison and Ned in the apartment. Allison reads from a newspaper.

ALLISON: Victim number twelve. "He asked me to hug him. He was in line behind me at the bank machine and he was sniffling — crying. I asked if there was anything I could do, and he said that he just really needed a hug. He said, 'Please don't be frightened. I've just been through so much.' So I hugged him and that's when I felt it. I felt very warm and then I felt wet and I realized it was blood. I realized he had stuck me — stabbed me — and then he was gone." *(Pause.)* He said his name was Ed. Her condition was upgraded to stable this morning . . .

NED: I don't care.

ALLISON: She got stabbed, Ned.

NED: Do I know her? I don't know her.

ALLISON: She's a human being.

NED: I want my paper back.

ALLISON: Can I just rip this article out?

NED: No.

ALLISON: Fine. *(She hands the paper back. A pause.)* Angela got a job.

NED: You should get one, too.

ALLISON: I'm looking . . . *(Pause. This is hard to do . . .)* Don't you guys have happy hours and shit? Maybe you could hook me up with someone from your work, you know?

NED: You're not their type.

ALLISON: What does that mean?

NED: You're . . . cheap.

ALLISON: Really? And what — not that I care what you think — makes me cheap?

NED: You are for sale. You are available for large quantities of money or goods. You have no intentions and no goals except a common lust for material gain.

ALLISON: And you're on Wall Street because . . . what?

NED: I'm getting tired of you. I let you into my home to perform a service and you have not performed it.

ALLISON: What do you want? A piece of ass? Is that all? If you're so fucking rich, call an escort service. Rent a babe. Stop whining. You want pussy so bad, go get it.

NED: I will have a woman that does not say "pussy" —

ALLISON: You go get her, Ned.

NED: I want a family. I want a nice, clean girl.

ALLISON: Yeah, well. You're a prize among men, Ned. You should have no problem.

(The door opens. Angela is home.)

ANGELA: I made five hundred dollars for hugging a writer! *(Approaching Ned, handing off bills.)* September. You'll have October by Monday. *(To Allison.)* Wanna drink on his expense account with me? *(Pause.)*

ALLISON: Let's go.

•   •   •

Back at SAFE headquarters (Evan's apartment, that is). A SAFE strategy meeting. Evan addresses the assembled group: Angela, Allison, Christopher, James, and Mary.

EVAN: Sociopaths have high thresholds, OK? This is really important. I've been doing some reading so we'll know what we're dealing with. *(Pause.)* A sociopath is defined as one who lacks the capacity to empathize, OK? They just can't do it. It's like . . . OK, a normal person sees a kid fall down and skin his knee and they're like, "Wow, that must have hurt. Poor kid." OK — a sociopath doesn't react like that. A sociopath sees a child fall and thinks "Better him than me." The only pain they notice is their own. *(Pause.)* And the sociopath's pain is really the problem. Scientific tests on incarcerated sociopaths have shown that they have higher pain and pleasure thresholds. Do you guys understand what that means?

(A silence.)

ALLISON: I knew a kid in school who could burn himself with matches and it didn't hurt him.

EVAN: Right. He's probably a sociopath now. They have a biological deficiency. Which is why they develop these extreme behaviors, see? They go to extremes because they are desperate to FEEL. *(Pause.)* I think the key to stopping Ed is not to hate him, but to pity him. And that begins with understanding him. *(Pause.)* Any questions? OK, the revised posters are here. *(Evan shows the revised composite. It is so vague and genderless as to be utterly useless.)* It's been pointed out to me that Ed looks really sort of . . . sexually . . . indefinite in the revised composite, but . . . Victim number thirteen thinks the voice was female, so . . . We're just covering all our bases and not committing to a gender.

(Pause.)

EVAN: Be SAFE, you guys.

(The meeting breaks up. James approaches Allison.)

JAMES: It's nice to see you again.

(A pause for recognition)

ALLISON: Oh! Wow. Hi. Thanks, you know, for hipping us to this. It could really work out great for us. We're really psyched.

JAMES: Excuse me?

ALLISON: We go to tons of bars, you know, and we meet tons of men, so . . . we can probably find him. Ed. I mean, I'm sure he drinks. He seems incredibly fucked up.

(James looks horrified.)

ALLISON: Are you OK?

JAMES: I don't think you should do that. I think you should —

ALLISON: Be SAFE. I know. Yada yada. I forget — what is it that you do?

JAMES: Do?

ALLISON: Work. Income. Money.

JAMES: Sorry. I have a very low rent and a small inheritance. So I don't actually work.

ALLISON: Oh. Did we talk about that?

JAMES: What?

ALLISON: The . . . inheritance/not working thing.

JAMES: I doubt it.

ALLISON: But it's small, huh?

JAMES: What?

ALLISON: Your inheritance.

JAMES: It's . . . ample. *(Pause.)* I've started writing.

ALLISON: Yeah? You should meet Christopher, then. He's a famous writer.

JAMES: I'm working on a teleplay.

ALLISON: What's that?

JAMES: Television?

ALLISON: Duh. Sure.

JAMES: So my time — days — are filled . . . with research. It's in the police/crime genre. So I'm doing research . . .

ALLISON: That's cool. I mean you were doing that anyway, right? Researching crime?

JAMES: I have a reason now . . .

ALLISON: That's good. A reason is good. I gotta go.

JAMES: I didn't mean "filled."

ALLISON: Sorry?

JAMES: My days are not . . . full. If you'd like to . . .

ALLISON: Well. Maybe. Call me.

(Allison starts to leave.)

JAMES: I don't have your number.

ALLISON: Um . . . The thing is I have kind of a definite idea of what I'm look-ing for.

JAMES: What is it?

(Awkward silence.)

ALLISON: It's hard to explain . . .

JAMES: But you said it was definite.

ALLISON: Right . . .

JAMES: You may speak freely.

ALLISON: Ummm . . . . Evan has my number. Call me. Do.

JAMES: *(Slightly aggressive.)* I'm going to. I will.

ALLISON: Yeah. OK. *(Pause.)* Don't . . . Don't make it sound like a threat when you ask a girl out. I mean you said speak freely, so I'm just telling you . . .

JAMES: That's helpful.

ALLISON: Call me.

JAMES: *(Too forcefully.)* I will! *(Realizing he has not taken her "note.")* . . . look forward to it.

ALLISON: Cool. See ya.

• • •

Lights fade. In darkness, Ned screams . . .

NED: I HATE THIS FUCKING CITY!!

(Lights up. Ned is disheveled and visibly enraged.)

NED: I SAID NO!

(A female police officer, Janice, enters.)

JANICE: You saw nothing?

NED: I was late. I had a date with a woman . . . He said, "Please help me" and I just . . . I HAD A DATE. And I kept walking and he pounced. He landed on top of me like a crow. It was like he came from above. He pinned me down and . . . A car alarm went off and scared him and then he left me . . . I missed my date. I joined a dating service, which was ex-pensive and —

JANICE: We think we have a suspect.

NED: I didn't see anything.

JANICE: Neither did the other victims. We're doing a voice line-up.

NED: I'm a busy man . . .

JANICE: It won't take long. Wait right here.

(Janice leaves, Mary Stone enters. She smiles at Ned — victim camaraderie — but he's not interested. The room gets darker. There is a series of Voices introduced by Janice. The Voices are those of other cast members. They may line up on stage for the following scene or deliver their lines from offstage — disembodied.)

JANICE: Voice one.

VOICE ONE: Can you help me?

JANICE: Voice two.

VOICE TWO: Can you help me?

JANICE: Voice three.

VOICE THREE: Can you help me?

JANICE: Voice four.

VOICE FOUR: Can you help me?

JANICE: Voice five.

VOICE FIVE: Can you help me? It's a rough, cold world when you're down on your luck . . .

JANICE: That's enough. Clear the stage.

(Janice re-enters. She waits for a response.)

MARY: *(Sadly.)* None of them.

JANICE: Mister . . .

NED: None. Nothing.

JANICE: You're certain?

MARY: I'll know it if I hear it, I'm sure I will. But from them — nothing.

JANICE: Let's get them back, do it one more time.

NED: I SAID NOTHING! I HEARD NOTHING! I SAW NOTHING! I told you: I CANNOT HELP YOU!

MARY: I saw. I heard. I want to help you . . . but. I can't.

• • •

Evan and Allison are having brunch with Christopher and Angela. There might be some coupling happening, but it remains to be seen . . .

EVAN: I'm a helper. That's really how I see myself . . . conceptually. In college — this was the eighties — and everywhere you looked it was like me-me-me. So I just took that all in and I said, "OK — you can judge it or you can change it." And I just got to work. *(Pause.)* Date rape was not yet really being talked about. I got really into that. Aggressively, like . . .

approaching women and just saying, "Look, we have a problem here and nobody's talking about it. Is there anything you feel like you need to tell someone?" And if they said no, I was like "Are you sure? 'Cuz I'm a listener. I can help." Sometimes it took like three, four approaches to get these women sharing. I broke down a lot of walls that way just . . . pushing them, you know? I'm still really proud of that. *(Pause.)* Suicide prevention. That almost got me kicked out of school. I totally ignored my course work. And I was like, "OK, Economics is important, History is important. But at three AM, I've got a human crisis live on the phone and a backpack full of books that are about . . . the past, right?" And I make a choice about what's important. *(Pause.)* I'm a helper, see?

CHRISTOPHER: Shit, I wish you'd been on my campus. I was so desperate. I had nowhere to turn. I couldn't tell the guys 'cuz they'd have laughed at me . . .

EVAN: Men fear emotion . . .

CHRISTOPHER: And I didn't want the women to see me as weak . . .

EVAN: Exactly.

CHRISTOPHER: I'm lucky to be alive I was so fucked up.

EVAN: I'm glad you made it.

CHRISTOPHER: My parents want me dead, though. I am not OK. I still warrant concern.

EVAN: But you can say that out loud to the three of us and that's a huge victory.

CHRISTOPHER: But I'm still desperate! Just because I can talk about it doesn't mean I don't need help!

EVAN: Nobody's saying that, man.

CHRISTOPHER: I need! I still need!

EVAN: You girls seem really giving. Coming to my meetings, helping your friend, Chris . . . You gotta be careful, though. Sometimes we forget our own needs because other people's needs seem so large.

CHRISTOPHER: Mine are large. My needs are very, very large.

EVAN: What do you two need?

(A long pause, they think.)

ALLISON: Money. We need money.

EVAN: For what?

ANGELA: To spend.

ALLISON: Duh.

EVAN: The money urge is a really interesting one . . . Statistics show that sixty percent of lottery winners wish they could give the money back. A surprisingly high number of them commit suicide. It doesn't make them happy. That's interesting, don't you think?

ANGELA: Yeah, but have you seen who wins?

ALLISON: They all live in like — the South. So they don't need money like people in New York do. For clothes and cover charges and clubs and rent. It's different with us.

ANGELA: They're giving all the money to the wrong people!

CHRISTOPHER: I find clubs really empty. All of it — loud music, liquor, drugs — they're just buffers against human despair.

ANGELA: We like buffers.

ALLISON: Buffers are OK. What's wrong with buffers?

CHRISTOPHER: *(To Evan.)* My sobriety has made me impotent.

EVAN: That's very common.

CHRISTOPHER: I need antidepressants to get out of bed, but they depress my libido.

EVAN: Have you ever seen an herbalist?

ALLISON: We have to go home now.

CHRISTOPHER: Fuck. See? Damn it. I open up and people find it alienating . . .

ALLISON: I just need to take a nap if I'm going to be beautiful by tonight. I wasn't even listening to you.

EVAN: What does being beautiful mean to you, Allison?

ANGELA: She wants a husband.

ALLISON: Like you don't.

EVAN: OK, I get it! The money functions as a sort of conduit to closeness. You want money to go out and you go out to find a partner. Closeness.

ALLISON: *(After some consideration.)* No.

EVAN: Marriage is pretty close, Allison.

ALLISON: It doesn't have to be. I met this girl . . . She got married to this homosexual guy whose parents are big, old money types and can't know that he's gay or they'd cut him from the will. So they got married and just . . . They live in a house in Tudor City and they both have like crazy shenanigans on the side.

CHRISTOPHER: That is so sad I can't bear it.

ALLISON: It is not so sad.

CHRISTOPHER: It is human tragedy on an epic scale. How can you not see that?

EVAN: OK, you guys: I think what Chris is saying — which I would echo — is that your friend's arrangement may be OK and we don't want to judge it, but it's maybe a little bit sad that that's the . . . level of communion that you aspire to.

ALLISON: Look around.

EVAN: I'm looking all the time, Allison. What do you see?

ALLISON: Needy people. Hungry people. Everyone has this look like they missed a few meals. It's . . . scary.

CHRISTOPHER: What about you — "gimme cash, gimme cash."

EVAN: *(Hand up, intervening.)* You want a partner who . . . has no needs?

ALLISON: That would be good. Yes.

CHRISTOPHER: You are unbelievable. I had coffee with James yesterday. He is crazy about you and you just stopped returning his calls.

ALLISON: Ick. I gotta go.

CHRISTOPHER: James is a smart guy. James has a lot to give. You would be lucky just to know him.

ALLISON: James? Let me tell you something about James. James reads about crimes in the newspaper, then he figures out where the victims live and he GOES TO THEIR HOUSES!

CHRISTOPHER: He goes there to help. He takes food and stuff. James is acting from an ancient and honorable tradition.

ALLISON: So you date him, you think he's so great. I gotta go.

(Allison and Angela prepare to leave.)

CHRISTOPHER: You think no one is good enough for you!

EVAN: Chris —

EVAN: My house, Tuesday. Unless Ed is . . . inactive over the weekend. Then there's no need to meet.

CHRISTOPHER: No meeting? But we could get together anyway. We could. We don't have to wait for Ed.

EVAN: Do you . . . want to?

CHRISTOPHER: James would want to. I want to. You can't just cancel on us like that. You can't.

EVAN: OK, we can meet even without an attack. I bought the food already, so . . . You're right. We can still meet.

• • •

Back at their apartment, Angela and Allison primp and prepare for the night ahead.

ALLISON: I don't think that no man is good enough for me.

ANGELA: What?

ALLISON: What Christopher said. I don't think that no man is good enough.

If you were a guy, you would be good enough! Why can't I find a boy version of you and you find a boy version of me?

ANGELA: Allison, I love you. But a boy version of you is not what I'm looking for.

ALLISON: I know. You can do better than me. You're together. You're not afraid.

ANGELA: Oh, I'm afraid.

ALLISON: Really? What are you afraid of?

(*Pause.*)

ANGELA: I'm afraid of winding up an old spinster in a dirty rented room eating tuna from a can because I couldn't make up my mind what to do with my life. What are you afraid of?

ALLISON: Sort of the same as you. Not getting it. Watching it on TV when I'm fifty and knowing I missed it.

ANGELA: But what is it?

ALLISON: I don't know. Comfort. Sort of. I mean, it isn't money — exactly — or fame. Although those would be great.

ANGELA: What is it, then?

(*Pause.*)

ALLISON: I don't know. I just feel sometimes like . . . like we don't know that many people who are . . . worth knowing. Sometimes I feel like you're the only person I know worth knowing and that's great, but . . . you can't just have one person in your life. That's not, like, safe.

ANGELA: (*Echoing Evan.*) You gotta be safe.

ALLISON: I'm serious.

ANGELA: (*Slightly condescending.*) So it's about knowing cooler people?

ALLISON: It's about mattering! I just keep thinking about this guy I went to junior high with. Jeremy Feldman. He was just this geek, this fucking greasy, pimply geek. But he wrote this book. *The Kid's Guide to Quitting Smoking.* All about how fucking hard it was for him when his parents quit smoking. And it got published and suddenly everybody wanted to be his fucking friend. All of a sudden people looked at him like he mattered. (*Pause.*) I just want to matter. The way they looked at us when we were making copies at the magazine . . . Angela they looked at us like we didn't matter!

ANGELA: So write a book.

ALLISON: I can't write. (*Pause.*) I can't act either and I'm not hot enough to be a model. Chelsea Clinton hangs out with Madonna and she doesn't have a talent. That can happen if, you know, you've got talented people near you, but —

ANGELA: You really think your life would change if you were hanging out with Madonna?

ALLISON: Of course it would.

ANGELA: Yeah, but what's fucked up about that, Allison, is that it's Madonna. I mean, you have no evidence that she's like, a good person or a wise person or . . .

ALLISON: That's what I want, OK. So kill me. You think the same way. You get all bent out of shape every time Naomi Wolf, like, breathes.

ANGELA: I'm smarter than she is.

ALLISON: It's the same thing. You want to matter to people you think are worth mattering to. You're the same as me even if you think you aren't.

(Pause.)

ANGELA: I read this interview with David Duchovny once . . . He was paraphrasing Barthes' idea, in *Camera Lucida,* that the reason we think we know famous people is because we spend lots of time with them in our homes — on TV and CD's, in the newspaper. The repetition of the image and the voice inspires the illusion of intimacy. He was just saying how fucked up it is to have tons of people feel like they know you or want to know you.

ALLISON: Well, boo hoo hoo David Duchovny. I mean, Michael J. Fox having Parkinson's . . . obviously it still sucks, but . . . you can't tell me it doesn't help a whole lot to have, like, Oprah and the whole fucking Senate care about you.

ANGELA: Maybe.

ALLISON: I don't want to get Parkinson's and have nobody care.

ANGELA: You're not going to get Parkinson's. But if you did, I would care.

ALLISON: Even if you had, like, a couple kids and some big job?

ANGELA: Of course.

(Pause.)

ALLISON: We should still have more friends.

ANGELA: Just to be safe.

ALLISON: Seriously, we should.

ANGELA: OK, let's go make some.

• • •

Allison's dream. Allison has fallen asleep and dreams of the night ahead. It's the usual bar-crawling scene but the people are . . . changed. Every actor plays a Bar Patron. *Bar Patrons should be costumed as to seem interchangeable, absurdly identical. Allison and Angela look vivid and out of place.*

ALLISON: They all look . . . the same.

ANGELA: If you're gonna be critical, we can just go home now.

ALLISON: Are you getting mad at me?

ANGELA: You want everything for nothing.

ALLISON: Where is this coming from?

ANGELA: Who do you think you are that you get to want everything?

ALLISON: OK, we'll talk to someone.

ANGELA: Who?

ALLISON: The one in the black . . . The one . . . God — tell me they don't all look the same to you.

ANGELA: Talk or we're leaving.

ALLISON: OK!

(Allison approaches a Bar Patron. The Bar Patrons speak too loudly and over-enunciate.)

ALLISON: Hi.

PATRON 1: Is it hot in here or what?!

PATRON 2: Is it just me or are they watering down these drinks?

PATRON 3: May I light that for you?

ALLISON: Light what?

ANGELA: If you're going to be critical —

PATRON 4: What'cha drinkin'?

ANGELA: Who do you like?

ALLISON: They're all . . . the same.

ANGELA: Oh — They're all the same and you're so special.

ALLISON: I didn't say that!

ANGELA: Choose or lose, Allison.

ALLISON: How am I supposed to choose?

BAR PATRON 2: You could try talking to us.

BAR PATRON 3: Talk? Why should we talk when we can dance?!

(Music begins. It is so loud as to make conversation impossible.)

(The Bar Patrons dance: loopy, exaggerated moves . . . not in time to the music, more modern-dance stretching than club bopping. The girls yell above the music.)

ANGELA: Who are you gonna dance with?

ALLISON: Nobody.

ANGELA: Nobody is ever good enough. You want, you want, you want. What about what they want?

ALLISON: I don't know what they want, they won't talk to me.

ANGELA: They're human beings, Allison.

ALLISON: I don't think they are.

(The music stops. The bar patrons stop dancing and stare at Allison.)

ANGELA: I have had enough. I can no longer be party to your dehumanization of your fellow man, your shallow superiority, your crass materialism. You don't need a boyfriend, you need HELP.

(Angela storms out of the bar.)

ALLISON: Don't leave me! *(Pause, computing it . . .)* I need . . . help.

(The Bar Patrons start to move in on Allison slowly, insidiously . . .)

BAR PATRONS: We'll help you.

PATRON 1: Everybody needs help.

PATRON 2: I need help.

PATRON 3: Just ask for what you need.

PATRON 4: I need a hug, will you hug me?

ALLISON: No!

PATRON 1: Want us to hug you?

(The Patrons are closing in on Allison.)

ALLISON: Please go away.

PATRON 2: Everybody needs help, Allison.

ALLISON: How do you know my name? I don't know you.

PATRON 3: Of course you know us —

PATRON 4: You've always known us.

ALLISON: I don't know . . . anybody.

(A DJ's Voice from offstage . . .)

DJ: *(Off.)* I got a special request here . . . it's to Ed from Ed. Thanks, Ed. Hit it, guys!

(The Bar Patrons scream with delight, abandon Allison, and hit the dance floor. They dance feverishly to Ed's request. The actress who has played Janice enters as Bartender.)

BARTENDER: Your friend said to give you a drink.

(Allison takes the drink and gulps it.)

ALLISON: Where is she? Is she here?

BARTENDER: *(Exaggerated and portentous.)* She? It wasn't a she, it was an Ed.

(Allison gags on her drink, stumbles onto the dance floor, and falls to her knees. The Bar Patrons dance over and around her and off the stage. Allison bolts up and screams.)

. . .

We are awake and in the girls' bedroom. Angela and Allison counsel Mary Stone.

ALLISON: . . . and the people there were plain of dress and masked of face. And though they spoke, they did not listen, and though they wanted they thought not to give. Because He said to them, "This shall be your punishment that you will never satisfaction know. Though you will see beauty you will know it not as such . . . and wisdom will it find you and you will beat it like a dog. But I have drunk the bitter liquid from the cup that is understanding and I see now folly and avarice and I see also salvation. This all is vanity. All this is vanity and chasing of the wind. That part's Ecclesiastes.

MARY: Your vision seems very bleak.

ALLISON: I'm a receptacle. I can't help that.

MARY: It's . . . interesting.

ANGELA: I think those wine coolers you drank were tainted.

ALLISON: So? The Indians use peyote — it still counts. *(Pause.)* We think you should date Ned.

MARY: Did he . . . mention me?

ALLISON: No.

MARY: But you think . . .

ALLISON: My vision says stop looking. My vision says: Stand in place and see the beauty where you are. Stop scamming and mine the richness in what you have been given.

MARY: Then . . . shouldn't one of you date him?

ANGELA: Hell no.

ALLISON: Ned hasn't seen what I've seen. Our beauty and richness escape him.

ANGELA: But he hasn't gotten close enough to you to hate you yet.

MARY: *(Not sure.)* I see . . .

ALLISON: Evan says you speak of loneliness.

MARY: I am lonely. I was resigned to it before the . . . attack. I was cloaked in my solitude, I was content. Now I'm restless. I feel broken open and vulnerable and yet somehow strangely . . . alive.

ALLISON: You're lonely, Ned wants a wife, and I have been chosen to make joy.

MARY: I don't know . . . He was rather attractive.

ALLISON: Call him.

(Angela and Allison leave Mary, thinking. A telephone begins to ring. It is

clearly a telephone but the ring is unusual . . . tinkly and mystical bells. Mary pulls out a phone. Ned enters with a portable phone and answers the ringing.)

NED: Hello?

MARY: Hello, Ned?

NED: Speaking.

MARY: Hi, Ned. This is Mary Stone. *(An awkward silence.)* I was attacked by Ed . . . ummm . . . we met at the voice line-up.

NED: Oh. Right. I can't help, you know. I was very clear about that.

MARY: Oh, that's not why I'm calling. I'm sort of . . . This is actually a personal call. I was just wondering if maybe you'd like to have coffee sometime.

(A slightly too-long pause.)

NED: Why?

MARY: I'm sorry?

NED: I can't help, you know. I said —

MARY: No, that's not why I'm calling. It's not about Ed, Ned. I mean we did meet because of him, but that's not why I'm calling . . .

NED: *(Too loudly.)* Are you asking me for a date?

MARY: I was thinking . . . yes.

NED: I don't know.

MARY: You mentioned that you'd been to a dating service, so I just thought . . . I'm sorry. If that was presumptuous. Are you seeing someone now?

NED: No.

MARY: Oh. *(A thinking silence)* But you don't want to have coffee?

NED: I don't know.

MARY: Just a coffee . . .

NED: I don't know.

MARY: I could come to you if that makes it easier. But I don't want to push.

(Pause.)

NED: Ok, I guess.

MARY: Where do you work?

NED: Downtown.

(Pause.)

MARY: Could you be more specific?

NED: *(A huge sigh — this is too much trouble.)* Just tell me where to go and I'll go. I guess.

MARY: Ummm . . . Edgar's, 84th and Broadway.

NED: When?

MARY: How about . . . now?

(Ned and Mary get rid of the phones and put on their coats. A bit of tinkly music and we are on Ned and Mary's date:)

MARY: I'm not generally so forward.

NED: Oh.

MARY: But since Ed . . . I don't know. Do you find that having come close to death makes you more . . . courageous? Outgoing, even?

NED: No.

MARY: I'm trying to deal with this in my therapy: the paradox of it . . . That being attacked is turning out to be the best thing that ever happened to me. I've made so many friends because of it. And I used to be such a shy person, I would never have reached out to another person. Making that phone call today was just . . . huge. *(Pause.)* This is — technically — the first date I've ever had. In my life. *(No answer.)* I'd like to have more. *(Still nothing.)* I've started wearing make-up. At Lord & Taylor you can hire a fashion consultant and so I bought some things . . . This doesn't interest you. Tell me about you, Ned.

NED: What?

MARY: You work on Wall Street?

NED: Yes.

MARY: That must be very exciting.

NED: It's good.

MARY: I heard you say you'd been to a dating service. I'm very intrigued by dating services. I wonder how you found it.

NED: In *New York Magazine.*

MARY: I mean the experience. How did you like it?

NED: How am I supposed to know? I didn't go on any dates. I made a tape. It took hours to make this one ten-minute tape and then . . . I didn't hear anything. For two months. I think business was not of the volume they had indicated. I think that they lied to me. They said they were showing the tape to people — women — but . . . no one called, so . . . I was considering a lawsuit when the call came. I set up the date, I was on my way there. She said she was small. She went to a seven sisters school — I was very clear that she be educated. And small. She said she was both educated and small. And then this thing happens.

MARY: Can't you . . . try again?

NED: She's not interested anymore.

MARY: Because of the attack?

NED: I might still sue that agency. They told me that my profile is "unsavory" now. That was the word she used not to date me: "unsavory."

(Mary puts her hand on Ned's.)

MARY: I don't find you unsavory.

NED: Don't do that.

MARY: See? I've become impetuous.

NED: Well, stop it.

MARY: You're very attractive.

NED: Thanks.

MARY: You seem very angry. Did Ed make you angry?

NED: No. Yes. I don't know. Stop looking at me like that.

MARY: Like what?

NED: You're on the make.

MARY: Aren't you?

NED: I'm trying to take a wife.

MARY: Is that different?

NED: Yes! Taking and making are different. And you're not my type.

MARY: Why not?

NED: You don't look like my wife.

MARY: What does your wife look like?

NED: She's smaller than me and she's educated but quiet.

MARY: That sounds like one of your roommates.

NED: And she's not a whore! She is not on the make. I am looking for her, but she is not looking for me.

MARY: You don't like me because I'm looking?

NED: You don't look right — I told you. You don't talk right either. You're too dark and too big and too pushy. You're just not right!

MARY: Well, you needn't be hostile about it.

NED: I don't like being pushed! I just don't like it when the wrong people push!

MARY: All right, this was a mistake. I don't know why you bothered even meeting me if you were so certain —

NED: I am not unsavory!

MARY: I didn't say that you were.

NED: You're unsavory, not me! What do you think of THAT?

MARY: I think you need help.

(Mary leaves Ned who does indeed look fired up and possibly dangerous. He simmers a minute, then storms out.)

• • •

Angela and Allison at home, alone. Allison tidies up the apartment and arranges snacks. Angela trails her, pitching in reluctantly.

ANGELA: I still don't think this . . . double-date thing is a good idea.
(The doorbell rings.)
ALLISON: Stand in place. Say hello.
(James and Christopher appear.)
ALLISON: My name is Allison. I'm so very pleased to meet you.
(They greet each other awkwardly and take seats. Everyone except Allison looks uncomfortable. Allison behaves like a Stepford wife.)
ALLISON: Did everyone have a nice day today? *(Silence. Then mumbled yeses.)* What did everyone do?
(Silence.)
JAMES: Christopher and I had a bit of lunch. We struck a pact . . . we were diligent to our craft in the morning. We wrote until noon and then rewarded ourselves with a meal.
ALLISON: That sounds lovely. What did you eat?
(Silence.)
CHRISTOPHER: I had a hamburger. Cheeseburger, actually.
ALLISON: With french fries?
CHRISTOPHER: Yeah.
ALLISON: James?
JAMES: I had an angel-hair pasta with a vegetable medley.
ALLISON: Mmmm. Delicious. There was a sauce, I presume?
JAMES: A mild Parmesan. Cheese.
ALLISON: Delightful. Angela, what did you do today?
ANGELA: You know what I did, Allison. I worked at the bookstore.
ALLISON: Yes, yes. Somebody has to bring home the bacon! Or in our case the chips and dips! *(Allison laughs, Angela looks disgusted.)* And how is the bookstore?
ANGELA: It's pretty much a bookstore.
(Silence.)
JAMES: Were there any . . . new arrivals of note? I allow myself one book in hardcover each month. It's a little luxury of mine that I'm loath to part with.
(Silence.)
ANGELA: I'm not really sure. I'm in special events.
(Silence.)

JAMES: Are there any particularly special events that we should know about?
(Silence.)

ANGELA: It's depression awareness month.

JAMES: Ah, how interesting.

ANGELA: We're doing screenings on . . . I think the eleventh. Free with a purchase over ten dollars.
(Silence.)

JAMES: Depression. Awareness. This new . . . awareness of . . . depression. Some may characterize it as an overawareness, but I really think, particularly with children, that we can't do enough by way of detection and prevention. A Jeffery Dahmer, for example, a Theodore Bundy . . . had these new stratagems of detection been in place for them, one wonders . . .

CHRISTOPHER: I wonder about myself! No one ever screened me for anything. I was morbidly obese in grade school. You'd think someone would have said something, asked me why I was so big. And sad. So big and so sad . . .
(Silence.)

ANGELA: God. Everything you say just stops a conversation cold. It's unbelievable. And he *(Indicating James.)* isn't a whole lot better. You guys are on a fucking date, you're talking about serial killers and obesity. What the hell is wrong with you?

CHRISTOPHER: We were picking up your slack, we were trying! You work in a bookstore, you don't even know what the new releases are.

ANGELA: I don't care what the new releases are.

CHRISTOPHER: You don't care about anything. Everything you say is on the surface. You don't try to connect on a deep level and you put down anyone who does.

JAMES: Christopher —

CHRISTOPHER: No — No — I've had it. I have feelings for you. I am trying to be close to you . . . I am ALL THE TIME trying to be close to you and I get nothing back!

ANGELA: *(Rising.)* A brief lesson in social interactions. Here's the surface, OK? YOU BEGIN ON THE SURFACE. You date on the surface. You buff that surface to a fucking shine and you make someone love you. *(Gesturing.)* This is under the surface. This is the "deep level" of which you speak. This is the great reeking, steaming pit of shame and sorrow and damage that WE ALL HAVE IF WE HAVE LIVED TO GROW UP. This is slop that no one wants to see and it is to be doled out carefully

IF AT ALL over a TEN TO FIFTY YEAR PERIOD. Somewhere in between the shine and the muck is where normal people converse.

CHRISTOPHER: So you admit to not being normal?

JAMES: I'd like to take responsibility. I took the turn. I spoke of Bundy. It was inappropriate. I apologize.

CHRISTOPHER: Don't apologize. You were trying. She's in no position to criticize when she isn't even trying.

ALLISON: *(Holds up a deck of cards.)* I anticipated this. I bought these especially for tonight.

JAMES: Are they playing cards?

ALLISON: Of a sort. It's a getting-to-know-you game.

ANGELA: I don't want to play.

ALLISON: You don't even know what it is.

ANGELA: Yes, I do. It's a queer new age parlor game for people who don't drink.

CHRISTOPHER: We can have a conversation without drinking, Angela.

ANGELA: We can have one without a card game, too, was actually my point.

ALLISON: *(Reading from box.)* "Fifty-Two Warm-Up is a gentle, noninvasive conversation cultivator. The game promotes emotional intimacy through moderately revealing questions."

JAMES: I think we should try it. We're all, in our different ways and by our own admissions, awkward in this arena. Some mild guidance might be useful.

CHRISTOPHER: All right. All right. I'll play if James does.

ALLISON: Question one: When was the last time you cried and why? Share only as much as your comfort level allows.

ANGELA: Well, gee, I wonder . . . would Chris like to start?

CHRISTOPHER: I'll start. I can start. I cried this morning. I was thinking about having sex with you. How we haven't done it yet and how even though that was my call, my decision it makes me feel . . . sad. I can't sport-fuck anymore. I need sex to be something more than anonymous animal release. I need it to mean something. I need the other person to want to know me and to care about me and I don't think you do.

ALLISON: Respond?

ANGELA: This is supposed to be noninvasive.

CHRISTOPHER: That was really hard for me to say!

ANGELA: No, it wasn't.

ALLISON: Respond.

(Silence.)

ANGELA: Once I had a temp job at a nonhealing wounds center. It was a place for people who, for one reason or another, had gaping wet sores on their bodies that didn't heal. They would come to get their sores cleaned out and redressed. Then they would go away and ooze through their dressings and have to come back for more . . . tending. It was a never-ending cycle of tending and oozing. And that's what I think of when I think of you. You're like a nonhealing wound. And I don't want to tend to you. Because I don't get anything out of it.

CHRISTOPHER: I could tend to you, too.

ANGELA: I'm not like you. I heal. I get over things. I don't have a "remember the Alamo" relationship to every bad thing that's ever happened in my life.

CHRISTOPHER: This is fantastic. This is the only honest moment I've ever had with you.

ANGELA: I just compared you to an open sore.

CHRISTOPHER: That's OK! I am an open sore, and finally for one minute I feel like you know me!

ALLISON: You see? It works! The game works! Angela?

ANGELA: What?

ALLISON: When did you last cry?

ANGELA: Junior High.

CHRISTOPHER: Be REAL!

ANGELA: I don't cry.

ALLISON: No, that's true. She doesn't cry. I've never seen you cry.

CHRISTOPHER: Why don't you cry?

ANGELA: It doesn't accomplish anything. I am nonreflective, forward thinking, and solution-oriented. Living with her, I have to be.

ALLISON: I'm a crier.

ANGELA: You cry over everything.

ALLISON: I know . . .

JAMES: *(To Allison.)* Perhaps you'd answer the question now.

ALLISON: I cried this morning. I was reading a book about JonBenet Ramsey.

JAMES: *(Relating a little too strongly.)* There's no shame in that! I've shed many tears of my own for little JonBenet. I find that case almost unfathomably painful.

ALLISON: I do, too. I guess. But that's . . . not why I cried. *(Pause.)* This girl who babysat her a few times got $5,000 from a magazine. The lady who cleaned her house got $20,000. These magazines wrote just enormous checks to anyone who ever knew her. *(Pause.)* It just seems like you can get a lot of money if you're in the right place when something really bad happens. Like that woman who went to the hospital for a caesarean and got a crazy doctor who carved his initials in her belly. She got millions of dollars. Just for having a scar. I would have a scar. It just seems unfair. Monica Lewinsky got to go to the Oscars and she wasn't in any movies! I want to go to the Oscars! There are all these people who are not as good looking and smart as I am and they are getting money and getting on TV and they didn't do anything except be nearby when something bad happened. It isn't fair! It just isn't fair! I don't have any money and nobody knows who I am! I want to do nothing and get money and have people know who I am! *(Silence.)* I'm sorry. It just . . . came out of me. I'm sorry. *(Pause.)* James?

JAMES: Yes?

ALLISON: Can you . . . help me?

JAMES: How?

ALLISON: Answer the question.

JAMES: Like Angela, I am not, by nature, quick to tears. I have cultivated . . . over years . . . a ritual for release. I take a book from my shelf. A murder book. I turn to the center and I see the photographs of the victims. I say their names. I imagine their last moments, their lost promise. I say their names. All of the prostitutes slain in Seattle who lost first their dignity and then their lives and saw no justice. Wendy, Gisele, Theresa, Virginia. I say their names and the tears come. Marcia, Amina, Opal, Denise. I imagine how they must have felt when they knew they were lost . . . Debra, Leann, Constance, Maureen. I break; I sob. *(Pause.)* I cried for Ed's victims this morning. I didn't have their pictures, but I didn't need them. I know these people. These people were unhappy. Have you ever asked a favor on the street? Have you? Change for a dollar or can I share your cab? Everyone is too busy, too full. These people were lacking. They had moments to spare. They did not have friends or lovers awaiting their arrival. ED IS PREYING ON THE INCOMPLETE and I won't have it! *(Silence.)*

ALLISON: Next question. Choose between a gift of flowers or fruit. Explain your choice. Angela.
(Silence.)

ANGELA: Are we talking cut flowers or a plant?

ALLISON: Cut flowers.

ANGELA: What kind of fruit?

ALLISON: That isn't the point! It isn't the point and you know it! James! Flowers or fruit?

JAMES: *(Defeated.)* Fruit. I don't like to see living things wither and die.

ALLISON: *(Nearly maniacal.)* Thank you! *(To Angela.)* Was that so hard? Christopher!

CHRISTOPHER: Fruit. When you say a gift of flowers my first associations are women and funerals. *(Writing.)* Which is kind of a cool title actually . . . *Women and Funerals.* So I'd prefer fruit.

ALLISON: Outstanding. *(To Angela.)* Do you see? Do you see how easy it is? DO YOU SEE HOW WELL WE'RE GETTING ALONG?!

. . .

Light scene shift to . . . a park bench on the edge of Central Park. Angela and Evan.

EVAN: I'm really glad you called me. I know it took a lot for you to ask for help.

ANGELA: Yeah yeah yeah. Can you help her?

EVAN: I'm still not clear what exactly the problem is.

ANGELA: She had a dream. She had a dream and she changed. I want you to deprogram her. Like they do with people who've been in cults.

EVAN: Are you saying her belief system has changed?

ANGELA: Right! She's different.

EVAN: Can you give me an example?

(Allison enters. She and Angela reenact a conversation that occurred earlier in the day.)

ALLISON: James and I went antiquing and I bought a hope chest!

ANGELA: I just don't know her anymore.

ALLISON: We found a retro diner with little teeny jukeboxes on the tables! We ate silver-dollar pancakes with fresh berries. Yum.

ANGELA: *(Turning around.)* Retro diner? We would not be caught dead in a retro diner.

ALLISON: You can listen to Buddy Holly while you eat.

ANGELA: I don't want to listen to Buddy Holly while I eat.

ALLISON: Suit yourself.

ANGELA: I never see you anymore.

ALLISON: I'll introduce you to my book club but you have to take it seriously.

ANGELA: What do you read?

ALLISON: Oprah books. Duh.

ANGELA: Allison, No!

ALLISON: The one we're reading now is about a wily and wise-cracking single mom who gets herself off welfare by opening a pretzel stand.

ANGELA: I feel like I don't know you anymore.

ALLISON: Angela, this is hard for me to say, but . . . it's getting hard to be around you. You're so negative.

ANGELA: I've always been negative.

ALLISON: I saw an ad in a magazine for antidepressants. It said welcome back. Welcome back with Paxil. I think you should look into it.

ANGELA: But I haven't gone anywhere to come back from. You're the one who's changed!

ALLISON: It's not that hard. You can do it, too!

ANGELA: I don't want to do it.

ALLISON: If you get a partner you can join us for salsa and merengue lessons at the Y.

ANGELA: I'd rather die.

ALLISON: *(Overreacting as though "die" is a buzz word.)* Die? Oh, no no. I am not going to die. I am in a *committed relationship.* I have a hobby which is antiquing which means ACCUMULATING BIG, THICK UN-WIELDY FURNITURE. I am here to stay. I have a Georgia O'Keefe calendar and I WRITE THINGS ON IT.

ANGELA: Allison, you're hysterical. Let's get a drink.

ALLISON: No drink. No more drink. A train came into my station and I got on it. You've got one idling in your station, but it won't wait forever.

ANGELA: You mean Chris? Let him go.

ALLISON: Suit yourself. I am not gonna be the girl at the bar anymore. I have spent too many nights chatting and charming and GOING HOME ALONE to wait for a phone call that never comes.

ANGELA: You didn't go home alone, though. You went home with me.

ALLISON: There's no security in female friendship. You know that. You're just keeping each other company until one of you falls in love and deserts the other.

ANGELA: Are you saying you're in love with James?

(Pause.)

ALLISON: We have common interests and goals. We share a value system. Also he has a rent-controlled apartment and a vacation home in Vermont both of which he's going to let me decorate. After I get my degree. I'm going back to school for interior design, did I tell you?!

ANGELA: You didn't.

ALLISON: It's gonna be fabulous.

ANGELA: But do you love him?

(Pause.)

ALLISON: Very few people get a grand prize, Angela. You can shrivel up and die waiting to be a winner or you can be a graceful runner up. The choice is yours.

ANGELA: That's the most depressing thing I've ever heard.

ALLISON: Choose or lose, Angela.

(Allison leaves.)

EVAN: Wow.

ANGELA: It's awful.

EVAN: It's very hard. What you're going through right now . . . When I did the crisis line at school so many of our calls were about this very thing.

ANGELA: Possession?

EVAN: I'm sure that's how you experience it. Seeing your best friend in a relationship can be incredibly painful.

ANGELA: But I'm not the problem. I'm not the one who got weird.

EVAN: People change, Angela.

ANGELA: Overnight?

EVAN: The twenties are formative years. People are finding their ways and it's absolutely normal for paths to diverge. It's one of the reasons youthful marriages fail.

ANGELA: I have to walk around.

EVAN: Do you want company?

ANGELA: No. I just need to think. I'm just going to walk home through the park.

EVAN: *(Looking at watch.)* OK. You've got two hours of daylight left. I do not want you in Central Park after dark. OK?

ANGELA: Whatever.

EVAN: Angela. I need you to respect my comfort level.

ANGELA: I won't stay in the park after dark.

EVAN: Call me if you need help.

(Evan leaves. Angela, alone, looks frightened.)

• • •

Later that evening . . . Evan's apartment. Angela, Mary, Christopher, Allison, James. Angela has a bandage over her heart, taped down amateurishly with an X of white surgical tape. She is flanked by Mary and Allison. Allison is sobbing.

ANGELA: Allison, I'm fine.

ALLISON: No, you're not! He got you in the heart!

ANGELA: Allison, he missed. He tried to stab me in the heart but he missed. I've got minor tissue damage, but it's really not a big deal. I'm fine. I think I can get disability, though.

ALLISON: Even if you're not hurt?

ANGELA: Oh, please. The psychological damage is gonna take like forever to go away.

MARY: I found that continuing to work after my attack really helped me. The mental stimulation and social interaction helped me stave off depression. *(Pause.)*

ANGELA: Whatever. I called this advocacy group for crime victims. My sense is there's a gravy train I can get on if I play my cards right.

ALLISON: This is all my fault.

ANGELA: It isn't. I mean it sort of is. It's not all bad, though. This guy called me —

ALLISON: Is he cute?

ANGELA: I have no idea. He's an artist. A photojournalist. He's doing this photo essay called "The Girls in the Park." It's gonna be pictures of, you know, girls who got attacked in Central Park. And all these famous girl rock musicians are writing little poems to go with the pictures. It's completely legit. Courtney Love wrote a haiku about Jennifer Levin, you know, from the preppie murder.

ALLISON: Oh my God! Who's gonna write about you?

ANGELA: Well, he mentioned this punk-folk chick from Portland, but I'd never heard of her and I was like, "Jennifer Levin gets Courtney Love. Come on. Can't we do better for me?" And he was like, "Jennifer Levin is dead and famous." Which is true.

ALLISON: How much is he gonna pay you?

ANGELA: That's the bummer. All the money is going to a foundation.

EVAN: Which one?

ANGELA: I don't know . . . The . . . Don't Walk in the Park Foundation? Who the fuck knows? It's not going to me. But the exposure makes it totally worth it. An agent called me.

ALLISON: No way.

ANGELA: Yeah! This woman called me this morning and she goes basically "I heard you got attacked, that really sucks. Have you thought at all of writing about it?"

ALLISON: What did you say?

ANGELA: I said it was really personal so the money would have to be good. And she said it was.

ALLISON: You're so lucky.

ANGELA: You just have to wait! Something will happen to you, too! You have to stay in the game, though. You can't drop out and . . . settle. You have to hold out for something extraordinary to happen. You just have to! *(Pause.)*

ALLISON: James, I'm breaking up with you.

CHRISTOPHER: Oh, I don't believe this!

ALLISON: I'm too young to settle. Sorry.

CHRISTOPHER: Because he's not rich or famous?

ALLISON: Because he's not . . . extraordinary. You don't have to be rich and famous but you do have to HAVE SOMETHING. I'm just not ready to settle for average.

CHRISTOPHER: You are the lowest of all life forms.

JAMES: Christopher, please —

ALLISON: So I want to be special? So what's wrong with that?

CHRISTOPHER: You're pathetic.

MARY: Allison only wants what everyone wants. She wants to be swept off her feet. Transported. Elevated. That lift in the chest and lightness of step which is unmistakably love.

ALLISON: Right. All of what she just said. I want that.

ANGELA: Me, too.

EVAN: You guys, we need to either give James a voice or end this conversation. I don't like to stifle anyone's expression, but I sense that feelings are being hurt.

JAMES: You're very kind, Evan, but you really needn't worry. I've sensed a distancing on Allison's part for some time. I wish her well and bear no hard feelings. She's a fine person and she deserves to be happy.

ALLISON: Omigod, thanks.

CHRISTOPHER: James is like THE BEST GUY I'VE EVER MET. I can't believe how cool he is. Why do the really great guys always get dumped?

ANGELA: *(To Chris.)* Not that we were ever officially dating, but I don't want to see you anymore.

EVAN: I'm gonna refocus for a sec if that's OK with everyone. I for one am really concerned about Angela's attack. I need to say that I feel violated . . . I feel my trust was violated, Angela, when you broke a promise to me and stayed in the park after dark. I also know that now is not the time to make this about me, so I'm gonna refocus again. We cannot lose focus. Our focus is Ed.

I'm concerned that Angela's attack may function as a blow to our morale. As a group. I mean, it's ironic, isn't it? This group is founded on the notion that increasing awareness can make a difference, can keep people safe. And for someone in the group to be attacked . . . I'm having a hard time dealing with that. It makes me feel like I've failed.

MARY: Oh, Evan, you mustn't feel that way.

ANGELA: Yeah, I totally blew you off. You were saying all the right stuff, I just wasn't listening.

EVAN: But if you're not listening, who is?

(Pause.)

CHRISTOPHER: Evan, I really wouldn't feel too bad. I mean . . . I wasn't gonna say anything, but . . . Angela's attack is dubious anyway. Look at the symbolism — the maudlin, sort of sledgehammer symbolism — inherent in the injury. Only hours after falling out with her best friend, Angela gets stabbed in the heart. I mean we don't need an FBI profiler to give us a read on that one.

ANGELA: Hello??! Are you high? I love Allison, I totally do. But not enough to shove a six-inch blade in my heart.

CHRISTOPHER: And miss. *(Pause.)* I should stop. I'm writing a piece about my experience with Ed for *The New Yorker*. It may be my next book.

ANGELA: *(That struck a nerve.)* Your experience! You don't have an experience — You never got near him!

CHRISTOPHER: I have a theory.

MARY: Ed is not a theory — He's a man!

CHRISTOPHER: That's my theory. Or rather, that's the theory that my theory debunks. I don't really think there is an Ed.

MARY: Oh, you don't??!!

EVAN: Go easy, man.

CHRISTOPHER: Look, it's my theory. You don't have to agree with it. It's my theory and I have a right to own it.

MARY: You're a deeply ugly person.

CHRISTOPHER: What is everyone getting so mad about?

JAMES: If I may . . . I feel I've become close to you.

CHRISTOPHER: Shoot.

JAMES: For the same reason your parents disowned you because of your last book, Mary is now having an angry reaction to the premise of your next book.

CHRISTOPHER: There's no comparison. I'm the first person to tell you I fucked with the truth in my first book. This is a hundred percent on the level. I don't believe there is an Ed. Or at least not the way you guys think there is.

MARY: You . . . weren't . . . hurt!

CHRISTOPHER: No one is more sympathetic to this shit than I am. When I get lonely and down, I self-destruct. I hurt myself. But I own up to it! That said, I've done way more work on myself than you people have. Ten years ago I might have been an "Ed victim" too.

(Mary is crying softly. Allison goes to comfort her.)

ALLISON: Do you see what you've done?!

CHRISTOPHER: Look, it's just my opinion. Just because I think maybe — I'm sorry, what is her name?

ANGELA: Mary.

CHRISTOPHER: Just because she seems . . . I dunno — sorta unstable to me . . . Just because maybe I think she faked her attack —

(Mary lunges toward Christopher.)

JAMES: Perhaps Christopher should leave.

CHRISTOPHER: I'm a member as much as anybody.

EVAN: I think James is right. This is a victims' rights advocacy group, and I'm starting to feel like you're victimizing the victims.

CHRISTOPHER: Fine. I've got all I need.

(Christopher leaves.)

MARY: *(Calling after.)* Ed is real!!

(Silence.)

JAMES: Perhaps a cordial, some wine for Mary.

EVAN: It's a sober house, man. If anybody wants to go out, though . . .

ANGELA: Are we not postering tonight?

EVAN: Umm . . . the thing about that is . . . *(Pause.)* I've been asked . . . they were really nice about it and totally grateful for our input, but . . . the police want us to stop circulating the composite. It just . . . looks like too many people. They feel like they're . . . wasting manpower and I, speaking on behalf of the group, told them we would respect that.

(Pause.)

ANGELA: Sorry I didn't see anything.

ALLISON: You didn't see *anything*?

ANGELA: No. *(Pause.)* I mean, I totally felt it. He pounced on me with, like, incredible force . . . He came out of nowhere. All of a sudden I felt this blow and this weight. Unbelievable weight. He had to be huge. I blacked out, so . . . I didn't see anything.

MARY: And that's not your fault.

(*Pause.*)

ALLISON: Well. Should we go drink?

EVAN: There's a documentary at the Film Forum about the refugee scene in . . . I forget where, but it's a refugee scene. I was thinking about catching the nine o'clock. Maybe we could make a kind of group outing of it.

ANGELA: I can't drink 'til my sutures come out, so . . . a movie would be great.

ALLISON: Mary?

JAMES: I would be very pleased to buy the lady a cordial after this unpleasant experience if she would consent to join me.

MARY: Thank you.

EVAN: OK, cool. Just close the door behind you. It locks on its own. (*They start to leave.*) And Mary. The only person we doubt here is Chris. OK?

MARY: Thank you.

(*Allison, Angela, and Evan leave. The lights dim slowly. James comforts Mary.*)

JAMES: I don't want you to be afraid.

MARY: I am afraid.

JAMES: It was a terrible thing that happened to you.

MARY: I was afraid before it happened.

(*Pause.*)

JAMES: Well. There is a lot to be . . . afraid of. (*Pause.*) I'd like to help you.

MARY: Don't say "help."

JAMES: Protect?

MARY: No one can protect anyone.

JAMES: Accompany. I'll accompany you. If you'll let me.

(*Mary and James kiss as the lights go out.*)

• • •

Lights rise on Allison, Angela, and Evan watching the movie, eating popcorn. We hear screams of refugees being thrown off boats. The film narrator speaks.

FILM VOICE: (*Off.*) There was no room on the boat, not a space to be had. The boat was full. The famine had made fiends of them all. Husbands pushed wives, and women disregarded their children. The water ran red with the blood of the rejected.

ALLISON: Ick.

EVAN: Dear God!

ANGELA: I find this really heavy handed.

EVAN: Ssssh.

ANGELA: "The blood of the rejected"?

ALLISON: This movie is nasty.

ANGELA: Let's leave.

ALLISON: Yeah, we don't like this movie. We're gonna leave now.

EVAN: Look at them! They're dying. They're killing each other!

ALLISON: Yeah and it's gross.

ANGELA: We have to leave.

EVAN: We have to help them.

(Standing, including the film audience.)

We don't have to sit here!

ANGELA: Right. We can leave.

EVAN: *(Shouting.)* We can help! I'm a helper and I CAN HELP!

(A collective SSSHHH from the film audience. Lights down on the movie-goers.)

• • •

One year later; split stage. Stage right, Christopher, in neurotic-tortured-artist mode, stands at a podium. He's reading at a bookstore to promote his new book. The assembled crowd is painfully small. Stage left, Angela and Allison. Angela holds a book — her book. Allison has a New York Times Book Review. *Both sides of the stage are lit.*

CHRISTOPHER: Thanks, umm, for coming. It seems like the rain, maybe, kept people away. Which . . . happens. I'm gonna read, umm, a piece from my book. The book is called *U.S. Drag.* That's a term coined by William Burroughs. It has to do with a peculiarly American kind of longing, depression, umm . . . The book is called *U.S. Drag . . .*

ALLISON: *(Reading.)* "The book is called *Cut Flower* by Angela Reynolds —

CHRISTOPHER: . . . The book is called *U.S. Drag* and the part I'm going to read is from the introduction . . .

ALLISON: Sayeth the *New York Times*, "A compelling feminist battle cry rises from the sludge heap of a post-Nirvana gen-X-austed wasteland. Reynolds transforms a random act of brutality and a city's gritty indifference into a radiant and rebellious coming of age . . . "

CHRISTOPHER: *(Reading:)* ". . . from the introduction. I begin hanging out with the Ed Squad to score points with a girl. The people I meet are nice and give me free — albeit bland — vegetarian food when I help with mailings. I feign interest in their mission and obsess about the girl . . ."

(From here on, the audience's focus alternates between Angela/Allison and Christopher. Maybe the actors go into soft freeze when not speaking, maybe lights direct our focus.)

(Angela practices for an upcoming reading.)

ALLISON: OK, let's try this again.

ANGELA: Hi, I'm Angela Reynolds and tonight I'll be reading from my book, *Cut Flower.*

ALLISON: Angela, the *New York Times* called you a saucy, sexy gen-X heroine. Do it like . . . "Hey, I'm Angela. I'm gonna read a little of my book *Cut Flower* if that's cool with everyone? You guys doing OK tonight?"

ANGELA: I'm a feminist heroine, Allison. I don't talk like fucking Jewel.

ALLISON: Fine. If you need to be Anne Sexton on Quaaludes, that's fine. I'll get up first, I'll be like . . . "Hey Boston! I need you guys to put your hands together for my friend, the radiant rebel, Angela Reynolds."

CHRISTOPHER: *(Reading.)* "I obsess. I obsess about the girl. After a few meetings, however, paranoia sets in. I start to think that the girl is just leeching off me for money and that I am going to be attacked by Ed. I have ample justification for both of these fears, but will herein confine myself to the latter.

"The thing is: Ed's victims have a lot in common. They are all single and reasonably successful. Most are well educated. Over half have been or are members of self-help organizations. Five have participated in dating services and three have either placed or responded to personal ads. They're lonely, dissatisfied people actively trying to improve their lives. They're messed up, but they're trying. They're a lot, I think, like me.

"I am further intrigued by the language these victims use to characterize their attacks. Ed begins to emerge, in my mind, as a bizarrely cuddly variety of serial attacker. Victims speak of being 'encompassed' and 'engulfed.' They talk about Ed like a lover, albeit a rather aggressive one. Yet none of them can provide a physical description. The composites they produce are useless.

"Are we, I begin to wonder, imposing unity and order on a bunch of disparate attacks that have nothing at all to do with one another? *(Pause.)* If they even occurred at all."

(Angela practices reading:)

ANGELA: *(Reading.)* "If the brutalized female of the eighties and nineties was 'asking for it,' her postmillennial counterpart takes the victim-as-aggressor paradigm one step further and actually enacts the violence upon herself. These self-assaulting women defy the laws of nature and the limits of their own bodies to accomplish acts of catastrophic violation. We are asked to suspend all reason and rationality to believe in a supernaturally powered suicidal superwoman."

ALLISON: I still think you should smile. The problem with the whole "pained" thing is that pain is boring. It's only interesting to the person who has it. Nobody else fucking cares.

(Christopher senses that his audience isn't with him. He begins pushing a bit.)

CHRISTOPHER: *(Reading.)* "A few years ago, I got a really bad migraine. My doctor wrote me three prescriptions and said take one of each. So I did. I went home, took my drugs, and lay down on my bed to wait for my pain to subside.

"A little while later, I heard my front door open and slam shut. I heard footsteps walk through my living room. I didn't move. They continued into my room and to my bed and I felt the person sit down beside me. I felt the weight. I felt it lie down beside me. I waited for . . . it . . . to pounce. Nothing happened. When I could no longer stand the terror, I turned around. I turned around to face the intruder and I found myself alone.

"Drug-induced hallucination? Vivid dream? How about religious visitation? How about a ghost? I believe that my afternoon visitor came out of me. I believe that lonely people pushed to their limits create their own heat, their own company. In 1996, mine cuddled up beside me in my apartment in San Francisco and we lay on my bed in the sun for a while. My visitor scared me, but also made me feel more alive in a time when I felt dead, mostly.

"In postmillennial Manhattan, a bunch of lonely people made their need flesh and called it Ed. I don't believe in the stigmata. I don't believe in a deity that makes statues in New Jersey weep and cripples walk after bank-breaking holidays to Lourdes. But I do believe in mind over body. I believe in trauma victims who make objects fly around and lights go on and off. I believe in cancers that mysteriously disappear. I believe in a breaking point that yields miracles some of which are ugly. I believe in a magic of the human mind that can never be proven or quantified, but I don't believe in Ed.

"If you allow for the possibility that the mind can heal you must, ergo, allow for the possibility that the mind can kill. Or at least kick you in the knees and steal your wallet."

(He closes the book. Angela tries a saucier, more "up" style.)

ANGELA: *(Reading.)* "Postmillennial self-assault theory is old school misogyny married to new-age junk science. Think Salem witch hysteria meets Uri Geller. Cotton Mather channeled through Shirley MacLaine."

ALLISON: The thing you're doing with your head is not working for me, but that was better. OK. Tomorrow we fly to Houston with the *Vanity Fair* people so you can take pictures with Darlie Routier.

ANGELA: Who?

ALLISON: Hot Texas death-row mom. Cut throat, black arms.

ANGELA: Oh, yeah.

ALLISON: My concept is that you, like, touch each other's scars, right? You touch her neck and she'll like put her finger between your breasts. It's sort of feminist solidarity meets soft core. We're pitching it like, "Look at these hot hacked-up women taking the blame for male violence. This is a travesty."

ANGELA: Oh my God, Allison. You were born for this.

ALLISON: I know.

ANGELA: How's the press on Christopher's book? Have you seen anything?

ALLISON: *(From memory.)* Quote: "A dense, bloated, navel-gazing exercise in faux spirituality, unwisely but appropriately titled *U.S. Drag . . .*"

ANGELA: Ouch.

ALLISON: He so deserves it. He fucking slandered you. Which reminds me, I have to call our lawyer and see where our suit is at.

(Allison starts to leave.)

ANGELA: If his book is tanking, maybe we shouldn't sue him.

ALLISON: Angela, you cannot feel sorry for him! A crazy man attacked you and Christopher is telling everyone he didn't exist!

(Angela looks thoughtful and uncomfortable. She's clearly reacting to Allison's mention of the attack. She's remembering something upsetting — but what is it?)

ALLISON: They're gonna catch him, Angela. He exists and they're gonna catch him. *(Allison raises the* New York Times Book Review.*)* The truth shall be heard. All will be revealed.

ANGELA: Right.

(Allison exits. Angela stands alone for a moment before following her.)

CHRISTOPHER: Thanks . . . everyone. For listening.

(A woman approaches Christopher. Her name is Christen, and she has short or severely pulled back hair. She hands Christopher a copy of his book to sign.)

CHRISTEN: That was a beautiful reading.

CHRISTOPHER: I'm a shitty reader.

CHRISTEN: I don't think so. Would you sign?

CHRISTOPHER: Absolutely. It was cool reading here, thanks for the invite. I like this place.

CHRISTEN: Thanks. We get some really great people reading here. Angela Reynolds read from *Cut Flower*. Have you read it?

CHRISTOPHER: No, I haven't.

CHRISTEN: I just thought 'cuz you know her . . .

CHRISTOPHER: We're not close.

CHRISTEN: Her book is really disturbing. But sexy, too. We were packed. I read it's gonna be a movie.

CHRISTOPHER: Good for her.

CHRISTEN: Drew Barrymore bought it for like crazy money.

CHRISTOPHER: Fantastic.

CHRISTEN: Has anyone bought your book yet?

CHRISTOPHER: Not yet.

CHRISTEN: That's too bad.

(*Pause.*)

CHRISTOPHER: I'm sorry. I can't believe I have to ask you this —

CHRISTEN: It's Christen. With a "C." It's like Chris plus ten.

CHRISTOPHER: Nice.

CHRISTEN: Thanks. (*Pause.*) You have an interesting theory. I'm not entirely sure I agree with it.

CHRISTOPHER: It's not a prerequisite for being my friend.

CHRISTEN: OK . . .

CHRISTOPHER: Want to fight me on it?

CHRISTEN: Not really. I just think if you're going to believe in hallucinatory attacks you have to believe in other forms of hallucinatory contact which you don't seem to be willing to address.

CHRISTOPHER: That's . . . valid. Like what other forms?

CHRISTEN: I don't know. Hallucinatory pickups, say . . .

CHRISTOPHER: I'm not ruling it out.

CHRISTEN: So I could say then that a guy who picks me up in a bar and fucks me and never calls me again possibly didn't call because he couldn't call because he never existed to begin with — I only imagined him.

CHRISTOPHER: Uh oh — do I know you or something?

CHRISTEN: Oh, you've always known me. (*Pause.*) I'm not trying to make you uncomfortable. I just think there are holes in your theory. I shouldn't have mentioned it.

CHRISTOPHER: Mention whatever you like. The book is published.

(He hands her the book back.)

CHRISTEN: You should look into that — phantom sex, I mean. If there are phantom assaults, well . . . Could be interesting.

CHRISTOPHER: Could be.

(Pause.)

CHRISTEN: Thanks again for coming. I'd offer you a ride but . . . someone has to put these chairs away and I don't have any help.

CHRISTOPHER: You need help?

CHRISTEN: I can't ask you to help.

CHRISTOPHER: I'll help.

CHRISTEN: *(Fast.)* Would you help?

CHRISTOPHER: *(Putting the moves on.)* I'll help you even though you hate my book.

CHRISTEN: I don't hate it. I just don't believe in it. You understand.

CHRISTOPHER: No, I don't, but . . . maybe you can help me.

(Lights out on impending romance, or something else . . .)

END OF PLAY

PERMISSIONS

As It Is in Heaven © 2002 by Arlene Hutton. Reprinted by permission of the author. Contact: Patricia McLaughlin, Beacon Artist Agency, West 30th Street, Room 401, New York, NY 10001. Dramatists Play Service, 440 Park Avenue South, New York, NY 10016.

Degas in New Orleans © 2002 by Rosary O'Neill. Reprinted by permission of Robert A. Freedman Dramatic Agency, Inc. Contact: Marta Praeger, Robert A. Freedman Dramatic Agency, Inc., 1501 Broadway, Suite 2310, New York, NY 10036.

Golden Ladder © 2002 by Donna Spector. Reprinted by permission of the author. Contact: Carolyn French, Fifi Oscard Assoc., 24 W. 40th Street, 17th Floor, New York, NY 10018.

Homecoming © 2002 by Lauren Weedman. Reprinted by permission of the author. Contact: Maryann Lombardi, Boulevard Artists, Inc., 2373 Broadway, #1508, New York, NY 10024.

Lapis Blue, Blood Red © 1995 by Cathy Caplan. Reprinted by permission of Douglas & Kopelman Artists, Inc. Contact: Douglas & Kopelman Artists, Inc., 393 West 49th Street, Suite 5G, New York, NY 10019.

Self Defense © 2002 by Carson Kreitzer. Reprinted by permission of the author. Contact: Judy Boals, Judy, Boals, Inc., 208 West 30th Street, #401, New York, NY 10001.

U.S.Drag © 2002 by Gina Gionfriddo. Reprinted by permission of the author. Contact: Bruce Ostler, Bret Adams, Ltd. 448 W. 44th Street, New York, NY 10036.